SAPPHO

BY

THOMAS McEVILLEY

SPRING PUBLICATIONS
PUTNAM, CONN.
2008

Published by Spring Publications, Inc.
Putnam, Conn.
www.springpublications.com

First Edition 2008

Cover design by white.room productions, New York

Printed in Canada

Part One, chapters 2, 3, 4, and 6 were published previously as: "Sappho, Fragment 94," *Phoenix* 25 (1971); "Sappho, Fragment Two," *Phoenix* 26 (1972); "Sapphic Imagery and Fragment 96," *Hermes* 101 (1973); and "Sappho, Fragment 31: The Face Behind the Mask," *Phoenix* 32 (1978).

Library of Congress Cataloging-in-Publication Data

McEvilley, Thomas, 1939-
Sappho / Thomas McEvilley. – 1st ed.
p. cm.
Includes bibliographical references and index.
ISBN 978-0-88214-574-7 (pbk. original : alk. paper)
1. Sappho–Criticism and interpretation. 2. Greek poetry–History and criticism. I. Title.
PA4409.M34 2008
884'.01–dc22

2008027231

∞ The paper used in this publication meets the minimum requirements of the American National Standard for Information Sciences – Permanence of Paper for Printed Library Materials, ANSI Z39.48–1992

CONTENTS

CARISSIMÆ UXORI

My deepest acknowledgement must go to James Vail whose keen intellect, matchless erudition, and warm and humorous personality made it possible for me to write this book; to Dominique de Menil whose years of support and encouragement welcomed this book into life; and to Klaus Ottmann, Editor in Chief of Spring Publications, who immediately merged with this book and produced it with meticulous care.

Art is various, verse develops unreachably.
See, from the mid-leaf born,
Growth may copy the cactus,
Yet adhere to its ancient root ...

– Vernon Watkins (from "Ode to T. S. Eliot")

PREFATORY REMARKS

I first wrote about Sappho in 1967–68, under the tutelage of James Vail in the Classics Department of the University of Cincinnati. The text that resulted – called "The Rosy-Fingered Moon: Imagination and Reality in the Poems of Sappho" – was my doctoral thesis. It was more or less an extended piece of New Criticism, meaning that in it I attempted a purely literary appreciation of the text, without much concern with referentiality, the text standing on its own, displaying its literary features for the delectation of readers – as it had done for thousands of years.

One chapter was devoted to each of six major fragments (1, 2, 16, 31, 94, 96) and other chapters dealt with groups of fragments (for example the hymeneal fragments and what I called the linking fragments). This from a corpus of 213 fragments recognized by Lobel and Page in their Oxford text of 1955 and by Voigt in her Dutch edition of 1971. Out of this 213 there are perhaps 70 that one feels one can at least partly understand, and eight or ten that are more or less complete (the six listed above, frr. 44 and 98, and perhaps a couple of others, such as 5 and 17).

Along with chapters on those major fragments, I presented a theoretical structuring of the corpus, which I divided into four groups depending on the attitude that the poet showed toward the content. In doing so, I deviated from the ancient Alexandrian editors' method, which had divided the fragments of Sappho's poems into groups depending on their meters rather than their content. In my categories the Group 1 fragments were more or less straightforward public and ritual songs, especially the epithalamia, but also including some fragments relating to the festival of the Adonia and a few others. Group 2 was comprised of the fragments that led Wilamowitz-Moellendorff to his *thiasos* theory (of a community of women dedicated to some temple where girls study music, dance, and other arts) – a kind of heartfelt re-approach to the inspired Aphrodisiac cultic vision that through the ages has been regarded as the center of Sappho's meaning. The overall theme of this group has been described, in one scholar's words, as "escape to a realm of beauty."[1] The Group 3 fragments involved addresses to and references to other adults of Sappho's class in sixth-century Mytilene. Here the *thiasos* or sheltered cultic atmosphere of the Group 2 fragments was replaced by a more secular, profane, and sometimes nasty mood of social and perhaps professional competition. Here are the snide references to Archeanassa and Gorgo as a married couple (fr. 213), the reproaches to both Sappho's brother Charaxus (fr. 5) and the contemporaneous poet Alcaeus (fr. 137), and the prayer that Aphrodite will be bitter to one Doricha (fr. 15). Group 4, finally, is comprised of a handful of fragments in which Sappho seems to refer to the distinctions among the first three groups, and to provide links between them, seeming to affirm that she meant to project these categories.

That entire text comprises Part One of the present book. It is the first of three layers of meaning that my encounters with the

1 E. Stehle, "Romantic Sensuality, Poetic Sense: A Response to Hallett on Sappho," in *Reading Sappho: Contemporary Approaches,* ed. E. Greene (Berkeley and Los Angeles: Univ. of California Press, 1996), 145.

Sapphic fragments have sedimented in my mind over a period of forty years.

After graduate school I submitted the chapters I liked best to various journals of classical philology; the chapters on frr. 2 and 94 were both published in *Phoenix*, and the chapter on fr. 96 in *Hermes*. Subsequently, the chapter on fr. 31 was also published in *Phoenix*.[2] These important parts of my vision of the Sapphic fragments were sympathetically received by various scholars.[3]

In the late 1970s, classical philology began to move into the background of my endeavors in favor of an increasing interest in philosophy and the visual arts. These matters occupied me for much of the 1980s and 1990s and after, resulting in a number of books, the most recent of which, in 2005, was *The Triumph of Anti-Art*.[4] I had it in mind during these years to develop my Sappho texts into a book, but put it aside for some time while other books moved out from my desk into the world.

Once, my attention swung back to the Sappho book, and I saw a new layer of meaning in the Sapphic fragments and wrote about it. At this time I had become involved in a mode of scholarly thought that one might call *Kulturwissenschaft*.

---

2 T. McEvilley, "Sappho, Fragment 94," *Phoenix* 25 (1971) 1, 1–11; "Sappho, Fragment Two," *Phoenix* 26 (1972) 4, 323–33; "Sapphic Imagery and Fragment 96," *Hermes* 101 (1973) 3, 257–78; "Sappho, Fragment 31: The Face Behind the Mask," *Phoenix* 32 (1978) 1, 1–18.

3 See, for example, L. Hatherly Wilson, *Sappho's Sweetbitter Songs: Configurations of Female and Male in Ancient Greek Lyric* (Milton Park: Routledge, 1996), 133, 138, 186, 190–92, and elsewhere; P. duBois, *Sappho Is Burning* (Univ. of Chicago Press, 1995), xi, 51f., 69–70, 141, and elsewhere; A. Pippin Burnett, *Three Archaic Poets: Archilochus, Alcaeus, Sappho* (London: Bristol Classical Press, 1998), 266 n97, 299 n60, 312 n100; the list could go on.

4 T. McEvilley, *The Triumph of Anti-Art: Conceptual and Performance Art in the Formation of Post-Modernism* (Kingston, N.Y.: McPherson and Company, 2005).

I now saw the Sapphic fragments less as the precious creations of an individual sensibility than as a kind of cross-section slice through a vast emerging wave of cultural history – a slice whose implications seemed to extend widely in both time and space. This is the text that comprises Part Two of the present book, "The Garden of the Graces: The Survival of Bronze Age Religious Motifs into the Modern Lyric Poem." It is characterized less by modern literary criticism than by an acknowledgement that these fragments point far back into prehistory and an attempt to deal with that fact. In those pages I attempted to dive deeply into the currents of ancient symbolism and psychology – more deeply perhaps than the New Criticism could light the way.

The Sappho project returned to the center of my life again after I began to retire from university teaching in 2005. Recently, at my home in the Catskill Mountains, I have added a new layer to what, it seems, will appear as a three-layered panopticon. This new section appears here as "The Clear-Voiced Song-Loving Lyre: Recent Explorations in Sapphic Studies." Each of the three layers represents the poet and her work in a certain way, and each represents my mind and its interaction with a finite body of text at a different stage of my life: Part One, the 1960s; Part Two, the years around 1980; Part Three, 2005–2008.

In the hope that what follows may be intelligible and useful to nonclassical scholars as well as to classicists, I have translated most of the Greek in the body of the text and much of it in the footnotes, and have frequently relegated more technical discussions to the notes. The main body of the text, then, should be intelligible all the way through to any student of literature.

The following abbreviations are used in the footnotes:

Αμ.	Ἀλκαίου Μέλη: *The Fragments of the Lyrical Poems of Alcaeus*, ed. E. Lobel (Oxford: At the Clarendon Press, 1927).
AP	*Anthologia Lyrica Graeca*, ed. E. Diehl, rev. R. Beutler (Leipzig: B.G. Teubner, 1952).
DK	H. Diehls, *Die Fragmente der Vorsokratiker*, ed. W. Kranz (Berlin: Weidmannsche Verlagsbuchhandlung, 1952).
GLP	C.M. Bowra, *Greek Lyric Poetry* (Oxford: At the Clarendon Press, 1936).
GMP	H.W. Smyth, *Greek Melic Poets* (London: Macmillan and Co.: 1900).
K.-A.	*Poetae Comici Graecae*, ed. R.Kassel and C. Austin, 6 vols. to date (Berlin: W. de Gruyter, 1983–).
LG	*Lyra Graeca*, ed. J.M. Edmonds (London: Heinemann, 1922).
LP	*Poetarum Lesbiorum Fragmenta*, ed. E. Lobel and D.L. Page (Oxford: At the Clarendon Press, 1963).
PMG	*Poetae Melici Graeci*, ed. D.L. Page (Oxford: At the Clarendon Press, 1962).
S&A	D.L. Page, *Sappho and Alcaeus: An Introduction to the Study of Ancient Lesbian Poetry* (Oxford: At the Clarendon Press, 1955).
Sappho	W. Schadewaldt, *Sappho: Welt und Dichtung. Dasein in der Liebe* (Potsdam: Eduard Stichnote, 1950).
Σμ.	Σαπφοῦς Μέλη: *The Fragments of the Lyrical Poems of Sappho*, ed. E. Lobel (Oxford: At the Clarendon Press, 1925).
Stud. Sapph.	A. Turyn, *Studia Sapphica, Eos* suppl. 6 (1929).
SuS	U. von Wilamowitz-Moellendorf, *Sappho und Simonides: Untersuchungen über griechische Lyriker* (Berlin: Weidmannsche Buchhandlung, 1913).

I use the numeration of Lobel and Page for the Lesbian fragments, except for a few cases where Diehl's numbers must still be used (indicated by "D").

The author in Eressos on the island of Lesbos chanting Sappho's poetry.
(Photo: Kent Hodgetts)

PART ONE

The Rosy-Fingered Moon

Imagination and Reality in the Poems of Sappho

I

Introduction

The Cologne papyrus (P. Köln Inv. 21351 and 21376)

We have about 200 lines of Sappho's poetry, their original order lost, in a little-known ancient dialect of a dead language. In addition, some strangled and unintelligible utterances, words and scraps of words, through which one tries to hear her voice.

Perhaps it is best to look at once at the question of who she was.[1] Says Strabo (13.617): "Sappho was contemporary with them," meaning Pittacus and Alcaeus. Eusebius: "Olympiad 45, year 2 (598 BCE): the poets Sappho and Alcaeus were in their prime." Athenaeus (599 BCE): "She belongs to the time of Alyattes, Croesus's father." The *Suda:* "...flourished (or was born?) in the 42nd Olympiad (612–609 BCE), as did Alcaeus, Stesichoros, and Pittacus." And Herodotus: that she chastised her brother for an affair with an Egyptian whore, Rhodopis, who flourished in the reign of Amasis (572 BCE).

Let us say, then, 630–565 BCE – which would place her squarely between Archilochus and Anacreon, and make her wrinkled and white-haired before she died. Her dialect shows that she was from Lesbos; all external and internal evidence, that she was a woman. And if we stand on the hill to the north of the little port at Mytilene, where Turkish women sleep in long gowns under the trees, and look across the water toward Asia Minor as the afternoon is turning into evening, we know we are doing one of the things she must have done sometimes. And that is, after all, a great deal.

1 Most of the material bearing on the question is conveniently collected by J.M. Edmonds, *LG* 1.140–81, and by M. Treu, *Sappho* (Munich: Heimeran, 1968), 109–27.

Nothing else in our scattered evidence can be taken seriously. Says the *Suda:* "Daughter of Simon, or of Eunominus, or of Eurygyus, or of Ecrytus, or of Semus, or of Scamon, or of Evarchus, or of Scamandronymous..."

Whence arose this confusion?

All women who led *public* lives seemed somewhat comical to male Athenians, and paid for it. Ten middle and new comic plays - six *Sapphos,* two *Phaons,* one *Leucadius,* and one *Leucadia* - paid Sappho off for having made love a theme of song. They have left us a tradition that later sympathizers of the poetess have treated with some bewilderment. "I understand," says Claudius Ælianus (*Varia Historia* 12.19), "that there was another Sappho in Lesbos, too - not a poetess, but a whore." And the *Suda:* "They say that this Phaon was loved by many women, including one Sappho - not the poetess, but another Lesbian, and that having no luck with him, she threw herself off the Leucadian Cliff." One can agree that these stories were about some other Sappho.

But what about these: "A sacred cult-leader," says Wilamowitz-Moellendorff. Leader of "an association of young women who devoted themselves to the cult of the goddess," Bowra explains. "A schoolmistress," Schmid says, getting down to the facts. "Pupils," adds Smyth, and "instructions," in (Treu clarifies) "good manners, style in dressing, and music," and, Burn points out helpfully, "she loved her pupils."[2]

What Sappho is this? Is this the voice behind our two hundred lines? Or is this, like the courtesan enamored of Phaon, some other Sappho of Lesbos, not the poetess, but a creation of later writers spinning yarns about an unknown thing?

---

2 *SuS* 73; *GLP* 188; W. Schmid and O. Stählin, *Geschichte der griechischen Literatur* (Munich: Beck, 1929), part 1, vol. 1, 420; *GMP* 228; Treu, *Sappho* (above, n.1), 145; A.R. Burn in his foreword to W. Barnstone's *Sappho* (Garden City, N.Y.: Anchor Doubleday, 1965), xi.

Maximus of Tyre (*Orations* 24.18) said:

> The eros of the Lesbian (if it is right to liken old things to new), what could it have been but the erotic practice of Socrates?
>
> For they seem to me to have practiced the same sort of love, the one of women and the other of men. And they both said that they loved many people and that they were captivated by all the fair. For what Alcibiades and Charmides and Phaedrus were to him, Gyrinno and Atthis and Anactoria were to the Lesbian, and what his rival practitioners Prodicus and Gorgias and Thrasymachus and Protagoras were to him, the same Gorgo and Andromeda were to her; sometimes she rebukes them, and sometimes argues with them and treats them ironically, just like Socrates.

Now, *is* Maximus saying that Sappho ran a school? (Did Socrates, indeed?) Is it not as lovers that he is comparing the two, rather than as teachers? And is he not a mannerist rhetorician anyway, practicing his comparisons?

There is another piece of evidence to support the schoolmistress theory; says the *Suda:*

> She was married to one Cercolas, a very rich man from Andros, and she had by him a daughter, named Cleis. She had three companions or friends, Atthis, Telesippa, Megara, toward whom she was said to hold a shameful type of affection. Her students were Anagora of Miletus, Gongyla of Colophon, and Euneica of Salamis.

Now some of this information reveals its source rather plainly. Cercolas of Andros ("Penifer from Virilia," as Mure aptly translates) is an obvious comic invention.[3] From where, then,

3 W.K. Prentice ("Sappho," *Classical Philology* 13 [1918], 347–60) is good on the influence of the comic material on our later biographies – and on other points, such as the daughter Cleis and the regrettable ambiguity of fr. 132. Seneca says (*Epistle* 88) that Didymus wrote on the question, Was Sappho a whore? And others portrayed her as a poets' slut, lying down for Archilochus, Anacreon, and Hipponax,

one wonders, did the *Suda* derive this word "pupils"? From a comic scene like the school scene in the *Clouds*? From the passage of Maximus just quoted? From a misunderstanding of Ovid's line, "Lesbia quid docuit Sappho, nisi amare, puellas?" (What did Sappho, the Lesbian, teach girls, but to love? [*Tristia* 2.365]), where *docuit* is far from indicating the activity of a schoolmistress? Or from someone else who had misunderstood one or the other? Does this evidence deserve to exert an extensive, even pervasive, influence on modern scholarship? There is disagreement on the question.

Most modern scholars have interpreted the poems as arising in the milieu of schoolgirls coming and going, presents sent from oversea homes, special loves and jealousies, precious pastimes ...[4] Certainly they have stretched the evidence

---

among others. Still we must beware, as Mure pointed out over a century ago (W. Mure, *A Critical History of the Language and Literature of Antient Greece,* vol. 3 [London: Longman, Brown 1850], 275), the error "of ascribing all the less favourable features of her portrait to the above polluted source, in their efforts to convert her into an ideal model of purity and excellence." Our comic fragments do not show whether or not she was portrayed on the stage as a whore. And, as Mure says, our ancient sources "describe the Æolian, and especially the Lesbian manners [as] refined and elegant it is true, but as notoriously voluptuous and profligate" (ibid., 305). A prostitute who killed herself for love of a ferryman? Or a schoolmistress with impeccable motives toward her pupils? The stories differ so widely as to suggest futility in the quest.

4 The view was familiar in the seventeenth century. In the nineteenth century, Wilamowitz-Moellendorff's enthusiastic development of it – he seems to have introduced the term *thiasos* to the Sapphic muse – gave it for a while universal prominence. The interpretations of Bowra, Theander, Perotta – even, to a surprising extent, that of Page – are rooted in the *thiasos* dream. A recent vigorous defence of it is R. Merkelbach's "Sappho und ihr Kreis," *Philologus* 101 (1957), 1–29. Merkelbach's main contribution to the argument: as pederasty grew out of the youths' barracks at Sparta, so lesbianism must have grown from *Mädchenbünde* in Lesbos; and if such existed, then obviously Sappho was leader of one – an appealing argument, but there is no evidence for the existence of *Mädchenbünde* in Lesbos or indeed anywhere in Greece. Neither Theocritus 18 nor Alcman's *Partheneion*

beyond all reason in so doing. And yet – the poems, when viewed in this way, *do* make sense. In fact, a certain special poignancy clings about them. And there *is* ancient evidence for it – if not the best...

Since almost all the external evidence must be suspected of comic pollution, a question arises about the quality of the internal evidence. Did Sappho present to us, in those 200 or so lines that we have, an image of what she saw, thought and did in the houses, streets, and pleasant hillsides of Mytilene? Surely, her poems contain image-words – words triggering memories of sense-impressions – but whether these images express her memory or her imagination remains a question; we must ask to what extent the poems are autobiographical. Some terminology will be helpful.

On the front of the stage, in the shadow – play of literature, are the *properties*, selected and arranged by the author; the supposedly real world in which the "action" of a novel or a poem takes place – the world in which the reader is expected to believe – what one might call the *hypothetical real.* [5]

But perhaps the author does not want simple belief. Perhaps he is drawn, too, by the excitement of wavering belief. Into the

---

is evidence of anything more than a group of girls who grew up in the same area, knew each other well, and met on Saturdays with the music teacher for choir practice. Sappho herself may have been the reason why female homosexuality came to be called "lesbian": indeed, the *Suda*'s testimony, for what it is worth, implies that other Lesbians of her day disapproved. And Merkelbach's premise, that pederasty grew out of the Spartan *συσσίτια*, is itself, somewhat speculative. The practice was probably common in the Near East, and the Lesbians, with Sardis only ninety miles away, were under strong Near Eastern influence.

5 Property, in the sense of "stage property," is Macneice's term (L. Macneice, *Modern Poetry* [Oxford Univ. Press, 1938], 91). Macneice, however, opposes it to "image," which I use in I.A. Richards's sense (*Principles of Literary Criticism* [London: Kegan Paul, 1925]) to mean any word triggering a memory of a sense-impression. Hence, some images are properties and some are not.

hypothetical real, out of that darker area at the back of the stage, he may introduce other images, not to be believed (not properties), but to ornament, enliven, complicate, and reveal the world of the properties – as do the vehicles of metaphors, similes, etc. Behind the hypothetical real of any literary work lies a potentially boundless and undefined other world, the *hypothetical unreal,* as vast as the author's imagination and not governed by a need for literal plausibility. Comparisons, metaphors, and similes link the two worlds, showing at what points the energies pass between them (tenor arising from the hypothetical real, vehicle from the hypothetical unreal). When he uses an *allegory,* an author darkens, for a while, the front of the stage, and directs our attention to that stranger and more distant area at the back – the hypothetical real is indirectly revealed as we gaze at the hypothetical unreal. Conversely, the *symbol* is a comparison in which only the hypothetical real is stated.[6] A property image is used by itself to establish links, to point to some part of that hypothetical unreal behind it. How, then, does one identify a symbol? It has neither the strangeness of allegory nor the forthrightness of the simile and the metaphor. It is the most elusive and delicate and (is it possible?) mocking of the various links between the two worlds. And this is its great appeal. Through the use of symbols the world of properties can maintain a surface of unruffled plausibility while still richly partaking of that unbounded world behind it. (And thus it is that claims of symbolism frequently arouse the ire of critics unwilling to believe that an author would demand that much of them.) Now to describe, in a brief overview, the hypothetical real and unreal of the Sapphic fragments.

---

6 An allegory goes usually from an object in the unreal to an abstraction or quality in the real; a symbol, from an object in the real to an abstraction or quality in the unreal.

In the shadow world of our 200 lines of Sappho, the hypothetical real seems at first to retain a smooth plausibility. The language has not, like even the simplest narrative passages in Pindar, been heated almost to madness in the furnace of metaphor. The links with the unreal are few and conventional (derived mostly from Homer) and they cluster in the few fragments of the traditionally ornate choral wedding song. (About half of the similes belong in the hymeneal fragments, though the latter comprise only a tenth of the whole.)

Half of the metaphors are merely ornamental epithets (usually a single compound word), and another quarter or so may be dead, or linguistic, metaphors. They never involve more than two words and almost never deal in daring or grotesque "Pindaric" compounds. They describe most of all the beauties of flowers and colors (rose, violet, gold, and black)[7] and female divinities. Synaesthetic metaphor lends sweetness to musical imagery, and nine musical metaphors, all previously unattested, may be Sappho's inventions.[8] Those describing erotic qualities of female beauty combine with

7 D.A. Campbell argues that we cannot be sure what color is signified in early *βροδο-* compounds. Homer's rosy-fingered dawn, like Sappho's rosy-fingered moon, may refer to white or yellow roses; pink or red dawns, Campbell says, are not mentioned before Hellenistic times. Sappho, indeed, does give Dawn golden slippers. Likewise *βροδόπαχυς*, "rose-armed," which Sappho uses of both Dawn and the Graces, may well mean white-armed, consistent with the Homeric λευκόλενος. (*Proceedings of the Classical Association* 65 [London, 1968], 34; see also his *Greek Lyric Poetry: A Selection of Early Greek Lyric, Elegiac and Iambic Poetry* [London: Macmillan, 1967], 280.)

8 Fr. 44.24: ἄυλος ἀδυμέλης, "sweet-songed flute"; fr. 71.5: *μέλος τι γλύκερον*, "some sweet song"; fr. 73.4: *ἀδύλογοι*, "with sweet words"; fr. 153: *ἀδύφωνον*, "sweet-voiced"; fr. 156.1: *πάκτιδος ἀδυμελεστέρα*, "more sweet-songed than the lyre"; fr. 185: *μελίφωνος*, "honey-voiced"; fr. 136: *ἰμερόφωνος*, "with desire in the voice" or, "aroused by the voice"; fr. 58.12: *φιλάοιδαν... χελύνναν*, "song-loving lyre"; fr. 103.10: *λιγύραν ἀοίδαν*, "sharp song"; fr. 71.6: *μελλιχόφων*, "soft-voiced."

flowers, music, and colors to make up about seventy percent of the whole.

These, then, are the ornate, or brightly lit, areas of the stage. In this world of rich, if muted, colors, sweet song, and erotic beauty we encounter seventeen gods, nineteen heroes and demigods, and eighteen plain humans – with a female eye to the characters as well as the coloration. Goddesses are mentioned thirty-three times, gods only thirteen; goddesses invoked at least ten times, gods... never. Alcaeus, the drunken warrior, mentions gods by name fifty-three times and goddesses only twelve times; in his fragments the greatest of the gods, Zeus, holds the lead (with eighteen occurences). But in Sappho it is Aphrodite, the greatest of the goddesses (fifteen); in her train come Dawn (five), the Muses and Graces (four), Hera and the Nereids. Zeus is only mentioned as somebody's father. Among the gods, only Eros is anywhere near the center of the stage.

Meanwhile back in the hypothetical real, the world of the eighteen human figures not from myth or art, all but one are women and girls, and that one is mentioned only once.[9] But everywhere are mentions of women and girls. Atthis, Andromeda, Gorgo, Gongyla, Pleistodika, Anactoria, Archeanassa, Gyrinno, Mnasidika, Timas... were these students in a school? Cult partners whom she led in dances on some green promontory? Objects of assignations in shadowed rooms? Or are they dreams encountered over the midnight oil, while fantasizing for a poem? We should not pretend that we know.

In the world where these figures move, nature counts only as a foil for emotional events. Place names are drawn from myth, indefinite and distant, piercing into the hypothetical unreal. The voice has a mysterious reluctance to specify the

9 I refer to the mention of some Cleanactidas, probably Myrsilus, in fr. 98.

times of day or the seasons of the year. Cut off in time and space, on that sweetly sounding stage (rose, purple, gold and black) peopled by women and watched over by goddesses, there is no hunger, thirst, heat, cold; the body feels only desire and its consequences, and the outside world is hardly in evidence. Into the hands of the actresses let us put six different types of stringed instruments, some flutes and castanets.[10] Around them the fragrances of hyacinths, roses, violets, honey lotuses, and the more modest chervil, anise, and celery. There is an ambiguous light from an unnamed source. The mood is one of happiness that passes, of desire that cannot be fulfilled. Let the play begin.

---

10 Fr. 103.12: the *λύρα*, "lyre"; fr. 58.12: the *χελύννα*, "tortoise shell (lyre)"; 118, the *λέχυ*, possibly the same as *χελύννα*; 156: the *πάκτις*, a kind of Lydian lyre; fr. 176: the *βάρβιτος* and *βάρομος* (?). From the marriage of Hector and Andromache (fr. 44), the *αὖλος ἀδυμέλης*, "sweet-voiced flute," and the rattle of castanets, *κρόταλοι*.

II

The Song of the Sacred Grove

(Fragment 2)

1a .ρανοθεν κατιου[

1 δεῦρυ † μεκρ̣η̣τα . π[ ] . ναῦον
ἄγνον ὄπ[αι τοι] χάριεν μὲν ἄλσος
μαλί[αν], βῶμοι δὲ τεθυμιάμε-
νοι [λι]βανώτωι·

—

5 ἐν δ' ὔδωρ ψῦχρον κελάδει δι' ὔσδων
μαλίνων, βρόδοισι δὲ παῖς ὁ χῶρος
ἐσκίαστ', αἰθυσσομένων δὲ φύλλων
κῶμα κατέρρει·

—

9 ἐν δ' λείμων ἰππόβοτος τέθαλε
τω̣τ . . . ι̣ρρινοις ἄνθεσιν, αἰ δ' ἄηται
μέλλιχα πνέοισιν [
[ ]

—

13 ἔνθα δὴ σὺ στέμ<ματ'> ἔλοισα Κύπρι
χρυσίαισιν ἐν κυλίκεσσιν ἄβρως
ὀμ<με>μείχμενον θαλίαισι νέκταρ
οἰνοχόαισον

—

† τούτοισι τοῖς ἐταίροις ἐμοῖς γε καὶ σοῖς.

1*a*. ὀρράνοθεν κατίοι[σα, Norsa; κα]ράνοθεν κατιοι[σα, Turyn. 1. δεῦρύ μ' ἐκ κρήτας ἐπ[ὶ τόνδ]ε ναῦον, Page; δεῦρ' ὔμ' ἐς ῥήτασ π[α]ρ [. . . . .]ε ναῦον, Schubart; δεῦρύ με κρήτας πρ[οκαλητ'] ἔναυλον, Gallavotti; δεῦρύ {ὐ} μ', ε<ῖ>κρῆτές μ[οτ ἐσαντο] ναῦ{γ}ον, Theiler/Von der Mühl; δεῦρύ με κρήτας τρ[ολίποιο]α ναῦον, Theander. 8. κατάγρει, Bergk. 11–12. μέλλιχα πνέοισι, <φόβαι δ' ἀπ'>ὀππά/νω κατίοι[σαι, Gallavotti. 17. τοίς ἐταίροις τοίσδεσ' ἔμοις τε καὶ σοῖς, Edmonds.

Come, for my sake, from Crete to this holy temple,
where is your lovely grove of apple trees,
and altars are smoking
with frankincense;

therein cold water sings through the apple branches,
and all the place is shadowed over with roses,
and from quivering leaves a magic sleep
flows down.

Therein a meadow with pasture for horses blooms with...
Flowers, and sweet
Breezes breathe
...

There, taking the garlands, Cypris,
into golden cups, luxuriously,
let the nectar mixed with good cheer
be poured like wine

(for these my friends and yours.)

The Text and the Question of Completeness

Seven lengthy samples of Sappho's work are known today, two handed down in books by ancient critics, all the rest discovered in modern times among the wreckage of the past. Fr. 2, "The Song of the Sacred Grove," was found in 1936 on an ostrakon in Florence.[1]

Faded ink, a broken upper right edge (removing several letters from each of the first six lines) and several mysterious blank spaces complicate the text, which is written out continuously, like prose. Spaces of about one character mark the ends of the first two strophes; a third such space, probably also intended to mark a strophe-end, follows *πνέοισιν* in line 11, where the scribe has unaccountably skipped from the middle of the third line of one strophe to the first line of the next. A similar space at the end of line 2 has not been explained, nor have spaces of about three characters each following the first words of lines 2 and 6. If line la is complete in two words – which amounts to saying, if it is the adonic line of a Sapphic stanza – then a larger space, possibly five or six characters, followed it. Does this indicate that line la is the end of a poem, and thus that we have the beginning of ours intact? We cannot be sure, as no other strophe ends so near the right edge. Let us look more closely.

---

1 First published by M. Norsa, "Versi di Saffo in un ostrakon del Sec. II a.c.," *Annali della Scuola Normale Superiore di Pisa*, ser. 2, vol. 6 (1937).

On paleographical grounds, line 1*a* would seem not to belong to our poem: the larger space following it; the fact that *κατιου*[is not Æolic, and *πνέοισιν* in line 11 does not reproduce the error; and that the only restoration of good pedigree (Norsa's *ὀρράνοθεν κατίοι*[*σα*) cannot stand at the end of a Sapphic stanza, but would suit nicely a dactylic meter.[2] But we are told that on other than paleographical grounds an earlier stanza is desirable, perhaps even necessary. Two arguments to this effect require close attention.

First, that in an invocation of Aphrodite the goddess herself must be mentioned at or near the beginning of the poem.[3] But the evidence is not nearly so clear as one might wish. Only twice in the Sapphic fragments can we be sure that we have the beginnings of poems with invocations – Ode 1, and fr. 103.8; they bear out the point, but are insufficient grounds for the formulation of a rule. In the other fragments, where we are always unsure that we have the beginning, we cannot say what may have been mentioned first. Further, it is possible that the invoking word δεῦρυ (hither) in the first line satisfied what requirements of prayer form Sappho felt and, indeed, that she may have had special reasons for witholding the name of the invoked deity until the end – precisely as Anacreon, the most Sapphic of the poets of the next generation, did in his fr. 12, beginning with the invoking word, but

---

2 Something like Turyn's suggestion, *καράνοθεν*, "from the mountaintop," although unattested elsewhere, may be the answer. See A. Turyn, "The Sapphic Ostrakon," *Transactions of the American Philological Association* 73 (1942), 308. C. Gallavotti ("L'ode saffica dell' ostrakon Fiorentino," *Studi italiani di filologia classica* 18 [1942], 190) suggests inserting a version of line 1a in the lacuna of lines 11 and 12, on the theory that the scribe, noticing his error in the third strophe, added the omitted phrase in the only space he had left. M.L. West suggests ("Burning Sappho," *Maia* 19 [1970], 316) that line 1*a* is a *paraphrase* of a preceding stanza – like Gallavotti's suggestion, a piquant and unproveable guess.

3 *S&A* 39–40.

witholding the name of the deity till the eleventh and final line. When Sappho deals with conventions based on Homer – as the prayer form is – there is *always* the possibility that she intends deliberately and pointedly to neglect or overturn some part of the received tradition. This argument can lead to no conclusion.

We are told repeatedly that the poem needs another stanza because Sappho's poems of this type have not four, but five.[4] The argument is Milne's (based on fr. 31), that the poems of Sappho's first book follow the pattern, theme-transition-variation-transition-recapitulation, which for the prayers is: invocation-transition-example of past (as in fr. 1) or mythological (fr. 17) epiphany-restatement of invocation.[5]

But a number of qualifications must be made. This structure is likely for fr. 5, almost certain for fr. 17, and certain for Ode 1 – but these are all prayers, and there is no poem that is not a prayer for which this structure can be confirmed. Now, isn't Milne's form only the standard Greek form for a prayer, already fully developed in Homer, and not a peculiarly Æolic lyric form at all?[6] And anyway, is Milne formulating a *rule* when he says, "Five is generally the limit to number of stanzas in these odes" (meaning the odes of Book 1)? Obviously he knows that Ode 1 is seven stanzas long and that only one poem (fr. 17) is certain to have had five. There is not enough material for a *rule* here.[7]

---

4 Turyn, "The Sapphic Ostrakon" (above, n. 2), 128, et al.

5 H.J.M. Milne, "The Final Stanza of φαίνεταί μοι," *Hermes* 71 (1936), 126–28.

6 For prayers, see F. Schwenn, *Gebet und Opfer: Studien zum griechischen Kultus*, Religionswissenschaftliche Bibliothek 8 (Heidelberg: C. Winter, 1927); G. Zuntz, "Zum Hymnus des Kleanthes," *Rheinisches Museum für Philologie*, n.s., 94 (1951), 337–41.

7 See Milne, "The Final Stanza of φαίνεταί μοι" (above, n. 5), 128. Some of Milne's "evidence" for his five-stanza rule and his arch form has simply disappeared (a new papyrus fragment has moved back the beginning of fr. 20 – out of the five-stanza range), some is incredibly

If, however, we accept a more relaxed version of Milne's argument – that the odes of Book I generally exhibit an arch or circular form – then fr. 2 can do very well with the four stanzas it has: the invocation being "theme," description of the grove "variation" or second theme, and repeated invocation, "recapitulation." If, on the other hand, we are strict about the rules – as if we knew the game – and demand five stanzas, transition passages (which are *rarely* in evidence in Sappho), and a clear verbal echo of the beginning at the end, then we must assume that our four stanzas are only the recapitulation and that theme, transition, variation, and second transition all occured in one action-packed stanza ending]ρανοθεν κατιου[or that our four stanzas are only the theme, and that the other elements occured in one stanza at the end. What an affront our poem would be to grace in structure. But let us turn our attention for a moment to the end of the poem, where a fifth stanza may have occured as well as at the beginning.

Line 17 does not occur on the ostrakon, but follows the last strophe as quoted by Athenaeus. It is not in the Æolic dialect; it is prose rather than verse, and the four words in it that have gender are all in the wrong gender. Yet it is a common view that this line leads into a new section of the poem.

Sappho and her companions, Norsa said, have performed a sacrifice in a shrine, received a sign of divine favor, and proceeded to request an epiphany for the feast that would follow; thus both earlier and later stanzas are missing. But Sapphic invocations, as far as we can judge, do not seem to arise from cult occasions, and, secondly, they begin the poems in which they occur (whether with mention of the divine

tenuous (we really do not know what is happening at the end of fr. 17), and some quite arbitrary (his belief that a new poem – "The Ode on Fortune," as he calls it – began at fr. 16.21 is insupportable).

name or not). More important, perhaps, are we to believe that Sappho expected the visible presence of Aphrodite at a feast? This "naive-realist interpretation," as West calls it,[8] seemed adequate to the first commentators. A postwar generation, however, spoke of a feast enriched by the *imagined* presence of the goddess, a revelry infused with the *feeling* of her nearness.[9] Perhaps so ... but is it proper to ask the goddess, even speaking figuratively, to act as servant at a mortal feast? (Setti suggests that Aphrodite participated in a feast of the gods that is going on at the same time as the mortal feast[10] – but really *τούτοισι* seems to suggest a single group of revelers.)

Rather than ask about the propriety of this banquet, let us ask whether there is any banquet at all; the lines on the ostrakon mention no mortal presence except Sappho. The banquet theory seems to rely unduly on the seventeenth line, the most corrupt and uncertain line in the text – if indeed it can be said to be in the text at all. Wrong in dialect, wrong in meter, wrong in gender, difficult in meaning, and ruinous to the circular structure of the poem, perhaps this clumsy line should be expelled from Sappho's poem and put back into Athenaeus's narrative – where, of course, a banquet lies ready for it. In the endless festive quoting of the deipnosophists, now and then one will extend the sense of the quotation past the end quote and bring it into playful reference to his dining companions. At 13.563*e*, for example, Myrtilus adopts the style and imitates the diction of the quoted author (as Athenaeus uses the word *ἑταίροις* in line 17) and brings the sense of the quotation to bear on the company in which he sits. And we should consider what is going on among the

8 West, "Burning Sappho" (above, n. 2), 308.

9 *GLP* 198, and W. Schadewaldt, *Sappho: Welt und Dichtung. Dasein in der Liebe* (Potsdam: Eduard Stichnote, 1950), 78–84.

10 A. Setti, "Il frammento saffico dell' ostrakon Fiorentino," *Studi italiani di filologia classica* 19 (1943), 125–47.

deipnosophists at the moment when the Sapphic passage is quoted: it is the discussion of wine. But it will be objected, perhaps Athenaeus is *paraphrasing* Sappho in this line. And we cannot be sure. He may, indeed, be paraphrasing some *other* passage of Sappho, such as fr. 160's *τάδε νύν ἐταίραις ταὶς ἔμαις τέρπνα κάλως ἀείσω*, "These delights now I will sing for my companions" (which seems very likely to come from a Sapphic stanza, as Diehl has it). But at 13.55*b*, Athenaeus's continuation of a quotation is definitely not a paraphrase of the quoted author (Apollonius Rhodius) - and it surely would have to be suspected of being one if we did not have the quoted context to compare. Line 17, really, will fit into Athenaeus's style more easily than into Sappho's and if he can take responsibility for it, we had better let him have it. When it is included in criticism of the poem it exerts a much stronger effect than its extremely questionable status can justify.

Finally, none of the arguments for either earlier or later stanzas is convincing; none of them is even very persuasive. It is time now to turn our attention to arguments for completeness of the poem, and first of all to the syntactical structure as described by Gallavotti.[11]

Each of the first three stanzas is made up of three enjambed clauses. Each of these clauses adds one item to the catalogue of features of the grove - altars, cold water, roseshade, glimmering leaves, etc. These are, let us say, the mosaic pieces from which the grove is constructed as we watch. In the fourth strophe, the grove being complete, Aphrodite appears within it; here the list-like three-clause structure is abandoned, and the poem runs smoothly to its end in one long clause. Superimposed on this clause structure is a pattern of initial words in the strophes: with *δεῦρυ* we begin, with

11 Gallavotti, "L'ode saffica dell' ostrakon Fiorentino" (above, n. 2).

ἐν δ' we continue, with ἐν δ' we continue again, and with ἔνθα we conclude, as the flower opens finally with the mention of the goddess.

Now, this is in no way a confused and unbalanced thing (as Milne's rules would suggest) possessing only part of its growth; it is a fully developed and nicely patterned organism. It seems clear that the structure is intentional, and doubtful whether another strophe anywhere could avoid ruining it. [12] Is it meaningless that the poem of Horace, which seems at least in part to be based on fr. 2 (*Odes* 3.18), is complete in four Sapphic stanzas?

In general, arguments against the completeness of the poem are based (however weakly) on concepts of convention and rule: the five-stanza "rule," the mention of the invoked deity at the beginning, the echo of the beginning at the end – arguments for its completeness, on an appreciation of the mature condition that the poem possesses as it stands. If we turn now to critical interpretation, we will find ample support for this division.

The Grove of the Goddess

The central question in the interpretation of fr. 2 is indeed the central question for all the Sapphic fragments: Does she mean it? Or, perhaps better: *How* does she mean it? Is it a record of personal experience? A ritual song? A conceit?

Those who see autobiography in Sappho's poems not unnaturally connect the apparent mention of Crete in the first line with the Parian Marble's exile in Sicily;[13] that is, she

---

12 For an *exempli gratia* restoration of a first stanza ending with line 1*a*, see W. Theiler and P. von der Mühl, "Das Sapphogedicht auf der Scherbe," *Museum Helveticum* 3 (1946), 22. It certainly does what can be done to make an interesting poem dull.

13 Thus Norsa, "Versi di Saffo in un ostrakon del Sec. II a.c." (above n. 1), 10.

stopped off at the one island on the way to the other.[14] The mention of Crete strengthens the view, basic to most criticism of this poem, that Sappho is referring to a real grove in a real geographical location. But in fact, this would be most unusual for her. As much as we would like to learn about Sappho's life from her poems, we must face the fact that she does not help us much. She does not, for example, use place names autobiographically. Let us survey them briefly, and tour, as it were, the geography of our 200 lines. What autobiography could one write from them?

Cyprus is royal (fr. 65) and the home of Aphrodite (fr. 35). *Panormos* and *Paphos,* like royal Cyprus, are homes of Aphrodite (fr. 35), and she is also invoked from *Crete* (fr. 2). There is a road to great *Olympus* (fr. 27.12); love's power sent Helen to *Troy* (fr. 16). Sappho longs to see the flowery banks of *Acheron* (fr. 95),

14 Thus a variety of readings meaning "to Crete" rather than "from Crete." K. Matthiessen has collected thirteen versions of line 1 ("Das Gedicht Sapphos auf der Scherbe," *Gymnasium* 64 [1957], 554–64); unfortunately many of them make good sense and are generally agreeable. W. Schubart ("Bemerkungen zu Sappho," *Hermes* 73 [1938], 303) followed by West ("Burning Sappho" [above n. 2], 316) would remove Crete altogether, translating "On the appointed days (of the festival)." A passage in Gregory of Nazianzus, however, offers some reason to retain it (see Q. Cataudella, "Saffo Fr. 5(4)–6(5) Diehl," *Atene e Roma,* ser. 3, vol. 8 [1940], 199), and it accords well with Hesychius's testimony (see C. Theander, "Zum neuesten Sapphofund," *Philologus* 92 [1927], 466) that Aphrodite was worshipped as Ἀνθεῖα (of the flowers) at Knossos, and with the only other mention of Crete in our Æolic fragments (which is discussed below, n. 15). West argues against the reading "from Crete" because it will not go with *ὀρράνοθεν* (from heaven) in line 1*a*, but this, it seems to me, argues rather against *ὀρράνοθεν* than against "from Crete." Omitting Crete altogether would have minor interesting results such as the possibility of fr. 35 (ἤ σε Κύπρος *καὶ* Πάφος ἤ Πάνορμος, "whether Cyprus and Paphos, or Panormos holds you") occuring earlier in this poem (which would make it look still more like the first stanza of Horace, *Odes* 1.30), but the reading "from Crete" is, as Page says (*S&A* 36), "the best sense with the least change." And the question does not strike me as crucial anyway.

and she will find fame there after death (fr. 65) because she has invoked the *Pierian* Muses (fr. 103). But a woman who had no share in the roses of Pieria will be forgotten when she goes to *Hades* (fr. 55). In fr. 44, where the frequencies of place names, personal names, and ornamental epithets are at their highest, consistent with the choral lyric style, we find: *Asia, Ida, Ilion* twice, *Plakia,* and *Thebe,* all literary references. Closer to home we find that *Lydia* is mentioned four times: Sappho would not trade Cleis for it (fr. 132); Anactoria's walk is to be preferred to the Lydian chariots (fr. 16); a gown of rare beauty is imported from there (fr. 39); a departed girl who assumes a sort of mythic status shines out among the Lydian wives (fr. 96). Similarly, *Sardis* is the source of an imported kerchief (fr. 98*a*), and perhaps is named in relation to the departed girl in fr. 96. It seems that Lydia and Sardis are mentioned not as geographical locations where events took place, but as symbols of wealth and a somewhat gauche monumentality to which Sappho opposes her subjective and internal value, ὄττω τις ἔραται. A *Lesbian* singer (who, judging from a remark of Ælius Dionysus [ap. Eusth. 11.1.129] was probably Terpander) towers over the singers of other lands (fr. 106). Altogether, nineteen place names are mentioned a total of twenty-seven times and only two seem likely to represent external facts about Sappho's life: a kerchief sent from *Phocaea* is praised as a lovely gift (fr. 101.3), and *Mytilene* is mentioned in a broken and unclear context probably involving Lesbian politics (fr. 98*b*3).

Here, perhaps, we can discern a certain spiritual autobiography, but no physical one; if anything, a veil is pulled down before our eyes. Sappho's place-names refer to the geography of the imagination, not the geography in which the body moves. It is not unreasonable to suppose that Sappho may have visited Crete – on the other hand, it cannot be said that there is any evidence for it at all. (The Parian Marble falls after our comic biographers and does not connect Sappho with Crete anyway.) The point is that such geographical associations seem irrelevant to her poetic purpose. Crete was connected with the cult of Aphrodite and with goddess worship in general, and it seems that Sappho could have no better reason to mention it.[15]

Turyn, looking, I think correctly, in spiritual geography rather than physical for the location of this grove, points out its similarities with Orphico-Pythagorean descriptions of the afterlife.[16] Most prominent is Pindar's dirge (114 Bowra):

> *τοῖσι λάμπει μὲν μένος ἀελίου τὰν*
> *ἐνθάδε νύκτα κάτω,*

---

15 Pace West, "Burning Sappho" (above, n. 2,), 316. See Diodorus Siculus, *Bibliotheca historica* 5.77.4–5, and Hesychius of Alexandria, *Lexicon*, s.v. Ἀνθεῖα. The fr. inc. auct. 16, *κρῆσσαί νύ ποτ' ὧδ' ἐμμελέως πόδεσσιν*, "Thus melodiously the Cretan girls once danced," seems to spring from the same sense of this Cretan ethos - which goes back to the famous Minoan gems, and was still clearly visible in the archaic period. Lobel and Page obstinately include this among the *Fragmenta Incertum Utrius Auctoris* (16), though it is indicated as Sapphic by its similarity to her fr. 154, the typically Sapphic *ἄπαλος* (eight times in Sappho, three in Alcaeus), the association of Crete and Aphrodite in fr. 2, the meter, which would fit Sappho's seventh book, and, above all, the subject and mood, which are distinctively hers. In favor of Alcaeus I find only his fr. 397, *τερένας ἄνθος ὀπώρας* - but this is a part of the common inheritance from Homer (e.g. *Odyssey* 9.449) and could be found anywhere - and *ἐρόεις*, which occurs once and possibly again in Alcaeus, never in Sappho. Many fragments preserved *sine nomine auctoris* (e.g. 105*c*, 108, 115, 129, 132, 140) are assigned to Sappho by Lobel and Page on less evidence. Though certainty is, of course, not to be hoped for here, it is nonetheless proper to treat the fragment as Sappho's.

16 Turyn, "The Sapphic Ostrakon" (above, n. 2), 312ff. The motif of the garden of the goddess, with apple trees and running water and a hint of initiatory rites, goes back at least to Sumerian cylinder seals. It is a typically Bronze Age motif that, in the Iron Age, becomes a symbol of a lost age of innocence (Eden), which might be recovered after death (Orphics), or reappear at a Millenium (Horace, *Odes* 3.18; Vergil, *Eclogues* 2), or (like the garden of the Hesperides) remain the impossibly distant goal of the hero's quest.

φοινικορόδοις δ' ἐνὶ λειμώνεσσι προάστιον αὐτῶν
καὶ τοὶ μὲν ἵπποισί<τε>γυμνασίαις<τε>, τοὶ δὲ πεσσοῖς,
τοὶ δὲ φορμίγγεσσι τέρπονται, παρὰ δέ σφισιν εὐανθὴς
ἅπας τέθαλεν ὄλβος·
ὀδμὰ δ' ἐρατὸν κατὰ χῶρον κίδναται
αἰεὶ θύα μειγνύντων πυρὶ τηλεφανεῖ παντοῖα
θεῶν ἐπὶ βωμοῖς.

In purple-rosed meadows is the space before their city
and shadowy with incense-fume and heavy
with golden fruits,
and some with horses, some with gymnastics,
some with games
and some with lyres enjoy themselves, and among them
the flower of happiness blossoms whole;
a lovely scent lies over their land
and sacrifices of all kinds are mixed forever with
fire far-shining, on the altars of the gods.

If Pindar's mood is quite different from Sappho's, still many images are shared (roses, incense, shadows, horses), and several words occur in both passages (λείμων, τέθαλε, χῶρος), suggesting, to Turyn at least, that both are imitating some third passage. In the afterlife of Ps.-Plato, *Axiochos* 371*c,* pure springs in flowery meadows recall Sappho's ὕδωρ ψῦχρον; and the phrase recurs again on an Orphic grave tablet. Guthrie says, "The word ψῦχρον means of course not simply cold, but refreshing... It is of the same root as *psyche,* soul... the word ψῦχρον in the Orphic line... literally means 'to be refreshed from evil.'"[17] Has Sappho then, "simply transferred the picture of paradisiacal landscape, known from Orphic poetry, from the paradise to the holy precinct of Aphrodite"?[18]

Let us, as a test, compare the following passage of Xenophanes (1.4–12):

---

17 W. K. C Guthrie, *Orpheus and Greek Religion* (London: Methuen and Co., 1935), 177.

18 Turyn, "The Sapphic Ostrakon" (above, n. 2), 315–16.

> *κρητὴρ δ' ἕστηκεν μεστὸς ἐυφροσύνης·*
> *ἄλλος δ' οἶνος ἑτοῖμος, ὅς οὔποτέ φησι προδώσειν,*
> *μείλιχος ἐν κεράμοις ἄνθεος ὀζόμενος·*
> *ἐν δὲ μέσοις ἁγνὴν ὀδμὴν λιβανωτὸς ἵησι,*
> *ψυχρὸν δ' ἔστιν ὕδωρ καὶ γλυκὺ καὶ καθαρόν·*
> *πάρκειται δ' ἄρτοι ξανθοὶ γεραρή τε τράπεζα*
> *τυροῦ καὶ μέλιτος πίονος ἀχθομένη·*
> *βωμὸς δ' ἄνθεσιν ἂν τὸ μέσον πάντῃ πεπύκασται*
> *μολπὴ δ' ἀμφὶς ἔχει δώματα καὶ θαλίη.*

> The crater stands full of good cheer,
> and other wine is ready, which swears it will never betray,
> sweet, and smelling of flowers in the cups;
> and among them the frankincense
> gives off its holy scent,
> and there is cold water both sweet and pure...
> In the midst of it all the altar is piled with flowers;
> round about, song and good cheer hold the halls.

And this, from Theognis (1249–52):

> *Παῖ, σὺ μὲν αὔτως ἵππῳ, ἐπεὶ σκιρτῶν ἐκορέσθης*
> *αὖθις ἐπὶ σταθμοὺς ἤλυθες ἡμετέρους*
> *ἡωίοχόν τε ποθῶν ἀγαθὸν λειμῶνα τε καλὸν*
> *κρήνην τε ψυχρὴν ἄλσεά τε σκιερά.*

> Boy, you are like a horse when, having had enough
> of running loose, you come back to our stables,
> desiring your rider and good pasture, your fountain
> fair and cold, and shadowy groves.

The readiness of everything, the frankincense already fuming, the cold water, the cups, the flowers, the altar piled high, all these remind us of Sappho's fr. 2; but Xenophanes is introducing a feast, not a paradisiacal scene. Has he used paradisiacal attributes to glorify his feast? Or is the Orphic paradise decked with festive imagery? Is Sappho alluding to paradise, introducing a feast, or both? Or neither? Is Theognis, in welcoming his catamite back, consciously using phrases suggestive of a return to paradise? Or is it merely a return for dinner, coupled with the ancient sexual metaphor of taming a horse? As so often in Greek poetry (and perhaps particularly in Sappho) we find that ritual, paradisiacal, and festal imageries overlap. Perhaps the Orphic authors, when framing their descriptions of paradise, merely dipped into the common fund of imagery for their purposes, as Sappho, Theognis, and Xenophanes did for theirs. A brief look at Horace, *Odes* 3.18, will be suggestive in this context.

Faune, Nympharum fugientum amator
per meos fines et aprica rura
lenis incedas abeasque parvis
aequus alumnis.

si tener pleno cadit haedus anno,
larga nec desunt Veneris sodali
vina craterae, vetus ara multo
fumat odore.

ludit herboso pecus omne campo,
cum tibi Nonae redeunt Decembres;
festus in pratis vacat otioso
cum bove pagus;

inter audaces lupus errat agnos;
spargit agrestes tibi silva frondes;
gaudet invisam pepulisse fossor
ter pede terram.

Faunus, lover of fleeing Nymphs,
you will step softly over my boundaries and through
my sunny acres, and you will go away
in good spirit toward my little charges,

if when the year is full a young goat falls
and the wine-bowl, Venus's accomplice, does not lack
ample wine, the ancient altar fumes
with heavy incense.

> All the cattle gambol in the grassy meadow
> when your December Nones come round again;
> all the district, on a holiday,
> idles among the cattle in the fields.
>
> The wolf roams among unfearing lambs;
> the forest sprinkles its rustic leaves on you;
> the spades-man, in gleeful three-time, beats the earth,
> his old enemy, with dancing feet.

Lines 7–8 recall lines 3–4 of the Sapphic poem rather closely, and are in the same position in their strophe. Further, the last three of the four strophes are arranged in tricola, as are the first three of Sappho's poem. (The cola are not enjambed, but this is typical of the difference between Horace's Sapphics and Sappho's own.) The rustic scene, the wine bowl, the mention of Venus, the smoking altar, the grove – perhaps the most striking similarity is the paradisiacal description in strophes 3 and 4, which has somewhat perplexed Horatian scholars. "The introduction of the miraculous element here into the account of the village festivities seems to us inharmonious," says T.E. Page, commenting *ad loc.*[19] But if Horace was basing his poem, in some respects, on the Sapphic passage, he may have seen clearly what is only dimly suggested to us, namely the conventional paradisiacal features of her grove.

Although Turyn's proposal remains no more than a strong possibility (not, I would think, a strong *probability*), let us consider for a moment what it means if it is so. Probably Sappho is not describing an afterlife; elsewhere she uses more conventional pictures of Acheron and Hades. To lend, however, to the worship of Aphrodite some of the atmosphere of a mystery cult might well suit her purpose. Surely the altar, golden cups,

19 Q. Horatii Flacci, *Carminum,* Liber IV, ed. T.E. Page (London: Macmillan and Co., 1883).

nectar, are more suggestive of a *sacrament* than a conventional banquet. Are there aspects to the worship of Aphrodite as Sappho understood it which she might present in an atmosphere suggesting *initiation*? The mysteries of Aphrodite...

Let us turn from the remarks of past scholars to the poem itself and see what we can make of it.

The Poem

Consider the only other long description of nature in early Greek lyric, Alcman's fr. 89, beginning with:

> εὕδουσιν δ' ὀρέων κορυφαί τε καὶ φάραγγες...
>
> The mountain peaks and valleys are asleep...

This, it seems, is a night world, still and silent, but not empty; beneath the silence, a current of potential energy runs. It is full of images of beasts and comes alive from the contrast between their teeming activity at day and their sleep at night.

The emptiness of Sappho's grove is deeper. It has a sense of unchanging, trance-like stasis. This stillness is neither night nor day, but timelessness. [20] Nor is mere sleep the psychological condition for such stillness: it is a κῶμα, or magic sleep, that drips from the tree limbs. This is a magical scene, like the house in the woods that is stumbled upon in fairy tales, where everything stands in readiness, but no one is at home. [21] This is as much the description of an inner condition, a readiness in the heart, as of an outer scene.

The grove, like the enchanted house, stands ready for a feast, a feast of some awesome and unseen power whose impending presence hangs over all. There are no celebrants, but

20 In the world of Sappho's poems, shadows are as apt to be cast by moonlight as by sunlight – and she is especially fond of the full moon. See frr. 34, 96, and 94D.

21 For Aphrodite ἐφίππος, see the scholia on the *Iliad* 2.820.

the sacred objects stand in order in the ritual place. There is no one who has lit the incense or tends it, yet it lies smoking on the altar. No voices sing the hymn, but the water of refreshment sings through the apple branches. There is no one either sleeping or waking, but from the flowers, leaves, and trees a magic sleep descends. There is no one to drink the sacred drink, but golden cups stand ready on the smoking altar. There is only the invisible presence of an observer who waits, slowly, methodically, with a rapt sensitivity to detail, noting the rich features of the landscape.

If the poem is complete in four stanzas (which is a very clear possibility) then surely it is a symbolic picture, describing a spiritual condition. Sappho herself (or, at least, the observer) is defined by the invocation, by her desire to have Aphrodite come and grant the nectar of joy;[22] Aphrodite, by her ability to do so and by her tendency to withold herself – as her name is witheld until the end of the poem. The description of the grove unfolds under the increasing tension of the missing name, which the reader, or auditor, familiar with the conventions of Greek prayer will feel the lack of at once. Finally, the emptiness of the grove is filled and the lack of the name supplied simultaneously by the mention of the goddess. The second invocation is elaborated until it has the force of an apparition: the prayer seems to be answered even as it is spoken. The goddess appears in the heart of the faithful devotee, pouring into ghostly cups immortal wine. At the same time, the halting, enjambed rhythm of the poem is purified and, like a flower blossoming, the verse runs

22 The suggestion of Theiler and Von der Mühl ("Das Sapphogedicht auf der Scherbe" [above, n.12], 25) is worth mentioning: that this nectar confers "the sweet dream of love" (den süßen Rausch der Liebe); thus, in the mood of magic sleep, Sappho meets the archetype that controls all such dreams. But the relevance of Catullus, Poem 99.2, *AP* 5.305, is questionable; Sappho, after all, is not bound by later events in a tradition she began.

smoothly to its end. The poem becomes an emblem, or visual pun, with Sappho, at the beginning, gazing across the intervening grove at Aphrodite, at the end.

Now if we ask again, where is this grove, we will see the immense suggestiveness of the poem, and the naivete of the question. The grove is a symbol and as such has not one identity, but many. It lies not only (if, in fact, at all) in the external world, but in the imagination of the poet. Further, it *is* the imagination of the poet, the grove of transformations, where visions are seen and the breaches in reality are healed. It lies locked in the verses of the poem; but it is poetry itself, that primal affirmative act rising from the love of beauty, which seems for Sappho, as much as (or possibly rather than) the sexual act, to have become the primary rite of Aphrodite. Fragment 2, in fact, as it creates in the heart of the reader the trance of paradise and the vision of beauty, *is* the grove that it describes.

Finally, it is the heart and what it longs for that are signified under the images of invoker and invoked. The grove is a general image of a relationship of desire and withholding, of emptiness and fullness, of art and life, which is acted out in various specific ways in the other poems. The inner rite that the lone suppliant plays in this still place is a central rite of life – the rite of the vision that alleviates, as in a magic sleep, the tension between dream and reality. Somehow the promise of happiness seems to have been fulfilled, but really it has only been imagined.

Sappho gazes across the grove at the goddess who gives joy in golden cups eternally.

III

The Devotees of the Goddess

(Fragment 94)

τεθνάκην δ' ἀδόλως θέλω·
ἄ με ψισδομένα κατελίμπανεν
↔
πόλλα καὶ τόδ' ἔειπέ[μοι]·
ὤιμ' ὡς δεῖνα πεπ[όνθ]αμεν,
Ψάπφ', ἦ μάν σ' ἀέκοισ' ἀπυλιμπάνω.
—
τὰν δ' ἔγω τάδ' ἀμειβόμαν·
χαίροισ' ἔρχεο κἄμεθεν
μέμναισ', οἶσθα γὰρ ὤς σε πεδήπομεν·
—
αἰ δὲ μή, ἀλλά σ' ἔγω θέλω
ὄμναισαι[....].[...]..αι
ὀ̣σ̣[σα μάλθακα] καὶ κάλ' ἐπάσχομεν.
—
πό[λλοις] γὰρ στεφάν]οις ἴων
καὶ βρ[οδων πλο]κ̣ίων τ' ὔμοι
καὶ [ ] πὰρ ἔμοι περεθήκαο
—
καὶ πό[λλαις ὐπα]θύμιδας
πλέκ[ταις ἀμφ' ἀ]πάλαι δέραι
ἀνθέων ἐ̣[βαλες] πεποημμέναις,
—
καὶ π[όλλωι λιπάρως] μύρωι
βρεντείωι.[ ]ρ̣υ[..]ν
ἐξαλείψαο κα̣[ι βασ]ι̣ληίωι
↔
καὶ στρώμν[αν ἐ]πὶ μολθάκαν
ἀπάλαν πα.[ ]...ων
ἐξίης ποθο[ ]α̣νιδων
—
κωὔτε τις [λόφος οὔ]τ̣ε̣ τι
ἶρον οὐδ' ὐ[δατος ρόα]
ἔπλετ' ὄππ[οθεν ἄ]μμες ἀπέσκομεν
↔
οὐκ ἄλσος.[ ].ρος
]ψόφος
]...οιδιαι
↔

1*a*. [Ἄτθιδ' οὔποτ' ἄρ ὄ]ψ[ομαι], Edmonds. 9. *αἴ δὲ μή, ἀλλὰ θέαν θέλω*, Schubart. 10. [σὺ δὲ] λ̣[ά]θ̣εαι, Wilamowitz. 11–12. Diehl. 13. Wilamowitz. 15. Athenaeus 15.674*c–d*. 17. ἐ̣[βαλες], Theander;

...Really, I want to die;
weeping she left me.

She said many things, and this:
"Alas, what terrible things we have gone through;
Sappho, truly I leave you against my will."

And I made her these replies:
"Farewell; go, and remember me,
for you know how we cared for you.

But if you do not, I wish to
remind you...
what tender and beautiful things we went through.

For many wreaths of violets
and of woven roses too,
and... you put around yourself at my side,

and many woven necklaces
made of flowers
cast about your soft neck,

and with much rich and royal
perfume elegantly you
anointed...

and upon a soft bed...
you satisfied desire
of tender young girls,

and there was no sacred hill,
nor temple, nor stream of water
whence we were absent,

no grove... the rattle (of castanets)..."

ἐ[*ράτων*], Schubart. 18. Wilamowitz, Diehl, et al. 24. *χόρος*, Blass; *γάμος*, Bowra. 25. *ἶρον οὐδ' ὐ* [*μέναιος εἶς*], Theander.

Meter and Text

Fragment 94 is identical in meter (glyconic, glyconic, glyconic with inserted dactyl) with fr. 101, which, according to Athenaeus, belonged in the fifth book of Sappho's poems. The meter of frr. 95 and 96 is similar (cretic plus glyconic, glyconic, glyconic plus bacchiac), and has led to the supposition that Sappho's fifth book contained various stanzas based on that complex and melancholy rhythm, the glyconic.

The only textual controversy of much importance centers on line 23, where the similarity of *ἐξίης πόθον* to Homer's phrase *ἐξ ἔρος εἵην*, to put aside desire (having satisfied it), seems to provide a clear reference to homosexual acts – possibly the only such reference in Sappho's fragments.[1] The appealing restoration *νε[ανίδων* (of young girls) – offered originally by Lobel, but since rejected by Lobel and Page – strengthens a suggestion that, even without it, is amply strong, as, of the six other uses of *ἄπαλος*, five describe girls in erotic contexts. Alternative restorations have been

1 "Possibly" because of fr. 99, col. 1, line 5, which Lobel and Page read ο.λ.ι.σ.β.. δοκο.ι.ς. περ.καθ....ενος. ὀλισβ-, if correct, must be ὄλισβος, "dildo," a word used elsewhere only by Cratinus and Aristophanes. A.W. Gomme points out, however, that both the lambda and the iota are highly questionable and that the fragment could as easily have been written by Alcaeus as by Sappho ("Interpretations of some Poems of Sappho and Alcaeus," *Journal of Hellenic Studies* 77 [1957], 255–66). Why anyone should be surprised to find the word in either poet – midway in the tradition between Archilochus and Anacreon – is a mystery to me.

found, but it must be said that none of them is as convincing as νεανίδων, and that νεανίδων itself is not entirely convincing.[2] The matter must be left unresolved.

The text I give contains some restorations, which, while far from certain paleographically, cannot be far wrong in sense (for example, Diehl's λιπάρως [elegantly] in line 18

---

2 C. Theander ("Studia Sapphica II," *Eranos* 34 [1936], 59–62) notes that (1) the use of ἐπί with the accusative in Sappho involves an allusion either to many places or to a general or customary place; (2) ἔρος is the word for sexual desire; πόθος usually means desire for someone or something absent (though he seems not to have noticed the erotic use at fr. 22.11); (3) ἄπαλος is used by Sappho of people, not of things – so a personal name must be restored; (4) since the girl is going away, she may have come from somewhere in the first place: she may, in fact, be the girl who has gone to Lydia in fr. 96. Hence his reading:

> καὶ στρώμν[αν ἐ]πὶ μολθάκαν
> ἀπάλαν πά[ρα μ]α[ι]όνων
> ἐξίης πόθο[ν ἄδυ νε]ανίδων

which he translates:

> et stragulis super mollibus (incubans) tenerarum ex Maeonibus
> expellebas desiderium suaviter virginum.

The proposed sense is: "When you first arrived, you missed your girlfriends and could not sleep; but now you have gotten over that – so why are you leaving?" He compares Xenophon, *Anabasis* 3.1.3. The obvious weaknesses of this are that the ambiguity still remains (*is* the allusion sexual or not?), and that Sappho elsewhere does not say Μαιόνων, but Λύδων. Edmonds (*LG* 1.242) ingeniously restores:

> ἀπάλαν παρ' [ὀπα]ṿọ́ων
> ἐξίης πόθο[ν ἄβρον Ἰ]ανίδων,

> (You) had from the hands of gentle serving maids all that
> a delicate living Ionian could desire.

Bowra (*GLP* 191 n2), echoing one of Theander's points, says, "though the Homeric phrases indicate satiety after the appetites have been indulged, πόθος indicated desire for someone absent, and the notion is that even this is set aside." Perhaps. But he, too, seems to have missed the use of πόθος at fr. 22.11.

and Edmonds's λόφος [hill] in line 24, neither of which occurs elsewhere in the fragments).

The Poem

Absense, separation, loneliness – these are Sappho's most typical moods, occuring also in frr. 1, 5, 16, 31, and 96 certainly, and probably in several others, including fr. 95. Also, the dramatic present in which someone looks back on a past conversation is one of her customary narrative devices (Ode 1, frr. 62 [probably], 95 [probably], and 134). The imagery overall is strikingly similar to that of frr. 2 and 96.

Yet though this is one of the longest and most typical of our Sapphic fragments, criticism has been disappointingly limited to biographical interpretations; this poem, in fact, has been appreciated as a mainstay of the biographical approach, and as little else.

Wilamowitz-Moellendorff regards Sappho's long speech to the departing girl as a window into the daily life of the *thiasos,* and scholars have followed him in this and have amused themselves by connecting the event with one or another of the names that the *Suda* has left us.[3] Bowra based his thoroughgoing biographical interpretation primarily on this poem and fr. 31. "Sappho looks back," he says of this poem, "on times which they have passed together, and enumerates

---

3 All of Sappho's editors have been too eager to restore proper names. Even Lobel gives us an uncertain Andromeda (at 68 *a*5 – δρομέδαν [by running] might be restored), – and a Doricha (in fr. 7.1) that seems quite unnecessary (Σμ. ad loc.).

For the influence of Wilamowitz-Moellendorff's view of this poem (*SuS* 48–52), cf. G. Perrotta, *Saffo e Pindaro* (Bari: Laterza, 1935), 34: "C'introduce nel chiuso mondo della poetessa, sicché noi possiamo dire d'avere agli occhi la vita quotidiana del tiaso" (There it is introduced into the closed world of the poetess, and therefore we can say that we have before our eyes the daily life of the *thiasos*).

activities that must have been the common round of their lives."[4] Here we encounter his central argument: "The simplicity of her manner has some of the qualities of the conversation which she claims to record, and it is hard not to believe that some such conversation took place, and that its substance was not entirely different from this record of it."[5] And again: "Her words are so unadorned that we take them literally."[6]

It is probably not necessary at this date to argue against the biographical interpretation of poetry. Those interested may peruse the very critical remarks of Wellek and Warren under "Literature and Biography" in their *Theory of Literature.*[7] The view that any piece of literature is a record of facts tends to rob it of artistic meaning by minimising, or even disparaging, the role of the imagination in it. Certainly, we would like to know about Sappho's life and to see how that knowledge might enrich the poems for us. (It might, of course, not at all.) But we have *no* sound facts on which to hang these poetic events. And even if we had, we would do well to ignore them after a moment, remembering, as Yeats says, that "the muse loves a liar, a gay and warty lad," and that poetry, while it may use external facts, is bound by no straight policies as to their chronology or perspective. (Perhaps, the more simple and sincere poetry sounds, the more it should be suspected of being a mask.)

Edmonds's *exempli gratia* restoration of line 1*a* (see the apparatus) may well be correct, in that it mentions both Sappho and the departing girl in one line. This unit is then doubled into two lines that define their differing attitudes: Sappho

4 *GLP* 100.

5 Ibid., 192.

6 Ibid.

7 R. Wellek and A. Warren, *Theory of Literature* (New York: Harcourt Brace, 1956), 75–81.

wishes to die;[8] the girl left her, weeping.[9] This doubled unit, of two lines, is in turn tripled into six lines that preserve the strict parallelism: one strophe, rather than one line, for each actor, and these strophes parallel in structure, the first line of each introducing a speech that fills the remaining two lines. This is the first section: three pairs of parallel statements increasing in length arithmetically. The fourth stanza begins Sappho's account of her recollections, and introduces a new structural section: until this point the two persons have been treated with exact equality and parallelism – then Sappho's side of it begins to outrun the girl's. Before considering this shift let us note how stanzas one to four are woven together by the repetition and development of key verbs placed prominently at the ends of lines.

At the end of stanza 1, *κατελίμπανεν* (she left me) expresses Sappho's point of view and calls forth as an echo in the girl's voice the *ἀπυλιμπάνω* (I leave you) at the end of stanza 2, while between them, at the end of line 4, the phrase *δεῖνα πεπόνθαμεν* (terrible things we have gone through) acts as a sad knot, tying them together. Sappho's own stanza ends with *πεδήπομεν* (we love you), a pathetic answer to

8 W. Schubart ("Neue Bruchstücke der Sappho und des Alkaios," *Sitzungsberichte der königl. preuss. Akademie der Wissenschaften* 1 [1902], 195–206) supposes that line 1 was spoken by the departing girl, a supposition denied by all later scholars except Gomme ("Interpretations of some Poems of Sappho and Alcaeus" [above, n.1]). While Gomme's argument (that if the subject changed in line 2, there would be a particle to indicate it) is a strong one, the structural symmetry of this part of the poem and Sappho's habit of beginning poems in the dramatic present seem equally weighty counterarguments.

9 Both Page (*S&A* 76) and Bowra (*GLP* 191) take *πόλλα* in line 3 with *ψισδομένα*, rather than with *ἔειπε*. The fact that each strophe is end-stopped makes this unlikely; the damage it does to the sense makes it practically impossible. Each girl has a speech, yet Sappho's is ten times as long. Thus she says that the girl said many things (*πόλλα*) of which she will repeat only one (*τόδ'*), but that she will give her own reply in full (*τάδ'*).

the verbs that have ended the first two stanzas. Μέμναισ' (remember me) at the beginning of that line is answered by ὄμναισαι (to remind you) at the beginning of line 10, and finally, in the prominent position at the end of that stanza, occurs the key phrase *καλ' ἐπάσχομεν* (beautiful things we have gone through).

The phrases *δεῖνα πεπόνθαμεν* and *καλ' ἐπάσχομεν* represent the two personalities, sum up the two speeches, and fix the emotional tension that the poem tries to resolve. (In the girl's speech, the most prominent position is given to *ἀπυλιμπάνω*. In Sappho's reply, *καλ' ἐπάσχομεν* has taken over the end of the stanza.) This structure of responding pairs of verbs interwoven in two or three significant positions acts as counterpoint to the other structure that we have observed and effects a transition. The plaiting of semantic signs with metrical positions is smooth and subtle, and distracts attention from the fact that the fourth stanza unbalances the parallel structure obtained in stanzas 1 to 3.

Stanzas 5 to 10 contain Sappho's recollections, explaining the phrase *καλ' ἐπάσχομεν*. To complete the structural pattern established at the start, an equally long reply by the girl would be needed, to justify her own reasons for saying *δεῖνα πεπόνθαμεν*. It seems unlikely that this happened, however. It would require a poem longer than any we know of in Æolic lyric, and would be a most un-Sapphic subservience to structural simplicity. It is more likely that we have lost only one stanza at the end, and that the structure evolves, at the same time regularly and dynamically, as follows: the first expression of the situation takes only one line, 1*a* (this, of course, is conjectural); this is doubled in lines 2 and 3; the new unit then is tripled into the parallel stanzas 2 and 3, which finally are quadrupled, the pair of responding stanzas being followed by the unit of stanzas 4 to 11. The discreteness of this last, largest, unit may be seen by the fact that each stanza in it, unlike the earlier ones, deals with one class of images (wreaths, necklaces, perfumes, sacred places), and that each begins with a καί, which has replaced the significant end-verb as the binding element.

Thus we are presented with four pictures, each expressing the situation in greater detail than did the last, in units that expand with mathematical regularity. The parallelism that was broken by the extension of Sappho's speech into the fourth strophe is seen, at the end, not to have been the structural key: that balance was deliberately created and just as deliberately destroyed. The extension of her speech – unprepared, and indeed prepared *against* – shows her private world surging up to outrun the bounds of form and balance. Yet the very unbalancing proceeds to establish a new, more comprehensive form and balance.

This type of artifice – of highly controlled shifts where, at first, form seems to have been overcome by passion, but then passion reveals itself as a new and greater form – is one of the things that impart to Sappho's best poems their almost electrical vitality. The impression of static yet vibrant eternality conveyed by fr. 2, for example, rises from its perfect, even pictorial, joining of form and content – Sappho, impatient in her longing, rising in the first line to gaze across the poem at Aphrodite who, being the desired rather than the desirer, arrives, stately and slow, only at the end; they are forever separated – and yet joined – by the intervening grove. It is a *tour de force,* and equally so is the dynamic evolution of fr. 94, where the two aspects, form and content, start in a kernel of unity (stanza 1), then gracefully diverge in a long slow arc that is in the end seen as a greater unity.

Turning now to content, we will discover that, in fact, the arc established by the expanding structural units and the path of its emotional development are one and the same, and that the two are bound by an expanding and receding experience of time, that is, by the dramatic sequence of events.

The questions that critics have been most concerned with are: how does Sappho feel toward the girl? what is the relation between the long passage of recollection and the rest of the poem? why does she choose the indirect method of narrating the conversation in the past tense? Two views have predominated.

"One feels," says Reinach," "that the poetess must have been experiencing a disappointment and that under this tender evocation she hides a reproach."[10] Wilamowitz-Moellendorff develops this further:[11] Sappho regards the girl's departure as a sign of unfaithfulness, and chides her for leaving after she has received so many favors. Through this particular event the general grief of Sappho's life is suggested: it is her fate to love and always to be left by those she has loved. Here Wilamowitz-Moellendorff quotes fr. 26: *ὄττινας γὰρ εὖ θέω, κῆνοί με μάλιστα πάντων σίνονται* (for those whom I treat well, they especially wrong me). Why, then, the apparently unnecessary device of portraying the event in the past? "It is an ingenious way," says Reinach, "to evoke the memory of their last affair."[12] Again, Wilamowitz-Moellendorff is more elaborate: the poem was written to be read to the girls who had stayed on after their friend's departure from the school so that they would hesitate to take such a step themselves.

10 T. Reinach, "Nouveaux fragments de Sappho," *Revue des études grecques* 15 (1902), 65: "On sent, l'on devine que la poétesse a dû éprouver une déception et que sous cette tendre évocation, se cache un reproche."

11 *SuS* 48–52.

12 Reinach, "Nouveaux fragments de Sappho," (above, n. 10), 64: "C'est une manière ingénieuse d'évoquer le souvenir de leur liaison passée."

What can be said in favor of this approach? That it is tender and sympathetic, surely; but not that it rests on evidence. Or that it has anything much to say about the *poem*. While Wilamowitz-Moellendorff often seems highly sensitive to Sappho's mood, still his settings in the school must, if regretfully, be regarded as figments. And anyway, he has used the poem to reveal the life; he has done next to nothing about revealing the *poem*.

Schadewaldt's view – shared by Bowra, and to some extent by Page – is that it is not bitterness but sorrow of separation (*Trennungsschmerz*) that bathes the poem in its sweet melancholy.[13] Sappho's essential emotion is love, but this leads to *Trennungsschmerz*, so she finds solace in memory. The poem's need for three levels of time results from the dilemma posed by the two emotions: at the time of leave-taking, Sappho, masterful in the presence of the beloved, consoled the girl with the treasure of memories she would take with her; but later, overcome by the grief of separation, she finds solace herself in the same memories *and* in the memory of how she had consoled the beloved girl. Schadewaldt rejects the idea that bitterness or reproach is involved and denies the relevancy of fr. 26, noting that the gender of κῆνοι makes it inappropriate. (He might with good effect have replied to Wilamowitz-Moellendorff's citation with fr. 41: ταὶς κάλαισιν ὔμμι νόημμα τὦμον οὐ διάμειπτον (my feeling toward you fair ones does not change).

Though this seems a fairly satisfying outline of the drama of the poem, it is at best an outline. It does not account for the increasing energy of the flow of words and images, and it appreciates the poem primarily as a revelation of Sappho's per-

13 W. Schadewaldt, "Zu Sappho," *Hermes* 71 (1936), 366; *Sappho* 115–19. Cf. the simpler view of Zuntz: *Amorem enim totum carmen spirat* (G. Zuntz, "De Sapphus carminibus," *Mnemosyne* 3.7 [1938], 88.)

sonality. But the poem works in a deeper and more satisfying way when it is considered not primarily as a self-revelation by the poet, but primarily as a work of art, that is, an artifact in which formal matters, i.e., the relations of theme to structure, are uppermost.

There are three time levels in the poem: the dramatic present, in which Sappho wishes to die; the time of the departure, which she remembers *in* the dramatic present; and the early life, which she remembers remembering at the time of the departure. This is the exact reverse of ordinary narrative order ("Once we lived happily together; then she left me; now I want to die"), and involves the emotions of all three times in the moment of speaking. The poem moves from present fact, to direct recollection, to indirect recollection, plunging ever deeper into the past. It is striking that the three sections into which the time levels divide the poem are the same as the three structural sections observed above. It can be assumed that their relationship is significant.

The present receives one scant line (possibly two, if we possessed line 1*a*); it is mentioned only to be rejected: "Really, I want to die." The wish to die, as elsewhere in Sappho, seems to be a metaphor for the rejection of present time, and memory, that shadowland where the present goes when it has died, may serve as a surrogate for physical death. In fr. 31 also it is in the pain of the present moment that Sappho says she is almost dying: death is an escape from that present, a rejection of it. The only other fragments where death is treated with extant context - frr. 55 and 147 - speak of it in the same breath with memory. Death, or memory, is an internal world that in some cases is preferred to the external one we call the present. In fr. 94 the wish to die is explained and, at the same time, fulfilled by the mind's turning inward to dwell in the past.

But is that past a strictly remembered one? Or does this death partake of the imagination as well as the memory? Bowra characteristically takes it as an unvarnished record of facts. "That this life," he says, referring to lines 12–29, "was entirely satisfying and happy seems clear enough."[14]

But I find this view difficult to accept. Sappho seems characteristically to begin her poems with some example of the difficulties of life, then to resolve the problem by affirming that art and imagination are creators of stronger, and healing, realities.[15] Furthermore, it is well known that Sappho does not explain her meanings, but acts them out. The very fact that the description in fr. 94 is of a life that seems totally happy should, I think, show us that it is either a partial or a total fiction – the healing imagination entering the domain of memory, to soothe the pain of life. After all, has the girl not said of their past, from *her* point of view, *δεῖνα πεπόνθαμεν* (what terrible things we have gone through)? What Sappho presents is an edited view, an *interpretation* of their past, one that bears the same relation to real life that the symbolic rite in fr. 2 bears to real rites. In the poem that immediately followed in the ancient edition (fr. 95), Sappho wishes to die and see the dewy lotus-bearing banks of Acheron. And so she does in fr. 94, also; she wishes to die, then turns inward to walk among imagined flowers on an imagined riverbank in another world. Death is co-extensive with a poetic region where imagination reigns and can supply what is lacking in life. The imagery of the three sections will bear this out.

Present life is an imageless void; in it there is only the stark wish to die. Turning inward, Sappho dwells for a while

---

14 *GLP* 191.

15 I would apply this description to almost all the long fragments: Ode 1, frr. 16, 31, 94, and 96. Fr. 2 is a *general* picture of the same thing, not using *examples*. Fr. 44, of course, is another matter.

in the direct past, suggested by the pain of the present. These seven lines are in a static and formal balance, like a treaty.[16] They are also abstract, containing no image-words except ψισδομένα (weeping). The fourth strophe, which breaks open the orderly formalism of these lines and effects the transition to a more remote reality, ushers in, at the same time, a wholly different mood and a new use of language. Stark and harsh in the present, formal and drab with weeping in the direct past, the language becomes free and ornamental. Images of beautiful objects and acts abound in what has been up to now an imageless poem.

The balanced, almost oppressive, orderliness of the first three strophes, and their lack of images, may be taken to show the mind's lack of freedom in them. The unbalancing fourth strophe is the striving against the bonds: as the poem, in this strophe, breaks loose from static form, so it breaks free from the grip of the world. When the mind has broken these limits it strains no more: the third reality is maintained for the remaining six strophes. That world is where Sappho wanted to be. The feeling, as the energy of the phrases increases and they become more rapid, is not grief, but triumphant agitation. It is the insistence that this is the greater reality.

And what is the nature of this reality? How is it portrayed? First, flowers (Sappho's most characteristic image) appear in the longest series in any of the fragments. Then perfumes, couches, desire; something possibly a wedding, possibly a stream of water; a sacred grove, the sound of castanets ... Is it a life of ritual acts or a life of festivities?

Ritual is suggested by ἶρον (a sacred object, as in Homer, or a temple, as usually after Homer), ἄλσος (a grove shrine), ψόφος (a rattling; used elsewhere only in fr. 44.25), and of course,

16 I refer to the balanced attention to the concerns of both parties as their relationship is put on a new footing. Also, ἀδόλως in line 1 suggests the language of treaties.

the flowers. As Schubart says, "There is no doubt that the floral ornament, the ointments, etc. were intended for the gods, if one considers the context, into which this description is inserted."[17] (See his reading of line 9 in the apparatus).

Yet, as in fr. 2, no rite as such is mentioned. We have, instead, two persons, presumably in love, who are placed in an environment of sacred objects, shrines, anointments, music, and a couch or bed. If any rite is suggested, it is the wedding rite. But this, clearly, is not a statement of past fact, but a suggestion arising from a group of symbolic objects – the homosexual lovers sanctified by and sanctifying in turn an environment suggestive of heterosexual marriage rites.

Jurenka, on the other hand, felt that these stanzas described a symposium.[18] On this side are: *μύρον* (unguent or perfume, used by Alcaeus in connection with drinking parties); the flowers and couches, and the fact that *ψόφος* in fr. 44.25 is used not of the wedding *rite,* but of the wedding *celebration.* Yet, as in fr. 2 again, there are no revelers; there is no wine; there is no hint of any specific festal occasion. The objects are in their places, but the activity is not named, and the scene is generalized in a tantalizing and ambiguous way. Once again we find that in Sappho ritual and convivial activities are suggested by the same imagery – and that neither seems to be merely (if at all) a description of past events. There is an emptiness, and a remoteness to the world they suggest, that cannot be accounted for by any historical realism.

---

17 Schubart, "Neue Bruchstücke der Sappho und des Alkaios" (above, n.8), 203: "Daß der Blumenschmuck, die Salben, usw., den Göttern zugedacht waren, kann man nicht bezweifeln, wenn man den Zusammenhang beachtet, in den diese Schilderung eingefügt ist."

18 H. Jurenka, "Die neuen Bruchstücke der Sappho und des Alkaios," *Zeitschrift für die österreichischen Gymnasien* 53 (1902), 294. Page (*S&A* 79) argues that the *στρώμνα* is strictly a bed for sleeping, but the word is not used elsewhere in Æolic.

Like the empty grove in fr. 2 and the empty night universe in fr. 96, this scene of halls, temples, and woodland groves, with garlands, perfumes, and music in abundance, seems created only for Sappho and her remembered companion. There is a symposium, but no guests; a round of cult activities, but no other worshippers – and no rite. It is a ghost city where Sappho and her friend may wander, as through a "forest of symbols" that suggest the condition of their hearts. Her wish is like Achilles' wish that he and Patroclus alone might raze the crown of Troy, wandering through the empty streets in a triumph of private happiness. It is a child's wish, typically homosexual, for a world where he (or she) and a best friend might do whatever they wish, disturbed by no one else at all.

In this empty place an entire symbolic lifetime is acted, in briefest suggestions, before our eyes. In the weaving of garlands, a preparation for marriage is shadowed forth; in the anointing, the wedding ceremony; its consummation, in the bed. A long married life of outdoor walks and visits to woodland shrines follows, where there is music everywhere, but no musicians to play it... Call this rather an *imagining about* the past than a record of it; how much of it is "based" on events in Sappho's life is impossible for us to know; that it is not primarily a record realistically presented seems plausible.

This imagined life will appear, as we go on, to be the central experience related in Sappho's poetry. It is a cult of the love of beauty (in flesh or in verse), under the auspices of Aphrodite, and presented by the poetess in her role as *vates,* as priestess and worshipper, at a cult that may have been known to no one else. Its central image is two persons in love in a ritual environment, with the goddess presiding who has poured this nectar in their cups. It is a great metaphor in which life itself (or at least the life devoted to the admiration of beauty) is the tenor; the wedding rite (or a shadowy and symbolic version of it), the vehicle – life is a wedding, in which the individual devoted to the love of beauty is wedded to it through an inner rite. Virtually all of the major fragments of Sappho take on greater meaning if we learn to look at them as aspects of this metaphor (as, I believe, she herself did).

But to call the traces of this imagined life, which can be found in most of Sappho's poems, merely a daydream arising from homosexual unhappiness[19] is not to do it justice. For these are poems, not daydreams, and there is a difference. The life she makes claims for, in which objects of sacred beauty and higher significance stream around us like blessings from goddesses, exists palpably in the poems, and through them other people – the readers, ourselves – may enter into it and undergo its transformations.

19 As, in effect, does Robert Bagg in "Love, Ceremony and Daydream in Sappho's Lyrics," *Arion* 3.3 (1964), 44–82.

IV

The Magic in Action

(Fragment 96)

]σαρδ.[..]
πόλ]λακι τυίδε̣ [ν]ῶν ἔχοισα
—
ὠσπ.[...].ώομεν, .[...]..χ[..]
σε θέαι σ' ἰκέλαν ἀρι-
γνώται, σαῖ δὲ μάλιστ' ἔχαιρε μόλπαι̣·
—
νῦν δὲ Λύδαισιν ἐμπρέπεται γυναί-
κεσσιν ὤς ποτ' ἀελίω
δύντος ἀ βροδοδάκτυλος † μήνα †
—
πάντα περρέχοισ' ἄστρα· φάος δ' ἐπί-
σχει θάλασσαν ἐπ' ἀλμύραν
ἴσως καὶ πολυανθέμοις ἀρούραις·
—
ἀ δ' <ἐ>έρσα κάλα κέχυται τεθά-
λαισι δὲ βρόδα κἄπαλ' ἄν-
θρυσκα καὶ μελίλωτος ἀνθεμώδης·
—
πόλλα δὲ ζαφοίταισ' ἀγάνας ἐπι-
μνάσθεισ' Ἄτθιδος ἰμέρωι
λέπταν ποι φρένα κ[.]ρ̣... βόρηται·
↔
κῆθι δ' ἔλθην ἀμμ.[..]..ισα τάδ' οὐ
νῶν τἄ[π]υστα νυξ[..()]πόλυς
γαρύει̣ [..()]αλον̣ [.....()].ο̣ μέσσον·
—
ε]ὔ̣μαρ[ες μ]ὲν οὐκ̣ α.μι θέαισι μόρ-
φαν ἐπή[ρατ]ον ἐξίσω-

---

1. ἀπυ] Σαρδίων, Wilamowitz-Moellendorff; ἐνὶ] Σάρδε[σιω], Edmonds. 17. κῆρ <δ'> ἄσαι βόρηται, Wilamowitz-Moellendorff. 18. ἄμμ' ὀ̣ξὺ̣ βοᾶι, Wilamowitz-Moellendorff. 19. νὺξ. πολύω[ς], Wilamowitz-Moellendorff. 20. γαρύε[ι δι'] ἀλὸς, Wilamowitz-Moellendorff.

23 σθ̣αι συ[..]ρ̣ο̣ς ἔχηισθ' α'[..̣()].νίδηον
[ ]το̣[...(.)]ρατι-
μαλ[ ].ερος
26 καὶ δ[.]μ̣[ ]ος Ἀφροδίτα
—
καμ̣[ ]νέκταρ ἔχευ' ἀπὺ
χρυσίας[ ]̣αν
29 ...̣()]απουρ̣[ ]χέρσι Πείθω
↔
[ ]θ[..]η̣σενη
[ ]ακις
32 [ ]......αι
↔
[ ]ες τὸ Γεραίστιον
[ ]ν̣ φίλαι
35 [ ]υ̣στον οὐδενο[
↔
[ ]ερον ἴξο[μ

...
... at Sardis ...
many times turning her mind in this direction,

since when we lived together
she held you like a manifest goddess
and took joy most of all in your singing;

now she shines out among the Lydian wives
like the rosy-fingered moon
when the sun has set,

outshining all the stars,
and it sheds its light on the salt sea
and the flowery fields alike,

and the fair dew is poured out,
and there bloom the roses
and tender chervils and blossomy honey-lotuses,

and, wandering far off,
she yearns for gentle Atthis
and her delicate breast is weighed down with desire,

her heart with grief, and she cries out for us
to come there ... things not unknown to us
... the night ... the sea ... in between ...

A third modern addition to the Sapphic corpus is fr. 96, the great companion piece to fr. 94 on the Berlin parchment, and in many ways the most mysterious of all the fragments.[1] Its general sense through line 20 is fairly clear. Someone (whom we might as well call Sappho) addresses a girl named Atthis whose beloved, another girl, has gone away to Lydia. Sappho likens the departed girl to the moon, in the longest simile that we have from her hand, and consoles Atthis with the thought that the departed girl is thinking of them, as they are thinking of her, and is longing for Atthis. It is uncertain whether the sixteen very fragmentary lines that follow belong to the same poem.

That seems simple enough, but there is much that is unclear, and one recent commentator considered a detailed understanding of the poem impossible – perhaps not even desirable. "What is hidden," Page says, "we cannot judge; what is revealed we observe to be devoid of anything profound in thought or emotion or memorable in language."[2] The question is what one feels is hidden in the poem, and what revealed. Surely, it *is* a difficult poem – perhaps the most difficult we have from Sappho – and perhaps the best. If we are

1 The publication details are the same as for fr. 94 (see above, chap. 3, "The Devotees of the Goddess," n. 1). The text I give is primarily that of Lobel and Page, with Wilamowitz-Moellendorff's readings preferred in two cases. My translation is only intended to show what I think the poem probably said grammatically.

2 *S&A* 95.

to discover its secrets, we must be prepared to deal patiently with the problems that the centuries have placed between us and the text.

The Text

The parchment does not tell us where the poem began. In our line 1 (which may or may not have been the second line of the first stanza of the poem) Wilamowitz-Moellendorff thinks he can see *σαρδίων*,[3] Edmonds, *σαρδη*;[4] Diehl, Lobel and Page agree that only *σαρδ-* can be read. It is generally presumed, because of *Λύδαισιν* in line 6, that this is a reference to Sardis; this is not certain, however, and Turyn, for one, chooses to disbelieve it.[5] Line 3 would seem to have contained a reference to a time when the girls were together, and Wilamowitz-Moellendorff's *πεδεζώομεν*, although unattested, is accepted by Diehl, and used here *exempli gratia*. In line 4, Lobel's *-σε θέαι σ' ἰκέλαν* is likely to be accepted as the solution of the parchment's *σεθεασικελαν*.[6] A disadvantage is that it makes Wilamowitz-Moellendorff's *ἔχεν* at the end of line 3 impossible, and some verb of thinking seems to be needed there. Μήνα in line 8 is impossible metrically, and Schubart made the obvious emendation, to *σελάννα*. But here the question arises, how *μήνα*, an uncommon word, got itself substituted for *σελάννα*, a common one. Beattie accordingly suggests that not the noun, but the adjective is corrupt, and offers *βροδοδακτυλήα μήνα*, "rosy-ringed moon," which is unattested elsewhere.[7] The passage is obelized by Lobel

3 See *BKT,* vol. 2 (1907), 15, and *SuS* 53.

4 *LG* 1.246.

5 *Stud. Sapph.* 61.

6 For a full discussion, see *S&A* 89.

7 A.J. Beattie, reviews of *LP* and *S&A* in *Journal of Hellenic Studies* 77 (1957), 320–22.

and Page because they do not like the definite article. In line 17 Wilamowitz-Moellendorff reads *κῆρ* (heart), *ἄσαι*, and *βόρηται* = *βάρηται* from *βαρέομαι*, (be heavy). But elsewhere in Æolic the root "heavy" appears as *βαρ-*. Zuntz's suggestion[8] that *βόρηται* is from *βορέομαι* (devour) is the only intelligible alternative presently available; thus he restores *κᾶρ* (fate) instead of *κῆρ*: "She wanders remembering gentle Atthis with desire, and a fate devours her delicate heart." The main objection is that *ζαφοίταισ'* must then be taken as a verb, and it appears more likely on other grounds to be a participle. Restoring a connective particle after *κῆρ*, we may translate the resulting chiastic zeugma as follows: "Wandering far off and remembering gentle Atthis, she is weighed down in her delicate breast with desire and in her heart with grief." In lines 18–19 Lobel and Page read *τόδ' οὐ* and *υστον* rather than *ταδ'ου* and *υσταν* (Wilamowitz-Moellendorff), but they acknowledge that the alphas are possible, and I have kept them because the stanza is meaningless without them. Lines 24–36 are too fragmentary for variant readings to be significant.

Allusiveness in Sappho

Some remarks about how to approach Sappho's meaning here are in order. The vocabulary and the range of images in our Sapphic fragments are both extremely limited; the poems give an impression of unusual consistency of idiom, and we would like to know how to account for that. Some will be satisfied with Lobel's view that she was bound by rules of a hypothetical "pure Lesbian vernacular,"[9] but that will seem to others to do an injustice to the artist's role in creating

8 G. Zuntz, "De Sapphus carminibus," *Mnemosyne* 3.7 (1938), 100.

9 *Σμ.* xviii–xx.

his or her own language. Gomme points out, quite rightly, I think, that other poets have adopted peculiar and characteristic vocabularies of very limited size for purely poetic reasons – creating a small sublanguage, as it were, highly selected and especially charged with the poet's sense of meaning – set off, in fact, from the vernacular of the day.[10] Now, Sappho's language is enough like Alcaeus's that we may call them both Lesbian. But it displays special peculiarities that cannot be ascribed to mere dialect conventions. The Sapphic fragments, for example, make no mention of wine although, as we have seen, festive imagery abounds; Alcaeus mentions wine ten time in a corpus not much larger than hers.[11] If we assume that Sappho regularly establishes her own usage and that her deviations from it are apt to be significant, then – *whether or not* she is working within the frame of a pure Lesbian vernacular, a thing impossible to ascertain – we may frequently find keys to her intentions.

For example, in line 2 the departed girl is τυίδε νῶν ἔχοισα, "turning her mind hither," but in lines 15–16 she is ἐπιμνάσθεισ' Ἄτθιδος (remembering Atthis). The first phrase does not occur elsewhere in the Sapphic fragments; μνάομαι, as in the second phrase, is her usual word for remembering. So why the alternative phrases? Turyn notes that recollection, in the Greek poets from Homer on, is powerful "ad affectionem oriundam," and supposes that Sappho had that connotation in mind in the word ἐπιμνάσθεισ'.[12]

---

10 "If then Sappho is stricter in her use of words and their forms, than Alkaios, it is because she is less true to the spoken vernacular. From this an important consequence follows. She has imposed this strictness on herself, she has made her own rules; and, that being so, she is allowed to break them." A.W. Gomme, "Interpretations of some Poems of Sappho and Alcaeus," *Journal of Hellenic Studies* 77 (1957), 263.

11 Sappho twice uses the verb οἰνοχοέω, but in both cases what is "wine-poured" is nectar. Wine itself is never mentioned.

12 *Stud. Sapph.* 65.

He cites abundant parallels from other authors, but let us just look for a moment at Sappho's own usage: Helen, when she abandoned husband and family, "did not remember" (*οὔδε ἐμνάσθη*) her parents and her child (fr. 16.11); in the same poem, Sappho is "remembering" (*ὀνέμναισ'*) Anactoria, whom she longs to see. In the scene of parting in fr. 94 we see, "Go now, and remember me, for you know how we loved you ..." Few examples, but they could not be stronger support for Turyn's suggestion. Conversely, fr. 129 suggests that "to forget" for Sappho meant "to cease to love":

> *....ἔμεθεν δ' ἔχηισθα λάθαν...*
> *ἤ τιν' ἄλλον ἀνθρώπων ἔμεθεν φίληισθα...*
>
> Have you forgotten me,
> or have you fallen in love with someone else?

All other occurences with context are not only harmonious with the equations "to remember" = "to love" and "to forget" = "not to love" but are enriched by them.[13] The common Homeric meaning of *μνάομαι* (to woo for a bride) comes to mind, and Theocritus 2.44–46 may be compared.[14] Sappho, though an innovator, was surely a Homerist also,[15] and it would not push the point too far to say that she intended the word *μνάομαι* in lines 15–16 to have connotations of wooing and marriage.

In line 2 of fr. 96, then, Sappho avoided the phrase, which has erotic connotations, and substituted a circumlocution, which perhaps was emotionally neutral ("Many times turning her mind in this direction"). In lines 15–16, after the eight-line simile (lines 7–14) has had its effect, and when

---

13 Fragments 55, 105*a*, and 147.

14 "Whether it is a woman or a man who lies next to him now, may he forget that mate as Theseus in Dia once forgot lovely-tressed Ariadne."

15 See *Stud. Sapph.* passim.

the departed girl is no longer thinking merely *τυίδε*, but specifically *Ἄτθιδος*, the erotic – or even hymeneal – phrase is used.

Now let's look at lines 4 and 5: "She held you like a manifest goddess, and took joy in your song above all." It is well known that Sappho's similes, and especially similes comparing humans to gods, are especially associated with hymeneal song.[16] Page, in attempting to refute the argument that such a simile in fr. 31 was a hymeneal allusion, says, "In 95.4 *θέαι σ' ἰκέλαν* is obviously not used as a compliment especially suited to a bride...,"[17] and it is possible that he has directly missed the point. Sappho uses such similes seven times, and either five or six of them are directly hymeneal and would seem to establish a convention within Sappho's extremely limited and consistent practice, which her hearers would be expected to recognize.[18] In that case, then, by virtue of the simile, Atthis and the departed girl are seen for a moment as potential bride and groom. But the past tense adds poignant commentary to this vision: the happy couple is separated; their possibility of happiness lies in the past. This suggestion will be strengthened shortly.

What of the rest of this stanza: "She took joy in your song above all?" Most of the musical images in the fragments are without context, but those that have context occur almost exclusively in connection with weddings; the only other occurence of the *μελπ-/μολπ-*root describes an activity at a wedding celebration (fr. 27.5).

---

16 See, for example, B. Snell, "Sappho's Gedicht *φαίνεταί μοι κῆνος*," *Hermes* 66 (1931), 75 n3.

17 Sic. This is a misprint for fr. 96.4.

18 Fragments 23.5, 31.1, 44.21, 44.34, and 111.5. I say five or six because, of course, the nature of fr. 31 is disputed. The traditional view is that it also is in some way a wedding song; the question will be considered elsewhere in this book. The last of the seven similes, fr. 68*a*3, is without context, but may well have been an allusion to hymeneal song.

And other such features appear. First, Sappho's use of nouns like "man," "woman," "girl," follows a very clear pattern. In the other occurences of γύνη, for example, the γύναικες, or matrons, are specifically distinguished from the πάρθενοι, or unmarried girls. Now, line 6 of fr. 96, if it said παρθένοισιν instead of γυναίκεσσιν, would be eminently appropriate for describing a bride among her attendant maidens (indeed, as I will argue, it could hardly be anything else). The departed girl, then, is seen for a moment as a bride in her bridal procession – but with what irony in that word γυναίκεσσιν: "Now she shines out among the Lydian *wives*..." The substitution of "wives" for "maidens" has the same poignancy of lost chance that the past rather than the present tense had in line 5.

Finally, let us consider in this light the obscure phrase in line 8, ἀ βροδοδάκτυλος μήνα (the rosy-fingered moon). It is rejected by Lobel and Page on the basis of Lobel's rule that there is no example in Sappho of noun + adjective or adjective + noun preceded by the article, except when the noun is a personal name.[19] Perhaps μήνα will not be accepted as a personal name, but then it will not fit the meter either. Schubart's σελάννα is not only obviously appropriate, but also removes the difficulty of the definite article, as Selene is a personal name as early as Hesiod (*Theogony* 371).

The result is that we have another comparison of a human to a god, and we are not surprised. In an epithalamium it is highly likely that first one partner, then the other was treated to the comparison with a god. Fragment 96, in a reserved, but not really disguised, fashion, seems to follow the path of a wedding song, accentuating the loneliness of the separated lovers by allusions to the bliss of loving union.

The peculiarity of the phrase "rosy-fingered moon" may be explained somewhat by this approach too. There is, of

---

19 Aμ. lxxvii and lxxxix.

course, no possibility that any Greek, almost, in fact, any modern, could miss the Homeric allusion and be unaware of the misplacement of the epithet. Was this sheer capriciousness? Hardly. Dawn is mentioned in Sappho primarily, if not exclusively, in epithalamic contexts; it is "golden-slippered, rosy-armed, shining mistress Dawn" who will awaken the lovers after their night of happiness – or if, as is likely, they are still awake, remind them of the return to the public world. The displacement of this adjective from the daylight, which will find them still together, to the wandering moon, which shines upon them in their sleepless and lonely separation, is another sign of the peculiar and troubling inversion of wedding song that can be discerned in fr. 96.

It may, however, be objected that these individual echoes of a wedding song are either too slight in some cases or too unsubstantiable in others to convince us. Clearly, they are possible; and when they explain what have been considered difficulties in the poem they take on some degree of probability. But they do not stand alone. They are, as it were, governed, and greatly increased in plausibility, by the striking similarity between the beginning of the simile in fr. 96 and another Sapphic passage, fr. 34:

> *ἄστερες μὲν ἀμφὶ κάλαν σελάνναν*
> *ἂψ ἀπυκρύπτοισι φάεννον εἶδος,*
> *ὄπποτα πλήθοισα μάλιστα λάμπηι*
> *γᾶν . . . .*
>
> The stars around the fair moon
> quickly hide their splendid light
> when at the full she shines
> upon the earth.

Several things may be said in support of the view that this was the hypothetical unreal, or vehicle, of a simile in a wedding song, and that the simile in fr. 96 is a conscious allusion to it.[20]

But before we proceed into the inner sanctum of the simile itself, we must pause to sketch out the broader context of Sapphic nature images in general, observing their patterns and availing ourselves of the principles that emerge from them.

Nature Images; the Symbolism of the Flower

In Sappho's poetic universe, the macrocosmic terms – the earth and sky – appear only in descriptions of imaginary or mythical events. Aphrodite descends through the *αἴθερος* (ether), to the *γᾶν μελαίναν* (dark earth, fr. 1). Eros, wearing a purple cloak, descends *ἐξ ὀράνω* (from heaven, fr. 54). Opinions are recorded as to what is the fairest thing on the dark earth (fr. 16). Sappho cautions herself not to try to embrace heaven with her two arms (fr. 52).

The winds, the sea, and geographical features appear principally as vehicles in similes. A girl is like the moon shedding light over the sea (fr. 96). Love falls on the heart like a wind on a mountain (fr. 47). And connotations acquired in similes carry over into ritual scenes: Love is like a wind (fr. 47), so sweet winds blow through Aphrodite's grove (fr. 2). Fields of flowers are nourished by the moon that is like a girl – and near Aphrodite's sacred grove lies a meadow of flowers (fr. 2). Golden flowers grow by some seashore (fr. 143).

20 Schadewaldt (*Sappho* 30) recognizes the possibility that this is a simile describing a girl, but not that it is hymeneal. R. Merkelbach ("Sappho und ihr Kreis," *Philologus* 101 [1957], 1–29.10) says, without arguing the point, "Sappho [vergleicht] die Braut mit dem Mond, der alle Sterne überstrahlt" (Sappho compares the bride to the moon, which outshines all the stars). It seems that the simile is not merely possible, but virtually certain, and that the hymeneal context also must have been there.

Someone wishes to die and see the lotus-bearing banks of Acheron (fr. 95). These images occur only in the hypothetical unreals of similes and metaphors, and in connection with gods and mythological references; they are not among the literal properties of the poems.

Birds are rarely mentioned; animals, hardly at all. A meadow is ἱππόβοτος (able to nourish horses), but no animals are said to be there, and the standard sexual symbol seems all that is intended (fr. 2). Some things, or persons, were like fauns, in a simile (fr. 58). The fleece of a white goat is offered to some god or goddess (fr. 40). Aphrodite's chariot is pulled by sparrows (Ode 1); in a metaphor, the nightingale is the messenger of spring (fr. 136); the swallow is Pandion's daughter (fr. 135); doves let their wings go slack, probably in fear (fr. 42). (And because of its close similarity to Alcman's fr. 82 we may suppose that this is from a simile describing girls.) Someone or thing is whiter than an egg (fr. 167), and Leda once found an hyacinthine egg (fr. 166). Again, the occurrences are all in similes, metaphors, ritual scenes, and mythological references.

Flora are far more abundant than fauna. Sappho and a departed friend had visited all the sacred groves (fr. 94). In Aphrodite's grove are walls of roses, and quivering leaves; and apples, symbols of awakening love,[21] hang from the boughs. In a hymeneal simile where the same symbolism is clear, the γλυκύμαλον (sweet-apple) hangs on the highest bough (fr. 105*a*). Love is like a wind among oak trees (fr. 47), and a bridegroom is like a slender sapling (shaken by that wind) (fr. 115). Dika is encouraged to weave slender shoots into wreaths for the Graces (fr. 81*b*). Overcome with passion at the wedding feast, Sappho becomes paler than grass (fr. 31). The Cretan maidens, dancing around the altar, bruise the

21 *GLP* 260/1.

tender blossom of the grass (fr. 93 D).[22] In the vehicle of the simile in fr. 96, dew, brought on by the moon, nourishes the flowers, and likewise the flowery banks of Acheron are wet with dew (fr. 95).

Overall, a pattern is clear: these nature images belong mostly to the hypothetical unreal. Where they belong to the hypothetical real, they are apt not to be properties of a literal kind, but to be chosen for their, usually erotic, symbolism.

Sappho's most common and pervasive nature image is the flower. The root *ἀνθ-* occurs altogether eleven times. Only one other noun, *παίς* (child or girl), occurs as frequently: ten times meaning "girl" and five times involved in conventional forms of address such as "child of Zeus." There are thirteen mentions of specific kinds of flowers, six mentions of garlands, and seven compound epithets involving flower names. On the other side, *παρθένος* (maiden) occurs eight times, *κόρα* (girl) twice, and about ten girls are mentioned by name. The two are Sappho's most common classes of images (followed by goddesses and musical images). Furthermore, they are inseparable.

Cleis is like golden flowers (fr. 132). A pretty girl was seen gathering flowers (fr. 122). A girl takes flowers in her hands and desire flies around (fr. 22). A girl with yellow hair should adorn it with garlands of flowers (fr. 98). A distant girl is like the moon as it shines on fields of flowers (fr. 96). Another girl who has gone once wove wreaths of flowers at Sappho's side (fr. 94). A girl abandoned by her lover, or possibly the hymen of a bride, is like a hyacinth trodden on the mountain path (fr. 105*c*). In a much damaged papyrus we have in one line "desire" and, two lines later, "flower" (fr. 78).

---

22 See above, n.15, chap. 3, where I argue that this fragment – which Lobel and Page reject – is Sapphic.

The mentions of specific flowers increase the profusion of uses. Walls of roses shadow in the sacred grove (fr. 2). Garlands of roses and violets are woven (fr. 94). In the moonlight simile, dew falls on rose and chervil blossoms and flowery honey lotuses (fr. 96). The roses of Pieria confer undying memory (fr. 55). Lotuses grow on the banks of the river of death (fr. 95), hyacinths in the mountains (fr. 105*c*), golden pulses by the sea (fr. 143). Wreaths are woven of anise (fr. 81*b*) and celery (fr. 191). We have a verb for weaving garlands (fr. 125) and a distinction between neck wreaths (ὐπαθύμιδαι) and head wreaths (στέφανοι). Isolated roses (fr. 74*a*4) and garlands (fr. 92.10) lie between the gaps of unreadable papyri.

It is clear that we are dealing here with a wider practice than we observed for the other nature images. The expected occurrences in similes and ritual passages are in evidence, but others seem to be properties in the hypothetical real. *All* of them (whose contexts are extant) occur in association with girls, with Aphrodite, or with death.

How, Wellek and Warren ask, does a symbol differ from an ordinary property image? "Primarily," they answer, "in the recurrence and persistence of the 'symbol.' An 'image' may be invoked once as a metaphor, but if it persistently recurs, both as presentation [hypothetical real] and representation [hypothetical unreal], it becomes a symbol, may even become part of a symbolic... system."[23]

Indeed, Sappho seems to stress the symbolic nature of this image openly in some passages, emphasizing its more than ordinary meaning. The Graces, she says, love well-flowered things, but turn away from what is not wreathed (fr. 81*b*). Oblivion awaits a woman who has no share in the roses of Pieria (fr. 55).

---

23 R. Wellek and A. Warren, *Theory of Literature* (New York: Harcourt Brace, 1956), 189.

Ancient critics attempted to explain the symbolism. Philostratus says (*Letter* 51), "Sappho loves the rose, and crowns it always with her praise, likening the beautiful ones among the girls to it," and let it go at that. Athenaeus (or Clearchus ap. Ath. 12.554*b*) makes a more ambitious attempt: "All lovers, weakened by their sufferings and melted by the sight of the fair, wax wanton; for it is of their very nature that those who think that they are blooming and beautiful should pick flowers. Wherefore Persephone's companions were said to be picking flowers, and Sappho says she saw

> *ἄνθε' ἀμέργοισαν παῖδ' ἄγαν ἀπάλαν*
> ... almost too pretty – a girl picking flowers ...

Surely all this is true: that flowers are symbolically associated with girls, and that what the images share (the *tertium comparationis*) is their perishability, and their beauty, which looks as if it could never perish. But Athenaeus, speaking in his own person (15.674*d*), adds a point of great importance: "Sappho urges the makers of a sacrifice to wreathe their heads, on the plea that what is the more adorned with flowers is the more pleasing to the gods." Unfortunately, Athenaeus does not tell us for what kind of sacrifice Sappho commends flowers. The fragment he proceeds to quote mentions only the Graces – goddesses of beauty and poetry, who are invoked by Sappho at least twice in the fragments, and at least once in connection with the Muses.[24] Pindar (*Olympian* 14) confirms for us their connection with the Muses, addressing them as "queens of song," and in a revealingly Sapphic passage (*Pythian* 6) says that the poet tills the garden of *Aphrodite* – or, *of the Graces*. But – aside from this silent and interior labor of the poet – there are no known rituals

24 Fragments 53, 103.8, and 128. The last may be a corrupt version of 103.8, or vice-versa.

performed in honor of the Graces. Let us look briefly at those rituals that do appear in Sappho, and especially at ritual passages in which flowers appear.

In the fragments of Sappho's hymeneals – songs written to be performed at a public, ritual event – flowers are not prominent; only the hyacinth in fr. 105*c* seems to belong to them. Neither do the fragments that hint at a rite of Adonis mention flowers. For what rite, then, are these blossoms to be woven into garlands?

Fragment 154 describes a rite, but does not mention the divinity:

> *πλήρης μεν ἐφαίνετ' ἀ σελάννα*
> *αἰ δ' ὠς περὶ βῶμον ἐστάθησαν*
>
> The moon shone full
> and the girls as they stood around the altar...

A full moon night, and a ritual of girls, out of doors; the scene in general will remind us of that in fr. 96. Fr. 93 D, similarly, tells much without telling all:

> *Κρῆσσαί νύ ποτ' ὦδ' ἐμμελέως πόδεσσιν*
> *ὤρχηντ' ἀπάλοισ' ἀμφ' ἐρόεντα βῶμον*
> *πόας τέρεν ἄνθος μάλακον μάτεισαι*
>
> The Cretan girls once danced thus tunefully
> around the lovely altar,
> bruising with their delicate feet
> the soft smooth blossom of the grass.

Again girls, around an altar, out of doors; the mention of Crete will bring to mind the invocation of Aphrodite in fr. 2.

Fragment 2 itself describes the ritual place more closely: altars, burning incense, golden cups; it is uncertain whether it is night or day; flowers, flowering branches, and the leaves of flowering branches frame the scene. Light creeps through the walls of roses, and a magic sleep flows down with it from quivering leaves; there is an extreme removal from the world. The mention of Aphrodite suggests a ritual of girls, but no girls are mentioned, nor is any ritual named or described.

We may be fairly sure that Sappho sometimes presented fictionalized pictures of rites. Himerius (*Orations* 1.4) says that Sappho would enter the bridal chamber after the wedding feast, make the bed, lead Aphrodite down from heaven in the Grace's chariot attended by a chorus of Loves, and, after binding the goddess's hair with hyacinths, would leave the bride and groom alone at last. It seems likely that he has taken a poem of Sappho, written in the first person, and paraphrased it.[25] Probably a similar fiction should be detected in frr. 2, 154, 93 D, and elsewhere, but at a much deeper level of her poetic life. Girls, an altar, flowers, a full moon, a goddess ... the fragments as they stand present a picture of a relatively undifferentiated symbolic rite.

It is differentiated in that it involves only female divinities – Aphrodite and the Graces – and in that, sometimes at least, it takes place at night and out of doors. Moonlight, music, and flowers are involved. Clearly the wedding-night vigil of the bridesmaids is implied. But nothing happens. No rite is performed, nor is any ritual occasion or purpose evident. The collection of these images seems, in itself, to be the point. They are presented *as if* they described an actual rite. As Kerényi says, "There have been and are ceremonies of love and friendship."[26]

In fr. 94 more flowers are mentioned than in any other fragment, and with them we find: unguents used in rites; a temple; a sacred grove; music ... But here the setting is

---

25 J.D. Meerwaldt attempts to reconstruct from Himerius's text a three-stanza hymeneal by Sappho ("Epithalamica I," *Mnemosyne* 4.7 [1954], 19–38, and "Epithalamica II," *Mnemosyne* 4.13 [1960], 97–110).

26 K. Kerényi, *Athene: Virgin and Mother in Greek Religion* (Putnam, Conn.: Spring Publications, 2008), 8.

entirely private, and seems perhaps more convivial than ritual. What is presented is not exactly a rite and not exactly a party, but some private meeting, probably of lovers, which involved the symbolic objects common to both. In this private scene the undifferentiated symbolic rite is acted out. *This* is the rite for which the altars fume in the sacred grove. Now reconsider fr. 96: girls, out of doors, a full-moon night, fields of flowers...

A typical scene in Sappho is of girls (never women) plaiting garlands for a rite that is never explained (fr. 125). What is dwelt on, rather, is their beauty as they do so and a certain unspecified sadness that this beauty evokes. On one level, this scene will be considered symbolic of preparation for marriage, and the sadness then may be thought to arise in part from the observation of the beauty of unmarried girls (of ungarnered blossoms) combined with the suggestion that when the flower is plucked, it dies – when the girl is married she is no longer the embodiment of a promise of eternal beauty ("And that is why," says Athenaeus, "Persephone is described as gathering flowers... " And what was Creusa doing when she was raped by the god? And Eurydice, walking "like Spring itself" among the sunny grasses?)

We must assume that these sentiments, in addition to being familiarly Greek, were characteristically Sapphic. In no other light can we see her choice of the flower as the key symbol of her work, and its unvarying association with young girls. It is beauty in its freshness, its immense and terrible delicacy, which the image suggests – that brief moment when the beautiful shines out at full power and assumes, for all its perishability, the stature of an eternal condition in the spirit if not in the body. The flower thus is the emblem of "the mysteries of Aphrodite" – that inner rite of the pure admiration of beauty, which Sappho presents – with the trappings of the wedding rite – as a paradigm of the proper activity of the soul.

But obviously there is more to it than that. Roses are not only Aphrodite's flowers, but equally the flowers of the Muses, and are worn to please the Graces, those "queens of song." For the poetess alone in her study, flowers symbolize poems, and garlands are woven for a still more generalized rite; it is, on this side of the coin, a symbolism of the poetic process – the rite in which the flowerlike beauty of girls is celebrated in an inner garden where such perishable stuff is transmuted into those timeless flowers: poems.

A Pause, and a Glance at Alcaeus

Before continuing, a brief summary is in order, since our course has led us far from our original subject. Investigating the connection of frr. 34 and 96, we looked at Sappho's nature imagery and found that it is mostly a part of the hypothetical unreal of the poems. Flowers, however, appear frequently both in hypothetical real and hypothetical unreal. When they occur in the world of properties (hypothetical real), they seem not to be literal, but symbolic properties. They are bound up with other images to form the outlines of a symbolic rite that works on several levels, involving admiration of the beauty of girls, devotion to the work of the Muses, and both admiration and sadness at the presence of beauty in the world in general and the impossibility of permanently possessing it. Our general conclusion about Sappho's nature images – that they do not describe the outside world so much as the world of the imagination – will profit from considering some things Sappho does *not* mention.

Is it day or night in the goddess's sacred grove in fr. 2? The shadows indicate day – but Sappho likes full-moon nights;

the mood of sleep indicates night – but Sappho thinks of the night as a time for waking. The ambiguity is probably intentional, and the time focus is indeed almost always vague in Sappho's poems.

Day is mentioned only once (fr. 43.9) and night twice (frr. 23 and 30, unless one accepts Wilamowitz-Moellendorff's reading of 96.19), and then only in epithalamia, where the terms indicate shifts from one stage of the rite to another. Dawn is far more prominent, with five mentions (frr. 58.19, 103.13, 104.1, 123, and 157), but all these again seem to be conventionally required by the themes of epithalamium or aubade. The sun is mentioned twice in conventional phrases, "to see the light of the sun" meaning "to be alive" (frr. 56.1 and 58.26) and once in the vehicle of a simile (fr. 96). The moon is more prominent, occuring in the two long similes, in the nighttime rite of girls (fr. 154) and in a poem generally attributed to Sappho, but declared "incertum auctoris" by Lobel and Page, fr. 93 D.

So day and night hardly occur and, even more conspicuously, the seasons are not mentioned at all – except once in a metaphor "Nightingale, sweet-voiced messenger of Spring" (fr. 136). Sappho describes a timeless world where the season, if it is suggested at all, is the poetically eternal springtime of young girlhood. And this is really an internal season. There is no awareness of the external calendar in Sappho, no wonder at spring, no meditation on the cycling of the year. The only season is the growing season of young girls; it is like spring because they are like early flowers, but it lasts all year because their growing season is not measured in months. Sappho's poetic world does not involve the seasons of the external world because they are irrelevant to it. A comparison with Alcaeus will make her position on such matters clear.

In Alcaeus, fr. Z 23 the onset of summer is described: the stars revolve, the hard season comes, Sirius burns through men's heads and knees. The discomfort of the external world calls for adjustment in the internal: his advice is, "Get drunk." We read, "Summer, when the sun pours bright heat on the earth." The poetically equivalent passage in Sappho is revealingly different: the moon pours silver on the earth (fr. 34 with Julian's addition). Night, when the external world is darkened and the lights within can be clearly seen, is Sappho's time; the moon, that reflective luminary whose radiance affects the eye, and the mind's eye, but not the body, is her favored source of light. In fr. Z 14 Alcaeus again presents us with external nature: "Zeus rains, a great storm from heaven, the streams of water freeze... Throw wood on the fire and break out the wine..." He is keenly aware of the external world and its seasons, the discomforts of summer and winter, and the steps to take to adjust to them. In Sappho these things do not even exist. Discomfort is inner passion, longing, and absence; its antidotes are love and fantasies of love, which feed not on wine, but on a sense of beauty. In Alcaeus we read, "the flower of tender autumn" (fr. Z 74), and, "I praise incoming flowery spring" (fr. Z 44). But in Sappho, where images of flowers are far more common, the blossoms of spring are never distinguished from those of autumn, or of summer.[27] The flower is not bound to the external world and is not a product of its seasons; it is an unchanging symbol of beauty that grows not from the earth, but from the imagination. The flower of spring is not more praiseworthy because it comes after cold winter;

27 The restoration ἠρίνοισιν ἄνθεσιν (with spring flowers) at fr. 2, line 10, is widely accepted and is perhaps correct; also, Demetrius says (*On Style* 166), "When Sappho sings of beauty, her words are full of beauty and sweetness, and so, too, when she sings of love and springtime and the halycon." Our existing fragments contain no mention of any season; but we would not be surprised to discover that, while the others were omitted, springtime may have formed a regular setting in her property world.

nor the flower of autumn more delicate because the more certain to die. All flowers are the same; they are nourished not by the sun, but by the moon,[28] and are most abundant in remembering (fr. 94) and in imagining (fr. 96). Furthermore, in Alcaeus, images of heat and cold are physical and arise from the weather, from external heat and cold. In Sappho, on the other hand, the heart grows cold from fear (fr. 42); cold sweat along with "subtle" fire arises from passion (fr. 31), and cold water (signifying spiritual refreshment) sings through the sacred grove (fr. 2); the heart burns with desire and is cooled by the appearance of the loved one (fr. 48). There are no other sources of heat and cold, but the heart and its imaginings; the external world, and with it to a great extent the body, are excluded, and the imagination appropriates their qualities, like all others, for its own.

I hope it seems as clear to others as it does to me that the two Lesbian poets differed radically in the relations they felt between imagination and reality. It is indeed a mistake to assume that the sound of honest emotion in Sappho's poems means that their shadow world had any existence outside her imagination. It seems, rather, that she has created in the poems a world in which that emotion may exist in its purest and clearest state. Indeed, her emotions may have grown and taken shape from the imagined world of the poems as much as it did from them. Alcaeus sees imagination primarily as a means to adjust to reality in the simple sense of the external world in which the body lives, politics take place, and so on. For Sappho it was a ship on which to drift with no anchor inward on the sea of poetry to a place remote from the outside world.

---

28 Boethius uses variants of this imagery twice. It is found also in the *Mahabharata* and the *Gita Govinda,* and in haunting and melancholy forms, has entered the modern world. "Lonesome," John Millington Synge's playboy says, "as the moon of dawn..."

Let us conclude this digression. Almost all of the sizeable nature passages, and many of the small ones, occur in similes. There is little or nothing to indicate that Sappho ever mentioned natural objects for their own sake. In fact, the contrary view is strongly indicated, that for Sappho external nature was principally an analogy or foil for internal events or a conventional source of decorative figures of speech.

The Similes

Can we, then, regard fr. 34 as anything but the hypothetical unreal of a simile? All the evidence of Sapphic imagery is in favor of it. Further, the Sapphic passage is based on a simile in Homer (*Iliad* 6.146ff.), and is followed in its turn by parallel similes in Bacchylides (8(9).27ff.), Meleager (*Palatine Anthology* 12.59), Horace (*Odes* 1.12.42–44), Ovid (*Metamorphoses* 2.722ff.), and Quintus of Smyrna (1.37–41). Finally, it is quoted by Eustathius as a comment upon another Homeric simile (8.555).

If fr. 34 was part of a simile (which I regard as virtually certain), then the likelihood is very great that it occured in an epithalamium. Most similes in Sappho's poems do; and, in particular, rather long similes involving nature imagery were typically epithalamic.[29] In fact, of the six long similes in the fragments, four (including fr. 34) were hymeneal, one (fr. 47) uncertain, and the last is the simile in fr. 96.

Further, the appropriateness of fr. 34 to a simile describing a bride among her attendant maidens is obvious. These lines from the Epithalamium of Helen (sung by a group of girls at night) will show the type. (Theocritus may, in fact, have been imitating Sappho here.)

---

29 Fragments 105*a*, 105*c*, and 115, among others, in Sappho. Examples from other poets – principally, of course, Catullus – would confirm the point.

Ἀώς ἀντετέλλοισα καλὸν διέφανε πρόσωπον
πότνια Νύξ, τό τε λευκὸν ἔαρ χειμῶνος ἀνέντος
ὧδε καὶ ἀ χρυσέα Ἑλένα διεφαίνετ᾽ ἐν ἀμῖν.

A lovely face does rising dawn reveal, O Lady Night,
or shining Spring when winter goes away, and
even so does golden Helen shine among her girlfriends.

Still, it may be objected, the simile in fr. 96 is not hymeneal; so perhaps fr. 34, being of the same type, was not either. But if we look closely at them we can tell a difference. Four similes in addition to fr. 34 have extended vehicles: frr. 47, 105*a*, 105*c*, and 96. 7–15. The two that are certainly from hymeneal songs (105*a* and 105*c*) are straight, or clear, in expression. There is no difficulty in supposing a clear analogy between their terms. They lack the sort of gloomy ecstasy or painful joy that characterizes the longer personal poems. In line with their function as public poems for festive occasions, they do not allow the discomfiting intrusion of personality into the ritually required expressions of praise. But the simile in fr. 96 is altogether different. It turns conventional metaphors inside out, as if to stress its own peculiarity, and extends the vehicle on and on with a loving tenderness that seems almost obsessive. It seems to some critics to have no sense at all, and is generally believed to lose hold of the thread that ties it to the poem at the beginning.[30]

Surely it is clear that fr. 34 belongs with frr. 105*a* and 105*c* in this manner, though its subject is the same as the simile in fr. 96.

---

30 Fragment 47, which may be more paraphrased than quoted by our source, is not much like Sappho at all. One cannot help suspecting that it was imitated from a lost fragment of Archilochus. It is most similar to fr. 130 among the Sapphic fragments, and fr. 130, in turn, is likely to have been imitated from Archilochus, fr. 249 (Lassere). Ibycus's rather different version of the love/wind simile (fr. 286 P) may indicate a common prototype.

Fr. 34	Fr. 96
The stars about the fair moon hide their shining light, when at the full it shines upon the earth...	At the setting of the sun the rosy-fingered moon outshines all the stars and pours its light upon the salt sea and the much-flowering fields...

It is difficult to imagine such a close similarity being insignificant in a nonformulaic poet. She is trying to catch our attention in one passage by echoing the other,[31] and we may be fairly sure that it is fr. 96 that does the echoing. Fr. 34 establishes the norm from which the other is the significant deviation.[32]

If fr. 34 was not in a hymeneal song, then the significance of the allusion and of the deviations is lost to us. But if it was, then everything falls into place. We are at liberty to presume an earlier or later stanza of fr. 34 with the word *πάρθενοι* (maidens), which in fr. 96 has become *γύναικες* (wives). Then the simile develops with an unusual amount of embellishment, appears to wander, and leads to an unexpected conclusion. It is the last in a series of inverted allusions to hymeneal song, and it controls the poem. We will now try to follow its course.

The passage is more difficult than may appear at first sight. In fact, the major critical question about the poem is not merely how the simile works, but whether it does so at

31 Cf. the allusion in Pindar, *Olympian* 3.42 to *Olympian* 1.1–2.

32 Also, certain of the later passages based on the Sapphic version of the Homeric simile have hymeneal overtones. Ovid's version clearly does, and Quintus may well be introducing Penthesilea with a hymeneal allusion in order to suggest that the young girl will be married to death, a familiar pathetic motif, and, at the same time, anticipating his later hints of a lost possibility of marriage between Penthesilea and Achilles.

all. The main problem is that, when it oversteps the "normal" bounds established by fr. 34, the simile seems to change in purpose. Blass says that it loses its original third term ("Überstrahlen" [outshine]) and adopts another ("das Erfrischende dieses Lichtes" [this invigorating light]).[33] A common impression is that around line 11 Sappho forgot her subject – "entraînée comme Ophélie par le courant fleuri de son rêve" (swept along like Ophelia by the floral current of her dream), says Reinach[34] – to which she returned with something like desperation in line 15. But Reinach's sympathy for the flower-charmed poetess is not universal. Page bluntly denies that the second part of the simile has any meaning. It is "simply a description of the appearance and functions of moonlight…nothing to do with the grief of Atthis for a lover lost."[35]

But Fränkel and others have claimed that the moonlit night does indeed have much to do with the lovers, as follows: the poem conspicuously lacks any environment in the dramatic present, any indication of indoors, outdoors, night, day, etc.; the reader naturally supplies this lack from the strongly described environment in the hypothetical unreal, often without realizing what has taken place. In other words, the night, which was mentioned originally only in the hypothetical unreal of a simile, becomes a part of the hypothetical real also; it replaces all the property images that we expect but that are not there. To put it bluntly, the hypothetical real of the poem is now taking place in *the vehicle of a simile.*

Schadewaldt elaborates the view: the moon, rising over the sea and shining on Sardis and Mytilene alike, unites the

33 F. Blass, "Die Berliner Fragmente der Sappho," *Hermes* 37 (1902), 456–79.

34 T. Reinach, "Pour mieux connaître Sappho," *Comptes-rendues de l'Académie des inscriptions et belles-lettres* (1911), 733.

35 *S&A* 95.

three women. The flowers suggest the presence of Aphrodite, and the space enclosed by the now semi-magical moon becomes a sort of sacred grove. "Raum trennt und Raum verbindet" (space divides and space unites).[36] The holy space resolves, by containing both, separation and union.

The basic point is, I think, secure. The reader is left with the impression that the distant girl, wandering up and down, and Sappho and Atthis thinking of her, are described on the actual moonlit night of the simile. Page objects: "It cannot be said that there is anything in the text to suggest or support (this notion),"[37] but it is difficult to see what he means. The text seems almost unavoidably to suggest it, and it is hard to see what kind of "support" it could give, being a poem and not a critical commentary. In a case like this, "support" is provided principally by a sense of artistic rightness, and this, I think, can be established.

The description of pale (as remembered) beauty, of imagined flowers nourished by reflected light and moistened by the most perishable of liquids, is poignantly evocative of the atmosphere of lover's absence. Further, it can hardly be denied that after the simile Sappho seems to feel that the parted lovers have somehow been brought nearer to one another. The distant girl, who, before the simile, was far off and painfully absent, now can actually be seen wandering up and down, remembering Atthis and wishing for Atthis and Sappho to come to her. But she can only be seen through the moonlight of the simile. Let us review what has happened.

The poem began with two subjects: the first and overtly stated one, in the hypothetical real, the separation of the two girls; the second, suggested by an orderly series of allusions to hymeneal song, and existing in the hypothetical unreal,

---

36 *Sappho* 121. See also, for this interpretation, G. Perrotta, *Saffo e Pindaro* (Bari: Laterza, 1935), 66f., and *SuS* 54.

37 *S&A* 94.

was the contrary of the first, the marriage of the girls. The simile began as an allusion to a hymeneal simile, but continued past the limit of that allusion and unexpectedly established the features of the hypothetical unreal as the actual properties of the poem: the two terms of the simile were not merely compared, but merged. The separated lovers' activity of remembering and imagining is not only symbolized (by the moonlight, etc.) but formally acted out by the movement of the hypothetical real and unreal into one plane. When the remarkable figure is over the two girls are united in thought of one another; they have been wedded, by a poetic trope, in the flowery fields, which the wandering moon rides over. But more can be said about this.

So far I have mentioned only the view that the description of the moonlight ceases, at about line 11, to be primarily (or at all) a comparison. This view is very fruitful and, I think, is correct. But the situation is more complicated than that. In fact, the integrity of the comparison can be defended also. Bowra, for example, says that, like the moon, the girl's beauty outshines all around her (this much from fr. 34); but further, "the moon nourishes the dew and the implication is that in a like way the girl gives life to all around her."[38]

But this, I think, does not go far enough, considering that the passage contains several of the property images we have interpreted as symbols. Flowers, for example, are symbols of girls, and as the moon exerts a nourishing influence on the flowers, so the departed moon princess exerts a fructifying influence from afar on Sappho and Atthis, nourishing love, which flows out like fresh dew, in their hearts. Further, both flowers and the moonlit night are symbols of that rite, which is on one level a substitute for the wedding rite; and on another, an end in itself. And it is this rite that is being performed here before

38 *GLP* 195.

us by a priestess and a devotee. By the end of the simile level is piled on level. As the moon wanders in the sky (searching for Endymion?) so the absent girl wanders in search of Atthis, colored, as Weigall points out, "like the red, rising moon, still tinged by the light of Atthis, her sun."[39] As the moon shines by reflected light so the girl shines in their imaginations rather than in their actual sight. As it nourishes nighttime rather than daytime flowers, so she nourishes dreams, rather than acts, of love. Indeed, the passage is so highly suggestive of reasonable poetic meanings that it requires a certain perversity to say that it is meaningless simply because no one of the levels is altogether more conspicuous than the others. That type of correspondence in poetry was over by Homer's time, if indeed it ever existed. With Sappho we are in the age when poetry works by a mass of suggestions so rich and, sometimes, so complicated that it can never be stripped down to a core of one-to-one equivalency. One may wonder why such a thing should even be desired.

The End

The great simile divides our remnant of the poem into three sections, taking the material that precedes the simile and transforming it into the third, or following, section with the return to the original situation. Turyn notes that if the reading ἄλον (sea) in line 20 is sound, the girl is wandering to and fro on the seashore, as Achilles did in the *Iliad* after the confiscation of Briseis (1.349), on the night before the funeral of Patroclus (23.59), and on the night after the funeral games (24.3); as Chryses did when insulted by Agamemnon (1.33), and Odysseus when longing for his homeland (5.156)

39 A. Weigall, *Sappho of Lesbos: Her Life and Times* (New York: Garden City Publishing, 1932), 122.

and when he thought himself betrayed by the Phaeacians (13.219).[40] Other citations (e.g. Pindar, *Olympian* 1.71 and *Olympian* 6.57) strengthen the point that it is a conventional scene, established by Homer, for a person grieving to wander distracted by the seashore, and especially at night.

We must remember, when considering this, not only that ἄλον in line 20 is uncertain, but that Sardis is not by the seaside, and that νύξ (night) in line 19 has been declared impossible by Lobel. We would not accept Turyn's view here at the loss of the very likely and appealing reading σαρδ- in line 1. But if the scene in the simile, which *is* a seaside scene, has become the scene of what follows, then we may accept both. Ζαφοίταισ' (wandering) in line 15 will bring to mind, for the reader familiar with Homer, the conventional scene of grief, and the return to the hypothetical real will turn smoothly on this hinge. But again there is more that can be said.

The feminine participle, περρέχοισ' (outshining) in line 9, followed by a paratactical string of clauses, leads naturally to the feminine participle ζαφοίταισ' (wandering) in line 15.[41] It must be stressed that no new subject (after σελάννα) for ζαφοίταισ' is stated: grammatically, the moon and the girl are not merely compared – *they are the same entity.* "The moon outshines the stars," the poem says, "sheds its light, nourishes the dew, and wandering thinks of Atthis and her heart is heavy." Really, there is no transition back from simile to main theme: the two are overlapped so as to become virtually one. And this, surely, is the strongest possible "support" for the view that the hypothetical unreal of the simile has become a property of the hypothetical real.

From line 18 on, lacunae dominate the text. In the seventh strophe the departed girl cries out, perhaps "for us to

40 *Stud. Sapph.* 59ff.

41 For the arguments against taking it as a third person singular present indicative verb, see *S&A* 91

come there," then there may be something about the sea in between. Line 20 is generally treated as the end of the poem, though the parchment is secretive on this point.

The eighth strophe seems to say, "It is not easy for us to equal the goddesses in beauty of form," which may seem an allusion to the second strophe of fr. 96, and so to resume an earlier theme of the same poem, completing the "ring" form *with a verbal echo.* Look, however, at the first line of fr. 94, "Truly I want to die, "and the echo two columns later, "A desire possesses me to die and see the banks of Acheron" (fr. 95.11–13). There is nothing else like them in the fragments – but here a difference in meters will convince us that two poems are involved. We must conclude that in the edition of Sappho's fifth book to which the Berlin parchment belonged, the poems were arranged within metrical groups with attention to similarities of themes and possibly similarities of phrasing (especially, perhaps, in the early strophes). Thus, strophe eight might well begin a new poem.[42]

In the ninth strophe Aphrodite appears, and in the tenth someone pours nectar from a golden bowl. There follows something about hands, and Peitho (daughter of Aphrodite, according to fr. 200). These lines are strikingly similar to the last strophe of fr. 2 – a description of nature with ritual elements is followed by a vision of Aphrodite pouring nectar with golden vessels. Perhaps then, fr. 96 continues as far as

42 R. Lattimore has questioned whether an Æolic lyric could begin with a *gnome* ("Sappho 2 and Catullus 51," *Classical Philology* 39 [1944], 185); G. L. Koniaris ("On Sappho fr. 16 (LP)," *Hermes* 95 [1967], 257–68), on the other hand, accepts the possibility without saying why. The longer fragments of Tyrtaeus and Mimnermus often begin with *gnomai,* and it is not unlikely that some of them began poems; and consider Phocylides: the gnomic tradition was lively indeed around Sappho's time. In Pindar we find *gnomai* beginning *Olympian* 1 and 11, *Pythian* 5, *Nemean* 4 and 6. And, really, isn't the beginning of Sappho's own fr. 16 a *gnome*?

line 29, and Sappho overtly connects the emotional union of Atthis and the departed girl with the symbolic rite for which the grove lay ready in fr. 2. I can suggest no connection to the main poem for what follows line 29.

If our poem ends at line 20, however, and lacks no more than one to four lines at the beginning, it already demonstrates (without the probably unnecessary verbal echo) what, with our meager evidence, we think of as the distinctive structural features of Sappho's lyrics: first, a situation of unfulfilled longing in the dramatic present; then, a shift to either a past or an imagined situation, practically unlimited in kind, which will generally be the longest section of the poem; when the poem returns to the original situation, the longing or frustration will have been tempered in some way by the sojourn in memory or imagination. While the situation in the dramatic present will be unchanged in any external way, the emotion with which it is imbued will have taken on a timeless quality suggesting a contentment beyond the reach of pain. The relation between the central part and the situation in the dramatic present is perhaps the most important key to the poems.

In the dramatic present in fr. 96, Sappho speaks to Atthis about her absent lover. The great simile, occupying the four central stanzas, joins the two girls through the vision of lands and seas joined by the nurturing moonlight, and casts Sappho, as the creator of the simile, in the role of love's helper (Aphrodite's *θεράπων*, a stand-in for Eros himself, as she suggests in fr. 159). When the original situation is restated, Atthis is no longer alone and abandoned. Her longing is reciprocated, and she and her lover clasp hands, as it were, over the sea, with Sappho presiding. The beauty, rather than the pain, of the separated, but yearning lovers has come to the fore. At line 20 the poem seems to hold its creatures in a sort of balanced perfection, and perhaps that signifies the end. Any conclusion on this point must, for the time being, remain uncertain.

V

The View from the Outside

(Fragment 16)

col. i ο]ἰ μὲν ἰππήων στρότον, οἰ δὲ πέσδων,
οἰ δὲ νάων φαῖσ' ἐπ[ὶ] γᾶν μέλαιναν
ἔ]μμεναι κάλλιστον, ἔγω δὲ κῆν' ὄτ-
τω τις ἔραται·
—]
πά]γχυ δ' εὔμαρες σύνετον πόησαι
π]άντι τ[ο]ῦτ', ἀ γὰρ πόλυ περσκέθοισα
κάλλος [ἀνθ]ρώπων Ἐλένα [τὸ]ν ἄνδρα
τὸν [πανάρ]ιστον
—]
καλλ[ίποι]σ' ἔβα 'ς Τροΐαν πλέοι[σα
κωὐδ[ὲ πα]ῖδος οὐδὲ φίλων το[κ]ήων
πά[μπαν] ἐμνάσθη, ἀλλὰ παράγαγ' αὔταν
]σαν
—
]αμπτον γὰρ [
]...κούφως τ[ ]οησ[.]ν
]με νῦν Ἀνακτορί[ας ὀ]νέμναι-
σ' οὐ] παρεοίσας,
—
τᾶ]ς <κ>ε βολλοίμαν ἔρατόν τε βᾶμα
κἀμάρυχμα λάμπρον ἴδην προσώπω
ἢ τὰ Λύδων ἄρματα κἂν ὄπλοισι
πεσδομ]άχεντας.
—
].μεν οὐ δύνατον γένεσθαι
].ν ἀνθρωπ[..(.)π]εδέχην δ' ἄρασθαι

---

12. *οὐκ ἐθέλοισαν*, Kamerbeek; *οὐκ ἀέκοισαν*, Theander; *αὔτικ' ἴδοισαν*, Milne. 13–14. *Ὦρος εὔκ]αμπτον γὰρ [ἔφυσεν ἆτορ]/[αἰ κέ τις] κούφως τ[ὸ νέον ν]οήσῃ*, Agar; *κύπρις εὔκ]αμπτον γὰρ [ὐπάγαγ' ἆτορ]/[ὄπποτ' οὐ] κούφως τ[ιν' ἐρᾶν π]οήσῃ*, Bignone; *ἠ μαλα γν]άμπτον γὰρ [ἔθος γύναικος]/[καὶ μάτει] κούφως τ[ὰ κὲν ἐν]νοήσῃ*, Diehl; *Ὦρος εὔκ]αμπτον γὰρ [ἀὲι τὸ θῆλυ]/[αἰ κέ τις] κούφως τ[ὸ πάρον ν]οήσῃ*, Edmonds; *κύπρις εὔκ]αμπτον γὰρ [ἀεὶ κατισχει]/ἆτορ, αἰ] κούφως [φρόνεον π]οήσῃ*, Fraccaroli;

coll. ii

[ ]
[ ]
—
[ ]
[ ]
[ ]
προσ[
—
ὠσδ[
[
[
τ' ἐξ ἀδοκη[τ
—

νήπιαν· κ]άμπτον γὰρ [ἔραντος ἦτορ]/[ἔλπεται] κούφως τ[ά τέ κε ν]οήσῃ, Jurenka; Ἴλιονδε εὔκ]αμπτον γὰρ [ἄγει τὸ θῆλυ]/[ἀ θέα] κούφως τ'[ἐς ὅ κεν ν]οήσῃ, Pesent.; καὶ μάλα γν]άμπτον γὰρ [ἔφυ βρότων κῆρ]/[καὶ μάτει] κούφως τ[άς ὅ κεν ν]οήσῃ, Sitzler; κύπρις ἄγν]αμπτον γὰρ [ἔθηκεν ἆτορ]/[ὅππτοτ οὐ κούφως τ[ιν' ἐρᾶν π]οήσῃ, Stella; θῦμος εὔκ]αμπτον γὰρ [ἔφυ γύναικες]/[τᾶς Ἔρος] κούφως τ[ρέπεται ν]οήσ[ι]ν, Theander; κύπρις ἄγν]αμπτον γὰρ [Ἔρον ἔπεμψεν]/[ὅς τέλει] κούφως τ[ά κεν ἀ ν]οήσῃ, Kamerbeek. 21–22. [εὖ μὲν ἴδ]μεν οὐ δύνατον γένεσθαι/[τοῦτ'] ἀν· ἀνθρώποις, π]εδέχην δ' ἄρασθαι, Wilamowitz-Moellendorff; [ὄλβιον] μεν οὐ δύνατον γένεσθαι/[πάμπ] αν ἄνθρωπ[ον π]εδέχην δ' ἄρασθαι, Milne. 23–24. e.g. [τῶν πεδειχον ἐστι βρότοισι λῷον]/[ἢ λελάθεσθαι], Edmonds; e.g. [τῶν ὑπάγηται θέας αὖτος αἴπερ]/[οὐκ ἀθέμιστον], Theander.

Some say a host of cavalry, others of infantry,
others of ships, is the most beautiful
thing on the dark earth – but I say it is
whatever one loves;

and it is very easy to make this understood
by everyone, for she who far surpassed
all mankind in beauty, Helen,
leaving her husband, that noble man,

and sailing away, went to Troy,
and she did not care at all for her child
or her parents, but ... led
her astray

... for bend ...
... and lightly ...
which now reminds me of Anactoria
who is not here,

whose lovely walk
and shining brightness of face
I would rather see than the chariots of Lydia
and foot soldiers with all their armor.

The Text

Another modern addition to our Sapphic corpus, fr. 16 was found on an Oxyrhynchus Papyrus (1231) and first published in 1914.[1] The left margin of the first column is missing in all but two lines, and strophes three and four have lost the right edge also. Oxyrhynchus fr. 2166*a*2, published by Lobel in the twenty-first Oxyrhynchus volume in 1951, supplied the left margin of strophe three and made all but the adonic line of that strophe more or less certain. Much scholarly literature of the intervening period is made less valuable by having been based on incorrect restorations of line 9.

The fourth strophe is still uncertain, and I have given in the apparatus a number of versions of it. Line 12 seems to have ended with a feminine participle on the subject of Helen's being led astray, and lines 13 and 14, it is generally agreed, contained observations on the fickleness of the female sex, and a subject for παράγαγ' (led astray). The latter is generally taken to be either Aphrodite or Eros; if Aphrodite, then line 15 may begin ἄ με, if Eros, ὄς με is possible. Κἄ με would presumably refer to all that has gone before. Still, the widespread agreement on the general sense of these lines should not blind us to the fact that they are almost entirely lost, and something quite different could have been there. Why, for example, could Paris not be the subject of παράγαγ'?

1 B.P. Grenfell and A.S. Hunt, *The Oxrhynchus Papyri: Part X* (London: Egypt Exploration Society, 1914).

All that is clear is that in lines 13 and 14 the transition is prepared from the mythological to the personal *exemplum.* (I have given in the critical apparatus several variant restorations of these lines to illustrate the amount of uncertainty that is often involved in a Sapphic text. Their sources can be found in the text by Theander referred to below, n.3.)

The one legible stanza above our line 1 is clearly from a different poem (fr. 15.9–12), so that we may be sure we have the beginning intact. The lack of the left margin, however, which would have contained the coronis, leaves us uncertain where the poem ends. The bottom edge of the papyrus is intact, showing that *col. i* ended with line 22. The top edge is gone, however, and the top of *col. ii* is missing down to line 6. After four more lines we have the coronis beginning a new poem. If, then, one assumes (as Edmonds does[2] and Theander seems to)[3] that the surviving upper edge for column 1 was the original upper edge of the papyrus, it follows either that our poem continued to line 32, or that a poem of only three stanzas intervened. But, as A. S. Hunt points out, there is no paleographical reason for this assumption, and the height of the papyrus must, finally, be considered unknown.[4] (Both Theander and Edmonds, however, base their interpretations on their view of the upper edge.)

We have, in short, three views of the length of fr. 16: either it was complete in 20 lines because at that length it completes the ring form we have encountered before; or, it was complete in thirty-two lines because what follows line 20 seems rather to comment on it than to begin a new poem; or, it was complete in some other number of lines, unascertainable due

---

2 J. M. Edmonds, "The New Lyric Fragments," *The Classical Review* 28 (1914), 73–78.

3 C. Theander, "Studia Sapphica," *Eranos* 32 (1934), 57–85.

4 A. S. Hunt, "The New Lyric Fragments," *The Classical Review* 28 (1914), 126–27.

to our ignorance of the height of the papyrus. The length of 32 lines has accommodated the biographical interpretations; the length of 20 lines, the formal ones.

The Interpretation

Edmonds, always the most confident of restorers and most persistent of biographical critics, suggests the following readings of lines 15–16:

> οὐ]δὲ νῦν Ἀνακτορί[α, τ]ὺ μέμνα
> δὴ] παρεοίσας.
>
> And now, Anactoria, you are forgetful of
> her though she is with you.[5]

When we observe the violent change that these few variants make in the poem as a whole, we must be sobered by the fact that they are all, or almost all, possible readings. (Hunt, in an article devoted to refuting Edmonds's readings of several new fragments, can take issue only with the δε of line 15.)[6]

Edmonds explains as follows: Sappho is in exile in Sicily; Anactoria and another woman, who is also a friend of Sappho, are living in Mytilene. "It gives point to the poem," Edmonds says, "if we imagine that Anactoria has fallen in love with a soldier." "Sappho says, in effect: You who are lucky enough to be with her still, have forgotten, it seems, a friend whom I would give anything to see again. For you have fallen in love. It is natural enough and I cannot blame you. But O that I might have the joy that you are throwing

5 Edmonds, "The New Lyric Fragments" (above, n. 2), 73–75. He explains *μέμνα* as an indicative standing for *μέμνασαι*.

6 Hunt, "The New Lyric Fragments" (above, n. 4), 126–27.

away."[7] The seventh stanza must have contained the third woman's name.

The point of this reading is to connect the poem with the third poem of the Berlin parchment, fr. 96. The belief that the girl who "now shines out among the Lydian wives" was Anactoria, goes back to Wilamowitz-Moellendorff. (The basis for it is that Maximus of Tyre mentions Atthis and Anactoria together.) Thus fragments 16 and 96 make up a larger drama: while Sappho is away, Anactoria, jilting Atthis, falls in love with a soldier, who thereafter takes her to Lydia to be his wife; upon her return, Sappho consoles Atthis with the thought that Anactoria *once* loved her, anyway, and even now may regret her decision.

Obviously, this is very fanciful. It is based on the unreliable story of the exile; and the third character is introduced *ex nihilo* from the desire to see in Sappho's poems a cross-referenced autobiography. Still, this interpretation has two considerable advantages; it explains neatly the mention of military forces in the first stanza and of Lydian armaments in the fifth (Anactoria has gone to Lydia with a soldier, but Sappho says, "I would rather see Atthis's face than the whole Lydian army"); and it explains the point of the mythological exemplum: as Helen, in the grip of passion, forgot her child and her parents, so Anactoria has forgotten Atthis.

Theander is somewhat more restrained, not introducing a third person: Sappho is in Mytilene, Anactoria in Lydia (the connection with fr. 96, he says, is probable); Sappho is planning to visit her, and says that when she gets there, whatever imperial splendors surround her, she will have eyes for Anactoria alone.His restoration of the sixth strophe is similar to Edmonds's.[8]

---

7 Edmonds, "The New Lyric Fragments" (above, n. 2), 74.

8 Theander's observations on the seventh strophe are worth noting: Apollonius Dyscolos (*On Syntax* 3.243) quotes fr. 33 to illustrate the use of εἴθε with the optative:

Both Edmonds's and Theander's views succeed in explaining the description of armaments, the mention of Lydia, and the mythologial exemplum. But the total lack of evidence for their biographical reconstructions cannot be exaggerated. Let us see what else is available. Fragment 16 is unique in our small corpus of monodic (private) lyric for containing, in miniature, all the elements of large-scale choral (public) lyric.[9] The first stanza is the only full example in monody of the priamel, a characteristic device of choral lyric (though found also in elegy and later prose).[10] Through a series of comparisons or contrasts the poet may appear to be leading up to his subject when actually he is already saying a good deal about it. Pindar begins (*Olympian* 1.1–8):

> Best of all things is water, but gold like a flaming fire
> shines through the darkness

> αἴθ' ἔγω χρυσοστέφαν' Ἀφροδίτα
> τόνδε τὸν πάλον λαχοίην.
>
> Would that I, O gold-crowned Aphrodite,
> might receive that lot.

A little later he quotes ἐρᾶν, ἔγω δὲ κῆν' ὄττω τις ἔραται. To illustrate εἴθε, Theander says that he could have opened any book, and probably would not have chosen one in Æolic; probably, then, he was quoting from memory (he is said to sometimes have quoted Homer from memory), and when, a little later, he came to ἐρᾶν, he would have thought of the same poem. Hence Theander inserts fr. 33 into the seventh stanza and suggests a sense like: "Would that I might see Anactoria again, a thing too wonderful to expect."

9 See esp. H. Fränkel, *Dichtung und Philosophie des frühen Griechentums. Eine Geschichte der griechischen Epik, Lyrik und Prosa bis zur Mitte des fünften Jahrhunderts* (Munich: Beck, 1962), 212.

10 "The principle theme is introduced as the climax of a series of popular subjects for comparison," says Page (*S&A* 55). And E. L. Bundy: "The priamel is a focusing or selecting device in which one or more terms serve as a foil for the point of particular interest." ("Studia Pindarica I: The Eleventh Olympian Ode," *University of California Publications in Classical Philology* 18.1 [1962], 5). Cf. Tyrtaeus 12 (Edmonds), and Plato, *Lysis* 211*d–e*.

> more than a great man's wealth.
> If you wish to sing of games, my heart,
> do not search the empty sky of day
> for another bright star
> more warming than the sun;
> nor shall we name any contest greater than the Olympian…

First water, then gold, then the sun – by the time the Olympic games, Pindar's actual subject, are mentioned, an aureole of elemental importance, cosmic richness, and eternal incorruptibility has already been cast about them. I will postpone for the moment a close look at Sappho's priamel.

In good Pindaric form, the priamel is capped by a gnomic proposition that is then glossed by a mythological *exemplum*. That the beauty of *the beloved* is the greatest beauty on earth is proved, Sappho says, by the fact that Helen left her husband and family and went to Troy, for Eros (?) led her astray. But why Helen? What is the connection between the *exemplum* and the priamel?

Before the publication of Oxyrhynchus fr. 2166*a*2, the crucial ninth line was restored, ὤστε πὰν] σέβας Τροΐας [ὄλεσαι (so as to destroy all the sacredness of Troy), or similarly, and scholars were at pains to determine whom, if anyone, Sappho blamed for the fall of Troy.[11] There is a reproach for Anactoria in the reference to Helen, says Croiset in a mood inherited from Wilamowitz-Moellendorff.[12] Kamerbeek exonerates Helen, restoring οὐκ ἐθέλοισαν (not willing) in line 12,[13] and Theander condemns her, restoring οὐκ ἀέκοισαν (not unwilling).[14] Bowra maintains that the

11 See, e.g., R. Hampe, "Paris oder Helena? Zu Sappho fr. 27a (Diehl)," *Museum Helveticum* 8 (1951), 144–46, written only months before the publication of Oxyrhynchus X.

12 M. Croiset, "Les Papyrus d'Oxyrhynchus," *Journal des Savants*, n. s., 12 (1914), 323.

13 J. C. Kamerbeek, "Sapphica," *Mnemosyne* 4.9 (1956), 97–102.

14 Milne's αὔτικ' ἴδοισαν (as soon as she saw him) strikes me as

whole point is that Sappho blames no one: Alcaeus, and their contemporary Stesichorus (to his great regret) had blamed Helen; but Sappho, like Homer, neither blames nor exonerates her: the reality of love is larger than such things. But then, why mention Helen? Page, who is outspokenly critical of this poem, sees it as a commonplace and unimaginative appeal for Homeric sanction of a personal statement. But the poems of Sappho we have considered have been so devoid of moral comment – even, perhaps, moral attitude – that we may wonder if any of that is to the point.

Some have been troubled by the use of the word κὰλλος, "beauty," to describe Helen. Isn't this merely sloppy writing? Page asks. If whatever one loves is the most beautiful thing, then how can Helen (who is not, after all, *everyone*'s girlfriend) be called the most beautiful? Koniaris provides the answer:[15] Helen, as the objective candidate for most beautiful, is called as witness and herself supports Sappho's subjective view.

When seen properly, the *exemplum* grows directly out of the priamel and smoothly and easily proves the correctness of Sappho's position. We have heard various witnesses (*οἰ μὲν, οἰ δὲ, οἰ δὲ* and finally ἔγω), now let us hear the testimony of an expert, someone who possesses the height of beauty already. But that is not all; the lyric persona asks: Where are all these ships, horses and men (these grand ranks from public choral song) going? What are they doing? And the mythological answer, which must follow the priamel, is obvious: they are merely following in the wake of Helen as *she* pursues the whim of the heart. Finally, all of the ships and armies too prove Sappho's point, the supreme and awesome power of female beauty – and its sweet dangerousness – are not merely affirmed, but *acted out* as the forces of nations

preferable to either of these; love in Sappho characteristically arises from seeing. This will be discussed later.

15 G.L. Koniaris, "On Sappho fr. 16 (LP)," *Hermes* 95 (1967), 257–68.

in the priamel pursue the mythical *exemplum,* Helen, into the poem.

Lines 13 and 14 evidently capped the myth with the traditional gnomic transition we expect in choral lyric from Alcman to Pindar. The context, the two words we can identify, and a parallel in Euripides' *Cyclops,*[16] indicate that some remark was made about the power Love has over women.[17]

Very likely, then, line 15 effected the transition from myth-capped-by-gnomism to the personal remarks introduced by the traditional relative clause so familiar from Pindar. The subject of ὀνέμναισ' (reminds) could be Cypris or Eros, or Helen, or the whole preceding situation.[18] The personal remarks, as expected, provide a second, and personal, illustration of the original proposition. Here Sappho returns to her own delicate and personal style after playing with the conventions of choral lyric – but, with a confident virtuosity, returns to the monodic mood while still *within the frame* of the choral lyric, putting the *sphragis,* as it were, on the piece. Her most typical subject, that of parting and separation, recurs at once, with only the lightest touch of its usual melancholy, in the adonic of the fourth stanza. Powerfully and smoothly the poem returns from the public to the private viewpoint (from public to private, from myth to life, from Helen to Anactoria), and *ironically,* also: veering intractably, as in the power of a magnet, toward Anactoria, the poem itself becomes yet another illustration of Sappho's proposition in line 4. With a sweet delicacy the lines grow suddenly into what we have awaited, like a melody set free. In a technique

16 See Hampe, "Paris oder Helena? Zu Sappho fr. 27a (Diehl)" (above, n. 11).

17 Kamerbeek ("Sapphica" [above, n. 13]) adduces Bacchylides' ἀγνάμπτους ἐρῶτας as a possible allusion to this passage. His and Theander's restorations here strike me as most graceful.

18 Cf. line 5 of fr. 31, where the τὸ seems to have a general antecedent.

we will recognize from fr. 2, the key name, witheld through the elaborate preparations for it, is released powerfully at the end. Helen transformed into Anactoria, the new avatar of that primal aphrodisiac splendor called *eros,* floats like the tenderest of understatements into Sappho's poem – at the same time striding through it like all the armies of history roaming loose, her *βᾶμα* (footstep), representing the marching of troops in stanza one, and her *ἀμάρυχμα λάμπρον* (brightness of face), the glitter of armor. (Surely Sappho was thinking of the already traditional metaphor – e.g. *Iliad* 14 – woman preparing for a tryst seen as champion preparing for battle.)

Beyond this, aesthetic analysis of the strophe is difficult – perhaps impossible. Bignone calls it, "una cosa tutta nuova e fresca, nostra, viva, presente" (something totally new and fresh, ours, alive, present)[19] and there are few passages in the poems we have discussed to which these adjectives might not be applied by one who would apply them here. Page, on the other hand, says, "This stanza was either a little fanciful or a little dull,"[20] and one has, as so often, the feeling that he simply does not like Sappho's poetry.[21] Let us confine ourselves for the moment to points that can be analysed objectively.

We have seen biographical arguments that account for the mention of Lydia in the fifth stanza. Schadewaldt argues,

---

19 E. Bignone, "Su di un nuovo frammento di Saffo," *Bollettino di filologia classica* 22 (1916), 13.

20 *S&A* 57.

21 G.M. Kirkwood, commenting on this remark of Page's ("Five Greek Lyric Books," *The Classical Journal* 52.2 [1956], 90) says, "Page seems bent on finding ways to deny emotional depth to Sappho's poetry." And J.A. Davison ("Sappho and Alcaeus," *The Classical Journal* n.s., 7.1 [1957], 23): "Those who find the last stanza of the poem almost intolerably moving can only feel that Page's comment... goes far to confirm a suspicion based on many other indications throughout his treatment of Sappho, that Page is rather out of his depth with Sappho and knows it."

perhaps more convincingly, that in the shadow of the Lydian empire and the sunrise of the great Greek fleets, disputes over types of weaponry were common – the old school aristocrat favoring infantry; the admirer of Lydia, cavalry and chariots; the progressive common man, the fleet.[22] Alcaeus, Z34, with its exclusion of all but footsoldiers' weapons (as in the Lelantine war) and its archaizing or Homerizing, is strong support for this. Sappho may, then, in the priamel, have been refering to actual poems on military subjects by the partisans of the different factions – including Alcaeus, Z34; the mention of Lydia was witheld until the end because in the second stanza the armaments of Greeks against Troy are suggested in illustration of the priamel, and this connection would be obscured by a prior mention of Lydia – which brings us back to the priamel itself.

If surely looks as if Sappho makes some ideological manifesto in strophe 1, but what exactly the message is is disputed. Theander, followed by Bowra and others, says that Sappho is contrasting masculine and feminine attitudes: some, being men, say a) b) c), but I, being a woman, say...it is what you love. I find it difficult, perhaps impossible, to deny this. Surely our *οἰ* and *ἔγω* provide a paradigm of male-female psychology that has not been surpassed. Sappho reduces the masculine fuss of armies and fleets, and empires rising and falling, to charms for the bracelet of her beloved.

Obvious as this may seem, not all agree on it. Wills calls this poem Sappho's "Umwertung aller Werte" (revaluation of all values)[23] and declares that Sappho's creed is not sexism, but subjectivism. He stresses the indefinite pronouns and the subjunctive mood of *ἔραται*:[24] "Sappho champions the

22 M. Treu, *Sappho* (Munich: Heimeran, 1968), 128 ff.

23 G. Wills, "The Sapphic 'Umwertung aller Werte,'" *American Journal of Philology* 88 (1967), 434–42.

24 But attention should be directed to an article by L. Rydbeck

the chaos of affectivity. She goes beyond Protagoras," Wills says, "in her vision of a beautiful and destructive anarchy."[25] And I, for one, find it hard to deny this meaning also to the passage – though it seems less prominent than the other, perhaps is merely a subheading of it.

But again, not all are satisfied. If Sappho means *whatever* one loves, says Koniaris,[26] then she does not disagree with the *οἰ μὲν*, who loved cavalry, the *οἰ* δὲ, who love infantry, or the *οἰ* δὲ, who love ships; her statement is merely a generalized induction based on theirs. She does not, therefore, mean, *whatever* a person loves, Koniaris argues, but whatever a person *loves*. It is eroticism that Sappho champions, and she imputes, no doubt rightly, other motives than erotic love to the *οἰ μὲν* and *οἰ* δὲ. "Τὸ *κάλλιστον* can materialize only in the 'beloved'; *τὸ κάλλιστον* can be grasped only by the 'lover.'"[27] (He does not, however, deal with the fact that *κῆνο* is neuter.)

Does it seem to the reader that one or another of these three -isms is Sappho's message here? It seems to me at least that all three are there. Gazing at us from behind these various modes of thought is the ironic persona of the poet who is aware that reality is complex, and is approaching its laws with flexibility, circumspection, and a willingness to embody contradictions. Why expect Sappho's answer to be simple? Why treat her as a primitive? She is already after the age of

("Sappho's *φαίνεταί μοι κῆνος*," *Hermes* 97 [1969], 161–66), where he argues that the Lesbian Æolic of Sappho and Alcaeus predated the Attic distinction between *ὅς* and *ὅστις*; that an "individual" use of *ὅστις* interchangeable with *ὅς* was common in early Ionic and probably Æolic also, and that *ἔραται* can be indicative, as in Theocritus 2.149.

25 Wills, "The Sapphic 'Umwertung aller Werte'" (above, n. 23), 441.

26 Koniaris, "On Sappho fr. 16 (LP)" (above, n. 15), 258.

27 Ibid.

Archilochus and the Δίος ἀπάτη, and was evidently – as this fragment so clearly shows – a woman of lively and varied intelligence, capable of viewing her cherished passions through others' eyes.

In fr. 16 she pretends to step for a moment out of her private vision and evaluate it in relation to the public world. From outside she validates the private and personal universe we saw the inside of in frr. 2, 94, and 96. Finally, this outside viewpoint is revealed as another trick of the poet. The choral form also leads inevitably to the personal statement; armies, empires, myths, all these ultimately lead back to the graceful walk of a girl, and her sparkling eyes. With a tender irony the moods of femininity, eroticism, and subjectivism are suggested and as quickly forgotten. As in Meleager: "A footstep – hers! Go back into my breast, my heart."[28] One must be in love to understand this logic.

And is this the end of the poem? We cannot be sure. Fr. 16 is strung taut between the imitated choral form and the delicate Sapphic style that peeps with some irony out of it. The question is which type of poem won out. Gnomic priamel, mythic *exemplum*, gnomic transition, personal *exemplum*, sphragis – one might expect another Pindaric element, a concluding prayer to a god. But the nicety of the poem in twenty lines is, I think, beyond dispute. If, in fact, Sappho carried the playful contrast between the two traditions out to the bitter end, we might almost be glad that we cannot see it. In that case our little poem could duplicate even the one regrettable feature of choral songs – their tendency to go on too long.

---

28 *Palatine Anthology* 12.147.

VI

The Face Behind the Mask

(Fragment 31)

φαίνεταί μοι κῆνος ἴσος θέοισιν
ἔμμεν' ὤνηρ, ὄττις ἐνάντιός τοι
ἰσδάνει καὶ πλάσιον ἆδυ φωνεί-
σας ὐπακούει

καὶ γελαίσας ἰμέροεν, τό μ' ἦ μὰν
καρδίαν ἐν στήθεσιν ἐπτόαισεν,
ὠς γὰρ⟨ἔς⟩σ' ἴδω βρόχε', ὤς με φώναι-
σ' οὐδ' ἒν ἔτ' εἴκει,

ἀλλ' ἄκαν μὲν γλῶσσα † ἔαγε † λέπτον
δ' αὔτικα χρῷ πῦρ ὐπαδεδρόμηκεν,
ὀππάτεσσι δ' οὐδ' ἒν ὄρημμ', ἐπιρρόμ-
βεισι δ' ἄκουαι,

† ἔκαδε μ' ἴδρως ψῦχρος κακχέεται † τρόμος δὲ
παῖσαν ἄγρει, χλωροτέρα δὲ ποίας
ἔμμι, τεθνάκην δ' ὀλίγω 'πιδεύης
φαίνομ' ἔμ' αὔται

ἀλλὰ πὰν τόλματον ἐπεὶ † καὶ πένητα †

---

7. Σμ: Ms. ὠς | γὰρ σἴδςβρόχεώς με φωνὰς οὐδ' ἐν ἔτ εἴκει.
9. LP: Cod. P. ἀλλὰ κᾷν | μὲν γλῶσσα ἔαγελεπτὸνδ'. 13. Cod. P. ἔκαδε μ' ἰδρῶς ψυχρὸς κακχέεται. κὰδ δὲ μ' ἴδρως κακχέεται, τρόμος δὲ, Ahrens; φαίνομαι † *S&A*; φαίνομ' Ἄγαλλι, Paton; φαίνομαι αὔτα, Thomson; φαίνομ' ἔγωγε, Milne; φαίνομ' ἀλαία, Bowra. See Manfredi (below, n. 1) for the new reading.
17. ἐπὲι γένηται, Diehl; ἐπὲι κεν ἦι τά (= ἐπὲι ἔστι), Wilamowitz-Moellendorff; ἐπεῖπεν· εἶτ' οὐ θαυμάζεις, κτλ. Bergk.

That man seems to me to be like the gods,
who sits opposite you
and hears you near
him speaking sweetly

and laughing attractively; but
it shakes the heart in my breast,
for as soon as I look at you,
I can no longer speak,

my tongue is broken to silence
and already a subtle
fire has run under my skin;
in my eyes is no vision,
my ears are humming,

a cold sweat pours down me, and trembling
seizes all (my body); I am paler than grass
and seem to be
almost dying...

But all must be borne, since... impoverished...

Fragment 31 – perhaps the most famous of all Greek lyrics – is preserved for us by Pseudo-Longinus (*On the Sublime* 10) who quotes it as an example of excellence in selection and organization of concrete details. Since we are dealing at last with parchment manuscripts rather than papyri or ostraka, we might expect the text to be plagued by fewer difficulties, but such is not the case. Although we are spared the irksome lacunae of the papyri, several lines are corrupt, and one major, perhaps insoluble, problem obstructs interpretation.

I have given in the apparatus the mss. readings of lines 7, 9, and 13, and in the text those of Lobel and Page. The sense of these lines seems clear enough and a review of their problems here is unnecessary. [1]

The most serious problem, as with fr. 2, is the end of the poem. "Longinus" quotes four stanzas to illustrate Sappho's objective description of the symptoms of passion in herself; there follows what seems to be a slightly corrupt Sapphic hendecasyllable, not part of the description of passion. Bergk and Hermann have restored it as a corrupt portion of "Longinus'" comment, thus leaving the poem complete in four stanzas. (Why would Longinus omit the rest of the stanza? Why would he quote one line more than is germane to his purpose?) But Wilamowitz-Moellendorff and others have restored it as the first line of a fifth and, presumably,

1 *S&A* 22, 24–25 may be consulted for a detailed discussion of the problems of these lines. In line 16 I follow M. Manfredi, *Dai papyri della Società italiana* (Florence: Le Monnier, 1965), 16–17.

final stanza. The question is so crucial that the main points in the controversy will be presented at once.

Structural Problems

In the discussion of fr. 96 I suggested that a free type of ring or arch form could describe it nicely. That poem was in Sappho's fifth book. Milne and others have concluded, for various reasons, that the poems of the first book followed stricter rules than the rest, specifically requiring a return to the original theme *and* a clear verbal echo, in the last stanza, of the first.[2] What do we find in fr. 31?

Thomson[3] (following Wilamowitz-Moellendorff) notes that τεθνάκην ... φαίνομαι (I seem about to die) in lines 15–16 echoes φαίνεται ... ἴσος θέοισιν (he seems like the gods) in line 1 – that is, *he* seems immortal; *I* seem about to die (i.e., mortal). He restored φαίνομαι αὔτα at the end, comparing *Iliad* 21.244/5 and 22.83/4, where αὔτα indicates the whole self after mention has been made of some part(s) of the self. The poem, then, is complete in the form:

> *He* seems like the immortal gods ... but *I*, poor mortal, seem about to die.

(Bowra, in the first edition of *GLP* [1936], concurs; in the second, he does not.)

But, Milne criticizes, the circularity proposed for these odes is not merely a matter of verbal echo, but of return to

---

2 H.J.M. Milne, "The Final Stanza of φαίνεταί μοι," *Hermes* 71 (1936), 126–28.

3 G. Thomson, "Two Notes on Greek Poetry," *Classical Quarterly* 29 (1935), 37–38. Cf. *SuS* 57. Thomson's article preceeded the publication of the Florence papyrus (see above, n. 1), which clarified line 16 as φαίνομ' ἔμ' αὔται. The new reading still allows his interpretation.

the original theme.[4] A theme is stated; a transition leads to a variation; another transition leads to a restatement of the theme, with a verbal echo of the first statement. In these four stanzas we have no variation or restatement, only the original theme. (It is a double theme, κῆνος and ἔγωγε, as in the *οἰ μὲν, οἰ δὲ, οἰ δὲ* theme of fr. 16.) Line 17 is a transition to a variation, which must still be followed by the second transition and the restatement. And, suffering under the five-stanza rule, Milne demands all of this in *one more stanza*.

It is hard to believe that the structure of Ode 1 could lead to such demands for fr. 31 (and fr. 2). In Ode 1 these elements are present, but there is something more, too: the fine balance with which they are distributed in the poem. It would seem that the theme-variation-theme rule and the five-stanza rule are grotesquely at odds with one another and should not be forced to cohabit in one poem. (In fr. 5 the theme seems to take up three of the five stanzas, but we do not know where the poem ended.)

A third view mitigates somewhat the stern demands of the ring.[5] Only Ode 1 and fr. 16, after all, exhibit conspicuous variation sections in their centers, with perceptible transition at at least one end. Perhaps we can say that the first stanza states the theme, "He is happy," or "They are happy"; the next three vary it, "I am not happy"; and a final stanza will need only to mention the man and girl again, probably in an offer of good wishes to the bridal pair. The *φαίνεται/φαίνομαι* echo, while significant, does not constitute a restatement of the theme; one stanza is lacking, but it will not be made to do as heavy duty as Milne lays upon it. The *gnome* of line 17 is a familiar form of transition back to the theme; the transi-

---

4 Milne, "The Final Stanza of *φαίνεταί μοι*" (above, n.2).

5 See, among others, *SuS* 57; A. Setti, "Sul frammento 2 di Saffo," *Studi italiani di filologia classica* 16 (1939), 195–221; B. Snell, "Sappho's Gedicht *φαίνεταί μοι κῆνος*," *Hermes* 66 (1931), 82 n3.

tion away from it was effected by the equally familiar relative clause in line 5.

A quite different point of view is worth considering. Lattimore, discussing Æolic lyric in general, says, "Alcaeus's famous ship-poem appears to begin with the most concrete type of description and to end with the drawing of a conclusion."[6] Further, Alcaeus, D 12 and Z 14+11 seem to have moral remarks following description, and many elegiac pieces observe this form. Perhaps, beside the ring-form, we may suppose another type of Æolic lyric: "descriptive passage ... followed by generalization or self-exhortation which grows directly out of the experience described."[7] Fragments 16 and 31, he suggests, may have been of this type.

It seems reasonable, as Lattimore argues, that a poet who wrote two or three hundred poems would use more than one general structure. But Lattimore's argument is extremely weak in its examples. Alcaeus's "famous ship-poem" is made up of two separate fragments, Z 2 and D 15, which, though they look nice together, may not be parts of one poem. Worse, Z 14 (*ὔει μὲν ὀ Ζεῦς*) and Z 11 (*οὐ χρῆ κάκοισι θῦμον ἐπιτρέπην*) of which we have an imitation in Horace (*Odes* 1.9) probably did not go together. It seems likely that such poems as Lattimore describes were written by early lyrists (other similarities, with *elegiac* practice, are persuasive), but there isn't any *evidence* for it. Indeed, it seems possible that Sappho's poems (at least those outside of the first book) had a great, possibly unlimited, range of form. One would not, for example, like to imagine either a ring or a gnomic ending to fr. 94 (though either is possible).

A last approach to the question must be considered. Catullus, in Poem 51, translates, or paraphrases, Sappho:

---

6 R. Lattimore, "Sappho 2 and Catullus 51," *Classical Philology* 39 (1944), 184–87.

7 Ibid., 187.

Ille mi par esse deo uidetur,
ille, si fas est, superare diuos,
qui sedens aduersus identidem te
spectat et audit

dulce ridentem, misero quod omnis
eripit sensus mihi; nam simul te,
Lesbia, aspexi, nihil est super mi
‹ uocis in ore; ›

lingua sed torpet, tenuis sub artus
flamma demanat, sonitu suopte
tintinant aures, gemina teguntur
lumina nocte.

That man seems to me to be like a god,
or (if this is no heresy) to surpass the gods,
who, sitting across from you,
gazes at you and hears you

laughing sweetly – which steals away my senses
in misery, for as soon, O Lesbia,
as I have looked at you,
the voice is gone from my mouth,

my tongue is numb, through my limbs
a light flame spreads, my ears ring
with their own noises, my eyes are darkened
with a double night.

And, in a fourth stanza interpreted by some editors as a separate poem (or fragment):

otium, Catulle, tibi molestum est:
otio exultas nimiumque gestis:
otium et reges prius et beatas
perdidit urbes.

Idleness, Catullus, does you harm:
you joy in your idleness and carry it on too long.
Even kings before now, and happy cities
idleness has ruined.

The connection of Catullus's *otium* stanza with the rest of his poem is about as uncertain as Sappho's fifth stanza.[8]

But isn't the coincidence *too* exact? It is argued that Catullus's remarks on *otium* are manifestly not a translation of Sappho's (apparent) remarks on poverty or deprivation. But his compression of her four stanzas into three shows that he is not following her literally. *His* poem, if it includes stanza four, exhibits the form that Lattimore suggests for hers.

Is a conclusion possible? Several arguments – ring form, gnomic cap, Catullan parallel – call for a fifth stanza. Nevertheless, none of them is unambiguous, and one sympathizes with Thomson that the poem seems complete in four, leaving the connection between its two subjects unstated. The contrary view seems too much based on the feeling that archaic poets could not leave anything unstated, i.e., that they were innocent of the techniques of understatement, implication, ironic suggestion – of the whole inner tension of poetry. It is time to inquire into the poem's content and see how it affects these questions.

Hochzeitlied *or* Liebeskummer?

The central controversy about the poem is well-known. Wilamowitz-Moellendorff regarded it as a *Hochzeitlied* (wedding song) sung by Sappho at the wedding feast of a girl who was leaving her *thiasos*.[9] He reconstructs the scene: "And now Sappho picks up the barbiton and sings her song, one

8 Against the *otium* stanza, see L.P. Wilkinson in J. Bayet, "Catulle: La Grèce et Rome," *Entretiens sur l'antiquité classique* 2 (Geneva: Fondation Hardt, 1953), 47; in favor of it, W. Ferrari, "Il Carme 51 di Catulle," *Annali della Scuola normale superiore di Pisa, Classe di lettere e filosofia* 7 (1938), 59–72, and Lattimore, "Sappho 2 and Catullus 51"(above, n.6).

9 *SuS* 58. It is not possible to mention all the literature on this question; I have selected the strongest carriers of the arguments.

of many she composed for the weddings of her pupils, full of bantering, of *fescennina iocatio*...even so she had sung for Atthis."[10] For several decades this view prevailed, especially after Snell's confident defense in 1931.

The simile in line 1, says Snell, is a conventional feature of hymeneal song, the εἰκάζειν.[11] Thus Himerius tells us (fr. 105*b*) that Sappho would liken a bride to an apple, a groom to Achilles and (in a fragment preserved by Hephaistion) to Ares. In the following lines, which, since they were quoted to illustrate meter, were probably the first lines of a poem, Sappho makes it clear that a simile describing the groom is in order in that position:

> τίωι σ', ὦ φίλε γάμβρε, κάλως ἐικάσδω;
> ὄρπακι βραδίνῳ σε μάλιστ' ἐικάσδω.
>
> To what, O dear bridegroom, may I well compare thee?
> To a slender sapling I may best compare thee.
> (Fr. 115)

Furthermore, in the description of the wedding of Hector and Andromache (fr. 44) Sappho calls the bride and groom "like gods." The first line of fr. 31, then, is the traditional *makarismos* (blessing) of poems celebrating an event in someone's life.[12]

Secondly, it is implied that ὤνηρ (man), with both the definite article and the demonstrative, *must* refer to the girl's husband or bridegroom: are we to believe, Wilamowitz-Moellendorff asks, that Lesbian girls of the seventh century sat

10 "Und nun nimmt Sappho das Barbiton und singt ihr Lied, wie sie so viele für die Hochzeiten ihrer Schülerinnen verfasst hatte, voll von Scherzen, von *fescennina jocatio*...sie hat ja auch für Atthis gesungen" (ibid.).

11 Snell, "Sappho's Gedicht φαίνεταί μοι κῆνος" (above n. 5), 72.

12 See Snell's examples, ibid., 75 n3.

in social, even romantic proximity with men to whom they were not betrothed?[13]

Sappho's description of her passionate reaction to the girl, then, is praise of the bride, typically indirect or reflected through a witness. It prefigures the erotic delights the groom is to have. It is not an expression of jealousy, as in Catullus's version.

We expect, at the end (i.e., in a fifth stanza) a farewell to the bridal pair, or an invitation to the maidens to sing the hymenaion, or something of that sort.

Some parts of this view were attacked by Bowra, who nonetheless accepted much. "It is unlikely that ὤνηρ means 'the husband,' for elsewhere Sappho uses γάμβρος for 'husband'; and Alcaeus twice uses ὤνηρ contemptuously to mean 'the fellow.'"[14] The simile is not necessarily hymeneal because the departed girl in fr. 96 thought Atthis like a goddess. The scene *is* a wedding feast (because nowhere else would a girl talk freely with a man), but the song is not a *Hochzeitlied,* that is, it was not performed at the wedding feast. There is need for a fifth stanza.

Setti more determinedly objected to every one of Wilamowitz-Moellendorff's and Snell's contentions.[15] Line 1 *is* a μακαρισμός, he says, but not an epithalamic one; those are less emphatic (just a single adjective) and must be conjoined with praise of the bride's beauty. Is it possible that an epithalamium would lack the terms νύμφα (bride) and γάμβρος (groom)? Is it possible that in an epithalamium the *reason* for the groom's happiness would not be stated? In the hymeneal fragments the tone is naive and direct. As for the segregation of the sexes, "the Lesbians," he says, "were not Muslims. On the contrary, one has the impression of a possibility of

13 *SuS* 58.

14 *GLP,* 1st ed. (1936), 216.

15 Setti, "Sul frammento 2 di Saffo" (above, n. 5).

relationships between men and women superior to that in Attica in the classical age."

Oddly, he does not deal with the crux of Snell's argument that the *μακαρισμός* should be an *εἰκάζειν*. Indeed, Sappho does say *ὄλβιε γάμβρε* (blessed bridegroom) (fr. 112), *φίλε γάμβρε* (dear bridegroom) (fr. 115), and *τίμιε γάμβρε* (honored bridegroom) (fr. 116), using only a single adjective for a *μακαρισμός*; but she also says (fr. 111.5–6):

> *γάμβρος εἰσέρχεται ἴσος Ἄρευι*
> *ἄνδρος μεγάλω πόλυ μέζων.*
>
> The groom comes in like Ares,
> much larger than a large man.

Setti calls this a special case, explaining that the groom was unusually tall. But what of Himerius's statement (fr. 105*b*) that she would liken the bridegroom to Achilles and *hold him like that hero in his deeds* – which surely requires a number of words. We will return to this.

Setti's attack weakened the Wilamowitz-Snell position, but it was still believed, for example, by Gallavotti in 1942 and Schadewaldt in 1950. More recently, Page has dealt what seemed to be the death blow. It is an attempt to whitewash Sappho's moral character, he says, by claiming that her expression of passion was only a conventional praise of the bride.[16] How could an expression of homosexual passion, he wonders, be appropriate at a heterosexual wedding? "What will the bridegroom make of it? With what pleasure will they listen, 'father and wedding guests,' to this revelation of Sappho's uncontrollable ecstasy? ... There was never such a wedding song in the history of society; and there should never have been such a theory in the history of scholarship."[17]

16 *S&A* 32.
17 *S&A* 33.

(Snell *had* commented, "We find it awkward that Sappho speaks so openly about her own love in front of the married couple.")[18]

Since Setti's and Page's attacks, Bowra has reneged on the wedding feast, and even Snell has recanted to the extent of saying the poem was not *performed* at a wedding feast.[19] Indeed, some recent commentators treat the wedding-song theory as a curiosity of the past.[20] But I think that the last word has not been spoken on this question; a review of the evidence will reveal some unexpected clarities.

First, it is claimed that a simile comparing a human to a god is an element of hymeneal song. This is refuted ("The reasoning hardly deserves refutation," says Page)[21] by two points: 1. Poets often use such terms on occasions other than weddings, and 2. Sappho herself, at fr. 96.4–5 uses such a phrase on a non-hymeneal occasion.

But objection 1 is not documented by either Setti or Page; what other authors do they mean? Comparisons with gods in direct terms such as *θεῳείδης, θεοείκελος, ἴσος θέοισιν*, are found principally in early epic, in a few places in Sappho, and in Plato where they are clearly somewhat ironic. The early lyrists, elegists, and iambists not only do not use them, but are, in some cases, at pains to say so; Alcman, for example, says of Hagesichora, at a moment when a *makarismos* is clearly in order, "She is not a better singer than the Sirens, for they are gods" (*Partheneion* 96–98). The exactitude of phrases

---

18 "Für uns ist es befremdlich, daß Sappho vor den Eheleuten so offen von ihrer eigenen Liebe spricht" (Snell, "Sappho's Gedicht *φαίνεταί μοι κῆνος*" [above n.5], 83 n1.

19 *GLP* 187 and B. Snell, *Gesammelte Schriften* (Göttingen: Vandenhoek & Ruprecht, 1966), 97.

20 G. Wills, "Sappho 31 and Catullus 51," *Greek, Roman and Byzantine Studies* 8 (1967), 167–97; G.L. Koniaris, "On Sappho fr. 31 (L-P)," *Philologus* 112 (1968), 173–86.

21 *S&A* 31.

such as "Akmon, the noblest of the demigods" (*Partheneion* 7)[22] will suggest that they did not use terms like "equal to the gods" freely. Simonides' encomium to Skopas (fr. 37) and his *Threnoi* quoted by Stobaeus (esp. fr. 18) may be regarded as explanations of this restraint. In brief, comparisons of humans to gods do not exist in Alcman, Alcaeus, Stesichorus, Archilochus, Tyrtaeus, Mimnermus, Theognis, Solon, Ibycus, Anacreon, Simonides, or indeed anywhere in Greek poetry of the seventh and sixth centuries except in Sappho.[23]

---

22 Cf. Alcaeus B 10.13.

23 Mimnermus (7.7) has *θέιος Ἰήσων*, but Jason was descended from Prometheus and the use of such adjectives for great figures from the heroic age had the epic sanction. Callinas (1.19) is more restrained in the only other passage of this type:

> *λαῷ γὰρ σύμπαντι, πόθος κρατερόφονος ἄνδρὸς*
> *θωήσκοντος, ζώων δ' ἄξιος ἡμιθέων*
> *ὥσπερ γάρ πύργον μιν ἐν ὀφθαλμοίσιν ὁρῶσιν.*

> When a brave man dies there is regret in all the people,
> and while he lives he is comparable to a
> demigod, for in their eyes he is like a tower...

And Tyrtaeus (1a col. 4 [6]) says,

> Like them, of august Hera ... when the Tyndaridae ...

but the *primum comparationis* is unknown. The irony of Theognis's "godhood" in these lines of his (337–40) is apparent:

> *Ζεύς μοι, τῶν τε φίλων δοίη τίσιν ὅι με φιλεῦσιν*
> *τῶν τ' ἐχθρῶν μεῖζον, Κύρνε, δυνησαμένων*
> *χ' οὔτως ἂν δοκέοιμι μετ' ἀνθρώπων θεὸς εἶναι,*
> *εἴ μ ἀποτεισάμενον μοῖρα κίχοι θανάτου.*

> Zeus, grant me repayment for the friends who love me
> and for the enemies who have been stronger, Kyrnus, than I;
> and then I will seem to be a god among men, if,
> when the lot of death comes for me, all my debts shall have
> been paid.

It does not need special pleading that none of these is comparable in the least to Sappho's explicit comparisons of humans to gods.

Only after Sappho, and only in a poet who seems to have been greatly influenced by her, and only in an erotic context, does anything like her comparisons with gods occur: Ibycus says of his favorite Euryalus, "You scion of the sweet Graces, darling of the fair-haired Muses, surely Cypris and tender-eyed Peitho nursed you amid blossoms of roses" (fr. 6). But this, of course, is not a comparison, and he probably is imitating Sappho anyway. When the Archilochus song at the games gave way to the full-blown *epinikion* the possibilities were increased; Simonides says of a boxing victor, "Neither the might of Polydeuces would have lifted hand against him, nor the iron child of Alcmena" (fr. 4). Which, of course, is not a comparison either. Perhaps it is Pindar whom Page and Setti are thinking of; but even in Pindar such comparisons are apt to be less direct and emphatic:

> I have praised the lovely son of Archestratus, whom I saw conquering by might of his hand beside the Olympian altar in those days, fair in body and touched by that youth that once kept shameless death away from Ganymede, by the power of the Cyprus-born.
> (*Olympian* 10.99–106)

Indeed, Pindar often follows Homer in the theological propriety of making descent from the gods a requisite for comparison with them. In any case, it is difficult to see what bearing evidence from Pindar (or the tragedians) could have on Sappho; he, of course, imitated her (using Æolic meters in twenty of the forty-six victory odes) and may have generalized into *his* type of encomiastic song a practice that she had used in *her* kind.

Surely Page and Setti are not thinking of Homer. Homer did not write occasional verse; such similes, in Homer's world, are not *μακαρισμοί,* but merely normal attributes. The point is that later poets, by using such a simile, would for a moment put their subject into Homer's world: this *was* the *μακαρισμός*. And Sappho seems to have begun it; and hence to have made her own rules. And now let's see what those are.

Of the eight similes of this type in her fragments, five occurred either in wedding songs or in songs that described weddings;[24] a sixth (fr. 68*a*3) has no identifiable context, a seventh (fr. 96.4) is best explained as a conscious echo of hymeneal convention, and the last is the example in fr. 31 that is under consideration. Furthermore, the overwhelming bulk of all similes in Sappho rise from the occasion of marriage: out of eleven similes with extant contexts, at least seven belonged to wedding songs. (This, marriage, is the "transforming" moment.) Snell seems to be vindicated in his opinion that the first line of fr. 31 would very likely be identified by an audience familiar with Sappho's practice as the beginning of a wedding song. We may compare Rufinus Domesticus (*Palatine Anthology* 5.94) for a play on the traditional *εἰκάζειν*:

> I call him blessed who looks on you, and thrice blessed
> who hears your voice, and he is a demigod
> who kisses your mouth: but a god, a god indeed
> is the man whose bed receives you as a bride.

Surely Rufinus is thinking of Sappho's poem, and lending strong support to the view that it is a wedding song.

Second, we are told that *κῆνος ὤνηρ* should be understood to mean "the husband" rather than "that man"; and this also has met with two objections: 1) that Alcaeus in two places (H 2.3 and D 14.7) uses it to mean simply "man,"[25] and 2) that Sappho herself says *γάμβρος* when she means bridegroom.[26]

---

24 Frr. 23.5, 44.21, 44.34, 105*b*, and 111.5.

25 *S&A* 31.

26 Setti, "Sul frammento 2 di Saffo" (above, n. 5), 202.

We have already seen that Alcaeus is an unreliable guide to the meaning of Sappho's poetry – spiritually distant from it as he was. She observed certain self-imposed rules of diction and imagery that he did not observe. For which we may be thankful once more, since the various words for human being make up one of the clearest cases of consistent patterning in her diction.

Sappho uses *γύνη* only of married women, *παρθένος* of unmarried (but nubile?) women, and *πάις* of young unmarried girls; in ritual contexts she may use *κόρα* also. The evidence for men is naturally much scantier, as they are mentioned more rarely, but suggests a similar set of distinctions.

Twice she uses *ἠίθεος* (unmarried man) and nine times *ἀνήρ*. In fr. 44 (which has more people in it than any other), the *γύναικες* went out "together with the *παρθένοι*" (lines 14–15) (i.e., they are different creatures), and then, in similar close conjunction, we read that the *ἄνδρες* yoked the horses to the chariots, and then something about the *ἠίθεοι*. The latter is taken by Page to modify *ἄνδρες*;[27] but is the sense, then, that the married women and the unmarried women and the unmarried men went out, but the married men stayed home? Rather, the close parallelism and proximity of the two pairs of terms – *γύνη/παρθένος, ἀνήρ/ἠίθεος* – suggests a parallel distinction, between married and unmarried men. We have, then, the sort of homey detail we would expect from Sappho's public songs: "The men drew out the (heavy) yokes, and the boys (it was, after all, a special day) drove." The distinction is suggested again at the end of the poem. The *παρθένοι*, we are told, sang a *μέλος ἄγνον*, and the *γύναικες* sang *ἐλελύσδω;* then *all* the men (*πάντες δ'ἄνδρες*) sang a lovely song to Apollo. Clearly, Sappho points out the generic use of *ἀνήρ* because she feels that it needs to be pointed out.

---

27 *S&A* 64.

Again: Helen had the noblest husband (ἄνδρα) of all mankind (ἀνθρώπων) (fr. 16.7). It seems clear: ἀνήρ when used specifically means "married man." The numbers of occurences of the different words will support this distinction: γύνη occurs but three times compared to seven for παρθένος; ἠίθεος but twice, to nine for ἀνήρ; it is as maidens, not as matrons, that Sappho is interested in women, but as husbands, not boys, that she is interested in men.

In sum, ἀνήρ occurs nine times and there is no case of which it can be said that it does not mean "husband" and several where it is clear that it does. The fact that Bowra and Page must go to Alcaeus to establish their point weakens it greatly: Alcaeus was not interested in these distinctions. Further, the point is treated as if it were an observation about the Lesbian-Æolic dialect; but rather, it is an observation about the practice of one poet. And that one poet was more interested in weddings and marriage than any other poet ever, and was one of the most careful and consistent in matters of diction. On this point, at least, she can be expected to get the words right.

What of the objection that γάμβρος should have been used instead in a wedding song? We must ask in which wedding song? The song at the feast, which fr. 31 must be if it is a wedding song, is precisely the one for which we have no evidence at all. Sappho's uses of γάμβρος are all at the entrance to the bridal chamber, and may have been limited to that stage of the ceremony. The word is not, after all, a universal Greek idiom for bridegroom: to Homer it meant son-in-law. The matter is uncertain. But the burden of the evidence is that κῆνος ὤνηρ in the first strophe would probably mean married man or bridegroom to Sappho's audience. In fact, it seems that ὤνηρ itself carried the desired connotation.

Finally, we hear that in Lesbos in the late seventh and early sixth centuries men and women would not have been together socially in such intimacy unless they were either married or getting married. To this it is objected 1. that we do not know (Bowra) and 2. that there is some suggestion of a greater possibility of relationships between the sexes at that time and place than in Attica in the classical age (Setti).

To the first objection it may be replied that we do know what Sappho and Alcaeus tell us, and that that is rather clear. In Alcaeus both men and women are mentioned, in groups and individually, but *never* together, except in the description of the *marriage* of Peleus and Thetis (fr. B 10). Further, we have from Alcaeus many poems dealing with social occasions (mostly *symposia*) of the type that this poem might be taken to describe (if it is not describing a wedding) – and women appear in none of them. In Sappho the evidence is even clearer: men are never even mentioned except in poems about weddings. No doubt other evidence would be welcome, but that which we have could not be clearer: there is no justification for assuming that an event other than a wedding may be described in fr. 31.

Setti's "suggestion of a greater possibility" is not documented. Is he thinking of Sappho's high education? Her participation in the profession of letters? The rumors of her affairs with Anacreon, Hipponax, and Archilochus? Whether women in general were highly educated and wrote poetry we cannot tell; but even if they were, the evidence is that they kept (or were kept) away from men to whom they were not married.

It seems that the three main points of Wilamowitz-Moellendorff's and Snell's argument are sound – perhaps sounder than they knew. What is clear is that the scene is probably a wedding, and that the poem begins with two elements of hymeneal song.[28] But we have only looked at the first stanza. It is in the following stanzas that the wedding-song theory encounters problems.

Setti's strongest argument, I think, is one that he himself did not develop fully: that the "tone" of fr. 31 is different from the "tone" of the known hymeneal fragments. According to Snell, stanzas two to four serve as praise of the bride. But we would expect in this place a comparison of the bride to a goddess, and direct praise of her beauty, her virtue, her handiwork; not this indirect acting out. And it is not merely the indirection that should not be there, but the unhappiness. Wilamowitz-Moellendorff described Sappho's wedding-songs as happy, joking songs – but surely this is no joke. As Page objects, the poem, if indeed sung at a wedding feast, was in incredibly, even absurdly, bad taste. I confess I cannot demur from this view. I find it almost inconceivable that stanzas two to four were *performed* as a conventional *Hochzeitlied*. This does not, however, tell us what type of poem it is. One difficulty faces all non-hymeneal interpretations: the presence of the man must be explained.[29]

If Sappho is not writing about someone's wedding, if it is a poem about passion, or about her specific passion for a certain girl, then why is the man mentioned at all? The traditional answer (flirted with by Page and presented strongly by Bagg[30]) is that the subject of the poem is not Sappho's love

28 Wills expresses a common hesitation when he objects that the wedding theory is "from outside," an "occasio ex machina" ("Sappho 31 and Catullus 51" [above, n.20], 168). But in fact all the evidence comes from within the Sapphic fragments; there are no external sources on the question.

29 The seemingly endless argument about whether ὄττις in line 2 has a definite or an indefinite antecedent strikes me as fruitless and, in fact, of little importance. Perhaps Rydbeck has silenced it at last (L. Rydbeck, "Sappho's φαίνεταί μοι κῆνος," *Hermes* 97 [1969], 161–66).

30 R. Bagg, "Love, Ceremony and Daydream in Sappho's Lyrics," *Arion* 3.3 (1964), 65.

of the girl, but her jealousy of the man. A variant of this (first proposed in 1816 by Welcker,[31] liked by Setti, and, more recently, by Wills) explains that it is not the man's favored position beside the girl that Sappho envies, but the man's composure under the onslaught of the girl's charms, which would reduce Sappho herself to idiocy. The question is, what is the antecedent of *τό* in line 5? If *ἰσδάνει καί... ὐπακούει* (that is, the *man*), then either of the above will work; but ordinary grammar (relative takes nearest antecedent) would favor *ἆδυ φωνείσας... καὶ γελαίσας ἰμέροεν* (that is, the *girl*); and how is the reader or listener to know that ordinary grammar is not in effect here?[32] Further, Sappho says, "When I look at *you* I cannot speak, etc.," (and the *σ'* of the mss. cannot lightly be disposed of as, for example, Beattie tries to do).[33] Page suggests, "When I look at you *being looked at by him*,"[34] but there seems little warrant for this in Sappho's regular practice. For Sappho, *seeing* a beautiful thing leads to *love;* it is always the *beauty* of the thing (not, say, its possession by someone else) that is the cause, and *love* (not jealousy) that is the result. (*Ἴδην* [to see] is, in fact, a key emotional word for her, as is *μνάομαι* [to remember].[35]) It seems that most frequently the jealousy theory is adopted not because the text recommends it, but as a result of rejecting the wedding theo-

31 F.G. Welcker, *Sappho von einem herrschenden Vorurteile befreyt* (Göttingen: Vandenhoek und Ruprecht, 1816).

32 I am inclined toward C. Gallavotti's view ("Studi sulla lirica Greca," *Rivista di filologia e di istruzione classica* 70 [1942], 117) that the entire first stanza is the antecedent.

33 A.J. Beattie, "Sappho fr. 31," *Mnemosyne* 4.9 (1956), 103–11. I regard his suggestion that it is the man for whom Sappho is overcome by passion as an oddity. Cf. "A Note on Sappho, fr. 1," *Classical Quarterly* n.s. 7 (1957), 180–83, where again he suggests that it is a man for whom Sappho is pining.

34 *S&A* 22.

35 Cf. esp. frr. 22.13–14 and 55.3, where "unseen" may well suggest "unloved." Turyn, *Stud.Sapph.* 33–41, has amassed an overwhelming list of parallels from Homer to Apuleius.

ry and being left with an extra, and very prominently placed, man to account for.

Koniaris asks us to see the poem as an encomium in which two witnesses, first some external man and then the poet herself, testify to the girl's beauty.[36] But what testimony does the man give? He shows none of the effects Sappho feels. And why is he compared to a god? That the poem is to some degree encomiastic is reasonable enough, but it (like fr. 16) is an encomium *disguised* within some other genre; and it is that other we must find out.

Bowra's view, which seems to hold the lead in Page's mind also – that the man is present because the poem describes some actual event at which he was present – strikes me as in every way the least satisfactory. "Its powerful impact," Bowra says, "comes from its air of reality, of being derived immediately and directly from Sappho's own experience."[37] Page goes on similarly: "Rarely, if anywhere, in archaic or classical poetry shall we find language so close to the speech of everyday."[38]

But if the man is in the poem only because he was at the event, then we must chide Sappho. If there had been other persons present would she have had to mention them too? Was she so primitive that she did not know how to omit what was artistically irrelevant? Are her poems no more than touchingly faithful recordings of actual everyday events? Her language, no more than everyday speech cleverly arranged into meters? Her psychology, no more than recently felt emotions honestly rendered? I will repeat my belief that Bowra's view (simplicity = truthfulness) may be directly wrong:

---

36 Koniaris, "On Sappho fr. 31 (L-P)" (above, n. 20).

37 *GLP* 187.

38 *S&A* 30. This position of both Bowra and Page seems contradicted by Page's declaration that "these poems are not spontaneous experiences of emotion" (*S&A* 85).

Pindar impresses me as more sincere than Sappho because he does not guard his words as she does.

To sum up: the view that the scene of fr. 31 is a wedding and that the song observes to some degree the conventions of a wedding song, seems called for by the three Wilamowitz-Snell arguments, by the fact that the man is present at all (which has not comfortably been accounted for otherwise), and by the apparent likelihood that the poem contained a fifth stanza, which can most easily and satisfactorily be reconstructed as a return to the persons of the bride and groom with a conventional statement of good wishes for them. Yet Setti's and Page's view that it is in impossibly bad taste for the poetess to praise the bride by declaring her own passion for her at a public event seems merited also. Let us suppose that Sappho meant to express both these things and, instead of assuming that one or the other of them must be explained away, let us see what kind of poem they make together.

The Poem

A comparison with an undoubtedly hymeneal fragment (fr. 112) will be instructive.

> ὄλβιε γάμβρε, σοὶ μὲν δὴ γάμος ὠς ἄραο
> ἐκτετέλεστ', ἔχηις δὲ πάρθενον † ἂν † ἄραο...
> σοί χάριεν μὲν εἶδος. ὄππατα δ' ⟨αὖτε νύμφας⟩
> μέλλιχ', ἔρος δ' ἐπ' ἰμέρτωι κέχυται προσώπωι
> ....τετίμακ' ἔξοχά σ' Ἀπροδίτα.[39]

> Happy bridegroom! The wedding you prayed for
> is fulfilled, and you have the girl you prayed
> for; your face is fair, but her eyes are gentle
> indeed and love is shed over all her beautiful face...
> Aphrodite has favored you exceedingly.

39 I have used Bowra's restoration of line 3.

It follows the general outline of fr. 31; a statement of the happiness of the man,[40] followed by the reasons for it, which consist primarily of a description of the beauty of the bride in terms (ἔρος ... ἰμέρτωι) that suggest that the singer desires her too. But how different it is. The tone is naive and direct; the mood is happiness shared by all; there is no hint that the singer and the bridegroom are not in harmony in their attitudes toward the event. So simple, even flat, is the language, and so childish the psychology that it is easy to believe that this is a commissioned poem, written to please an audience of ordinary tastes. Fragment 31 could almost be a violent, even cruel, parody of this, laying bare the face behind the mask, as it were, the harder, stronger, uglier psychology of the adult, that lies behind the feigned happiness of popular culture and its public events. Let us review it once more.

At the end of the first stanza the reader (or auditor) familiar with Sappho's poetry will assume that this is a wedding song. Then a change, a type of emotional surprise typical of Catullus, one of Sappho's greatest imitators, occurs. To sketch out, *exempli gratia,* the dramatic situation: Sappho has been asked (hired?)[41] to write or sing the wedding song, and she has begun nicely; then the sight of the bride puts her out of control. Her public impersonal role is eclipsed by her internal, personal reaction. She is shaken to the heart; her tongue falls silent (i.e., the impersonal public song ends; but the inner song of passion continues though the tongue be

---

40 I am not convinced by Wills's claim that ἴσος θέοισιν means, by Homeric precedent, *strong as the gods,* and is therefore not appropriate to a hymeneal μακαρισμός. In a new age and context, with new conventions, there is no reason why it should not refer to general happiness or well-being, as Snell says.

41 The possibility should be considered. Pindar says that once poets did not toil for gold, and now they do (*Isthmian* 2.6–8). But he does not say what poets. Was it Orpheus and Musaeus, perhaps? Herodotus (1.24) says that the Lesbian poet Arion of Methymna, in the generation *before* Sappho, went to Italy and Sicily and made a fortune.

still). The public song has been taken over by the private one. The public event is now ignored, and the private event is carried out to its exaggerated end, when Sappho seems almost to be dying – then calls herself back with the words, "But all must be borne boldly," and something (about a poor singer *having* to work for his or her dinner?) that the manuscript has lost. This transition must remind one of the famous Catullan ending "At tu, Catulle, destinatus obdura" (But you, Catullus, resolutely endure), and it seems likely that Catullus learned from Sappho this sudden change indicating the irrational imperium of passion. Presumably, then, she returned to the public song, the conventional congratulations to the bride and groom standing in ironic, even horrible contrast to the painful inner song that intruded before them.[42]

We have, it is true, been led to this view by a desire to avoid two great internal problems: the awkwardness of the end if it is a wedding song, and the awkwardness of the beginning if it is not. There is more to recommend it than its convenience, however; let us consider certain points of imagery.

Nowhere else is Sappho's imagery comparably physical. Not only does she mention the body far more than usual, but she uses words that are at variance with her usual practice, and the variation is always in the direction of the cruder, more physical words. Let us disabuse ourselves of the notion that it is even possible, much less creditable, for a great poet

42 Cf. G. Perrotta, *Saffo e Pindaro* (Bari: Laterza, 1935), 48: "La poesia dell' ode e nel contrasto tra la prima strofe e l'altri: tra la gioia dei due innamorati felici e l'ardore disperato di Saffo" (The poetry of the poem is in the contrast between the first strophe and the others: between the joy of the two happy sweethearts and Sappho's despairing passion). Since *ὤνηρ*, in Sappho, seems more strongly to suggest "husband" than "bridegroom," we should mention the possibility that, whereas the whole is a bitter parody of a conventional wedding song, the word "husband" (if such it is) contains an ironic pathos not unlike that of "matrons" in fr. 96.6–7.

to simply lapse into everyday speech, without being aware of the poetic significance of each word.

Καρδία (heart) occurs nowhere else in Sappho. Her regular word for the organ in which erotic responses are located is *θῦμος*. The words are interchangeable in Homer, but seem to have received more definition from Archilochus. He uses *θῦμος* only once in the fragments (fr. 118 Lass.), clearly not meaning a physical thing, but something like "will." *Καρδία* we find three times, always with a strong hint of physical meaning (*καρδία ἰαίνεται, καρδία πλέως, ὑπὸ καρδίαν*). Whether we may assume that the word was associated by Sappho with Archilochus (and hence with blunt expression of physical fact) is uncertain; but it is fairly sure to be a break with her usual practice, and the phrase *καρδίαν ἐν στήθεσιν* (the heart in my breast) indicates that the physical organ itself is meant, which is strongly at variance with her usual avoidance of bodily imagery and does not occur elsewhere.

In line 9 *γλῶσσα* (tongue) is probably aimed at a similar effect. It occurs two other times with context: "If your tongue had not been cooking up something evil to say..." (fr. 137.4) and, "When anger spreads in the breast, the yapping tongue must be guarded" (fr. 158.2). The first, in Aristotle's context (a reply to an indecent poem of Alcaeus), refers not to ordinary speech, but to poetry, and it seems likely that the second one also was in castigation of some ill-tempered poet (possibly even Archilochus). Yet Sappho does not ordinarily refer to the organs of speech when talking about poetry, but to the voice; someone is called *λιγύφωνος* (clear-voiced) (fr. 30.8); someone else (Mika?) *μελλιχόφων* (soft-voiced) (fr. 71.6); maidens are *μελίφωνοι* (honey-voiced) (fr. 185); a girl is *ἀδύφονον* (sweet-voiced) (fr. 61). The difference between these passages and the two with *γλῶσσα* is that in the latter two the poetic act is viewed unfavorably; poets are reproached, as if they had not behaved like poets, but like ordinary people. Hence no musical image is used: the words are presented as the products of the tongue alone. In line 8 of fr. 31 it seems that Sappho says that she *became* silent, since, indeed, she says ὀυδ'... ἔτ' εἴκει (no longer do I speak); but she was not involved in the conversation between the man and the girl. Does she refer to her inability to continue singing the wedding song? Her tongue is broken to silence. The emptiness of the song, its failure to express her true feelings, overrides the polite duty.

We see also πῦρ (fire), which does not occur elsewhere in the fragments, and ψῦχρος (cold), used once of water (fr. 2.5) and once of the spirit (θῦμος) in birds. Only in fr. 31 are the physical sensations of heat and cold a part of Sappho's poetic world. Ἀκούαι (ears) are nowhere else mentioned. Ἴδρως (sweat): the phrase is from Homer (e.g. *Odyssey* 11.599); it is not to be expected in Sappho's ordinary imagery where a heart may be weighed down by grief or fluttered by desire, but where the fact that bodies sweat will elsewhere find no cause to be mentioned. Τρόμος (a tremor): like other socially awkward qualities of the body, it is not mentioned elsewhere, but τρομέροις (trembling) appears in a poem (fr. 21.4), which evidently described in unpleasant terms the bodily decrepitude of old age.

In Sappho's general practice, parts of the body are mentioned only as containers of erotic beauty. (This is true also of the old age fragment just referred to, where the point is that they no longer have it.) They usually occur in decorative compounds (καλλίκομοι [fair-haired], βροδύπαχυς [pink-armed], εὔποδα [lovely-footed]) or modified by her typical adjectives for feminine beauty (ἄπαλαι δέραι [delicate throat], ἰμέρτωι προσώπωι [lovely face], ὄππoτα μέλλιχ' [gentle eyes], ἐράτοισ φόβαισιν [beautiful tresses], etc.), and in conjunction with her most typical imagery as seen in the other poems: hands are to weave garlands with, hair is to twine them in, etc. Fr. 31 departs conspicuously from all of these generalities. How are we to understand it in relation to the poems that we have discussed earlier, which we should regard as representing the mainstream of Sappho's poetic imagery and diction? There is a strikingly clear and reasonable relationship that fits well with our view of Sappho's intelligence as a poet.

We have supposed, from the other poems, that in Sappho's poetic world she presents young girls in an idealized poetic environment where they live among symbols of their erotic beauty and symbols drawn from ritual, especially the wedding rite; their life is a constant rite of preparation for loss of maidenhood. But in fr. 31 she presents us not with this dream of beauty, which she, as poet, controls, but with *the real thing – an actual wedding.* By excluding from it all the symbols of beauty (flowers, songs, etc,) and describing for the first and only time the actual body, its unpleasant lack of control, its inability to fulfill the mind's idealized desires, its ugly pain and crude helplessness, she makes explicit the difference between the real and the poetic worlds. Consider the pathos and irony, the great wit, of what is accomplished here. The pathos is that she must confess that she hates in the real world what she loves in the imagined one; the irony that while she portrays the disintegration of certain conventions of song (the conventional public song proves unable to contain true passion), she forces the two realities finally to cooperate in another – if incredibly tense and explosive – song.

And only here, of all the poems, is Sappho at center stage. Elsewhere she consoles another girl who is at the center of the poem, or invisibly watches over the grove of the goddess who stands at the center, or follows a departed companion (who is at the center) down the lanes of memory or imagination – but here she is present *in the flesh,* and at the dead center of the poem, in a reality that is an affliction to her alone. Now for once death appears. For once, the grim facts of bodily death become overwhelmingly clear and close: she is mortal; her tongue of songs is broken; sweat pours down her body. Here the basic lyric-erotic mysticism (or nightmare) is first fully presented – the identification, inherited *in semina* from Archilochus (whose true successor Sappho is), of eros and thanatos, of love and death. At the edge of reality this meeting takes place. At that tormented boundary between the imagined and the perceived, the desired and the enforced, the private and the public songs, the initiate of Aphrodite's mysteries lies, as Archilochus said, "dead with love, pierced through the bones by the horrible pains the gods have sent me."

But wait, Catullus! Stiffen your spine! Be firm!

VII

The Figure in the Doorway

(Ode 1)

ποικιλόθρον' ἀθανατ' Ἀφρόδιτα,
παῖ Δίος δολόπλοκε, λίσσομαί σε,
μή μ' ἄσαισι μηδ' ὀνίαισι δάμνα,
πότνια, θῦμον.
—]
ἀλλὰ τυίδ' ἔλθ', αἴ ποτα κἀτέρωτα
τὰς ἔμας αὔδας ἀίοισα πήλοι
ἔκλυες, πάτρος δὲ δόμον λίποισα
χρύσιον ἦλθες
—]
ἄρμ' ὐπασδεύξαισα· κάλοι δέ σ' ἆγον
ὤκεες στροῦθοι περὶ γᾶς μελαίνας
πύκνα δίννεντες πτέρ' ἀπ' ὠράνωἴθε-
πος διὰ μέσσω,
—]
αἶψα δ' ἐξίκοντο· σὺ δ', ὦ μάκαιρα,
μειδιαίσαις ἀθανάτωι προσώπωι
ἤρε' ὄττι δηὖτε πέπονθα κὤττι
δηὖτε κάλημμι,
—]
κὤττι μοι μάλιστα θέλω γένεσθαι
μαινόλαι θύμωι· τίνα δηὖτε πεῖθω
ἄψ † σαγην † ἐς σὰν φιλότατα; τίς σ', ὦ
ψάπφ', ἀδικήει;
—]
καὶ γὰρ αἰ φεύγει, ταχέως διώξει·
αἰ δὲ δῶρα μὴ δέκετ', ἄλλὰ δώσει·
αἰ δὲ μὴ φίλει, ταχέως φιλήσει
κωὐκ ἐθέλοισα.
—]
ἔλθε μοι καὶ νῦν, χαλέπαν δὲ λῦσον
ἐκ μερίμναν, ὄσσα δέ μοι τέλεσσαι
θῦμος ἰμέρρει, τέλεσον· σὺ δ' αὔτα
σύμμαχος ἔσσο.
—]

---

1. *ποικιλοφρον*, some mss. 19. *μαι/βαι σαγηνεσσαν*, cod. P; *καισαγηνεσσαν*, alii.; *μαῖσ' ἄγην*, Wilamowitz-Moellendorff; *και σ' ἄγην ἐς ϝὰν*, Edmonds; *ἄψ τάγην ἐς σὰν*, Page.

Splendor-throned immortal Aphrodite,
child of Zeus, wile-weaving, I beseech you,
do not overwhelm with troubles and with sorrows,
mistress, my heart;

but hither come, if ever at other time,
hearing my voice from afar
you heeded, and leaving your father's house
of gold, you came,

yoking your chariot; and fair swift
sparrows drew you around the dark earth,
fluttering fast their wings from heaven
to mid-sky,

and quickly were here; and you, O blessed one,
smiling with your immortal countenance,
asked what now I had suffered, and for what
now I called you,

and what most of all I longed for
in my mad heart: whom now shall I persuade
to come to your love? Who, O
Sappho, is hurting you?

For if now she flees, soon she will follow,
and if she does not accept gifts, she will give them;
and if she does not love, quickly she will love,
even unwilling...

Come to me now, too, and free me
from harsh anxiety,
and whatever my heart longs
to have fulfilled for me, fulfill it! And be,

yourself, my ally.

The Text

Ode 1 is the longest and best preserved poem in Sappho's corpus, and the only one to come with a manuscript tradition. Dionysius of Halicarnassus quotes it (*On Literary Composition* 23); Oxyrhynchus Papyrus 2288 preserves the all-important coronis, indicating that we may be sure we have the end of the poem; Hephaestion (83) cites line 1 to illustrate the Sapphic hendecasyllable, indicating, on the (perhaps questionable) principle[1] that metricians quote always the first line of a certain meter, that, for once (and once only) we seem to have the beginning of the poem as well; and that it was the first ode in the first book of the Alexandrian edition of Sappho.[2] For Dionysius it was an example of the smooth and flowery style (*γλαφυρὰ καὶ ἀνθηρα σύνθεσις*) in which Sappho, among the lyrists, exceeded Anacreon and

1 See Lobel, Σμ. xv.

2 An attic hydria of about 430 BCE (National Archaeological Museum, Athens, 1260; Collingnon-Couve, 1241) shows Sappho holding a book whose first column contains the line *ἀερίων ἐπέων ἄρχομαι ἀλλ' ὀνάτων* (words of air, but fair to hear, I sing), evidently an elegiac pentameter. "This introductory poem," says Edmonds (*LG* 1.181n3), "apparently stood first in S.'s own collection of her poems." But at least as early as Plato's time she was the subject of elegiac epigrams; the Atticism of this line indicates that an epigram containing it was prefixed to some Attic edition of Sappho. A letter of Julian the Apostate (30) implies that an iambic motto began Sappho's poems. The question should remind us how very little we know about early editions of the lyric poets, or, indeed, about what kind of publication they wrote for.

Simonides; Hesiod surpassed other epic poets; Euripides, other tragedians; and Isocrates, other orators. He praises its harmonious smoothness and coherence.

In line 1, half the mss. of Dionysius read *ποικιλόφρον'* (of varied purposes, or moods, or wiles), attested by Alcaeus (D 11.7) and Euripides (e.g. *Hecuba* 131); and half, *ποικιλόθρον'* (of the painted, or richly wrought, throne), a *hapax legomenon.* But Hephaestion and the papyrus both give theta (though dotted in the papyrus by Lobel and Page), and it is used here, as it were, from custom. Even so, what does it mean? Ποικιλόθρονος or *ποικιλόθρονον*? The latter would mean "with various flowers" (i.e., woven on her robe); compare *Iliad* 22.441: *ἐν δὲ θρόνα ποικίλ' ἔπασσε* (and in it she wove varied flowers) with its close verbal echo, *Iliad* 14.214–21, and Theocritus 2.59 for Aphrodite's possession of an elaborately embroidered robe.[3] Surely this meaning is possible, perhaps even preferable.

In line 19 there is a more serious problem: two readings of the codices, both problematical, are given in the apparatus. Wilamowitz-Moellendorff, choosing codex P, assumes an active verb *μάω*, which Page calls "non-existent"[4] (it is cited by *LSJ*, but only in the perfect with present sense). Μαῖσ(αι) as a second person singular of *μαίομαι* is questioned by Lobel and declared "a monster" by Page.[5] Page's argument (that P should not be followed here because the *μαι-* could come from *μαινόλαι* in the line above) seems to me to be weakened by the fact that the copyist of P first wrote *βαισαγην* and then, evidently applying a critical eye to his work, corrected

3 For this interpretation of the first word see G.M. Bolling, "Poikilos and Throna," *American Journal of Philology* 79 (1958), 275–82; M.C.J. Putnam, "*Throna* and Sappho 1.1," *The Classical Journal* 56.2 (1960), 79–83 and L.B. Lawler, "*Pepoikilmena Zoia*," *The Classical Journal* 56.8 (1960), 349–51.

4 *S&A* 9.

5 Σμ. 16; *S&A* 9.

it to μαισαγην. Edmonds's change of sigma to digamma follows the majority of the mss. with the slightest change, but makes awkward sense: "Whom shall I persuade to lead you also into her affection," or, in his own words, "Whom shall I make to give thee room in her heart's love?"[6] Oxyrhynchus Papyrus 2288 (published in 1951), however, does not seem to read either μαι- or και- here; Lobel and Page give ̣]̣σαγην, allowing only one letter before the bracket and suggesting either psi or phi after it. Ἄψ (cf. fr. 34.2) is the obvious candidate, and Page writes it, leaving both Dionysius's and the papyrus's sigma unexplained.[7] "It looks as if σαγην hid some word for 'come,'" says Bowra,[8] and I think we must be content with that.

There are two lesser questions. According to the punctuation of the papyrus, χρύσιον (golden) in line 8 modifies δόμον (home); Wilamowitz-Moellendorff, however, says that anyone who would take χρύσιον with δόμον "has no feeling for Greek word order" (hat kein Gefühl für griechische Wortstellung).[9] Headlam[10] brings Apuleius, *Metamorphoses* 6.6 into evidence, where Vulcanus aurifex, the goldsmith, makes Aphrodite's chariot "more precious through the very loss of the gold (ipsius auri damno pretiosum)." Further parallels accrue on both sides: Pindar, *Nemean* 10.88: οὐρανοῦ ἐν χρυσέοις δόμοισιν (in golden homes in heaven) (and *Pythian* 3.94, *Isthmian* 4.60, and elsewhere); Homer, *Iliad* 5.722: δίφρος δὲ χρυσέοισι … ἱμᾶσιν (a chariot with golden reins) (and *Iliad* 25.503, *Iliad* 10.438, *Hymn to Demeter* 431). Perhaps neither claim is superior, except that Sappho herself says

6 *LG* 1.185.

7 *S&A* 10.

8 *GLP* 199 n1.

9 *SuS* 45 n1.

10 W. Headlam, "Notes on the Greek Lyric Poets," *Classical Review* 14 (1900), 6.

elsewhere (fr. 127): δεῦρο δηὖτε Μοῖσαι χρύσιον λίποισαι (come hither, Muses, leaving your golden), and we can hardly restore anything but a word for home.

Κωὔκ ἐθέλοισα in line 24 falls under the shadow of Lesbian vernacular enthusiasts by not occuring elsewhere in Sappho, and only once irregularly in Alceaus (fr. 66). Page attacks it enthusiastically in light of his peculiar interpretation of stanza 6 as a comment not on divine power, but on human fickleness: "If today she is running away from you, tomorrow you will be running away from her."[11] Hence he favors Knox's κὀύ σε θέλοισα in line 24: she will love you even when you are sick of her. [12] Page's connection of διώκειν and φεύγειν does not seem solid (διώκειν is used of wind driving a ship, of a charioteer driving horses, etc.), and there is little else to recommend his interpretation here.[13] That Sappho is praying for the advances of a loved one with the intention of rejecting these advances is in no way clear and seems a gratuitous attribution of perverse motives to the poetess. Perhaps the specter of doubt hangs over ἐθέλοισα on dialectal grounds, but it is not enough to merit a defense.

---

11 *S&A* 14f.

12 A. D. Knox, "On Editing Hipponax: A Palinode?" *Studi italiani di filologia classica,* n. s., 15 (1938), 194 n3.

13 Homer even uses διώκειν intransitively (*Iliad* 23.344 and 23.424), where there is no question of a fleeing party. And G. L. Koniaris cites Plato, *Symposium* 191d and *Theaetetus* 168 ("On Sappho Fr. 1 [Lobel-Page]," *Philologus* 109 [1965], 30–38). Page's interpretation of this stanza (like his emendation τάγην in line 19) has aroused much disagreement: from A.W. Gomme ("Interpretations of Some Poems of Sappho and Alcaeus," *Journal of Hellenic Studies* 77 [1957], 284); A.J. Beattie (reviews of LP and *S&A* in *Journal of Hellenic Studies* 77 [1957], 321); A. Cameron ("Sappho and Aphrodite Again," *Harvard Theological Review* 57 [1964], 237); and Koniaris (loc. cit.).

Does She Mean It?

Ode 1 is a kletic hymn with a specific request for a favor from the god. It is one of the mainstays of a certain attitude (from Wilamowitz-Moellendorff to Treu) that regards "piety" as an outstanding quality of Sappho. But did not Paul warn us about the prayers that are prayed in public? Let us ask the obvious question: Does she mean it?

Bowra thinks so, saying, "The appearance of Aphrodite must be treated as an actual experience," but adding circumspectly, "it is never easy to get to the heart of religious experience."[14] Pfeiffer, Perrotta, and Schadewaldt are in general agreement that the poem should be taken at face value: it is a prayer she expects to be answered, and a vision that she has actually seen. Wilamowitz-Moellendorff was sufficiently embarrassed to suppose that not a waking vision, but a dream, which Sappho believed, in good Homeric fashion, to be an actual visitation, is here narrated.[15] But, Bowra says rightly, "there is no hint that it is a dream."[16] Page retreats further: all Sappho *saw* was a flock of sparrows; these she has elegantly ornamented for the entertainment of her friends.

West is more outspoken, referring to "the naive realist interpretation, which assumes that Sappho's earlier prayers had habitually been greeted by mass descents of sparrows."[17] And Cameron calls it "an exercise in a literary genre, charming indeed...but...not to be taken seriously as a religious utterance."[18]

A decision on this question in light of our current *Zeitgeist* may seem obvious, but the poem did not come from

---

14 *GLP* 202.

15 U. v. Wilamowitz-Moellendorff, *Der Glaube der Hellenen* (Berlin: Weidmannsche Buchhandlung, 1932), 2.111.

16 *GLP* 202.

17 M. L. West, "Burning Sappho," *Maia* 19 (1970), 308.

18 Cameron, "Sappho and Aphrodite Again" (above, n. 13), 1.

our time – it is best to look closely at the evidence since the question is basic to understanding Sappho.

The invocation is conventional in its use of compound adjective epithets of epic type, and a genealogy.[19] Compare *Iliad* 16.233–34:

> Ζεῦ ἄνα, Δωδωναῖε, Πελασγικὲ τηλόθι ναίων
> Δωδώνης μεδέων δυσχειμέρου…
>
> Zeus, Dodonaion Lord, Pelasgian, living afar,
> ruling wintry Dodona…

Homeric *Hymn to Dionysus* 7.1:

> ἀμφὶ Διώνυσον, Σεμέλης ἐρικυδέος υἱόν…
>
> Of Dionysus, the son of glorious Semele, (I will tell)…

Anacreon 3.1–3:

> γουνοῦμαι σ' ἐλαφηβόλε
> ξανθὴ παῖ Διὸς ἀγρίων
> δέσποιν' Ἄρτεμι θηρῶν…
>
> I sing of you, the shooter of deer,
> yellow-haired huntress, child of Zeus,
> mistress of wild beasts, Artemis…

It must be noted, however, that Sappho's epithets do not seem to be actual cult titles – at least one is her coinage, and the traditional mention of powers and of places ruled is absent. It is, in fact, an abbreviated invocation that suggests

---

19 For the conventions of Greek prayers in general, see E. Norden, *Agnostos Theos: Untersuchungen zur Formengeschichte religiöser Rede* (Leipzig: Teubner, 1913); F. Schwenn, *Gebet und Opfer: Studien zum griechischen Kultus,* Religionswissenschaftliche Bibliothek 8 (Heidelberg: C. Winter, 1927); G. Zuntz, "Zum Hymnus des Kleanthes," *Rheinisches Museum für Philologie,* n. s., 94 (1951), 337–41; R. Pfeiffer, "Gottheit und Individuum in der frühgriechischen Lyrik," *Philologus* 84 (1929), 137–52.

the conventional features while not parading them in full array – much as, in fr. 31, the *makarismos* and εἰκάζειν are compressed into one: the allusion is still clear.

The invocation leads to a request for aid made in one of the two Homeric ways: either the suppliant can claim that he has done a service to the god and deserves one in return, as Chryses (*Iliad* 1.39–41) says:

> εἴ ποτέ τοι χαρίεντ' ἐπὶ νηὸν ἔρεψα,
> ἢ εἰ δή ποτέ τοι κατὰ πίονα μηρί' ἔκηα
> ταύρων ἠδ' αἰγῶν...
>
> If ever I roofed a shrine pleasing to thee
> or burnt for thee fat thighs
> of bulls and goats...

or he may cite as precedent a past service that the god rendered freely, as Diomede (*Iliad* 5.116–17) says:

> εἴ ποτέ μοι καὶ πατρὶ φίλα φρονέουσα παρέστης
> δηΐῳ ἐν πολέμῳ, νῦν αὖτ' ἐμὲ φῖλαι, Ἀθήνη...
>
> If ever with kindly thought you stood by my father
> in baleful war, now me also do thou love, Athena...

and Achilles (*Iliad* 16.236–37):

> ἠμὲν δή ποτ' ἐμὸν ἔπος ἔκλυες εὐξαμένοιο,
> τίμησας μὲν ἐμέ...
>
> Once indeed you hearkened to my words when I prayed
> and honored me...

The appeal is made, as regularly in Homer, with an aorist imperative. The precedent is followed by a repetition of the appeal in standard language: ἠδ' ἔτι καὶ νῦν, Achilles says in the next line. The appeal for the god to be σύμμαχος (ally), which ends the poem, is equally conventional; compare Archilochus, fr. 86 (Lass.):

> *κλῦθ,' ἄναξ Ἥφαιστευ, καί μοι σύμμαχος γουνουμένῳ*
> *ἵλαος γενεῦ...*
>
> Hear me, Lord Hephaistos, and as my ally
> be generous to my supplication...

And Æschylus (*Choephoroi* 1–2 and 19):

> *Ἑρμῆ χθόνιε, πατρῷ' ἐποπτεύων κράτη*
> *σωτὴρ γενοῦ μοι ξύμμαχός τ' αἰτουμένῳ...*
> *...γενοῦ δὲ σύμμαχος θέλων ἐμοί...*
>
> Chthonian Hermes, guarding thy father's power,
> be savior to me, and ally, as I pray...
> ... and be my ally willingly...

Clearly, the poem obeys the conventions for prayers that were established by Homer and varied little for centuries. But there are problems. For example, the sanction, or record of precedent, is disproportionately long. Again let Diomede and Achilles show us the norm; Diomede (*Iliad* 5.115ff.):

> Hear me, child of aegis-bearing Zeus, Atrytone,
> if ever with kindly thoughts you stood by my father
> in baleful war, now me also do thou love, Athena.

And Achilles (*Iliad* 16.236ff.):

> Once indeed you hearkened to my word
> when I prayed and honored me
> and oppressed greatly the people of the Achaians;
> now again accomplish my prayer...

Diomede's prayer (*Iliad* 10.284ff.) is the only example of a sanction comparable in length to Sappho's:

> ... follow with me as when with my father
> thou didst follow, noble Tydeus, into Thebes,
> when he went as a messenger from the Achaians;
> and them he left by the Asopus,

the bronze-chitoned Achaians,
and a honeyed word he bore to the Cadmeians there,
but on his way back he devised terrible deeds,
with thee, brilliant goddess,
for eagerly thou didst stand by him;
even so now stand by me.

First, Homer's desire to present a little story in the frame (and possibly to suggest paternal precedent for the Doloneia) has caused him to unbalance the elements of the prayer. Sappho's unbalancing is even greater – five of seven stanzas devoted to one element, the sanction. Has she, too, another motive than efficacious prayer?

Second, the invocation, far from containing the proper cult epithets, actually strives for unconventional and imaginative effects, toying with Homeric usage by making up two new epithets (*ποκιλόθρον'* and *δολόπλοκε*), traditional in form, but not in content.

Third, the traditional *σύμμαχος* has seemed inappropriate here; Archilochus used it as a soldier, Orestes as a would-be assassin claiming the sanction of military-style retaliation. In Sappho's ode it necessarily conjures up the somewhat ironic metaphor of the woman in love as a soldier striding to battle.

Surely we can recognize in the first of these irregularities Sappho's private convention of unexpectedly shifting the weight of a poem from its announced present subject to some remembered or imagined event in the past; in the second, her tendency to treat religion as an aspect of poetry; and in the third, her playful antinomy between great and public events (such as war) and minor private ones (such as romance), which is stated with all possible clarity in fr. 16. Is this, then, a conventional prayer? Or is it, like frr. 16 and 31, grounded somewhat in the tension between the choric and monodic styles, hence peculiarly Sapphic and literary? Let us look at the heart of the poem where its great vitality resides, the epiphany.

"This poem," Bowra said in his first treatment of the question,[20] "with all its accuracy and truth to nature, is after all a religious poem, concerned with an experience which can only be called mystical." He compares Pindar's claim that he met the hero Alcmaeon on the road to Delphi and notes that "all Greece believed that Philippides saw Pan on Mount Cyllene in Arcadia in 490."[21] But aren't these examples very few? And are they, in fact, to the point at all? The story of Philippides represents popular superstition and can tell us little or nothing about the credulity or skepticism of the educated classes who wrote poems in the difficult Æolic meters. As for that wilful and erratic genius, Pindar...who knows? He may well have meant it, but even so his epiphany is so different from Sappho's as to have little bearing on it.

Cameron makes the point: "There is generally," he says, "a certain suddenness and unexpectedness in epiphany, as when Athena appears to Achilles, or the *οἰοπόλος δαίμων* meets the Argonauts. So Pindar himself met Alcmaeon; *ὑπάντασεν ἰόντι γᾶς ὀμφαλὸν παρ' ἀοίδιμον.*[22] In Sappho this element of suddenness is absent, as is also the element of astonishment and fear, or pleasure mixed with fear, which such appearances commonly produce."[23] In Homer the true parallels are in the fictional epiphanies (as in the approach of Apollo in *Iliad* 1, or of Poseidon in *Iliad* 23) "in which Homer describes the gods *as actors in the story,* whose

20 *GLP* (1st ed., 1936), 193.

21 *GLP* 202f.

22 "He stood up before me as I was going toward the songful navel of the earth" (*Pythian* 8.59).

23 A. Cameron, "Sappho's Prayer to Aphrodite," *Harvard Theological Review* 32 (1939), 6.

actions he can describe as accurately and fully as those of his other characters..."[24]

Surely, on one level Sappho's description of Aphrodite's flight is in the tradition of Hesiod's endlessly elaborated description of the Heliconian Muses at the beginning of the *Theogony;* each poet, at the beginning of his (or her) book, asks in a conventional and prettified way for the sanction of his or her patron goddess. Theognis's initial appeal to Apollo is rather detailed also. So Dante was to describe Love in the *Vita Nuova,* specifying the clothing, the gait and the demeanor of the god, and the precise hour of the day at which the god appeared to him – and (in chapter 25) stating forthrightly that he has based these fictions on those of the ancient love poets. When we glance over the traditions of epiphanies in general we find that the "accuracy and truth to nature," the detail, of Sappho's description really should exclude the use of the word "mystical": Plotinus and Nicholas of Cusa knew no way to be so clear about what they had seen, but were forced to speak in painful riddles of that "darker than any mystery."

Yet Bowra would include Sappho among those "for whom the excitements of love possessed a definitely mystical character";[25] and, while not wishing to exclude Sappho from this group (all awakened humanity), we must complain that Bowra seems to confound two traditions here. Is Sappho, with her epiphanies of love gods and goddesses, in the tradition of St. John of the Cross ("O night that joined the lover to the beloved bride, transfiguring them each into the other") or of, shall we say, Robert Herrick ("Love and myself (believe me) on a day/At childish push-pin (for our sport) did play..."[26])?

---

24 Ibid., 7; my italics.

25 *GLP* (1st ed., 1936), 103.

26 "Love's Play at Push-Pins," in *Works of Robert Herrick,* 2 vols., ed. A. Pollard (London: Lawrence & Bullen, 1891), 1:19.

The one uses erotic love as a metaphor for epiphany; for the other, epiphany is a metaphor for erotic love. Granted that erotic bliss may drip with mystical rapture – it is, then, *in the form of the beloved* that the god or goddess appears – not as an outside advisor in frustrated moments. We may doubt that the *desire for* sexual favors (or their Tuscan equivalent) is ever a plausible source for actual mystical experience.

In early Greek literature only Pindar returning to the earth's umbilicus and meeting Alcmaeon along the way looks even remotely like a mystic's epiphany. Much closer to Sappho in time, tradition, and tone is this of Anacreon (fr. 13):

> *σφαίρῃ δηὖτε με πορφυρῇ*
> *βάλλων χρυσοκόμης Ἔρως*
> *νήνι ποικιλοσαμβάλωι*
> *συμπαίζειν προκαλεῖται…*

> Once again golden haired Eros
> throws his purple ball at me
> and calls me out to play
> with a girl in colored sandals…

So Sappho herself even said that she saw Eros *ἐλθόντ' ἐξ ὀράνω πορφυρίαν περθέμενον χλάμυν* (coming from heaven wearing a purple cloak) (fr. 54). Surely Chameleon was right to suggest that this poem of Anacreon's (with its second stanza, and in its Æolic meter) was, as it were, "dedicated" to Sappho.[27] As our ancient testimonia amply show,[28] Anacreon was considered the most Sapphic of ancient poets. Surely no other poem is so like this one of Sappho's as Anacreon's "hymn" to Dionysus (fr. 12):

> *ὦναξ, ὧι δαμάλης Ἔρως*
> *καὶ Νύμφαι κυανώπιδες*
> *πορφυρῆ τ' Ἀφροδίτη*

---

27 See *PMG*.

28 They will be discussed in chap. 12, "Varia," below.

συμπαίζουσιν ἐπιστρέφεαι
δ' ὑψυλὰς ὀρέων κορυφάς
γουνοῦμαί σε, σὺ δ' εὐμενὴς
ἔλθ' ἡμίν, κεχαρισμένης
δ' εὐχωλῆς ἐπακούειν·
Κλεοβούλωι δ' αγαθὸς γένεο
σύμβουλος, τὸν ἐμόν γ' ἔρω-
τ', ὦ Δεόνυσε, δέχεσθαι.

O Lord with whom conquering Eros
and the dark-eyed Nymphs
and sparkling Aphrodite
play as you wander the high crests of mountains,
I kneel to you; be favorable,
come to me, hear and be gracious to my prayer;
be a good advisor to Cleuboulus,
and tell him, O Dionysus, to accept my love.

Is it a coincidence that Anacreon's poem is in an Æolic meter? That the epithets, as in Sappho's poems, are not traditional, but newly minted? That both the names are witheld until the end – a practice we will observe, among his predecessors, in Sappho and nowhere else?

Indeed, the whole tradition of secular hymnody in monodic lyric is under suspicion of frivolity: Proclus, our only ancient source, states that the hymn was sung by a stationary chorus.[29] It is not certain that Sappho's hymns, or Anacreon's, or Alcaeus's were considered the real thing (that is, religious songs) in antiquity; private statements about reality, lyric wanderings, erotic and sympotic jests making playful use of choric forms – but not hymns like the choric hymns.

The positions of Sappho and Anacreon within this tradition seem fairly clear. His versions are typically smaller, lighter, and less reminiscent of choral style; only one step farther lie the *Anacreontea* – Love plays about the lip of the

29 See *GMP* xxix.

wine cup, or on the strings of the lyre. The lack of complex artifice in Anacreon, who suggests choric conventions with light and unelaborated strokes, confident that his meaning will be clear, indicated that such play between the two styles in erotic contexts was familiar already from the work of his predecessors. Sappho obviously was the main one. And before her we may put Alcman, of whom Athenaeus says (13.600ff.):

> Archytas the writer on musical theory
> maintains according to Chamaeleon
> that the originator of love songs was Alcman,
> and that he was the first to give out to the schools
> song that was licentious...

Will we be asked to take this love epiphany from Alcman, fr. 58 seriously?:

> *Ἀφροδίτα μὲν οὐκ ἔστι, μάργος δ' Ἔρως οἷα <παῖς> παίσδει,*
> *ἄκρ' ἐπ' ἄνθη καβαίνων, ἅ μή μοι θίγηις, τῶ κυπαιρίσκω.*
>
> It is not Aphrodite, but wild Love,
> who plays like a child, "Do not touch me,"
> walking down the tips of the flowers
> of the little galingale.

Alcman's love-songs presumably *were* choral (he "gave them out to the schools," says Athenaeus), though they would hardly be called hymns. Sappho, in adapting the genre, joins it with the hymn, bringing a certain irony to bear on both the monodic subject and the choral form.[30] Anacreon adopts her

30 For the influence of Alcman on Sappho, cf. Alcman, frr. 48 and 49 with Sappho, fr. 96.9–14. Alcman, fr. 59*a* illustrates a purely "Sapphic" strain in his work; his love songs and his concentration on young girls would surely have appealed to her. Other similarities have been noted here and there in this book.

playful style and, perhaps under his influence, Ibycus (in the "Encomium to Polycrates" [fr. 282*a*]) attempts to follow suit. Here the history of *genres* develops before our eyes. Ibycus, who hailed from the Dorian west and was already composing in strophe, antistrophe, and epode under the tutelage of that prototypical chorus master, Stesichorus, has not mastered the light touch of the eastern monody to which he wishes to convert. He states openly, and rather heavy-handedly, that he has now changed his arena and will clothe personal, erotic subjects in the armor of the chorus, fighting love's battles with all the alarums of war. And surely that is part of what Sappho, at the doorway to her poems, means too.

The tradition of mocking the great, the martial, the masculine, the public event by giving its trappings to the trivial, the erotic, the effeminate, the private event flows on through the Roman elegists, through Provence, the cavaliers Lovelace and Suckling, to strange forms in Baudelaire ("I climb the siege-works like a chorus of worms crawling on a corpse – you are cold") and pretty echoes in Yeats ("And maybe what they say is true / of war and war's alarms, / but oh that I were young again / and held her in my arms"). Homer glimpses it in his lighter moments (the "arming" of Hera for the seduction of Zeus),[31] and perhaps Archilochus developed it; but it is above all a Sapphic theme (though her emphasis seems more on exalting the small than belittling the great). It is stated in the guise of a credo in fr. 16 and placed, by the ancient editors, at the entrance to her world.

The tradition is clear; that Sappho belongs in it is beyond dispute. So what is the problem? Anacreon's own words tell us that he leapt from the Leucadian cliff (fr. 31) in despair at love; no one treats the statement as autobiography. Why

31 M.C.J. Putnam's thesis that Sappho had in mind throughout this poem the appeal of Hera to Aphrodite in *Iliad* 14 is well worth mentioning ("*Throna* and Sappho 1.1" [above, n. 3]).

should the same patent joke about Sappho have given rise to scholarly controversy in our century? It is because her mask is on more firmly; her surface is smooth and unruffled; she is like Sophocles in this, the smiling face of the poet (who knows both realities) elusive behind the still mask.

Let us consider again our original question: Does she *mean* it? Perhaps she *means* it as much as Dante *means* his apparitions of Love; as much as Rilke *means* his Duino angel; as much as Robert Graves *means* his white goddess – as a group of symbols radiating her particular sense of life, locating the center, so to speak, of herself and her world. But as a prayer literally meant, made with a hope for specific effects – come now. Reason lies on the other side.

The Emblem on the Door

Why did the Alexandrian editors put this poem first, as the greeting in the doorway, as it were, of Sappho's book? In part, no doubt, because a poetry book *should* begin with a prayer. But one expects a prayer to the Muses or to Apollo, a request for blessings on the poetic undertaking, not this appeal for romantic help.

Is it because for Sappho the erotic and poetic powers appear as two sides of the same symbolic coin, the roses of Pieria and the roses of Cypris woven into one garland? Indeed, Sappho, in the understanding hands of her unknown Alexandrian editor, seems to present success in her book of poems in the guise of romantic success. But there is more. Should we not expect in this position a paradigm, an announcement (acted out, rather than stated, as usually with Sappho) of poetic theory and/or personal values?

Aphrodite is mentioned in the first line, and a kletic hymn develops, with Homeric models. But, strangely, the epithets are new and ingenious; they announce through their form that their roots are in Homer, but through their content that a new life has entered song: it is grand in its source (ποικιλόθρον') but guileful in its methods (δολόπλοκε); Aphrodite, not Apollo, is its patron. The compact between love and song has been made, once and for all, and she has become the leader of the Muses.

She is asked to relieve some unspecified pain and weariness. The sanction describes a past occasion when she did so, and, typically, our sense of location in the poem is undermined at once. As the vehicle of the lone simile becomes the environment of fr. 96, now the past arrival and conversation of Aphrodite enter the foreground, the dramatic situation, of Ode 1: Sappho calls; Aphrodite comes. As in fr. 2, we seem to see the prayer being answered even as we hear it being asked. In the descent from heaven is a regular Greek picture (the Apollonian) that reaches fulness in Pindar: the gods' homes are gold (the great virtue of which, as Sappho herself was the first to point out, is that it is imperishable; see fr. 204); but on the earth are sorrow and weariness, transient cares that change yet seem always the same – the deep sky lies between. (Cf. fr. 52: *ψαύην δ'οὐ δωκίμωμ' ὀράνω* † δυσπαχέα † [I do not hope to embrace heaven with my two arms].)

At the center of the poem, at the division between the two worlds, as it were, Aphrodite, the goddess, meets Sappho, the mortal, and "smiling with her immortal countenance, asks what now..." There is no grimness, no majesty of divinity; she comes as Thetis came to Achilles, like a mother to her crying child, and, like Thetis again, asks what the trouble is – though of course she knows.[32] The human is presented as an unruly child or an untrained beast, whose "wild heart" (*μαινόλαι θῦμωι*) the divinity must "tame" (*δάμνα*).

32 See T. Krischer, "Sappho's Ode on Aphrodite," *Hermes* 96 (1968), 1–14, for the comparison with Thetis's epiphanies to Achilles.

In stanza five, at last, the complaint is specified: "Who now do you want to love you? Who is hurting you, O Sappho?" This is to be the primal plaint of the world at whose doorway we stand, the world of Sappho's poems; here all the vitality of life is grounded in the interpersonal; all its motivation, in emotions.

But it is the goddess's attitude that is most revealing. "What *now,* O Sappho, what *this* time?" There is, in the indulgent smile, the mildly chiding repeated δηὖτε – a sense, as Castle says, of "the wisdom of long experience... that this anguish has happened before and will surely happen again, that the woes and joys of particular loves are vain and transient..."[33] Of course. Aphrodite, being a goddess (an archetype, a universal), knows only (or primarily) the universal aspect of being; Sappho, a mortal, is caught in the web of ephemerality. Though she can converse with the archetype in her mind, and perceive the wisdom of it's broader view, still she is caught in the desire of the moment. The girl is not named because she herself is of no importance; she represents the endless succession of desires in which humanity is caught (the *anima*). Here again Sappho presents with her light and feminine touch a view that would be developed more aggressively by Pindar (*Pythian* 8.95–97):

> *ἐπάμεροι· τί δέ τις; τί δ' οὔ τις; σκιᾶς ὄναρ*
> *ἄνθρωπος. ἀλλ' ὅταν αἴγλα διόσδοτος ἔλθῃ,*
> *λαμπρὸν φέγγος ἔπεστιν ἀνδρῶν καὶ μείλιχος αἰών.*
>
> Creatures of a day! What is it to live? What is it not to live?
> A dream of a shadow is man! But when a brightness,

33 W. Castle, "Observations on Sappho's *To Aphrodite,*" *Transactions and Proceedings of the American Philological Association* 89 (1958), 76. I am not convinced by Koniaris's argument ("On Sappho Fr. 1 [Lobel-Page]" [above, n. 13]) that Aphrodite can never advise that Love be taken lightly; Aphrodite did not write the poem; and anyway, it is not Love that is in question here, but individual loves.

> sent from god, comes down, then there is a radiance,
> a light, on man, and life is sweet...

And Aphrodite, too, though she knows that Sappho is in a trap that she will not escape, responds with that sweet light. Like a totally indulgent mother she grants all that is asked: "Love will be yours above all; they will not be able to resist you..." We can sense here the loneliness of a woman who dealt with imaginings of distant gods and made to them the cry for human love. The starkness of desire is more pathetic when it is prettified. In stanza seven, like a child who, while perceiving the greater wisdom of the adult, remains unregenerate in its demands, Sappho repeats her request.

The fluttering, sparrow-drawn chariot descending from the timeless mansions in the sky, the eternal smile of the divine and fertile mover of all life, the goddess and Sappho speaking like epic mother and child across the cosmic (indeed, ontological) border that divides them like an exquisitely detailed and superbly wrought cameo – this little scene sparkles in the frame of mortality, between the insistent, repeated requests. If this poem was, indeed, the first in Sappho's book, we may suppose it was because the Alexandrian editors perceived its terrible acuteness as a picture of the human condition; and because it is in a sense typical of all of her poems; *and* because it is simpler than many of them – even if that makes it a little less interesting.

VIII

A Garland of Rosebuds

Born from the cactus flowers of Archilochus, most of Sappho's poems still seem, in John William Mackail's words, "to be, without effort and without hesitation, at the central heart of poetry."[1] "Without effort," however, will not apply to frr. 16 and 96, with their mannered imitations of choral style; and, in light of these newer fragments, Ode 1 and fr. 31 take on also a cunning and elusive air. In these, and in the expanding waves of fr. 94, we hear, along with the nightingale's outpouring, the artifice of the mocking-bird. But Mackail did not know these newer fragments. He referred to the famous short fragments when he said, "We read a few simple words simply put together; we admire them and pass on; and then we find that there is some witchery in them that makes us go back, and again back, and yet again back, to make sure we have not missed something, to try to find what it is in them that moves us so... and in the end we find... that the magic and mystery still seem, as they seemed at first, just beyond our reach."[2]

Shall we object, in light of our new long fragments, that, in context, Sappho's simple words seem not to have been so "simply put together" after all? It is ironic, and yet just recompense, that the destruction or mutilation of all Greek books between Homer and the fifth century has sensitized us to a new "genre" of a strange and intense power, the "fragment" (a pointing hand broken from an archaic statue, a

1 J.W. Mackail, *Lectures on Greek Poetry* (London: Longmans, Green and Co., 1911), 92.

2 Ibid., 101.

one-line Heracleitean pronouncement reverberating in ancient darkness). Ezra Pound and others have imitated the Sapphic fragments; they are freer than the haiku or the stornello and in a way more suggestive. They are sculpted for us by Tyche herself, pure gifts of the goddess, the freshness of her hand, as well as Sappho's, still on them. They combine a personal and an impersonal making, a concrete and a universal force.

The six longer pieces we have looked at share many features: hints of choral structure; a shift from present dramatic time to a central section of memory, myth, or imagining; imagery of the beauty and love of girls, goddesses of beauty and love, and cult objects; an almost total exclusion of practical or everyday objects. These are two-thirds of the long fragments. Is it reasonable that the greater part, perhaps two-thirds, of Sappho's poems were of this type? We will keep this question in mind while rummaging among some of the smaller fragments, those rosebuds (or fallen petals, perhaps) in which the glory of Sappho's roses, as Meleager so nicely calls them, is still sweetly and freshly hinted.

Fr. 22

]βλα . [
]εργον, . . λ'α . . [
]ν ῤέθος δοκιμ̣[
]ησθαι

—

]ν̣ ἀνάδην χ . . [
δ]ὲ μή, χείμων[
] . οισαναλγεα . [
]δε

—

.] . ε̣ . [. . . .] . [. . . κ]έλομαι σ . [
. .] . γυλα . [. . .]α̣νθι λάβοισα . α . [
. .]κτιν, ἆ̣ς σε δηὖτε πόθος τ̣ . [
ἀμφιπόταται

—

τὰν κάλαν· ἀ γὰρ κατάγωγις αὔτ̣α[
ἐπτόαισ' ἴδοισαν, ἔγω δὲ χαίρω
καὶ γὰρ αὔτ̣α δήπ̣ο̣[τ'] ἐμεμφ[
Κ]υπρογεν[ηα
—
ὡ̣ς ἄραμα̣[ι
τοῦτο τῶ[
β]όλλομα̣[ι

In lines 10–12 we may have, "she taking up the lyre (?), and desire for her fluttered around you again," in which case "the fair one" of line 13 goes unexplained; or, ignoring the "you," "when she takes up the lyre, desire flutters around the fair one again." Then: "For her dress shook you when you saw it" (assuming *αὔτας* in line 12), or, "For the dress shook her when she saw it" (assuming *αὔταν*), "and I rejoiced." Then: "For I too once reproached the Cyprus-born," or, "for *she* too..." Perhaps: someone has renounced love, then falls in love again, and Sappho, knowing (with Mimnermus and, later, Lucretius) that to renounce Aphrodite is to renounce life, is glad. What is clear, despite grammatical ambiguity, is "the trembling sensitiveness of the Aiolian" (as Smyth puts it[3]) – desire flowing from the fluttering of a dress and shaking the viewer's heart; beauty (the Cyprus-born) incarnate, at the heart of life, in young girls. The "fragment genre" can proffer the single detail – as here a girl's garment – in poignant isolation:

Fr. 92

[
[
π̣ε̣[
κρ[. . . . .]περ[
πεπλον[. . .]π̣υ̣σ̣χ̣[
κα̣ικλ̣ε̣[. .]σαω[
κροκοεντα[

3 *GMP* 229.

πεπλον πορφθ[ρ........]δ̣εξω̣[.]
χλαιναι περσ̣[
στεφανοι περ[
καλ[.]ο̣σ̣σ̣α̣μ̣[
φρυ[
πορφ[υρ
τ̣α̣π̣α̣[
[
π[

a gown (?)...
saffron-yellow...
a gown of purple...
wearing (?) veils...
garlands around...
beautiful...
purple...
and soft (?)...

Fr. 39

...πόδας δὲ
ποίκιλος μάσλης ἐκάλυπτε, Δύδι-
ον κάλον ἔργον.

...a colorful gown hid her feet,
a pretty, Lydian one.

How many fragments of archaic korai convey this same living moment?

The fall of a gown about a pretty ankle – O Cyprian!

Fr. 57

τίς δ' ἀγροΐωτις θέλγει νόον.....
ἀγροΐωτιν ἐπεμμένα σπόλαν.....
οὐκ ἐπισταμένα τὰ βράκε' ἕλκην ἐπὶ τῶν σφύρων;

What rustic wench charms your mind...
wearing her rustic shawl...
ignorant of how to draw her gown about her ankles?

Objects of beauty, in general, go undescribed in Sappho, or are described by one stroke of detail – a gown *παντοδάπαισι μεμειχμένα χροίαισιν*, "in which all colors mingle" (fr. 152) – because their beauty is certified first by their ability to arouse desire. This effect is presented in many shades, from Homeric:

Fr. 47

> Ἔρος δ' ἐτίναξέ μοι
> φρένας, ὡς ἄνεμος κὰτ ὄρος δρύσιν ἐμπέτων.

> Love shook my heart like the wind
> falling on oak trees on the mountain.

to typically Sapphic:

Fr. 48

> ἦλθες, † καὶ † ἐπόησας, ἔγω δέ σ' ἐμαιόμαν
> ὂν δε ἔψυξας ἔμαν φρένα καιομέναν πόθωι.

> You came ... and I had longed for you,
> and you cooled my heart, which had been burning
>   with desire.

to inimitably Sapphic:

Fr. 49

> ἠράμαν μὲν ἔγω σέθεν, Ἄτθι, πάλαι ποτά ....
> σμίκρα μοι πάις ἔμμεν' ἐφαίνεο κἄχαρις.

> I loved you once, Atthis, a long time ago ...
> you seemed to me a little and graceless girl.

Or rather, let us give it Swinburne's treatment:

> *I loved thee* – hark, one tenderer note than all –
> *Atthis, of old time once* – one low long fall
> Sighing – one long low lovely loveless call
> Dying – one pause in song so flamelike fast –

Atthis, long since in old time overpast –
One soft first pause and last.[4]

Desire is at the center; the acts that rise from it are noted only sparingly:

Fr. 36

καὶ ποθήω καὶ μάομαι…

I desire, I long for…

Fr. 38

ὄπταις ἄμμε

You burn me…

Fr. 46

ἔγω δ' ἐπὶ μολθάκαν
τύλαν κασπολέω †μέλεα· κἂν μὲν τε τύλαγκας ἀσπόλεα·†

I will stretch my limbs upon a soft cushion…

The object that contains beauty; the desire that rises always from *seeing* it – and soon the love-god holds sway, entering the heart unscrupulously in any guise. Sometimes in a grand descent from above:

Fr. 54

ἔλθοντ' ἐξ ὀράνω πορφυρίαν περθέμενον χλάμυν…

…coming down from heaven in a purple cloak…

---

4 "On the Cliffs," in A. C. Swinburne, *Songs of the Springtides* (London: Chatto & Windus, 1880), 57–58.

Sometimes like a sudden storm:

Fr. 47

Ἔρος δ' ἐτίναξέ μοι
φρένας, ὡς ἄνεμος κὰτ ὄρος δρύσιν ἐμπέτων.

Love shook my heart like the wind
falling on oak trees on the mountain.

Sometimes like a creeping serpent:

Fr. 130

Ἔρος δηὖτε μ' ὀ λυσιμέλης δόνει,
γλυκύπικρον ἀμαχανον ὄρπετον...

Eros, once again, the limb-loosener, shakes me,
the bittersweet, the creeping, irresistible thing...

Here, he receives that basic coinage expressing, as fr. 31 does, the confusion of the senses under the onslaught of desire, *γλυκύπικρον* (bittersweet). And elsewhere also he is christened, as is Aphrodite, with new-coined epithets for his new age in song:

Fr. 172

ἀλγεσίδωρος

...pain-giving

Fr. 188

μυθόπλοκος

...myth-weaving...

The reaction of the poet's *persona* (the lyric "I") to this new universe ruled by beauty, by the eye that sees it, and by the implacable god of the heart, is understandably sometimes confused:

Fr. 51

οὐκ οἶδ ὄττι θέω· δίχα μοι τὰ νοήμματα.

I do not know what to think; I am of two minds.

Sometimes unsure of herself:

Fr. 120

ἀλλά τις οὐκ ἔμμι παλιγκότων
ὄργαν, ἀλλ' ἀβάκην τὰν φρέν' ἔχω…

But I am not of a hostile temper;
rather, I have a quiet disposition…

Frequently it must turn to prayer:

Fr. 86

] ̣ ακάλα ̣ [
] α̣ἰ̣γιόχω λ̣α̣[
] ̣ Κ̣υ̣θέρη' ε̣ ̣ ̣ ομ[
]ο̣ν ἔχοισα θῦμο̣[ν
κλ]ῦθί μ̣' ἄρας αἴπ[
]ας π̣ρ̣ολίποισ̣α κ[
] ̣ πεδ' ἔμαν ἰώ[
] ̣ ν χα̣λέπαι ̣ [

… the aegis-bearer…
… Cytherea…
… having spirit…
… hear my prayer…
… leaving…
… for me…
… sorrows…

And sometimes dreams:

Fr. 134

ζὰ . . . ἐλεξάμαν ὄναρ Κυπρογενηα

I spoke with the Cyprus-born in a dream . . .

Fr. 63

Ὄνοιρε μελαινα[
φ[o]ίταις ὄτα τ' ὔπνος [
—
γλύκυς θ̣[έ]ο̣ς, ἦ δεῖν' ὀνίας μ[
ζὰ χῶρις ἔχην τὰν δυναμ[
—
ἔλπις δέ μ' ἔχει μὴ πεδέχη[ν
μηδὲν μακάρων ἐλ̣[
[—]
ο̣ὐ̣ γάρ κ' ἔον οὔτω[̣ ̣́
ἀθύρματα κα ̣[
—
γένοιτο δέ μοι[
τοὶς πάντα[
—

Dream . . . (child) of black night . . .
wandering where sleep . . .
sweet god, my terrible pain . . .
without having the power . . .
I do not hope to share . . .
nothing of the blessed ones . . .
for not thus . . .
playthings and . . .
may there be for me . . .
all . . .

Dream is invoked as a god (cf. *Iliad* 2.8) who can grant all wishes. The coronis ( ) indicates the end. The vocative ὄνοιρε either begins the poem (in which case gnomisms about the different lots of men and gods form the Variation section framed by the two prayers) or begins the Recapitulation section of a poem perhaps thirty lines long.

Fragment 95, the third great fragment from the Berlin parchment, may also describe a dreamed epiphany, and pained musings, under the influence of erotic stress, on the mortal condition:

1 ου[
↔
ἦ̣ρ' ἀ[
δηρατ̣[
4 Γογγυλα̣[
↔
ἦ τι σᾶμ' ἐθε̣[
παισι μάλιστα̣[
7 μας γ' εἴσηλθ' ἐπ̣[
↔
εἶπον· ὦ δέσποτ', ἐπ̣[
ο]ὐ μὰ γὰρ μάκαιραν̣ [
10 ο]ὐδὲν ἄδομ' ἔπαρθ' ἀγα[
↔
κατθάνην δ' ἴμερός τις [ἔχει με καὶ
λωτίνοις δροσόεντας [ὄ-
13 χ̣[θ]οις ἴδην Ἀχερ[
↔
.]..δεσαιδ' .[
.]..δετο .[
16 μητι..[
↔

spring...
too late...
Gongyla...[5]

or what sign...
for the girls above all...
Hermes (?) came...
I said, O master...
for not a goddess...
I enjoy nothing...

---

5 Cf. Ezra Pound's translation: "Spring.../Too Long.../Gongula..." ("Papyrus," in *Ezra Pound: Poems and Translations,* ed. R. Sieburth [New York: Penguin/Library of America, 2003], 289).

a certain desire takes me, to die
and see the lotus-bearing dewy banks of Acheron…

Perhaps: Gongyla asks Sappho if a sign has appeared to her (in what connection we cannot know, but no doubt it was erotic); Sappho replies that a god came to her; and she told him that she wished to die *unless* (?) some request or other were granted. Hermes is strongly suggested in lines 7 and 8, and probably his function as ψυχαγωγός will explain why here alone we have a male divinity answering Sappho's prayer.

Finally, let us look at two small pieces that do not proclaim the Sapphic *persona* to which we have grown accustomed.

Fr. 102

γλύκηα μᾶτερ, οὔτοι δύναμαι κρέκην τὸν ἴστον
πόθωι δάμεισα παῖδος πραδίναν δι' Ἀφροδίταν.

Sweet mother I can no longer work my loom
being mastered by desire for a boy, through slender
Aphrodite.[6]

Here, it would seem that the lyric "I" is not the controlling voice of the other fragments we have looked at. Further, the lines are quoted by Hephaestion, and thus would seem to be the beginning of a poem. But no other extant fragment clearly begins with a dramatic voice, that is, a person other than "Sappho" speaking. Also, the subject here seems to be heterosexual love. There is, thus, a good deal of cogency to the supposition made by Bowra among others, that "this is a song of an ancient and widespread kind, a *chanson de toile*, such as girls sang over the loom, lamenting their loves."[7] It does, indeed, convey the childlike mood of much folk poetry,

---

6 So the line is always translated. But in Sappho's ordinary practice πάις would mean "girl."

7 *GLP* 134.

but polished into the finished gracefulness of Sappho. There is, however, virtually no external evidence on archaic Greek folk songs. The possibility that it occured in a wedding song must at least be mentioned.

Fr. 94D

δέδυκε μὲν ἀ σελάννα
καὶ πληΐαδες, μέσαι δὲ
νυκτες, παρὰ δ' ἔρχετ' ὤρα,
ἔγω δὲ μόνα κατεύδω.

The moon has set
and the Pleiads, it's the middle
of the night, time passes,
and I lie alone.

Preserved by Hephaestion *sine nomine auctoris,* this fragment has been attributed to Sappho at least since the sixteenth century, but is relegated by Lobel to the *Fragmenta Incerta Auctoris* ("Equidem ne Æolicum quidem esse arbitror"[8]), and cast out by Lobel and Page altogether. According to Lobel and Page, the mss. read ἁ σελάνα, ὤρα and καθέυδω; further, μέσαι and παρά they will not accept as Æolic.

Various authors have defended the little poem, perhaps best Gomme,[9] who notes that the best ms. of Hephaestion reads σελάνα with ν written above (a second ν written above the ν, as if a correction: "unmistakable evidence that the poem is Lesbian"[10]), and that μέσαι and παρά both occur in Alcaeus. Hephaestion quotes the poem in a discussion of the Æolic poets. To which of them, then, is it to be assigned? Surely not Alcaeus. The sentiment, the μέν, δέ, δέ, δέ foil (as in fr. 16)

8 Σμ. 72.

9 "Interpretations of Some Poems of Sappho and Alcaeus," *Journal of Hellenic Studies* 77 (1957), 265. (See also B. Marzullo, *Studi di poesia eolica* [Florence: Le Monnier, 1958], 1–60, and A. Massimi, "Schedae Sapphicae," *Giornale italiano di filologia* 12 [1959], 26–35.)

10 Ibid., 266.

and the meter (which, like the fragment just discussed, can be regarded as a kind of rising Ionic) will all direct it to Sappho. The citation *sine nomine auctoris* is a problem Lobel and Page have lived with elsewhere (Hephaestion quotes Ode 1 without naming Sappho), and Lobel's objection to the article with σελάννα really is a tempest in a teapot.[11] No doubt, our Sapphic corpus contains some items that should not be there (I for one am suspicious of fr. 47), but, granted the meager evidence we have from which to form our texts, these lovely lines should be restored to the Sapphic muse.

Quoted by Hephaestion – therefore we have the beginning of the poem. But do we have its end? The similar priamel in fr. 16 (where, also, major conditions in the outside world were used as foils for a private and romantic condition) led on to other things. Yet if the original poem was longer, then here our "fragment genre" has been felicitous indeed.

The wheeling heavens, the blackness of night outside the window when the moon has set, a lonely bed – it is a haunting and melodious theme that has echoed down the ages.[12] And its few words are richly suggestive. Line 1: the moon, as Clay points out, in a world alive with myth, does not merely set – she returns to the arms of her beloved, Endymion. Likewise the Pleiads sink into the sea to the bed of their husband Poseidon.[13] All nature proceeds in the cosmic rhythm to its

---

11 Gomme (ibid.) lists eight "irregularities" in Sappho's use of the article, and eleven from Alcaeus, any one of which could cover the present case. See also D. Clay, "Fragmentum Adespotum 976," *Transactions and Proceedings of the American Philological Association* 101 (1970), 124, on this question.

12 Smyth (*GMP* 243) quotes Scottish and German songs on the same theme, and see the version of Housman quoted by Clay, "Fragmentum Adespotum 976" (above, n. 11), 125.

13 See Clay, "Fragmentum Adespotum 976" (above, n. 11), 125–26. He points out that Sappho is said to have written a version of the Selene/Endymion myth – the earliest version known: see the Scholia

mating. Only "Sappho" stands outside this rhythm, in a primal vision of erotic loneliness, listening painfully as (in line 3) "time passes," or, "the watchman passes on his rounds,"[14] or, "the time for marriage passes (in my life)…"[15] The star of morning announces the approach of dawn, but the poetess will not now sing the bittersweet, "Oy dieus! oy dieus! de l'albe tan tost ve!" of her Provencal successor, nor will she now wish the night could be twice as long (see fr. 197). If it is a complete poem (which is more than possible), then it is among the finest work in short genres that the Western tradition has produced.

Neither this poem nor fr. 102 (discussed just prior to it) can have come from the kind of poem we have become accustomed to from Sappho. Both are typically Sapphic in style – but typical not of the erotic poems, but of the hymeneal fragments. Their subject also – the loneliness of unmarried girls – is clearly connected with the epithalamic subject. But neither of them seems likely to be from a wedding song. We should assume that a "Complete Works of Sappho" would reveal some (probably few) poems in which she adopted the *persona* not of the lover of young girls, but of the young girl herself. And we should not be surprised that in these poems Sappho's very distinctive and highly crafted symbolic idiom should have given way somewhat to the traditional idiom of folk poetry, in recognition, no doubt, that the minds and personalities of the girls she dreamed about were not so complex and difficult as her own. Now let us turn our attention to the wedding songs themselves, since our divagations have brought us at last within their aura.

---

in *Apollonium Rhodium vetera,* ed. C. Wendel (Berlin: Weidmannsche Buchhandlung, 1934), at 4.57–58.

14 E. Fraenkel, "*Vesper Adest* (Catullus LXII)," *The Journal of Roman Studies* 45 (1955), 1–8.

15 Massimi, "Schedae Sapphicae" (above, n. 9).

IX

The Hymeneal Songs

Other poets, says Himerius (*Orations* 1.4), "were bold enough when it came to singing of, say, Hera; but the mysteries (ὄργια) of Aphrodite, both in singing to the lyre and in making epithalamies, they left to Sappho alone." Demetrius (*On Style* 132) also mentions weddings as one of Sappho's most common subjects or occasions. Himerius's distinction between the mysteries of Aphrodite as Sappho sang them to the lyre and composed them in epithalamia points to the dichotomy between the private, monodic (and homosexual) side of her mask and the public, choral (and heterosexual) side.

A fuller view of Sappho may emerge by balancing the private voice of the monodies with the public voice of the ephithalamia. But there is a basic problem: deciding which fragments are hymeneal and which are not. Regrettably we don't know how Sappho' poems were arranged in the Alexandrian edition.

Identifying the Epithalamia

Servius, commenting on Vergil's *Georgics* (1.31), says, "Sappho, quae in libro qui inscribitur epithalamia ait" (Sappho who says in the book entitled Epithalamies . . .). But citations from Sappho elsewhere are given by serial numbers of books, never by titles, and the poems in the numbered books were arranged primarily by meters, not by subject matter. Perhaps, then, Servius had a different edition.

Wilamowitz-Moellendorff supposes that the epithalamia alone were gathered into a separate book, perhaps because they alone allowed of neat topical arrangement. This book – if it existed – may have had its own manuscript tradition and may have been extant later than the others.[1] Thus Himerius, who lived in the fourth century (and only quotes and mentions Sappho's epithalamia), could have seen this book – though much of Sappho, supposedly, had already perished. The Berlin Parchment (published in 1907 and containing frr. 94, 95, and 96), by proving that the fifth book was extant in the sixth century CE, refutes the latter part of Wilamowitz-Moellendorff's hypothetical account, but it may still be supposed that the Alexandrian editors separated Sappho's wedding songs from her other poems because they alone were choral. Our papyrus finds, however, indicate that the last poems of Book 1 (frr. 23, 27, and 30 – the intervening ones cannot be identified) were hymeneal and also the last two poems of Book 2. Thus the evidence of Servius and that of the papyri seem to be at variance. Several solutions have been proposed.

Edmonds proposes an early edition, perhaps Sappho's own, arranged by subjects, with the epithalamia forming the last book; when the Alexandrian editors then dealt the various books out into their eight or nine metrical categories, the epithalamia would naturally come last in each.[2] The problem is that we find no other mention of a topical arrangement. If the two editions were extant simultaneously, as Edmonds supposes, we would expect a mixed mode of citation; we have, instead, fourteen references to Sappho's books by number, and only one (Servius's) by title.

---

1 U. von Wilamowitz-Moellendorff, "Textgeschichte der griechischen Lyriker," *Abhandlung der königlichen Gesellschaft der Wissenschaften zu Göttingen. Philologisch-historische Klasse,* N.F. 3 (1900), 72.

2 *LG* 218f.

Page has suggested that those of Sappho's wedding songs that were written in the meters of the first eight books were put at the ends of those books; those whose meters fit nowhere were gathered in a, presumably small, book at the end.[3] There are problems to this "solution" also. Were all of Sappho's metrically unusual poems epithalamia? And should we not expect fr. 110 (in meter ⏓⏓–⏖–⏖–⏖––) to have fitted into the second book with fr. 44 (⏓⏓–⏖–⏖–⏖–⏑–)? The fifth book, in comparison, seems to have contained a variety of meters.[4]

---

3 *S&A* 125f.

4 M. Treu (*Sappho: Lieder* [Munich: Ernst Heimeran Verlag, 1968], 171) draws attention to fr. 6 (LP) in this connection:

(*a*)] ωσδα̣ [
] κακκ[
]ʃ ατρι[
]ε̲ κτα̣ ̣[
(*b*)] [/]̣[
]̣ +θᾰ̄[
] / στείχ[
] ὤσιδω̣[
] τὰσετ̣ [
] ποτνια ̣[
]χρυσοπ̣[
]κᾰππο[
]̣ ανμ[
]κ̣ᾶρα ̣[
]̣[

Lines 7–11, Treu points out, look rather like a waking song: line 7 echoes fr. 27, and in line 10 no Olympian name but Ἄυως (Dawn) can be restored (hence in line 11 either χρυσοπεδίλλος [golden-slippered], used by Sappho of Dawn at frr. 103.13 and 123, or χρυσόπαχυς [golden-armed], used by Bacchylides [5.40]). Yet a marginal number puts this fragment at line 500 of Book 1 and Oxyrhynchus Papyrus 1231 tells us that that book had a total of 1,320 lines; on the principle that the hymeneals are gathered at the ends of books, Book 1 must have had 800 lines of hymeneals, a figures that is astonishingly high. We might note also that while fr. 23 seems hymeneal, fr. 24, which fol-

It is possible that the Alexandrian editors distinguished between the terms *hymenaion* (meaning any kind of wedding song) and *epithalamion* (meaning just the ἐπιθαλάμιον κατακοιμητικόν, the lulling song outside the chamber, which seems to have been the most important of the wedding genres).[5] In that case, fr. 30, which ends Book 1 and seems to be a διεγερτικόν, or waking song, and fr. 44, which, if it is a wedding song, was probably sung at the banquet, fell naturally into the metrical books, and the κατακοιμητικά were gathered into a separate book, called Epithalamia, at the end. This would fit with the common assumption that the κατακοιμητικόν (the bedding song) was, as Smyth puts it, "the most important of the bridal songs."[6] It is this type that Theocritus and Catullus imitate from Sappho.

Page and others have made much of Oxyrhynchus Papyrus 2294 (fr. 103) in this connection. It seems to be a librarian's bibliographical list:

]. ω̣[
]σ̣α̣ν ἐν τῶι . [
]. δὲ (δέκα) κ(αὶ) ἑκάστης ὁ (πρῶτος)[
]. εν τὸ γὰρ ἐννεπε[.]η προβ[
]. ατε τὰν εὔποδα νύμφαν [
]τα παῖδα Κρονίδα τὰν ἰόκ[ολπ]ον [
]. ς ὄργαν θεμένα τὰν ἰόκ[ολ]πος α[
].. ἄγναι Χάριτες Πιέριδέ[ς τε] Μοῖ[σαι
].[. ὄ]πποτ' ἀοιδαι φρέν[...]αν . [

---

lowed it in the edition represented by Oxyrhynchus Papyrus 1231, does not. There are other reminders that our knowledge of the arrangement of Sappho's poems is very imperfect. Lobel thinks that they were arranged alphabetically within books, and there is some evidence for a topical arrangement of fragments within the same metrical group.

5 See R. Muth, "Hymenaios und Epithalamion," *Wiener Studien* 67 (1954), 5–45.

6 *GMP* cxv.

]σ̣αιοισα λιγύραν [ἀοί]δαν
γά]μβρον, ἄσαροι γὰρ̣ ὑμαλικ[
]σε φόβαισι θεμένα λύρα ̣ [
] ̣ ̣ η χρυσοπέδιλ<λ> [ο]σ Αὔως
] ̣   στίχ(οι) πλ[ ]
] μετὰ τὴν πρώτην [
]φέρονται ἐπιγεγρα[
ἐπιθα]λάμια
] ̣ υβλίου καὶ βέλτιο̣[ν
]
]ροπ ̣ ̣ ̣ ̣[̣ ̣] ̣ϵ ̣[

In line 3 we see: "Ten (poems?) and of each the first (line?)"; lines 4 through 13, then, are the first lines of poems, and in line 14 we see, "130 (or, since the third digit is lost, from 130–139) lines," then, in line 17, the title "Epithalamia." The question is whether this title refers upward or downward. Page argues that the horizontal strokes above and below the end of the word mark it as a new heading, i.e., the book of Epithalamia is to follow.[7] But in fact, lines 5 (containing *νύμφα* [bride]) and 11 (*γάμβρος* [groom]) clearly seem to be from hymeneal songs; the invocation of the Muses in line 8 looks like choral, not monodic style, and line 13 ("golden-slippered Dawn") might well begin a waking song, and so forth. If lines 1–16 are, as Page would have it, a list of a non-hymeneal book (Book 8), with its few hymeneals gathered at the end, then it is strange that fully seven out of ten (all following line 5) should be hymeneal. If, on the other hand, the title refers upward, and lines 1–16 are the list of the book of epithalamia, then there were only ten of those, which does not seem enough for a poet to whom, as Himerius said, all others gave place in making epithalamies.

Treu's suggestion might fit better, that fr. 103 is a list not of an entire book, but of a selection of poems to be performed at

7 *S&A* 116–19.

a specific wedding, a program for the evening.[8] If he is right, then the fragment says nothing about Sappho's book of epithalamia, but tells a great deal about ancient weddings. Above all, it seems that at a full-scale wedding as many as ten major songs would be sung, not to mention brief offerings like the toasts at modern weddings. The early entries, presumably for the wedding banquet, show us praise of the "lovely-footed bride"; the waking songs come last. Lines 15–17, then, will be restored as "All after the first are gathered under the title Epithalamia," and the first poem, presumably, will have come from the end of some other book.

Finally, the list does not help much. In fact, there is no bibliographical or paleographical evidence that helps identify which of Sappho's fragments are from hymeneals. It is necessary to use less direct evidence, and certain principles seem to apply.

First, all the fragments that Lobel calls "abnormal" (which show "epic intrusions" in dialect and, in meter, epic correption and mute+liquid not making position)[9] are or may be hymeneal. Also, all the fragments in epic hexameters are or may be hymeneal. In general, then, elements of heroic dialect, heroic meter, or (much less clearly) heroic theme, may be taken as suggestion (not proof) that the fragments in which they occur are hymeneal. There are in addition some fragments that show a clear appropriateness to some part of the wedding ceremony and may be assigned to that part at least *exempli gratia.* And finally, there is the evidence from other authors. We have Theocritus's "Epithalamion of Helen" (*Idyll* 18), Catullus's so-called Roman (Poem 61) and Greek (Poem 62) Epithalamia,[10] and the processional songs at the ends of

8 Treu, *Sappho* (above, n. 4), 167ff.

9 See Σμ. xxviff. For a complete list of the abnormalities in the Sapphic fragments see *S&A* 65–67.

10 Catullus, Poem 62 is usually called the "Greek epithalamion,"

Aristophanes' *Birds* and *Peace* (which, although they are parodies, are parodies *of* something). Theocritus's and Catullus's epithalamia were clearly influenced by those of Sappho, and whenever we find a Sapphic fragment echoed in one of them, we can reasonably (though still somewhat *exempli gratia*) call it hymeneal.

In short, the prospects for arriving at a conclusive reconstruction of a book of hymeneals or a Sapphic program of hymeneals are slight. Still, we can feel the mood and texture of these songs, for which Sappho was best known in antiquity.

Stages of the Wedding

A full program of Sapphic hymeneals unfolded in four stages to follow the four stages of the wedding. Similarly, the marriage theme was treated in four different styles,

---

but there are problems. It is as certain as such things can be that Catullus is imitating Sappho in several passages of this poem, and the inference that other passages of it are probably imitated from lost passages of Sappho is plausible. Further, the passages of Sappho that seem to be the prototypes of the Catullan passages are all the same in meter (except where textual corruption is almost certain), so that Catullus's poem may have been a close imitation of one specific poem of Sappho's, as his Poem 51 is a close rendering of her fr. 31. We might hope, then, tentatively to reconstruct a whole hymeneal poem of Sappho from the Catullan parallel. But, unfortunately, the poem by Catullus cannot be reconciled with our conception of either a Greek or a Roman wedding. (See E. Fraenkel, "Vesper Adest [Catullus LXII]," *The Journal of Roman Studies* 45 [1955], 1–8.) It seems to be a song of a Greek type, placed in an artificial (viz., imagined) ceremony that has some Roman and some Greek traits. Scholars have not been sensitive enough to this point. Neither Bowra nor Smyth, for example, discusses the problem, yet one (Bowra) assigns Catullus, Poem 62 to the banquet, and the other to the stage outside the bridal chamber. They are missing the point that this poem is not a "real" epithalamion performed at an actual wedding as at least some of Sappho's were. It is a literary set piece that reflects elements of her style, but complicates, rather than clarifies, other matters.

and the marital event illuminated from four points of view. Within this four-part structure the basic event is that the bride is transferred from her father's house to her groom's. A banquet in the afternoon at the bride's father's house (*θοινή γαμική*) was the first scene of song. In later Attic custom, the women sat apart from the men, the bride veiled among them; the Æolic practice is unknown. None of the fragments can definitely be assigned to this stage, but we know pretty well what such poems were about; ancient portrayals of weddings shared by gods and heroes concentrated on the banquet scene (e.g. Pindar, *Pythian* 3.87ff., *Nemean* 4.105ff.; Euripides, *Iphigenia at Aulis* 703ff., 1036ff.; Apollonius of Rhodes, *Argonautica* 4.790; Catullus, Poem 64.305ff.; and the François Vase), and we may suppose that the narration of myths, and especially of mythic weddings, went on at the banquet – the divine or semi-divine event gracing by analogy the human one. Snell remarks that a mythic wedding is recounted "for the greater glory of the occasion."[11] And Smyth: "The transference of a human institution to the divine sphere... dignified the marriage of commonplace people."[12] As no definite example of the song in the banquet hall survives, one cannot say whether it was monodic (like the songs of Phemius and Demodocus in the *Odyssey*), or choral, like later ceremonial verse. Many short songs may have been sung in the course of the banquet (as in fr. 41 the gods pay their respects to the groom), and some of them must have been monodic, not unlike the toasts at a modern wedding. To this context, also, the fragments expressing the point of view of the bride's parents might reasonably be assigned.

---

11 B. Snell, *The Discovery of the Mind in Greek Philosophy and Literature*, trans. T.G. Rosenmeyer (New York: Dover Publications, 1982), 62.

12 *GMP* cxvii.

After the banquet (perhaps when the evening star rose, as in the Roman custom), the company escorted the bride to her new home in a festive procession (the *νυμφαγωγία*) attended (at least in epic scenes) by flute, lyre, and dancing (see *Iliad* 18.491ff. and Hesiod, *Shield* 272ff.). Aristophanes' processionals involve bawdy joking, and something like Catullus's *fescennina jocatio* would seem most likely, in the Greek practice, to fit here.

Outside the bridal chamber, the third and main movement, with its several subdivisions, took place. Before the *κατακοιμητικόν*, the bedding or lulling song, a mock *ἀγών* may have taken place, the unmarried girls attempting to protect the virginity of the bride, and the unmarried men to sacrifice it.[13] From inside the bridal chamber, through windows open to the evening air, the couple heard the *ἐπιθαλάμιον κατακοιμητικόν*, or bedding-song-outside-the-chamber, sung either by a chorus of girls (as in Theocritus, *Idyll* 18), by a mixed chorus (as in Æschylus, fr. 43), or, possibly, by hemichori divided by sex (as in Catullus, Poem 62). This is the only hymeneal song of which we have complete examples, but unfortunately it seems that these (Theocritus's as much as Catullus's) were literary set pieces in imitation of Sappho rather than actual epithalamia for performance at weddings. Theocritus's use of the Æolic dialect is an acknowledgement that he, like Catullus, was imitating one or more of Sappho's epithalamia. His chorus of girls begins with mildly bawdy joking at the groom's expense, proceeds through a brief lamentation for the bride's loss of virginity to praise of her beauty and handiwork, and ends with good wishes for them both, for the night's sleep and the general future. The imagery is drawn mostly from nature; there is no narration of myth. Catullus's Poem 62 takes the form of a debate between two hemichori: the girls lament

13 See J.D. Meerwaldt, "Ephitalamica II," *Mnemosyne* 13 (1960), 106–10.

virginity about to be lost; the boys defend sexual union. The imagery again is from nature, not from myth.

After the *κατακοιμητικόν* the company left the bridal pair to their own devices for most of the night and returned at or shortly before dawn to sing the *ἐπιθαλάμιον διεγερτικόν* or waking-song-outside-the-chamber. Æschylus, fr. 43 suggests that boys and girls both sang this song.

The first "movement" (the banquet song) is characterised by epic grandeur; the second (the *νυμφαγωγία*), by light-hearted banter; the third (the *κατακοιμητικόν*), by a tender awareness of sexual union as part of nature's beauty and mystery; and the last (the *διεγερτικόν*) (probably), by a call to return to the world of daily business. Obviously, in one such night several songs (perhaps the ten suggested by fr. 103) would be sung, and in the case of an aristocratic wedding in Sappho's time it is likely that some (if not all) of them were specially written for the occasion. Someone had to write them, to arrange and rehearse the chorus and the musicians, and to oversee the actual production. It would seem likely that Sappho herself performed these functions a number of times, and if the legend that her family was wealthy is wrong (the evidence wavers), this may be how she earned her living. In any case, the traces of all this can be found in her work, and it is time to look at them now.

Reconstructing the Wedding Song

Here is how Homer describes it:

> And so they were banqueting in the high hall, the neighbors and relatives of godlike Menelaos, and enjoying themselves; and among them a sacred minstrel sang to the lyre, and two tumblers leapt up and down through the midst of them, as he began his song.
>
> (*Odyssey* 4.16–19)

The scene is inside the great hall. The guests have eaten and drunk in the flare of the torches. Some sign (perhaps the entrance of tumblers) indicates the beginning of the song. The poetess reaches for her lyre, the chorus, perhaps just of girls, rises and begins in a stately mood. Something like their song can be recovered from fragments:

Fr. 127:

> *δεῦρο δηὖτε* Μοῖσαι *χρύσιον λίποισαι*...
>
> Come hither, Muses, leaving your golden home...

Fr. 124:

> *αὔτα δὲ σὺ* Καλλιόπα
>
> Even you yourself, Calliope

Fr. 128:

> *δεῦτέ νυν ἄβραι* Χάριτες *καλλίκομοί τε* Μοῖσαι
>
> Come now, tender Graces and fair-haired Muses

Fr. 103.8

>]. . *ἄγναι* Χάριτες Πιέριδέ[*ς τε*] Μοῖ[*σαι*
>
> ...sacred Graces and Pierian Muses...

A mythical wedding, sometimes one at which gods or heroes were present (Peleus and Thetis, Kadmos and Harmonia, Menelaos and Helen are all candidates) is conjured up to shed its grace on the Iron-Age proceedings at hand. ("And you all went, you gods, to the weddings, and you yourself feasted among them and held the lyre, O friend of the wicked...," says Hera to Zeus [*Iliad* 24.62f.].)

Fr. 141:

κῆ δ' ἀμβροσίας μὲν
κράτηρ ἐκέκρατ'
3,4 *Ἔρμαισ δ' ἔλων θέοισ' ὠινοχόαισε.*
κῆνοι δ' ἄρα πάντες
καρχάσι' ἦχον
7,8 *κἄλειβον ἀράσαντο δὲ πάμπαν ἔσλα*
τὼι γάμβρωι.

And there stood a wine-bowl full of ambrosia
and Hermes, taking the pitcher, poured it out for
the gods, and they all took the cups and poured a libation
and prayed for all good things for the groom ...[14]

For the honor of the family (and, indeed, of human life in general) the grandeur of the public event must be enhanced by heroic myth. In fr. 44 (possibly the earliest extant epyllion) we seem to possess such a song from Sappho's hand:

Fr. 44

Κυπρο̣ .[ ]ας̣·
κάρυξ ἦλθε̣ θε̣[ ]ελε̣[...] . θεισ
Ἴδαος ταδεκα ...φ[..] . ις τάχυς ἄγγελος
3a < >
τάς τ' ἄλλας Ἀσίας . [.]δε . αν κλέος ἄφθιτον·
Ἔκτωρ καὶ συνέταιρ̣[ο]ι ἄγοι̣σ' ἐλικώπιδα
Θήβας ἐξ ἰέρας Πλακίας τ'ἀ .[..]νάω
ἄβραν Ἀνδρομάχαν ἐνὶ ναῦσιν ἐπ' ἄλμυρον
πόντον· πόλλα δ' [ἐλί]γματα χρύσια κἄμματα
πορφύρ[α] καταύτ[..]να, ποί̣κ̣ιλ' ἀθύρματα,
ἀργύρα̣ τ̣' ἀνάρ̣[ι]θ̣μα [ποτή]ρ[ια] κἀλέφαις.
ὢς εἶπ'· ὀτραλέως δ' ἀνόρουσε πάτ[η]ρ̣ φίλος·
φάμα δ' ἦλθε κατὰ πτ̣όλιν εὐρύχο̣ρ̣ο̣ν φίλοις.
αὔτικ' Ἰλίαδαι σατίναι[ς] ὐπ' ἐυτρόχοις
ἆγον αἰμιόνοις, ἐ̣π̣[έ]βαινε δὲ παῖς ὄχλος

14 Fr. 141 is irregular in one word, *ἄρα*, and is metrically unclassifiable.

γυναίκων τ' ἄμα παρθενίκα[ν] τ ̣ ̣[̣ ̣] ̣ σφύρων,
χῶρις δ' αὖ Περάμοιο θυγ[α]τρες[
ἴππ[οις] δ' ἄνδρες ὕπαγον ὐπ' ἀρ̣[ματ
π[ ]ες ἠίθ̣εοι, μεγάλω[σ]τι δ̣[
δ[ ] ̣ ἀνίοχοι φ[̣ ̣ ̣ ̣ ̣] ̣[
π[΄]ξα ̣ ο[
< *desunt aliquot versus* >
ἴ]κελοι θέοι[ς
] ἄγνον ἀολ[λε-
ὄ̣ρ̣μαται̣[ ]νον ἐς Ἴλιο[ν
αὖλοσ δ' ἀυ[μ]έλης[ ]τ' ὀνεμίγνυ[το
καὶ ψ[ό]φο[ς κ]ροτάλ[ων]ως δ' ἄρα πάρ[θενοι
ἄειδον μέλος ἄγν̣[ον ἴκα]νε δ' ἐς α̣ἴθ̣[ερα
ἄχω θεσπεσία̣ γελ̣[
πάνται δ' ἦς κὰτ ὄδο[
κράτηρες φίαλαί τ' ο'[̣ ̣ ̣]υεδε[̣ ̣] ̣ ̣ εακ[̣] ̣[
μύρρα καὶ κασία λίβανός τ' ὀνεμείχνυτο
γύναικες δ' ἐλέλυσδον ὄσαι προγενέστερα[ι
πάντες δ' ἄνδρες ἐπήρατον ἴαχον ὄρθιον
Πάον' ὀνκαλέοντες ἐκάβολον εὐλύραν,
ὔμνην δ' Ἔκτορα κ Ἀνδρομάχαν θεοεικέλο[ις.

Σαπφο[ῦς μελῶν
β

Cypr – ... The herald came ... Idaos ... the swift messenger [missing line] "and of the rest of Asia ... the deathless story; Hector and his comrades are leading a glancing-eyed girl from sacred Thebe and Plakia ... tender Andromache, in ships over the salt sea; and many golden bracelets and purple robes ... varied bangles and countless silver cups and things of ivory." So he spoke, and straightway [Hector's] father rose up, and the story went through the wide-wayed city to his friends. At once the sons of Ilos led the mules beneath the well-wheeled carriages, and all the throng of matrons went up together with the [fair?]-ankled maidens, and apart from them the daughters of Priam. And the men led horses underneath the yokes ... youths most of all ... [were?] charioteers ... [unknown number of lines missing] like gods ... sacred ... rose up ... to Ilion, and

> the sweet-voiced flute was mixed with the lyre and the clatter of castanets; and in a clear voice the maidens sang then a sacred song and the divinely-sounding echo went up to heaven... to everyone along the road... bowls and cups... myrrh and cassia and frankincense were mingled; and the women who were older sang crying out with a loud voice, and all the men sang a lovely song calling on Paean far-shooter, lord of the lyre, and they sang of Hector and Andromache the godlike ones.
>
> The second book of Sappho's songs.

This strange fragment (found in Oxyrhynchus Papyrus 1232, published in 1913) is rejected by Wilamowitz-Moellendorff, Lobel ("almost certainly supposititious"), and Bowra ("not Sappho's"), although Oxyrhynchus Papyri 1232 and 2076 firmly place it at the end of Sappho's second book. Page's defense of *πορφύρα* and *ἀργύρα* as Homeric-style contractions of Ionic forms (*πορφύρεα* and *ἀργύρεα*) (rather than as Attic forms) seems to have allayed doubts.[15] It is presumed to be a wedding song because: 1) It occurred at the end of a book; paleographic evidence, while not complete for all books, shows that Book 1 ended in several hymeneals and that the poem preceding fr. 44 in Book 2 was hymeneal. 2) It displays very conspicuously the abnormalities associated with the certainly hymeneal fragments.[16]

---

15 Wilamowitz-Moellendorff, "Neue lesbische Lyrik," *Neue Jahrbücher für das klassische Alterthum* 38 (1914), 229ff.; Lobel, Αμ. xvii; Bowra, "Earlier Lyric and Elegiac Poetry," in *New Chapters in the History of Greek Literature. Third Series: Some Recent Discoveries in Greek Poetry and Prose of the Classical and Later Periods,* J. U. Powell, ed. (Oxford: The Clarendon Press, 1933), 13; Page, "The Authorship of Sappho b2 (Lobel)," *The Classical Quarterly* 30/1 (1936), 10–15.

16 The fragment is epic, rather than Lesbian, at about twenty points (Lesbian forms given in parentheses): 1.6: *ιερας* (*ῑρας*); 1.7: *ἐνί* (*ἐν* or *ἐνν*); 1.11: *ἀνόρουσε* (*ὀνόρουσε*); 1.12: *κατά* (*κατ*), *πτόλιν* (*πόλιν*), *φίλοις* (*φίλοισι*); 1.13: *ἐύτροχοις* (*εὔτροχοις*); 1.16: *περάμοιο*

3) Its primarily dactylic meter reminds, again, of those fragments.[17] 4) It describes a wedding. Page remarks that "there

---

(περάμω); 1.21: θέοις (θέοισι); 11.23 and 26: ἐς before a vowel (εἰς); 1.33: ὀνκαλέοντε (ὀνκάλεντες); omission of temporal augment in lines 11 (ανόρουσε), 26 (ἴκανε), and 31 (ἐλέλυσδον); vowel before mute+liquid scanned short in lines 8 (ἐλίγματα χρύσια) and 14 (ὄχλος); epic correption in line 5 (συνέταιροι ἄγοισ'); hiatus between lines 9 and 10, 27 and 28.

17 Page (op. cit. [above, n. 3], 318), following A. M. Dale ("The Metrical Units of Greek Lyric Verse, I, II, III," *The Classical Quarterly* 44 [1950], 138–48 and 45 [1951], 20–30, 119–29), notes that the dactylic nature of lines commencing with the Æolic base seems to arise from the prolongation of the choriambic nucleus. Page remarks, "The common appellation 'Æolic *dactyls*' is misleading." But it seems that Sappho herself was misled. Her other examples of Æolic dactyls are frr. 110*a*, 115, 130, 131, 136, and 146, of which 110*a* and 115 are certainly hymeneal, and 136 and 146 may have been. It is clear that she associated epic dactyls with hymeneal song, and, it seems, Æolic dactyls also. In fr. 44 it would seem that Sappho herself was impressed by the *dactylic* nature of the lines, despite their apparent origin from the prolonged choriamb, and hence allowed them, like epic dactyls, to draw with them features of epic dialect and theme. The fact that the hymeneal fragments are dominated by these two meters, both dactylic in sound if not in origin, is hardly an accident. Finally, it should be noted that this is the only stichic poem known from either Sappho or Alcaeus – and surely Sappho has made it stichic in order to underline the fact that it is an imitation of an earlier age – specifically of the stichic dactyls of the epic.

But the situation seems to have been more complicated. Gregory Nagy (*Comparative Studies in Greek and Indic Meter* [Cambridge, Mass.: Harvard Univ. Press, 1974]) has argued that the Æolic meters originated earlier than the heroic dactylic hexameter. A situation is implied in which Æolic and Ionic poets made different metrical choices at some time in the Late Bronze and Early Iron Age. The basic choice is this: on the one side there is the dactyl (–⏑⏑), which seems to bring a certain meaning with it. Specifically, dactylic hexameter is a kind of marching rhythm; it forges every onward into the future without a pause (except the caesurea, a rhythmical pause artfully distributed in the line and exerting a tremendous modulating force on the onward-thrusting energy of the dactyls). On the other side is the choriamb (–⏑⏑–). I suggest that it is more a dancing than a marching rhythm. The dactyl is like a top-heavy object, always falling forward. But the is no recorded evidence incompatible with the hypothesis that 44 was a hymeneal song, sung at a real wedding."[18] But he has understated the case; in fact, all the evidence that we possess (though it is, of course and as always, less than we would like) points positively toward this hypothesis.

But what *kind* of wedding song can it be? It has nothing in common with the Theocritean and Catullan examples, but rather with the processional song at the end of the *Birds*. The latter, however, like the Theocritean and Catullan examples, contains the traditional Pherecratean refrain Ὑμὴν ὦ Ὑμέναιε, which is conspicuously absent from fr. 44. Obviously, that a mythic wedding is told to glorify the festivity means that it is not a waking song. And by elimination, then, we place it at the feast, recalling Snell's observation that a mythic wedding is told to glorify the festivity.[19] But this conclusion is not certain; there remains the possibility that this fragment is neither hymeneal nor even Sapphic.

---

choriamb closes the loop and comes back constantly to where it began. Instead of marching, it pirouettes. It has a sense of completeness as of a cyclicity that is fulfilled again and again – whereas the dactyl is forever rushing forward. By stringing choriambs together ancient poets approached the other, the dactylic tradition. –∪∪––∪∪– becomes, for the sake of the onrushing speed of speech, –∪∪–∪∪–. Thus out of choriambs grew the so-called Æolic dactyls and, as Dale suggests, the dactylic sound of Æolic dactyls drew them closer to the epic line and promoted a conflation – hence Sappho's fr. 44. Historically it seems that the epic dactyls took over the Æolic dactyls and appropriated them into the epic discourse, though their meaning when they began may have been very different.

A second major choice that early Æolic poets made was the anceps – a metrical position in which either a long or a short syllable could occur with no consequences in either case. This may linger from a very early prosodic stage before the counting of longs and shorts. In a way the two ancipitia that begin the Sapphic line remind one of the Homeric caesura. They open up an unfathomable abyss in the line from which the rest of the line then grows or springs or blossoms.

18 *S&A* 74.

19 See Snell, *The Discovery of the Mind* (above, n.11).

Assuming the poem *is*, as the evidence suggests, a hymeneal banquet song, then the poet has omitted the *primum comparationis* – the bride and groom – and has left the rather obvious connection between the myth and the occasion unstated. (The bride and groom may have been mentioned at the beginning of the poem, but then we would expect another mention at the end.) But lest anyone miss the point, Sappho modernizes the heroic wedding, giving it the *σατίναι* (chariots), incense, and castanets of sixth-century Lesbos. The metaphorical relationship works both ways: as the Lesbian bride and groom are transported into the hyperreality of legend, so Hector and Andromache are transported into the earthly realm of real sixth-century custom. The profusion of musical imagery, the use of the adjective *ἄβρα* (delicate) for the bride[20] (while the groom receives no adjectives), the concentration on luxurious and lady-like trinkets, all seem typically Sapphic. But there is no passion, there is no personality; there is none of the special insight into the intensity of the perishable moment that gives Sappho's better poems their power. Page compares fr. 44 to Bacchylides at his best, and here alone in his remarks on Sappho does he seem overgenerous (or, indeed, even generous). Does the comparison with Hector and Andromache seem odd or ill-omened?[21] In the garlanded banquet hall, in the light of the torches and the heat of the wine, only the mythic grandeur, it seems, was felt. Theocritus, after all, chose Helen and Menelaos! And Sappho herself on another occasion (as meter and epic correption tell us) may have chosen a yet stranger vehicle for the myth in the marriage hall:

---

20 Fr. Inc. Auct. 26 (LP) (line 2: *εὔποδα νύμφαν αβ*[]) should be assigned to Sappho on analogy with this passage and fr. 103.5 (]̣*ατε τὰν εὔποδα νύφαν*).

21 As J.T. Kakridis argues, "Zu Sappho 44 LP," *Wiener Studien* 79 (1966), 21–26.

Fr. 142:

> Λάτω καὶ Νιόβα μάλα μὲν φίλαι ἦσαν ἔταιραι
>
> Leto and Niobe once it seems were friends...

After the mythic narration, the chorus sings, in a more tender mood, of the bride's beauty, with some pious admonitions and a reminder that they will stay up all night in her honor. Again the good taste of the mythic *exemplum* is not subjected to close scrutiny:

Fr. 23:

] ἔρωτος ἠ̣λ̣π̣[
]
—
]τιον εἰσιδωσ[
]Ἐρμιόνα τεαυ[τα
] ξάνθαι δ' Ἐλέναι σ' ἐίσ[κ]ην
]κες
—
] ̣ις θνάταις, τόδε δ' ἴσ[θι,] τὰι σᾶι
] παίσαν κέ με τὰν μερίμναν
]λ̣αισ' ἀντιδ[̣ ̣] ́ [̣]α̣θοις δ̣ὲ̣
]
—
]τας ὄχθοις
]ταιν
παν]νυχίσ[δ]ην

> of love... (for) when I look at you... Hermiona (was not?)
> such... and liken you even to yellow-haired Helen...
> but know this: for mortals... your... every care...
> the shores... stay up all night...

Epic simile, gnomic transition, personal remarks; the bride is likened to Helen, the groom (as Himerius tells us) to Achilles. Aphrodite has cast a shining mist about their heads... Inwoven with the brightness of their praises are comments, always favorable, on the advantages of their union:

Fr. 148:

> ὀ πλοῦτος ἄνευ † ἀρέτας οὐκ ἀσίνης πάροικος
> ἀ δ' ἀμφοτέρων κρᾶσις † εὐδαιμονίας ἔχει τὸ ἄκρον †
>
> Wealth without virtue is a bad living mate, but the
> combination of the two brings the height of happiness

and on the unimportance of physical beauty, if one or the other of them (in this case, it seems the groom) should lack it:

Fr. 50:

> ὀ μὲν γὰρ κάλος ὄσσον ἴδην πέλεται <κάλος>,
> ὀ δὲ κἄγαθος αὔτικα καὶ κάλος ἔσσεται.
>
> He who is fair to see is fair,
> but he who is good will soon be fair also.

And perhaps, attention was paid to the loss that the bride's parents were about to suffer, and to their generosity:

Fr. 109:

> δώσομεν, ἦσι πάτηρ
>
> We will give, said the father...

To the New Home

Now the epic narration and the songs of praise or good wishes are ended. Perhaps (as in the *deductio* of a Roman wedding) the bride has disappeared for a minute and now reappears, newly garlanded and adorned, ready for the bridal procession, the *νυμφαγωγία*. The company, having rested and drunk and been entertained after dinner, rise in a lighter mood to escort the couple playfully to their bridal chamber.

Says Hesiod (*Shield* 273–80):

> Some in a well-wheeled chariot were bringing a bride to her husband, and the bridal song swelled all around, and far-off rolled the gleam of the blazing torches, held in the hands of maidservants who went in front, delighting in the festival; and playful choirs of youths followed them, singing with gentle lips to the shrill song of the pipes, and the echo shivered around them. And the girls led on the lovely dance to the lyres.

And Homer (*Iliad* 18.491–96):

> From their chambers they led the brides through the city with blazing torches, and the great bride-song rose up. The young men eddied about in their dancing while among them the flutes and lyres gave cry. And women, each standing in the doorway to her house, admired them as they passed.

It is the cool twilight of the north Ægean. Emerging from the bride's childhood home, the wedding party makes its way by torchlight through the streets, above the moonlit harbor, toward the groom's home. The young girls sing in chorus, inviting the women who lean from windows of houses they pass to come with them:

Fr. 27:

]κ̣αιπ̣[
]̣.[̣.]̣.[̣.]ν̣ος[
3]σι·

—

. . .]̣. καὶ γὰρ .η σὺ πάις ποτ[
. . .]ι̣κ̣ης μέλπεσθ' ἄγι ταῦτα[
. .] ζάλεξαι, κἄμμ' ἀπὺ τωδεκ[
7 .]δρα χάρισσαι·

—

σ]τείχομεν γάρ ἐς γάμον· εὖ δε[
κα]ὶ σὺ τοῦτ', ἀλλ' ὄττι τάχιστα[
πα]ρ̣[θ]ένοις ἄπ[π]εμπε, θέοι[
11]εν ἔχοιεν
—
] ὄδος̣ μ[έ]γαν εἰς Ὄλ[υμπον
ἀ]νθρω[π]αίκ ̣[

for you also once were a girl … come, dance … hold converse with us … and honor the … for we are going to a wedding; and you will do well to come too; quickly now, send out your girls … the gods … may have … a road to great Olympus … mankind … [22]

The season is springtime; the night is sweet and blossomy. But soon the procession reaches its goal. The bride passes through the perfumed and garlanded doorway to be presented at the household altar, while her friends, prevented by the best man, stay outside. As the groom escorts her to the door, they line the path and sing:

Fr. 111:

ἴψοι δὴ τὸ μέλαθρον·
ὐμήναον·
ἀέρρετε τέκτονες ἄνδες·
ὐμήναον.
γάμβρος † εἰσέρχεται ἴσος † Ἄρευι,
ἄνδρος μεγάλω πόλυ μέζων.

Fr. 106:

πέρροχος, ὡς ὄτ' ἄοιδος
[ὐμήναον.]
ὀ Λέσβιος ἀλλοδάποισιν

22 I see no need to follow Diehl (ad loc.), Theander ("Atthis and Andromeda," *Eranos* 44 [1946], 65), and Treu (*Sappho* [above, n. 4], 192) in their view that this is addressed to Andromeda or some other hypothetical "rival" of Sappho.

Raise the roofbeam high
(hymeniaon!)
O carpenters.

The groom comes in like Ares
(hymeniaon!)
taller than a very tall man.

(Towering like the poet of Lesbos
(hymeniaon!)
over those of other lands.)[23]

Now the virgins play at rescuing their friend, and make light of the guards at the door:

Fr. 110:

θυρώρωι πόδες ἐπτορόγυιοι,
τὰ δὲ σάμβαλα πεμπεβόηα,
πίσσυγγοι δὲ δέκ' ἐξεπόναισαν

The doorman's feet are seven cubits long
and his sandals needed five oxhides,
and ten shoemakers labored at them.

It is a light and homely verse, with echoes of work songs and folk songs.

But now the *ἀγών* of youths and maidens enters a more serious stage. The epithalamion proper, investigating the sorrow and the beauty of the end of childhood, and the entrance into the mysteries of sexuality, is underway. The virgins

---

23 I give this fragment with the emendations recommended by Lobel (Σμ. 49); also, Edmonds's addition of fr. 106 here strikes me as useful *exempli gratia*.

I would not rule out Kirk's interpretation of this fragment as a joke on the ithyphallicism of the groom ("A Fragment of Sappho Reinterpreted," *The Classical Quarterly* 13 [1963], 51f.). Both Aristophanes and Catullus give us the feeling that there *should* be a rather coarse humor here.

lament the loss of their friend, who now stands outside the course of nature as they know it and unaccountably goes not home to her mother, but to a man's house, at dusk.

Fr. 104:

> *ἀστέρων πάντων ὁ κάλλιστος*
> *Ἕσπερε πάντα φέρων ὄσα φαίνολις ἐσκέδας' Αὔως,*
> *† φέρεις ὄιν, φέρεις αἶγα, φέρεις ἄπυ † μάτερι παῖδα.*
>
> ... fairest of all the stars ...
> Hesperus, you who bring back all that shining
> Dawn scattered, you bring the lamb, you bring
> the kid, you bring the child back to its mother...
> (But her you bring not home again ...) [24]

Even as the marital event transpires in the perfumed stillness within, one girl takes the role of the bride and sings:

Fr. 107:

> *ἦρ' ἔτι παρθενίας ἐπιβάλλομαι;*
>
> Even now do I cling to maidenhood?

She calls out to her girlhood, now fleeting, and the chorus replies in response:

---

24 In Catullus, Poem 62 the rising star signaled the end of the banquet, but that does not seem the point here. E. D. Floyd's restoration, *αἶγα φέρεις ἔπερον τε, φέρεις ἄπυ μάτερι παῖδα*, is appealing in its smoothness, but the line misses the third *φέρεις* (see "Sappho's Word for 'Sheep,' 104 A. 2 [L.-P.]," *The Classical Review*, n.s., 18/3 [1968], 266–67).

Iliad 22.317–18 is a possible source for fr. 104*b*:

> *οἷος δ' ἀστὴρ εἶσι μετ' ἀστράσι νυκτὸς ἀμολγῷ*
> *ἕσπερος, ὃς κάλλιστος ἐν οὐρανῷ ἵσταται ἀστήρ...*
>
> As is that one star among all the stars in the dead of night,
> Hesperus, who is the fairest star in the sky...

Fr. 114:

(νύμφη). παρθενία, παρθενία, ποῖ με λίποισα † οἴχηι;
(παρθενία). † οὐκέτι ἥξω πρὸς σέ, οὐκέτι ἥξω †.

(Bride): Maidenhood, maidenhood, leaving me,
whither away?
(Maidenhood): No longer will I stay with you,
no longer stay...

The chorus of girls laments the sacrifice of the beauty of maidenhead to the busy desires of manhood:

Fr. 105*c*:

οἴαν τὰν ὐάκινθον ἐν ὤρεσι ποίμενεσ ἄνδρες
πόσσι καταστείβοισι, χάμαι δέ τε πόρφυρον ἄνθοσ...

Like the hyacinth in the mountain, which the
shepherd men tread underfoot, and on the earth
the purple flower (lies crushed)...

And the chorus of young men replies, describing the girl who would hold back from marriage as a last rose of summer, left to wither alone...

Fr. 105*a*:

οἶον τὸ γλυκὺμαλον ἐρεύθεται ἄκρωι ἐπ' ὔσδωι,
ἄκρον ἐπ' ἀκροτάτωι, λελάθοντο δὲ μαλοδρόπηες,
οὐ μὰν ἐκλελάθοντ', ἀλλ' οὐκ ἐδύναντ' ἐπίκεσθαι.

As the sweet apple blushes on a high bough, high upon
the highest, and the apple pickers have forgotten it –
No, they did not forget it; they were not able to reach it.[25]

---

25 Frr. 104, 105*a*, and 105*c* are assigned here on analogy with Catullus, Poem 62. Whether or not Sappho's hymeneals used boy and girl hemichori is a matter of guesswork. Unfortunately Catullus's poem, though probably based on one of Sappho's, is not close enough to interpret these lines for us. See J. A. Davison, "A Marriage Song of Sappho's," in *FromArchilochus to Pindar* (London: Macmillan,

The question of maidenhood being, by this time, rather academic, the two hemichori make up their differences and proceed to praise the bride in loftier imagery:[26]

Fr. 108:

ὦ κάλα, ὦ χαρίεσσα

O fair, O blessed (maiden) ...

Other girls pale beside her:

Fr. 34 :

ἄσρερες μὲν ἀμφὶ κάλαν σελάνναν
ἄψ ἀπυκρύπτοισι φάεννον εἶδος,
ὄπποτα πλήθοισα μάλιστα λάμπηι
γᾶν.........

The stars around the fair moon
quickly hide their gleaming light
when at the full she shines
upon the earth ...[27]

1968), 244, for the interpretation I have given. The common view that the hyacinth is a girl who gave herself thoughtlessly to the first-comer, and the apple a bride (possibly of slightly advanced age) who has waited her time is quite reasonable also.

Frr. 105*a* and 105*c* have both been questioned by Lobel (Σμ. xxvii and 47) on metrical and dialectal grounds. For a lengthy discussion the reader may consult B. Marzullo, *Studi di poesia eolica* (Florence: Le Monnier, 1958), 61–114.

26 The sequence that follows is based on Theocritus, *Idyll* 18, where the chorus first jokes at the groom's expense and laments the bride's loss of virginity, then praises her beauty and handiwork, and finally wishes them both well for the night's sleep and the general future, with a reminder that they will be back at dawn. With fr. 108, cf. *Idyll* 18.38, and with fr. 34, *Idyll* 18.20–28.

27 See above, chap. 4, "The Magic in Action," for the idea that this fragment should be regarded as hymeneal.

And not only her beauty, but her handiwork is so fine that:

Fr. 56:

οὐδ' ἴαν δοκίμωμι προσίδοισαν φάος ἀλίω
ἔσσεσθαι σοφίαν πάρθενον εἰς οὐδένα πω χρόνον
τεαύταν

I do not think that in all time to come any girl
will see the light of the sun who is the equal of
this one in skill...

Now the chorus turns its attention to the groom:

Fr. 115:

τίωι σ', ὦ φίλε γάμβρε, κάλως ἐικάσδω;
ὄρπακι βραδίνωι σε μάλιστ' ἐικάσδω.

To what, O dear bridegroom, may I well compare thee?
To a slender sapling I will best compare thee.[28]

He is congratulated on the beauty of his bride:

Fr. 113:

οὐ γὰρ † ἑτέρα νῦν † πάις ὦ γάμβρε τεαύτα

There is no other girl such as yours, O bridegroom...

And the pleasures he even now is enjoying are described to him tenderly:

Fr. 112:

ὄλβιε γάμβρε, σοὶ μὲν δὴ γάμος ὡς ἄραο
ἐκτετέλεστ', ἔχηις δὲ πάρθενον † ἂν † ἄραο...
σοὶ χάριεν μὲν εἶδος, ὄππατα δ' <αὖτε νύμφας>
μέλλιχ', ἔρος δ' ἐπ' ἰμέρτωι κέχυται προσώπωι
.............τετίμακ' ἔξοχά σ' Ἀφροδίτα

28 Cf. Odysseus' praise of Nausicaa in *Odyssey* 6.162f.

> Happy bridegroom the wedding you prayed for
> is fulfilled, and you have the girl you prayed for;
> Your face is fine, but her eyes are gentle indeed
> and love is shed over all her beautiful face...
> Aphrodite has favored you exceedingly.[29]

Perhaps the perfect tense in line 2 indicates that the couple has been alone now for some time. In any case, in time the songs draw near their end, and the chorus, imagining that the couple is drifting off to sleep, lulls them gently:

Fr. 151:

> *ὀφθάλμοις δὲ μέλαις νύκτος ἄωρος...*
>
> On (their) eyes black sleep of night...

Fr. 126:

> *δαύοις ἀπάλας ἐτάρας ἐν στήθεσιν.*
>
> You may sleep on the breast of a tender companion.

And soon,

Fr. 149:

> *ὄτα πάννυχος ἄσφι κατάγρει*
>
> When nightlong (sleep?) holds them...

the chorus gently bids them goodbye:

Fr. 116:

> *χαῖρε, νύμφα, χαῖρε τίμιε γάμβρε, πόλλα...*
>
> Farewell, bride, farewell, honored groom...

---

29 I have used Bowra's restoration in line 3. See *GLP* 218.

Fr. 117:

† χαίροις ἀ νύμφα †, χαιρέτω δ' ὀ γάμβρος

Farewell, bride, and may the groom fare well…

And goes elsewhere.[30]

Where does the chorus go? Theocritus (*Idyll* 18.13–14) mentions nightlong activities that groups of girls engaged in (παίσδειν, he says), and from which the bride will now be absent. Beyond that, nothing is known. Presumably they would be absent for several hours before returning to sing the waking song.

In any case, in time the stars have wheeled in the heavens, and Hesperus, from whom the song began, has sunk and now rises again, heralding Dawn. The chorus of virgins, at the end of their bridal vigil, returns and sings again as the first birds are heard:[31]

Fr. 30:

νύκτ[. . .] . [
—
παρθενοι δ[
παννυχισδο . [.]α . [
σὰν ἀείδοι . ν φ[ιλότατα καὶ νύμ-
φας ἰοκόλπω.
—
ἀλλ' ἐγέρθεις, ἤϊθ[ε
στεῖχε σοὶς ὑμάλικ[ας
ἤπερ ὄσσον ἀ λιγύφω[νος
ὔπνον [ἴ]δωμεν
—

30 Cf. Theocritus, *Idyll* 18.49: χαίροις ὦ νύμφα, χαίροις εὐπένθερε γάμβρε. Frr. 56, 126, 149, and 151 are included here more or less *exempli gratia*.

31 Æschylus, fr. 43 suggests that the waking songs were sung by both boys and girls; in that case, fr. 30 may have been amoeban, lines 2–5 being sung by the girls and lines 6–9 by the boys, calling their friend back to their company.

night . . . maidens . . . all night long . . . sing your love
and your violet-bosomed bride's. But wake up,
step out with the bachelors, your peers . . . as for us,
we shall see no more sleep than will that shrill-voiced bird . . .

The groom is commanded to recommence activities of his former life; the honeymoon already is over. And with remarks again on their own tiredness, and a mood of return to the everyday world, they conclude:

Fr. 43:

]α̣ι̣·
—
]
]λ̣ετ̣α̣ι̣
—
][[κ]]αλος
] ̣ ἄκαλα κλόνει
—
] κάματος φρένα
]ε̣ κ̣ατισδάνε[ι]
—
] ἀλλ' ἄγιτ', ὦ φίλαι,
], ἄγχι γὰρ ἀμέρα.
—
]
]
] ̣
]
]
]

peaceful . . . tired at heart . . .
sits down . . . but come, dear girls . . . for day is near.

The coronis indicates the end.

X

The Biographical Question Again

There is no reason to believe that Sappho herself or any of her contemporaries left a written account of her life; at least, no ancient author mentions one. Chameleon's *Sappho* is lost, and we are left with scraps of information. The only one early enough to come from a contemporary account, or from an unpolluted oral tradition, is Herodotus's story that Sappho rebuked her brother for running with Egyptian whores. Our main sources are not only much later, but highly questionable in motive as well as in authority: Ovid's "Letter from Sappho to Phaon" (*Letters of the Heroines* 15); the Oxyrhynchus biography (late second or early third century CE); and the *Suda* (tenth century CE), along with mentions in Aristotle, the Parian Marble, and late authors such as Athenaeus and Maximus of Tyre. All material except the anecdote in Herodotus falls under the shadow of Athenian New Comedy.

Modern authors, faced with this discouraging array, but still understandably curious about the poetess and eager to believe that we know her, react variously. Some give free reign to imagination and construct clairvoyances inspired, one would think, more by love than by learning.[1] Others, donning, however happily, the uncomfortable yoke of the evidence, construct minimal biographies from "those waifs and strays

1 See, e.g., among those which are not outright frauds, A. Weigall, *Sappho of Lesbos: Her Life and Times* (New York: Garden City Publishing, 1932); M. Goldsmith, *Sappho of Lesbos: A Psychological Reconstruction of her Life* (London: Rich & Cowan Ltd., 1938); and É. Mora, *Sappho: Histoire d'un poète et traduction intégrale de l'œuvre* (Paris: Flammarion, 1966).

of Sappho ... and others" (as Symonds calls them[2]), which they feel are most likely to be true. The version presented by A.R. Burn may be taken as a representative example:

Sappho was an aristocrat, the daughter of Scamandronymos and Cleis, born in the late seventh century, with brothers Eurygyus, Charaxus, and Larichus. She married young and had a daughter whom she named after her mother; her husband probably died early. She was small and dark, and not beautiful; a poetess revered in her own day, who, in competition with rival lady teachers, taught music, poetry, and the various womanly accomplishments to young girls of good family, many of whom were sent from overseas to her school, and to some of whom she formed romantic (and perhaps sexual) attachments. She may have been exiled, with other nobles, under the tyranny of Pittakos, going to Sicily. The end of her life is unknown.[3]

Now, we may admit ungrudgingly that all of this *might* be true. But how much of it is *probably* true and how much merely *possible* (in an infinity of other possibilities) is another matter altogether. Let us look at each item.

That Sappho was an aristocrat: the only evidence is Athenaeus, *Scholars at Dinner* 10.424*e*: "The highest born youths used to pour wine among the ancients... And the beautiful Sappho many times praised her brother Larichos as wine-pourer in the city hall of the Mytilenaeans." But Athenaeus does not say where such praises were uttered, whether in her poems, on the comic stage, or in some text like Ovid's "Letter to Phaon." And one wonders if his light and glorified view of noble society, not of the ancient Mytilenaeans or the Æolians, but merely of "the ancients," is really evidence for anything except the attitudes of Athenaeus's own society.

2 J.A. Symonds, *Studies of the Greek Poets*, 2 vols. (New York: Harpers and Brothers, 1880), 1:291.

3 A.R. Burn, *The Lyric Age of Greece* (London: Edward Arnold, 1960), 227–39 and 243; and Symonds, *Studies of the Greek Poets* (above, n.2).

The names of her relatives: Herodotus (*Histories* 2.135) names her father Scamandronymos and is followed in this by most later authors. The Pindaric scholiast, however, names him Eurygyus and the *Suda* shows how varied the tradition was, saying, "Simon or Eunominus or Eurygyus or Ecrytus or Semus or Scamon or Euarchos or Scamandronymos..." There is uniformity among weak authorities for naming her mother Cleis, but the name does not occur elsewhere, and one wonders, considering its suggestions of "a ball and chain," if it was not a comic coinage. Charaxus is named by Herodotus, Larichus by Athenaeus (as quoted just above); the *Suda* and the Oxyrhynchus biographer name all three. The two names from Herodotus, surely, are stronger than the others, but are more or less useless for all that.

That she married, and married young: The *Suda* says she married a wealthy man, one Cercolas of Andros. The name is an obvious comic fabrication, and there is no other evidence for her marriage. The Oxyrhynchus biographer omits it altogether. That she married *young* is, perhaps, an assumption based on the belief that if she had been aware of her confirmed homosexuality she would not have married at all.

That she had a daughter, who was named after her mother: Various late ancient sources (including, again, the *Suda*) mention the daughter, Cleis, but we cannot be sure that they had any evidence other than our own fr. 132 ("I have a fair child, like golden flowers, my beloved Cleis..."), which, as Prentice points out[4] is quite ambiguous. Suppose the ancients, led on (like the moderns) by the similarity of names, mistranslated lines that meant only, "I have a lovely girlfriend, etc."? The use of *ἀγαπάτα*, of an only child, is attested elsewhere, but is not invariable.

---

4 W.K. Prentice, "Sappho," *Classical Philology* 13 (1918), 347–60.

That her husband died early: This is based on the presumption that a prominent homosexual lady must be unencumbered by a husband.

That she was small and dark and not beautiful: The tradition seems to have started with Ovid (*Letters of the Heroines* 15.31ff.), who thus explains why Phaon jilted her. He is followed by Maximus of Tyre (*Dissertationes* 24[18]7), the scholiast on Lucian (*Imagines* 18), and the Oxyrhynchus biographer. Plato, on the other hand, calls her "the beautiful Sappho" (*Phaedrus* 235*b*) and is followed, again, by the light-hearted Maximus (24[18]7), by Athenaeus (10.424g), and by Julian (*Epistola* 30). Are such statements any more "evidence" than, say, Homer's testimony that Helen was "fair-haired" or Hera "white-armed"?

That she was revered in her own day as a poet: There is external evidence only in Ovid's *Letters of the Heroines* 15.35–36: "I have a name that fills the world." But, really, this is a reference to the state of her reputation in Ovid's time, not in her own. In certain of the fragments she expresses a hope for immortality as a poet, and we may conclude that she was ambitious; but we have no way to assess her reputation in her lifetime.

That she taught girls in an atmosphere somehow like a school: This is an unwarranted assumption based on Maximus of Tyre and a single word of the *Suda,* which may in turn have been based on a misunderstanding of a line of Ovid (see above, chap. 1).

That girls came from overseas to learn from her: This is based on the names Anagora of Miletus, Gongyla of Colophon, and Euneica of Salamis, preserved by the *Suda,* and on the mention, in fr. 101, of a gift sent from Phocaea. But if Mytilene, as Burn himself makes abundantly clear, was a metropolitan area drawing merchants and their families from afar, it is obvious that girls from other cities must have lived there without having been sent for the sake of any school – as the families of modern business men follow them from city to city where their jobs may call them.

That she taught music, poetry, and various womanly accomplishments: There is no external evidence for statements of this type, yet they continue to be made on the flimsiest of internal grounds. Treu, for example, says "there the young girls learned: fine manners and elegance of dress,"[5] etc. But really, do fragments like 39 ("a vari-colored gown hid her feet, a fine Lydian one"), 57 ("what country wench charms your heart... wearing her country clothes... not knowing how to draw her gown about her ankles") and 98 ("My mother said that in her youth it was a great adornment if one had hair bound with a purple ribbon, but to have hair more yellow than a torch, bound with blossoming flowers, is the finest thing of all") really imply that Sappho taught elegance of dress in a girl's finishing school? All that these fragments say about Sappho is that she had an active concern for grace and fashion in her acquaintances; they have no bearing on the school hypothesis, which may or may not be true, but cannot invoke the direct support of *any* of the fragments.

That she formed homosexual attachments: This may be the only indisputable piece of Sappho's biography that we have.

That she was exiled under Pittakos and went to Sicily: Only the Parian marble stands behind this statement, which it offers along with dates for Cecrops, Theseus, the rape of Persephone, and so forth.[6] It might be true. But Phaon was connected with Sicily, and it is equally possible that a comic playwright invented the exile in order to get her into proximity

5 "... die jungen Mädchen da lernten: feine Sitte, und Eleganz der Kleidung." (M. Treu, *Sappho* [Munich: Heimeran, 1968], 145.)

6 Cicero's mention (*In Verrem* 2.4.57) of a statue of Sappho at Syracuse lends some slight support. But the Syracusan tyrants were culturephiles of the first order. The statue by Silanion (fourth century BCE), or a copy of it, is in the J. Paul Getty Museum of Art, Malibu, Calif.; see H. von Heintze, *Das Bildnis der Sappho* (Mainz and Berlin: Florian Kupferberg, 1966).

with him. Consider Ovid, *Letters of the Heroines* 15.11: "Phaon, you frequent the distant fields of Typhoean Ætna," and 15.15: "Now the Sicilian girls come as new prey for you."

That the end of her life is unknown: Burn wisely ignores the tradition that she leapt from the Leucadian rock – while admitting other information that smells of the same comic sources.

It is striking how similar Burn's biography is to that offered by the disparaged and ridiculed *Suda*. Other scholars draw the lines elsewhere, according, it would seem, to their tempers. Campbell, for example, says that the poetess was orphaned at age six[7] (presumably thinking of Ovid's lines, "Six birthdays had passed for me when I gathered the bones of my parent, early dead..." [*Letters of the Heroines* 15.61–62]), and perhaps there is reason to this, for why would Ovid make up such a fact?

The other letters do not show similar novelistic detail.[8] Still, Ovid's lines seem to suggest only the death of one parent, presumably (judging from fr. 98) the father, and indeed it might be more realistic to treat the "Letter of Sappho to Phaon," in the company, as it is, of letters from Helen to Paris, Hero to Leander, and so forth, as total fiction. In any case, Ovid's source, if indeed he had one, is unknown. Page, treading what seems the wisest course, accepts only the Herodotean story, which, of course, (pace Page) tells us nothing about Sappho herself.[9]

---

7 D. A. Campbell, *Greek Lyric Poetry: A Selection of Early Greek Lyric, Elegiac and Iambic Poetry* (London: Macmillan, 1967), 261.

8 There may, however, be more to this than meets the eye. None of the early mss. of the *Letters* includes the "Letter to Phaon," and neither does P, the best ms. Those that contain it seem to treat it as a similar work of unknown ancestry, either prefixing or annexing it to the text. Of course, if it is not by Ovid, then differences in the treatment of Sappho are of unknown significance.

9 *S&A* 48–51.

In the end, none of the external sources is helpful. They offer mere wisps of smoke, and when these have been blown away it seems that there is no one behind them. Sappho, under their cover, has gotten away.

Presumably we would find some part of her lurking, however disguised and fragmented, in our few lines of her poems–if we knew how to interpret them. All prominent Sapphic scholars have interpreted the poems as straightforward and literal pieces of autobiography; in this approach Page differs from Wilamowitz-Moellendorff only in degree, feeling, as he does, that while the fragments *are* autobiographical they are so few and slight as to provide little or no information. Some have felt that this approach is restrictive and banal, and have found, in concentrating on the artistry of many of the fragments, the presence of a controlling imagination so deep and thorough that one must be prepared for the possibility that the very persons and events in the poems were in some way imagined. The property world that the poems present seems to display symbolic properties far more prominently than literal ones. (Even literal properties, of course, are not necessarily faithful to any external facts.) Lobel's "pure Lesbian vernacular" seems to be a misreading of a private symbolic system. (And, of course, even in a vernacular tongue the imagination may move with freedom.) But we have considered so far only a part of the corpus.

Two fragments (5 and 15) are confirmed by the reasonably strong evidence of the Herodotean anecdote as autobiographical. Interestingly, they present us with a world of literal properties that has little or nothing in common with the properties of the poems thus far considered. In other words, there is a cleavage *within the normal fragments* between those that grow from the private imagination of the poet and those that grow from the public world of sixth-century Mytilene.

Fr. 5 (The Propempticon for Charaxus):[10]

Κύπρι καὶ] Νηρήδες ἀβλάβη[ν μοι
τὸν κασί]γνητον δ[ό]τε τυίδ' ἴκεσθα[ι
κὤσσα ϝ]ọị θύμωι κε θέλῃι γένεσθαι
πάντα τε]λέσθην,

—

ὄσσα δὲ πρ]όσθ' ἄμβροτε πάντα λῦσα[ι
καὶ φίλοισ]ι ϝοῖσι χάραν γένεσθαι
.... ἔ]χθροισι, γένοιτο δ' ἄμμι
.... μ]ηδ' εἴς·

—

τὰν κασιγ]νήτον δὲ θέλοι πόησθαι̣
]τίμας, [ὀν]ίαν δὲ λύγραν
]οτοισι π[ά]ροιθ' ἀχεύων
]̣να

—

]̣εισαΐω[ν] τὸ κέγχρω
]λεπαγ[..(.́)]αι πολίταν
]λλωσ̣[...]νηκεδ' αὖτ' οὐ
]κρω[]

—

]οναικ[ ]εο[ ]̣ι
]..[.]ν· σὺ [δ]ἐ̣ κύπ̣[..]..[..(.)]να
]θεμ[έν]α κάκαν [
]ι.

—

Cypris and Nereids, grant that my brother come hither
safely, and such things as he desires in his heart,
may he accomplish them all,

and such things as he did badly before, may he atone
for them all, and be a joy to his friends ... to his enemies,
and may there be for us ... not one.

May he wish to do ... honor to his sister,
and the ... of grievous sorrow wherewith before afflicted ...

---

10 Fr. 5 was recovered mostly from Oxyrhynchus Papyrus 7 (B.P. Grenfell and A.S. Hunt, *The Oxyrhynchus Papyri*, 15 vols. [London: Egypt Exploration Fund, 1898–1922), with three lines (15, 17–18) added from P. Oxy. 2289.6 (E. Lobel, *Oxyrhynchus Papyri 21* [1952]).

... heeding ... of the little grains(?) ... of the citizens
... again not ...
... and do you, Cypris ... setting aside ... evil ...

Sappho prays to the Nereids and, probably, Aphrodite for her brother's safe return and for a reform in his ways that will please his friends while disgruntling his enemies. There is a reference to past sorrows, in which, it seems, Aphrodite had a part, an implication that his sister has been unhappy with him, and something about citizens. It is possible that the story behind this poem is given by Herodotus, *Histories* 2.134 ff.:

> Rhodopis was Thracian by birth, slave of Iadmon, the son of Hephaestopolis, and fellow slave of Æsop the writer of stories ... She came to Egypt in the company of Xanthus of Samos in order to pursue her trade and was ransomed at a great price by a Mytilenaean, Charaxus, the son of Scamandronymous and brother of the poetess Sappho. So Rhodopis, at her freedom now, stayed in Egypt and, being very attractive, acquired great wealth ... Her fame grew so great that all the Greeks knew by name Rhodopis ... But when Charaxus returned to Mytilene after setting her free, Sappho taunted him a great deal in a poem.

Strabo (*Geography* 17.1.33) says that Herodotus's Rhodopis was called Doricha by Sappho (Rhodopis, "rosy-cheeked," is presumably only a nickname), and the following stanza, evidently the end of a poem, appears to rise from the same affair.

Fr. 15.9-12:[11]

Κύ]πρι κα[ί σ]ε πι[κροτ΄..]ạν ἐπεύρ[οι
μη]δὲ καυχάσ[α]ịτο τόδ' ἐννεύρ[οι
Δ]ῳρίχα τὸ δεύ[τ]ερον ὠς πόθε[ννον
εἰσ] ἔρον ἦλθε.

11 Fr. 15 is from Oxyrhynchus Papyrus 1231, fr. 1, *col. i* (B.P. Grenfell and A.S. Hunt, op. cit. [above, n.10]).

> Cypris, and may she find you more bitter, and may
> she, Doricha, not boast, saying this, how he came a
> second time to her longed-for love. [or: how
> she came a second time to such a desirable affair] ...

Even here some shadows hang over the evidence. Fr. 5 seems to have been written before Charaxus's return, not after, and it does not precisely *taunt* him. Further, Athenaeus says (*Scholars at Dinner* 13.596*b*) that Herodotus was mistaken in identifying the famous Rhodopis with the Doricha mentioned by Sappho. And what, if anything, the fragments tell us about Sappho's character is questionable; Page discerns in them "a want of discretion and good temper," while Lesky perceives "the warmth of sisterly love."[12]

In any case, these fragments are conspicuously different from the others considered. Here alone do terms of moral censure or approval make an appearance: *ἄμροτε* (sinned), *ἔχθροισι* (enemies), and *κάκαν* (evil) are words that we will seek without success in the erotic poems while the most typical features of those poems – maidens, flowers, terms for beauty, musical imagery – are absent here. Furthermore, the viewpoint is not private, but public: Charaxus is exhorted not to love his sister, but to do honor to her, and the mention of *πολίταν* (citizens) at once removes us from the world of inner fancy and directs us to the world of outer life; Aphrodite here is not the benign goddess of the idealized revery, but a deity to be invoked in curses – no longer sweet, but "bitter" Aphrodite.[13] If the other major fragments seem to portray

12 See *S&A* 51 and A. Lesky, *A History of Greek Literature*, trans. C. de Heer and J. Willis (London: Gerald Duckworth & Co., 1966), 139.

13 Sappho's invocation of the Nereids rather than Poseidon may rise from the same preoccupation with female divinities that the erotic poems display, but Plutarch implies that there was an actual cult of the Nereids on Lesbos (*Banquet of the Seven Wise Men* 20; see S. Wide, *Lakonische Kulte* [Leipzig: B. G. Teubner, 1893], 224), and the praise of the Nereids in B 10 of Alcaeus (who normally prefers male

a dreamworld of impossible beauty, these two sound like real life.

Fr. 137, which Aristotle preserves as an exchange between Alcaeus and Sappho, is similar:

> *θέλω τί τ' εἴπην, ἀλλά με κωλύει*
> *αἴδως ....*
> *αἰ δ' ἦχες ἔσλων ἴμερον ἢ κάλων*
> *καὶ μή τί τ' εἴπην γλῶσσ' ἐκύκα κάκον,*
> *αἴδως †κέν σε οὐκ† ἦχεν ὄππα-*
> *τ' ἀλλ' ἔλεγες †περὶ τῶ δικαίω†*
>
> I wish to say something to you, but modesty
> prevents me...
> If you had desire of noble or fair things, and your
> tongue were not cooking up something base to say,
> shame would not cast down your eyes, but
> you would speak with propriety...

The meter is the Alcaic stanza, elsewhere not used by Sappho. Presumably the first two lines are from a poem of Alcaeus to Sappho; the latter four, some part of her reply. If this is true, then strong support is lent to the otherwise unsupported view that Alcaeus and Sappho frequented the same circles in Mytilene and hence that she was probably of aristocratic family; but Stephanus, for what his opinion is worth, denies that the male speaker is Alcaeus, and we cannot be sure.[14] That some indecent proposal has been made to the poetess herself is perhaps likely, but in no way certain from the text. The tone throughout sounds more playful than quarrelsome.

We know, however, that neither *αἴδως* (shame) nor the root *δίκ*- (right or justice) occurs elsewhere in the fragments,

---

deities) points the same direction.

14 Blass points out evidence in Cramer's *Inedita* that this may be a poem from one hand recounting a dialogue between lovers – not necessarily connected with either Sappho or Alcaeus. See F. Blass, "Zu den griechischen Lyrikern," *Rheinisches Museum für Philologie*, n.s. 29 (1874), 150.

and the root κάκ- (evil) is shared only by fr. 5 and one other:

Fr. 3:

]δώσην
—
]ύτων μέντ᾽ ἐπ[
κ]άλων κἄσλων, σ̣[
.́]λοις, λύπηις τέμ[
]μ᾽ ὄνειδος
—
]οιδήσαις . ἐπιτ .[
].́ αν, ἄσαιο . τὸ γὰρ .[
]μον οὐκ οὕτω μ̣[
] διάκηται,
—
]μηδ̣[ ]. αζε, [
]χ̣ις, συνίημ[
].ης κακότατο[ς
]μεν
—
]ν ἀτέραις ε[
]η φρένας, εὔ[
]α̣τοις μακα[
]
—
]α̣[

Little can be done by way of restoring or translating this,[15] but what remains is significant enough. Ὄνειδος (reproach) occurs nowhere else in the fragments; κάλων κἄσλων (fair and good), only in the reproach to Alcaeus; κάκος (evil), only in the poem on Charaxus and the reproach to Alcaeus. Ὀιδήσαις (swollen or troublous) expresses disgust, as does

---

15 J.M. Edmonds's attempts may be consulted in "Three Fragments of Sappho," *The Classical Review* 23 (1909), 99–104, and "The Berlin Sappho Again II," *The Classical Review* 35 (1921), 139–41. He takes it as a reproach to Charaxus (as did Diehl) because of the "elder-sisterly" tone. But really... do we even know that she was older?

ἄσαιο (to be glutted or to loathe). *Λύπηις* (pain) echoes *ὀνίαν λύγραν* (distressful pain) of fr. 5.10. The poem seems to have been primarily concerned with moral judgements, and to have lacked altogether the imagery of "gardens of the nymphs, weddings, and love affairs" that, as Demetrius tells us (*On Style* 132), "are found in all the poems of Sappho."

Fr. 20:

]επι ̣ ε̣σμα[
]ε, γάνος δὲ και̣ ̣ ̣[
3]
—
τ]ύχαι σὺν ἔσλαι
] . ενος κρέτησαι
]ας μελαίνας
7]
—
]έλοισι ναῦται
] μ̣εγάλαις ἀήται[ς
]α κἀπὶ χέρσω
11]
—
̣́]μοθεν πλέοι ̣[
] δετα φόρτι' εἰκ[
] νατιμ' ἐπεὶ κ ̣[
15]
—
] ρέοντι πόλλ̣ ̣ ̣[
]αιδέκα̣[
]ει
19]
—
]ι̣ν ἔργα
] χέρσω [
] ̣α
23]
—
´] ̣ ̣[

The subject, at least after line 8, where a new poem may begin, is a sea voyage. "Great winds" (line 9) and "to the shore" (line 10) imply storm and, possibly, shipwreck. But Sappho seems in general unconcerned with the state and its travails, and we must not hasten to liken it to the allegory in Alcaeus, Z 2. Schadewaldt connects it with the Charaxus affair, Schubart with the exile in Sicily; the fragment offers no support for either view.[16] Φόρτια (cargo) in line 13 reminds us of πολίταν (citizen) at fr. 5.14, an image that directs our gaze to the world of goods, trade, and citizens, which we would expect of Mytilene in the early sixth century. Again, the imagery of the erotic poems is absent.

Several fragments of very uncertain nature may perhaps be included in this group.

Fr. 121:

> ἀλλ' ἔων φίλος ἄμμι
> λέχος ἄρνυσο νεώτερον·
> οὐ γὰρ τλάσομ' ἔγω συνοί-
> κην ἔοισα γεραιτέρα...
>
> But if you are my friend
> seek a younger bed(mate),
> for I will not bear to
> live with (you), being older.

Similarity in subject would seem to associate this with fr. 137 (quoted above in this chapter), yet it has none of the rude and moralizing diction of the latter. It is possible that neither fragment is properly autobiographical, and that both were exercises in a standard theme, the Rejected Suitor dialogue.

---

16 *Sappho* 137; W. Schubart, "Bemerkungen zu Sappho, Alkaios und Melinno," *Philologus* 97 (1948), 315.

Fr. 58:

].[
].δα[

]
4].α

]ύ̣γοισα[ ]
].[..]..[ ]ι̣δάχθην

]χ̣υ θ[.΄]ο̣ι̣[.]αλλ[.......]ύταν
8].χθο.[.]ατί.[.....]εισα

]μένα ταν[....ώ]νυμόν σε̣
]νι θῆται στ[ύ]μα[τι] πρό̣κοψιν

]πων κάλα δῶρα παῖδες
12 .]φιλάοιδον λιγύραν χελύνναν

]ντα χρόα γῆρας ἤδη
]ντο τρίχες ἐκ μελαίναν

]α̣ι, γόνα δ' [ο]ὐ φέραισι
16]ησθ' ἴσα νεβρίοισιν

17 ἀ]λ̣λὰ τί κεν ποείην ;
] οὐ δύνατον γένεσθαί

19] βροδόπαχυν Αὔων
20 ἔσ]χατα γᾶς φέροισα[

]ο̣ν ὔμως ἔμαρψε[
]άταν ἄκοιτιν

]ι̣μέναν νομίσδει
24]αις ὀπάσδοι

ἔγω δὲ φίλημμ' ἀβροσύναν,] τοῦτο καί μοι
τὸ λά[μπρον ἔρος τὠελίω καὶ τὸ κά]λον λέ[λ]ογγε.

This is beyond restoration. But we see in lines 13–15 references to old age – wrinkles and grey hair – and these lines will remind us of Alcman, fr. 26 (P), where he laments his inability any longer to dance with the young girls of the choruses. If it is Sappho's own old age referred to, then lines 10–12 may reminisce of finer days ("gifts and young girls and the clear-voiced, song-loving lyre..."). We see, in lines 19ff., the traces of Eos going to her lover Tithon ("rose-armed Dawn... bearing the limits of the earth... still clasped... husband..."). And in lines 25–26, which are restored from Athenaeus:

> I love delicacy (luxuriousness?), (hear?) this, and for me
> the bright and the fair belong to desire for the sun.

The last line has always been looked at as if it meant something, and many have struggled with it. Roche translates, "For me glitter and sunlight are one society," which is not what the Greek says, and Barnard, "Love has his share in the sun's brilliance and virtue," which is a fantasy.[17] Athenaeus says, "(Sappho) refused to separate refinement from honor... making it clear that the desire to live comprehended for her the bright or famous and the beautiful and honorable; and these belong to virtue." But there is no mention of virtue. Athenaeus is right, however, in seeing what our modern translators miss, that for Sappho "to see the sun" means to live, and "desire for the sun" means "desire to live." Perhaps the speaker is growing old and is relinquishing attachment to "the bright and the fair," as not appropriate for one about to leave life. There is no good reason to assume that Sappho is speaking here in her own person though indeed that may, as Athenaeus implies, be the case. The key word is ἀβροσύνη (delicacy, luxuriousness, refinement), which she does not use elsewhere in the fragments, and we will look briefly at the four things to which she applies the adjective ἄβρος.

---

17 *The Love Songs of Sappho,* trans. P. Roche (New York: Mentor, 1966), v; *Sappho: A New Translation,* trans. M. Barnard (Berkeley: Univ. of California Press, 1958), #6.

Fr. 140.1:

κατθνα<ί>σκει, κυθέρη', ἄβρος Ἄδωνις· τί κε θεῖμεν;

He is dying, Cytherea, the delicate Adonis, what shall we do?

Fr. 44.7:

ἄβραν Ἀνδρομάχαν ἐνὶ ναῦσιν ἐπ' ἄλμυρον

(Bringing) delicate Andromache in ships over the salty sea.

Fr. 128:

δεῦτέ νυν ἄβραι Χάριτες καλλίκομοι τε Μοῖσαι

Come hither now, delicate Graces and fair-haired Muses...

Fr. 2.13ff.:

ἔνθα δὴ σὺ στέμματ' ἔλοισα κύπρι
χρυσίαισιν ἐν κυλίκεσσιν ἄβρως
ὀμ<με>μείχμενον θαλίαισι νέκταρ
οἰνοχόαισον

Do you come hither, Cypris, and, taking the garlands,
pour delicately, in golden cups, the nectar mixed with joy.

All are in connection with gods or legendary figures; two describe objects of erotic desire; two, the goddesses of love and beauty – all of them describe things lost or distant or unattainable. Always and only for gods and heroes (and perhaps for those whom the service of poetry exalts into such realms) *ἀβροσύνη* is the *divine* quality of love and beauty, the paradigm that lies behind every object desired on the dark earth – every *ὄττω τις ἔραται* (whatever one loves).

Fr. 21 seems to deal with a similar theme.

]

—

]. επαβολης̣[

]α̣νδ' ὄλοφυν [.....]ε̣.

] τρομέροις π.[..]ạλλα
5]
—
] χρόα γῆρας ἤδη
]ν ἀμφιβάσκει
]ς πέταται διώκων
9]
—
]τας ἀγαύας
]ẹα, λάβοισα
] ἄεισον ἄμμι
13 τὰν ἰόκολπον.]
—
]ρ̣ων μάλιστα
]ας π[λ]άναται

> lamentation... with trembling (limbs?)... the skin old already... encompasses... (Eros?) flees (the old?) pursuing (the young?)... of the noble girl... taking the (lyre?)... sing for me the violet-breasted one... especially... wanders...

Again, a speaker who appears to be old reflects on old age and on the fact that Eros is for the young, then finds in songs of youth and beauty a nostalgic pleasure. These two fragments – 58 and 21 – constitute our only evidence that Sappho herself lived to old age.

Several short fragments have been made much of by biographical critics, on the (rather weak) basis of the testimonium of Maximus of Tyre (*Orations* 18.9):

> What his rival craftsmen, Prodicus, Gorgias, Thrasymachus, and Protagoras were to Socrates, that Gorgo and Andromeda were to Sappho, who sometimes takes them to task, and at others refutes them and dissembles with them exactly like Socrates.

It is probable that these remarks were based on Sappho's poems rather than on any independent biographical source; in fact, they may have been based on some of the very fragments we have.

Fr. 131:

Ἄτθι, σοὶ δ' ἔμεθεν μὲν ἀπήχθετο
φροντίσδην, ἐπὶ δ' Ἀνδρομέδαν πόται

Atthis, it has become hateful to you
to think of me, and you fly to Andromeda...

Fr. 133:

ἔχει μὲν Ἀνδρομέδα κάλαν ἀμοίβαν...
Ψάπφοι, τί τὰν πολύολβον Ἀφροδίταν...;

Andromeda has a fair bargain (?)...
Sappho, why gracious Aphrodite...

Fr. 144:

μάλα δὴ κεκορημένοις
Γόργως

... to those who have had enough of Gorgo...

Fr. 155:

πόλλα μοι τὰν Πωλυανάκτιδα παῖδα χαίρην

A fond farewell I bid to Polyanax's daughter.

Fr. 82:

εὐμορφοτέρα Μνασιδίκα τὰς ἀπάλας Γυρίννως

Mnasidika is prettier than the gentle Gyrinno.

Fr. 213:

]..[.].τ...[
. ..[..].σε εμα κ' Αρχ̣εάνα[σ-
σα Γόργω<.> σύνδυγο(ς)· ἀν̣τὶ τοῦ
σ̣[ύν]ζυξ· ἡ̣ Πλειστοδίκη
τ]ῆ̣ι̣ Γ̣[ο]ρ̣γ̣οῖ σύνζυξ μ̣ε-
τ̣ὰ τ̣[ῆς] Γ̣ογγύλης ὀν[ο]μασθή-
σετ[αι· κ]οινὸν γὰρ τὸ ὄν̣ο-

μ[α .]ε̣δ . ται η κατὰ τῆ̣ς̣[.]...
α̣[...] Πλ[ε]ι̣σ̣τοδ̣ίκη[..]ν
ὀνομ]α̣σθη̣σε̣τ̣[αι] κυ-
]η̣[ ] . α̣τ̣ε̣τουτ
] . νο̣ αν

Lines 2–3 may be a quote from Sappho: "My ... and Archeanassa the husband (or, as later, associate or comrade) of Gorgo"; then a grammarian's comment, that Sappho has used the form *σύνδυγος* instead of *σύνζυξ*; then the commentator is evidently paraphrasing the Sapphic passage: "Pleistodika along with Gongyla will be called the husband (wife? comrade?) of Gorgo." Is Pleistodika the same person as Archeanassa, or, as Gallavotti suggests,[18] should we translate: "Pleistodika will be comrade for my Gongyla and for Gorgo Archeanassa," where Archeanassa ("great lady") is understood as an ironic title alongside the ironic use of terms like "marriage" and "husband"?

Fr. 68*a*:

]ι̣ γάρ μ' ἀπυ τὰς ἐ . [
ὔ]μωσ δ' ἔγεν[το
] ἴσαν θέοισιν
]ασαν ἀλίτρα[
Ἀν]δρομέδαν[.] . αξ
]αρ[...] . α . . κ . [.]α
]ε̣ον δὲ τρόπον α[.] . ύνη[
]κ̣ορο̣ν οὐκατισ . ε . [
]κ̣α[.....] . Τυνδαρίδαι[ς
]ασυ[.]...κα[.] χαρίεντ' ἀ . [
]κ' ἄδολον [μ]ηκέτι συν[
·β· ·κη·
]μεγαρα . [..]ν̣α[...]α[

---

18 C. Gallavotti, "Auctarium Oxyrhynchium," *Ægyptus* 33 (1953), 159ff.

Judging from the simile in line 3 (ἴσαν θέοισιν [a girl equal to the gods]), it may seem that the terms of a wedding song are sarcastically applied to Andromeda and some other girl, possibly the *Suda*'s Megara (see line 12). One or the other of them is called a "sinner" (line 4), and what follows looks vaguely hortatory and reproachful.

Clearly these fragments hint of gossip from within some social group. But it is doubtful that we will ever know what was going on here, and somewhat surprising that Page takes the bait so eagerly, saying, "Andromeda was evidently another Sappho, the leader of a company of young women," and, "There was another leader of a rival society, Gorgo," altogether as if he believes in Wilamowitz-Moellendorff's *thiasos*.[19] Other scholars also bind these fragments within a frame provided by the rather light remarks of Maximus, which, as I have argued,[20] perhaps should not be taken so seriously. We may note, however, that κάλαν used in a moral sense (fr. 133) and κεκορημένοις (fr. 144), as well as the generally bitter tone of these fragments, will associate them with frr. 5, 15, and those discussed with them in this chapter.

Surely, if any of the fragments are likely to be autobiographical in the sense of dealing with unimagined facts, it must be those quoted in this chapter; both internal imagery and our strongest external authorities (Herodotus and Aristotle) give warrant for the conclusion. And so different is the moralizing and emotionally depressed tone of these fragments from the sensuous and enraptured tone of the others that such difference cannot be without significance.

Are these poems not also less interesting than the others? Does it not appear that a flatter and less gifted aspect of the poet's mind is at work here? Two observations must be made. First, that several of these poems seem to have dealt with

---

19 *S&A* 133–34.

20 Above, chap. 1, "Introduction."

heterosexual love and to have arisen from shallower depths of the poet's spersonality. Second, that all these poems seem to show her in contact with the outside world – her historical life, her biography –, while the others show her in that sacred inner garden of Aphrodite to which the "real" and unblessed people and events of Mytilene did not penetrate. To some extent the "historicity" of the poems discussed in this chapter testifies against the historicity of the erotic poems. We have encountered in the two groups of fragments two different property worlds; the autobiographical nature of the one is likely on both internal and external grounds; the symbolic nature of the other on internal grounds *and* through its contrast with the first, which functions as a sort of indirect external evidence for it. That both groups are "normal" in dialect should not mislead us: they do not come from the same life; they do not speak of the same world.

What, then, of Atthis, Anactoria, and Gyrinno? I consider it likely that the historical Sappho, whoever and whatever she was, knew persons with those names. But what relationship she bore to them it is not given to us to know. Perhaps she was the stately aristocratic priestess, revered far and wide as poet and worshipped by lovely young girls. Or perhaps they were the town beauties and she a commercial versifier and hanger-on of their group, who hardly knew them except in her dreams. Who knows, and again who knows?

The few great poems by Sappho we have are ours now to value and understand as we will. The poetess herself wanders, lost to us, in those same mists where Homer lies.

XI

The Linking Fragments

Fragments of Sappho, then, seem to fall into three groups: a traditional, ritual group discussed in chapter 9; a newfangled erotic group whose imagery is to a considerable extent based on the traditional ritual imagery (chapters 2 through 8); and an autobiographical group that describes the world that Sappho shared with the general citizenry of Lesbos in the sixth century BC (chapter 10). The internal evidence for this division is rather strong. Indeed, certain poems in the erotic group (most notably frr. 16 and 31) seem to display implicit awareness of the distinction between the inner world of the religio-erotic hymn and the outer world that brings a sensitive poet to something close to satire. But this is not all; there are in addition some fragments that refer openly to the two realities, comparing them, and judging, always, the inner poetic one as higher.

Fr. 55:

κατθάνοισα δὲ κείσηι οὐδέ ποτα μναμοσύνα σέθεν
ἔσσετ' οὐδὲ † ποκ' † ὕστερον· οὐ γὰρ πεδέχηις βρόδων
τῶν ἐκ Πιερίας· ἀλλ' ἀφάνης κἀν Ἀίδα δόμωι
φοιτάσηις πεδ' ἀμαύρων νεκύων ἐκπεποταμένα.

When you die you will lie there and there will be
no memory of you at all, for you do not share
in the roses of Pieria, but unseen in the house
of Hades, too, you will wander among the shadowy dead,
having flown away (or, fluttering among them).

Is it any wonder that Meleager called Sappho's poems "roses"? She herself calls the gifts of the Muses roses, and also calls girls roses and says that Aphrodite's garden is where such roses grow. This double metaphor provides a key to Sappho's view of poetry that is amply borne out elsewhere: only the poetry of ideal love is true poetry. The woman who had no share of the Pierian roses will be forgotten, and for Sappho forgotten means unloved; also she will be unseen, and in Sappho one sees only loved things – "Love comes in at the eye," as Yeats said. Not to share in the Pierian roses means not to be a true poet; but the symbol is doubly effective: not to be a poet means not to be a lover: love exists most truly in poetry, in the imagination. (In the real world the sight of the loved one can be a nightmare; consider fr. 31.) This woman of no education (for whom Stobaeus tells us fr. 55 was written) has not worshipped in the magic rose-garden of Aphrodite's mysteries; to worship there means to ennoble oneself by loving, which in turn means to write poems, hence to share in the roses of Pieria. The initiated lover leaves poems, and hence is remembered (loved) through them forever; such, as the event has proved, was to be Sappho's case, and well she knew, or hoped, it.

Ælius Aristides, in paraphrasing either the poem that contained fr. 55 or a similar one, says:

> I think you must have heard also how Sappho boasted to some women who were reputed happy, saying that the Muses had given her real happiness, and made her enviable, and that when she died she would not be forgotten
> (Fr. 193)

From such poems also came fr. 147:

μνάσασθαί τινά φαιμι † καὶ ἕτερον † ἀμμέων

I say that someone will remember me hereafter...

and fr. 32:

> αἴ με τιμίαν ἐπόησαν ἔργα
> τὰ σφὰ δοῖσαι
>
> They (the Muses?) made me honored,
> granting me their works.

In the tone of these fragments there is a certain defensiveness, an impulse, ill-restrained, to protest too much. That those other women *seemed* to be happy (τῶν εὐδαιμόνων δοκουσῶν εἶναι γυναικῶν, says Ælius) can only mean that they were successful in the external world; but the *real* happiness, Sappho says (τῷ ὄντι ὀλβίαν), is when the internal world is blessed by the gifts of the Muses. Evidently Sappho said that those smug women *really* should envy *her* – and is this the attitude of one who is successful in love and external affairs? Does it not rather sound as if the Gyrinnos and Anactorias and Atthises gave their favors to those other competent women, and that Sappho raised against such crude success her worship in the garden of the imagination?

The worship of Aphrodite, and the worship of the Muses: it is easy indeed to imagine a conflict between them. But Sappho, the first fanatic devotee in the new tradition of Alcman and Mimnermus, refused to submit to this conflict, and insisted on having them both.

Fr. 65:

.....] . . . α[
—
.....]ρομε[
.....] . ελαṣ[
—
.ροṭήννεμε[
Ψάπφοι, σεφίλ[
—]
Κύπρωι̣ β̣[α]σίλ[

κ̣αίτοι μέγα δ.[
—]
ὄ]σσοις φαέθων̣ [
πάνται κλέος [
—
καί σ' ἐνν Ἀχέρ[οντ
—
..[......]ν̣π̣[
—]

Someone (perhaps Aphrodite herself) tells Sappho that she is dear to the queen of Cyprus and will have fame (in every girl's heart?) after she has gone to Acheron. The sense is, of course, conjectural, but here Sappho's claim to immortality seems to be based on her service to Aphrodite, as in fr. 55 it rests on service to the Muses – the two spiritualities that are fused in the symbol of the rose. Indeed, Sappho once referred to herself as, along with Eros, the servant of Aphrodite (fr. 159), and in fr. 150, addressed to her daughter (as Maximus of Tyre tells us), she says:

οὐ γὰρ θέμις ἐν μοισοπόλων † οἰκίαι
θρῆνον ἔμμεν' · οὔ κ' ἄμμι τάδε πρέποι

It is not right that the *threnos* should be sung
in the house of those who serve the Muses;
this would not be proper for us (or, for me).[1]

It is a poetic decree – a limitation of the proper sphere for poetry – made as a mouthpiece of the Muses; and it is one that would not have been commonly accepted. The *threnos* is attested as early as the *Iliad* (e.g. 24.721), where it is sung round the biers of both Hector and Patroclus. It seems to have been the early type of elegiac verse,[2] and in any case

1 Sappho seems often to use the ("journalistic" or "royal"?) first person plural; its use here is no proof that there were other poets in the house. Cf. frr. 21.12, 24.3–4, 38, 147, and 121.1.

2 See Horace, *Ars Poetica* 77.

was almost certainly a respectable poetic *genre* by Sappho's day. It is surprising to hear that it has no place in the Muses' servant's house. We might recall that Sappho seems in other fragments to deny the propriety of polemical, satirical, and obscene verses also.[3] We can only conclude that the *threnos* is not proper to one who serves the Muses because one who serves the Muses serves Aphrodite also – and sings only of love. Hence the musical imagery, which is so common in Sappho, occurs only in connection with girls, weddings, and praises of the beauty of girls. The service of song and the service of love are the same; they are two aspects of that greater service I have called a symbolic rite in Sappho.

These passages not only define Sappho's view of her own poetic activity, but clearly differentiate it from activities that other people engage in. There is, in fact, a certain tone of alienation; she seems always to be aware that her private activities are of a spiritually different quality, and to resent the baseness of the outside world. Those people who *seem* to be successful and happy, but to whom the Muses will not grant immortality, are successful in the world of Sappho's brother, Charaxus, and his lover, the hetaera Doricha (Rhodopis), of the *πολῖται* and *φόρτια* of frr. 5 and 22; they know nothing of the world of fr. 2, where Sappho performs her service of love and song, hoping to drink immortality from golden cups.

Other poems conveyed the same somewhat lonely message not through discursive comment on poetry, but in the plastic language of symbolic images.

3 Frr. 137 and 158.

Fr. 81*b*:

> σὺ δὲ στεφάνοις, ὦ Δίκα, πέρθεσθ' ἐράτοις φόβαισιν
> ὄρπακας ἀνήτω συναέρραισ' ἀπάλαισι χέρσιν·
> εὐάνθεα † γὰρ † πέλεται καὶ Χάριτες μάκαιραι
> μᾶλλον † προτερην †, ἀστεφανώτοισι δ' ἀπυστρέφονται.
>
> Do you, O Dika, weave with your dainty hands garlands
> of anise-sprays, and bind with them your lovely hair;
> for true it is that the blessed Graces love well-flowered
> things and turn away from that which is not garlanded...

The fragment is filled with highly connotative language typical of Sappho: Ἄπαλος (soft, tender, delicate) occurs only in the company of her most personal and highly charged images: a girl twines garlands around her "delicate" neck (fr. 94.16); they lie on "soft and delicate" beds (fr. 94.22); flowers in the moonlight are "tender" (fr. 96.13); a girl gathering flowers is "tender" (fr. 122); one lies on the bosom of a "tender" companion (fr. 126); Gyrinno is "tender" (fr. 82*a*). Ἔρατον, in its only other occurrence, describes the footfall of Anactoria in fr. 16; ὄρπαξ, the slender bridegroom (fr. 115.2). Flowers, of course, are everywhere, and the Graces, for Sappho as for Pindar, were goddesses of poetry as well as of beauty in general and to be invoked along with the Muses (fr. 128). It would be obstinate indeed to interpret this fragment as the straightforward advice of a simple-minded woman when, as we have seen, Sappho is far from being either straightforward or simpleminded. Surely this is an invitation, couched in symbolic terms, to develop a new spirituality and participate in an entirely new world – the world of art and imagination in which Sappho herself lived. Surely the unflowered things from which the Graces turn away are those women who have no share in the roses of Pieria – but one does not don those garlands lightly.

Let us look finally at one of the most undervalued and misunderstood of the fragments, the gentle and beautiful "song to her daughter," fr. 98:[4]

(*a*)

1 ..].θος· ἀ γάρ με γέννα̣[τ’
—]
σ]φ̣ᾶς ἐπ’ ἀλικίας μέγ[αν
κ]όσμον αἴ τις ἔχη<ι> φόβα<ι>ς̣[
4 π̣ορφύρ̣ωι κατελιξαμέ[να πλόκωι
—]
ἔ̣μμεναι μ̣άλα τοῦτο δ̣[η
ἀ̣λλα ξανθοτέρα<ι>ς ἔχη[ν
7 τ̣α<ῖ>ς κόμα<ι>ς δάιδος προ[φέρει πόλυ
—]
σ]τεφάνοισιν ἐπαρτία[ις
ἀ̣νθέων ἐριθαλέων· [
10 μ]ι̣τράναν δ’ ἀρτίως κλ[
—]
11 π̣οικίλαν ἀπὺ Σαρδίω[ν
...].αονιασπολεις [
. . .

(*b*)

σοὶ δ’ ἔγω Κλέι ποικίλαν [
οὐκ ἔχω πόθεν ἔσσεται [
3 μιτράν<αν>· ἀλλὰ τῶι Μυτιληνάωι [
—]
. . .

].[

παι.α.ειον ἔχην πο.[
6 αἰκε̣..η̣ ποικιλασκ...(.)[
—
ταῦτα τὰς Κλεανακτίδα[
φύγας †..ι̣σαπολισεχει†
9 μνάματ’· .ἴδε γὰρ αἶνα διέρρυε[ν
—

4 Fr. 98, from the so-called Milan-Copenhagen papyrus, was first published by A. Vogliano; fr. 98*b* in "Nuove Strofe di Saffo," *Philologus* 93 (1939), 277–86; fr. 98*a* in *Sappho: una nuova ode della poetessa* (Milan: Ariel, 1941). I give Page's text (*S&A* 97ff.) except for line 6 where I prefer Lobel's emendation.

(*a*)

For she who bore me used to say that in her youth it was a great adornment for a girl to have her hair bound with a purple ribbon. But it is better to have hair more yellow than a torch, bound up with wreaths of blossoming flowers (or, but it is better for a girl who has hair more yellow than a torch to bind it etc). Just now ... a gay ribbon from Sardis ...

(*b*)

I do not know whence will come a gay ribbon for you Cleis; but for a Mytilenaean ...

...

These relics of Kleanactidas ... the fugitive ...

government (?) ... For these wasted terribly away ...

We cannot be sure that 98*a* and 98*b* belong to the same poem. Lines 98*b*.1–3 stood at the bottom of the column (beneath 98*a*.1–12 and 98*b*.4–9), with dashes before each line in the left-hand margin. This peculiar notation has led to their insertion in the gap between 98*a* and 98*b*, on the presumption that they may have been omitted accidentally from 98*a* and appended later. We may, then, have one poem in 98*a*.1–12 and 98*b*.1–3, and another in 98*b*.4–9. The marginal ἀνω (above), which would be expected, however, is missing. And, indeed, 98*b*.1–3 is as strongly bound to 98*b*.4–9 by its mention of Mytilene (the *only* one in the fragments) and the latter's reference to government and Kleanaktidas, as it is bound to 98*a*.1–12 by the shared imagery of the hair ribbon. We do not know, but 98*b*.1–3 seems rather to bind the other two together, and it is for the time being best to proceed on the assumption that we have here one poem. As for the placing of lines 98*b*.1–3, it is not terribly important whether they come before or after 98*b*.4–9, and I follow the consensus in placing them before and doing without the missing ἀνω.

The lines are usually interpreted as belonging to a poem written in exile: Sappho and Cleis are in Sicily, where the rich garments of Lydia are not available as they were in Mytilene, and the mother consoles her daughter, who wants a pretty headband, with the thought that flowers would be better anyway. But the exile mentioned might just as well (perhaps better) be that of Kleanactidas, i.e., Myrsilus. It is equally plausible that for unknown reasons, possibly involved with the political references in the last stanza (sumptuary laws passed by Pittacus?), Sappho is unable to get her customary luxuries in Mytilene and suggests an alternative to Cleis.

Whatever the political circumstances may have been (and who knows?), such considerations fail as usual to deal with the poem as a poem. This fragment is linked as strongly as possible to both the worlds of Sappho's "normal" poems; references to politics link it to the public world of Mytilene, and Sappho's most basic and pervasive symbol – flowers for binding in a girl's hair – place it in the private and symbolic world of the mysteries of Aphrodite. One must be interested in politics first and poetry a poor second to interpret this poem in the light of the Parian Chronicle and not in the light of fr. 81*b* and others.

The central action of the poem is the typically Sapphic presentation of conflicting realities: the familiar antinomy between the public and the private worlds. The imported Lydian ribbon, like the Lydian armaments of fr. 16, represents the public world of goods, citizens, and ships that the autobiographical fragments portrayed; over against it Sappho sets the central image of her religio-erotic poems, flowers for a girls hair, expressing symbolically what the generalization *ὄττω τις ἔραται* conveyed in fr. 16. The exhortation that Dika received in fr. 81*b* – to enter the garden of the imagination where the Muses and Aphrodite tend the blossoms of songs and loves – is followed by an ugly picture of the alternative – the outside world of Mytilenaean politics, exile, and Kleanax's son. The latter is the overbearing and sinister masculine world – identified by the *only* male name in the fragments; the former, the gentle and cloistered world of women. It is desire for Lydian imports that embroils one in the problems of the outside world; peace in the garden of Aphrodite follows from devotion to the beauty of simple flowers.

Fr. 81*b* explained its symbolism directly: to bind one's hair with flowers means to earn the favor of the goddesses of beauty and poetry, i.e., to serve them. Fr. 98, on the other hand, is a *tour de force* of immense subtlety. As in fr. 16, Sappho toys with the conventions of the choral song to emphasize, by contrast with the sweep and size of choral technique, the stronger delicacy of her own preoccupation with Anactoria's footstep. As in fr. 31, she uses the conventions of public wedding song to set off the extreme privacy of her own emotions, and as in fr. 2, she disguises as a conventional invocation the symbolic picture of her relationship with love. Thus in this poem she uses the conventions of a mother's defensive response to a request from her child to present a plea for the beauty of poetry. The smoothness with which the pieces of the disguise are put together is perhaps greater than for any other poem; everything follows reasonably from the possibly fictitious, but totally believable request of a young girl for a pretty ribbon: "My mother advised ribbons, but I chose[5] to wear flowers in my hair, and would wish the same for you; but you want a ribbon now, and I do not even know where I can get one, for the ugly business of politics blights our world."

The lightness with which the picture is sketched, the gentleness of the exhortation, does not make it any less likely, only more to be admired. The world of beauty, of the Muses,

5 In paraphrasing thus I prefer to think that in line 6 Sappho gives her own view as distinct from her mother's; it might, however, be a continuation of her mother's advice.

the Graces, and Aphrodite, is sketched in one sure and delicate stroke: it is the world where a girl wears flowers in hair more yellow than a torch. There is no care, no age, no death; a flower is a girl is a poem, and a poem is young forever. Outside the door of the house where the Muses' servant lives, ordinary men are singing the *threnos* as they waste away beneath the heel of Kleanax's son.[6]

---

6 It is probable that fr. 71 was a poem of this type also.

]μισσε Μίκα
]ελα[. . . .]λά σ᾽ ἔγωὐκ ἐάσω
]ν̣ φιλότ[ατ᾽] ἤλεο Πενθιλήαν̣[
]δα κα̣[κό]τροπ᾽, ἄμμα[
] μέλ̣[ος] τι γλύκερον .[
]α μελλιχόφων[
]δει, λίγυραι δ᾽ ἄη[
] δροσ[ό]εσσα[
. . .

The girl Mika is reproached for choosing the friendship of ladies descended from Penthilus (the legendary leader of the Æolic migration to Lesbos). The Penthelidae were even more immersed in Lesbian politics than the Kleanactidae – and even more stained by it. In Sappho's day Pittacus married into the family. It seems that they were all the same to Sappho, and that she exhorted her friends not to become involved in politics at all; and that they were not impressed by her advice. In fr. 71, as in fr. 98, it seems, the world of politics was contrasted to the world of "sweet song … gentle-voiced … clear-sounding" (lines 5–8), which Mika, ill-advisedly, had abandoned.

XII

Varia

Sappho's Date in Lesbian History

Scholarly approximation of the dates of Sappho's life range from about 630–570 BCE to 612–555 BCE. The specific date 612 is given by the *Suda* (in the first notice on Sappho). Another specific date, of 598, is given both by the Parian Marble and in Eusebius's *Chronicle*.[1] None of these is a good source, but they are what we have to work with. The ancient custom was to give just one date where we would give two, and unfortunately there is some ambiguity about what that one date meant. It seems that it did not mean birth. Usually it is interpreted as a *floruit*, "was flourishing," which traditionally meant "was forty years old." There is also the matter of *Olympiads;* when the *Suda* says 612 it means the four-year period 612–609. In that case Sappho may have been born as early as 652 BCE, a date that in general seems a bit too early. So perhaps a slightly sloppy researcher might be using *floruit* to mean "was born" rather than "was at full flourishing" – in which case the 612–555 dating follows. This period in Lesbos can be briefly described.

In many Greek states (for example, Corinthia and Samos) the traditional aristocratic oligarchies had been displaced by the (usually demagogic and economically progressive) tyrants whose reigns prepared the way for the democracies of the fifth century. In perhaps 610 BCE one Melanchros disrupted the ruling clique of Mytilene (the Penthelidai) and

1 Ancient sources on Sappho's life are gathered by Edmonds in *LG* 1.140–81.

briefly ruled as tyrant, until he was overthrown in turn by a counterrevolution of nobles led by Pittacus (one of the Seven Wise Men of Greek archaic tradition), and some version of oligarchy was restored. In about 606 an expanding Athens took thought for the first time of the wheat supplies from the Black Sea area and attacked the small Mytilenaean stronghold of Sigeon on the Trojan Plain at the mouth of the Hellespont. Pittacus led the Mytilenaean forces (among whom was the poet Alcaeus) and killed the Athenian general in single combat. Nevertheless, when the dispute, after some years, was referred to Periander of Corinth for judgement, he upheld the Athenian claim. A second aspiring tyrant, Myrsilus, descendant of Kleanax, rode in on the unrest with the support of the former anti-tyrant Pittacus, whose fortunes, after the loss of Sigeon, may have been in eclipse. The noble faction, including Alcaeus, was driven into exile at nearby Pyrrha (fr. 98 may somehow refer to this period) where, when Myrsilus attacked them, he probably died. Pittacus was now, however, estranged from the other nobles by his support of Myrsilus and was himself declared dictator by the anti-oligarchic crowds. He drove the noble faction off of Lesbos altogether this time. (Sappho's exile to Sicily, if indeed it existed, may belong here. The date is perhaps 590.) For ten years Pittacus held power, fending off an alliance of the exiled nobles with the Lydian king Croesus, and is credited with altering through diplomacy Lydian plans to conquer the Æolic islands. Resigning his office in perhaps 580, he lived for ten more years and gained a reputation as a wise man. In what manner the Mytilenaean government continued after his death is unknown. This series of events is referred to only once in the fragments of Sappho.

The Size of the Sapphic Corpus

One recent guess (Barnstone's) refers to "the more than five hundred poems by Sappho," but this figure will hardly do. It is apparently the result of multiplying nine (the number of Sapphic books according to Tullius Laurea and the *Suda*) by 1,320, the number of lines in book one according to a Pindaric scholiast[2] and an Oxyrhynchus Papyrus,[3] and dividing by twenty-two, the average number of lines in the first two odes. But there are better ways to approach it. First of all, if our bibliographical fragment (fr. 103) describes Book 8, as Page argues, then that book had only about 136 lines. Book one survives in more fragments than any other and was composed in the stanza named for Sappho and should hardly be taken as the norm – it was very likely the longest of the books by far. Using a mean length between what was probably the longest book and what was probably the shortest (Book 8) we reach a total of about 6,500 lines. If the poems were an average of twenty lines long (which seems as likely as any figure), we have a total of 325 poems – which may still seem surprisingly large. If, on the other hand, we are not convinced that fr. 103 describes Book 8, we will still note that nearly a third of our extant intelligible lines belong to Book 1; perhaps, then, Book 1 comprised as much as a third of the original work. This assumption leads to a total of 3,960 lines and 198 poems. These two pairs of figures may stand as somewhat nervous high and low limits.

---

2 *Scholia Vetera in Pindari Carmina,* ed. A. B. Drachmann, vol. 2: Scholia in Pythionicas (Leipzig: B. G. Teubner, 1910), 5–6.

3 Oxyrhynchus Papyrus 2076.

Myth and Religion in Sappho

The following testimonials have come down:

Scholiast Ap. Rhod. 4.57:

> Concerning the love of Selene, Sappho and Nicander in the second book of the *Europa* write, and it is said that Selene comes to Endymion in this (the Latmian) cave...

Aulus Gellius, *Attic Nights* 20.7:

> Homer says that (Niobe) had six sons and six daughters; Euripides, that there were seven of each; Sappho, nine; Bacchylides and Pindar, ten...

Servius, *Commentary on the Æneid of Vergil* 6.21:

> Some take it that there were seven boys and seven girls whom Theseus set free, and so says Plato in the *Phaedo* and Sappho in her lyrics...

Himerius, *Orations* 13.7:

> ... like the choir-leader of the Muses himself, when both Sappho and Pindar send him in a poem, adorned with golden hair and lyre, and drawn by swans, to Mt. Helicon, where he dances with the Muses and Graces.

Servius, *Commentary on the Eclogues of Vergil* 6.42:

> Prometheus, after creating man, is said to have ascended to heaven with Minerva's help and, lighting a torch at the wheel of the sun, to have stolen fire, which he showed to man. Angered by this, the gods sent two evils over earth, fever and disease, as Sappho and Hesiod relate.

Pausanias, *Description of Greece* IX 29.8:

> Sappho the Lesbian, learning the name of Oitolinus from the words of Pamphos, sang of Adonis and Oitolinus alike...

Further, the following fragments:

Fr. 135:

τί με Πανδίονις, Ὤιρανα, χελίδω...;

Why, Irana, does Pandion's daughter, the swallow, (awaken me)?

Fr. 142:

Λάτω καὶ Νιόβα μάλα μὲν φίλαι ἦσαν ἔταιραι

Even Leto and Niobe once were friends.

Fr. 166:

φαῖσι δὴ ποτα Λήδαν †ὐακίνθινον† πεπυκάδμενον εὔρην ὤιον

They say that Leda once found a hyacinthine egg, covered ...

Fr. 186:

Μήδεϊα

Medea

Fr. 140:

κατθνα⟨ί⟩σκει, Κυθέρη', ἄβρος Ἄδωνις· τί κε θεῖμεν;
καττύπτεσδε, κόραι, καὶ κατερείκεσθε κίθωνας.

He is dying, Kytherea, the delicate Adonis, what shall we do?
Beat your breasts, O maidens, and rend your garments.

Fr. 168:

ὦ τὸν Ἄδωνιν

Oh, for Adonis

That Sappho should have been interested in the immensely rich and expressive symbols and images of mythology is no surprise; many points in our meager evidence, however, are difficult to account for. Were the stories of Selene and Endymion, Leto and Niobe, Theseus and the Minotaur, and Prometheus's theft of fire, narrated in extended "epyllia" of the type of fr. 44? If so, then fr. 44 is probably not a wedding song and surely the overall impression of the corpus would change if to our three types of poems we added another, the pure mythical narrative. P. Fouad 239 may provide us with a second poem of that type, numbered by Lobel and Page as Alc. 304:[4]

col. i	*col. ii*
]σανορες̣ ̣ ̣[	
]μ̣αι τὸν ἔτικτε Κόω ̣[	. . .
Κρ]ονίδαι μεγαλωνύμω̣<ι>	ε̣μμ[
]μέγαν ὄρκον ἀπώμοσε	και̣ ̣[
]λαν· ἄϊ πάρθενος ἔσσομαι	ρ̣ ̣ε ̣[
] ̣ων ὀρέων κορύφα̣ι̣ς’ ἔπι	ω ̣ ̣ ̣[

4 Lobel and Page attribute the fragment to Alcaeus because in *col. ii* of the papyrus a nu-movable makes metrical position, and this is more characteristic of Alcaeus (five times) than of Sappho (twice). See E. Lobel and D. L. Page, "A New Fragment of Æolic Verse," *The Classical Quarterly,* n.s., 2.1/2 (1952), 1–3. But as Treu points out (*Sappho* [Munich: Heimeran, 1968], 163), three of the Alcaic examples occur in one papyrus, and one more such find could alter the situation comparably for Sappho. Further, the meter belongs to Sappho's second book and is not used by Alcaeus, and the subject matter of *col. ii* seems characteristically Sapphic. If the poem occured in Sappho's second book, which seems likely enough, we must again consider whether it was hymeneal; like fr. 44, it is strangely, even perversely, appropriate to such an occasion.

]δ̣ε νεῦσον ἔμαν χάριν·
] ̣ε θέων μακάρων πάτηρ·
]ολον ἀγροτέραν θέοι̣
] ̣σιν ἐπωνύμιον μέγα·
]ερος οὐδάμα πίλναται·
] ̣[̣] ̣ ̣ ̣ ̣ α̣φόβε[̣ ̣]ʹ ̣ ̣ω·

μοισαν ἀγλα[
πόει καὶ χαρίτω ̣[
βραδίνοις ἐπεβ ̣[
ὄργας μὴ ᾽πιλάθε ̣[
θ̣ν̣άτοισιν· πεδʹ ̣χ[
]δ̣αλίω[

... whom the maiden of Koos bore
... to the great-hearted son of Kronos
... swore a great oath
... I shall be forever virgin
... on the peaks of the great mountains
... this bow my gift
... the father of the blessed gods
... the wild goddess the gods
... a great name
... no Eros approaches

Clearly, it is the story of the birth and character of Artemis, and may indeed be a part of the poem on Leto and Niobe, which is mentioned in fr. 142 and in Aulus Gellius; further, *col. ii* may well have contained the description of Apollo as choir leader of the Muses, mentioned by Himerius. Unfortunately we do not know how long the poem was.

Perhaps, on the other hand, these stories were more briefly told, as allusions or precedents forming the middle sections of poems, as the story of Helen is used in fr. 16. Fragment 17 is another example of the type.

πλάσιον δη μ[
πότνι᾽ Ἦρα σὰ χ[
τὰν ἀράταν Ἀτ[ρέιδαι
4 τοι βασίληες·
—
ἐκτελέσσαντες μ[
πρῶτα μὲν περι̣ ̣[
τυίδ᾽ ἀπορμάθεν[τες
8 οὐκ ἐδύναντο
—

πρὶν σὲ καὶ Δί’ ἀντ[
καὶ Θυώνας ἰμε̣[
νῦν δὲ κ[
12 κὰτ τὸ πάλ̣[αιον
—
ἄγνα καὶ κα̣[
π]αρθ[εν
ἀ]μφι.[
16 [ ]
—
[ ]
18 .[.].νιλ[
ἔμμενα̣[
[?]ρ̣ἀπικε[

Hera and, it seems, Zeus and Dionysus, are invoked to stand by the speaker as of old they stood by Atreus's sons in some crisis or other, perhaps involving a sailing voyage. Lines 7–8 suggest that ships were becalmed, and lines 13–14 bring to mind the sacrifice of Iphigenia; however, Hera was not the goddess invoked at Aulis, according to our other versions of that story. The suggestion in τυίδ’ (hither), line 7, is that the sojourn of part of the fleet at Lesbos on the way home from Troy is the subject. The appeal to Zeus, Hera, and Dionysus (the so-called Lesbian triad) supports this view, but according to our other versions, only Menelaus (not "the Atreidai," as line 3 has it) was present at the time. That it is a propempticon of some kind is likely enough, but to guess at the circumstances would be unprofitable.

The reference to Pandion's daughter (fr. 135) is very likely from an aubade, a little form that one would not be surprised to find was typical of Sappho; compare frr. 123 (ἀρτίως μεν ἀ χρυσοπέδιλλος Αὔως [Me just now golden slippered Dawn...]), 197 (Libanius, *Orations* 12.99, says that Sappho prayed that the night would be twice as long), and 157 (πότνια Αὔως [mistress Dawn]). Countless little gems in the *Palatine Anthology* echo and elaborate these themes.

The references to Adonis (which are the earliest evidence of his cult among the Greeks) and Oitolinus are somewhat more complex in their ramifications. Certainly, Sappho, with her interest, however private and peculiar, in Aphrodisiac cults, would have dealt somewhere with the story of Adonis. But fr. 140 looks like the text of a rite, arranged antiphonally for priestess and chorus of girls. There is nothing else like it in the fragments, but the great appeal of its direct style and basic message associate it with frr. 102 ("Sweet mother I can no longer work my loom...") and 94D ("The moon has set, and the Pleiads..."), which are themselves somewhat anomalous and have frequently been explained as exercises in traditional folk genres. Shall we, in the light of this fragment, see Sappho as the nineteenth century saw her, as a priestess leading girls' rites of lamentation for Adonis or, as is more customary today, as a literary dilettante writing exercises in various genres? Perhaps either view is more conditioned by the age in which it was formulated than by the evidence.

The matter is complicated somewhat by the ancient connection of Sappho with Phaon. Servius says (*Commentary on the Æneid of Vergil* 3.279),

> Phaon, when he was a ferryman accustomed to carry passengers from Lesbos to the nearby continental shore for money, once carried Venus, who had taken the form of an old woman. For this service she gave him an alabaster box of unguent that, when used daily, made women fall in love with him. Among these was one who, when she could avail nothing with him, is said to have thrown herself from Mt. Leucates, whence now comes the custom of hiring people once a year to leap from this mountain into the sea.

Strabo (*Geography* 10.452) shows Sappho's place in the story and provides a source for it:

> This rock holds the temple of Apollo Leucates
> and the leaping place that is supposed to cure love
> and where, as Menander says, "Sappho first,
> pursuing in desire the proud Phaon, leapt from
> the far-seen rock."

The connection of Phaon with Aphrodite, with the Anatolian mainland, and with the institution of annual, probably springtime or late-winter, sacrifices, likens him suspiciously to Adonis himself; this impression is strengthened by his violent death (mentioned by Ælian, *Historical Miscellanies* 12.18, and others) and by Athenaeus's testimony (*Scholars at Dinner* 2.80):

> Cratinus says that Aphrodite, when beloved by Phaon,
> hid him among the fair wild lettuces, but Marsyas
> the Younger says it was among the growing barley.

Phaon's name, "shining one," associates him with Apollo (on whose feast day the Leucadian rite was performed), and we may well have, in these scattered testimonia, the relics of an Anatolian dying god, associated with the new vegetation in springtime, with the goddess of sexuality, and with the dying and reborn sun of the winter solstice.

We may suppose, then, that Sappho sang of Phaon, as of Adonis, in his role as a dying lover of Aphrodite, lamenting for him as a devotee of the goddess, and that the Attic comic playwrights with their penchant for satirizing myth as well as history, merged the two in creating an absurd story about Sappho. (That both Athenaeus [*Scholars at Dinner* 13.70] and the *Suda* [s.v. Phaon] associated the story with the *other* Sappho, the courtesan, may show their awareness of its comic origin.)

It would seem that Sappho had a general interest in gods of this type (a quality that accords well, I think, with what we know of her from her poems). Dioscorides, in the *Palatine Anthology* (7.407), describes her as follows:

ἢ καὶ Ὑμὴν Ὑμέναιος ἔχων εὐφεγγέα πεύκην
σὺν σοὶ νυμφιδίων ἵσταθ' ὑπὲρ θαλάμων,
ἢ Κινύρεω νέον ἔρνος ὀδυρομένῃ Ἀφροδίτῃ
σύνθρηνος μακάρων ἱερὸν ἄλσος ὁρῇς·
πάντῃ, πότνια, χαῖρε θεοῖς ἴσα, σάς γὰρ ἀοιδάς
ἀθανάτας ἔχομεν νῦν ἔτι θυγατέρας.

Either Hymen Hymenaios, holding the gleaming
pine torch, stands with you by the bridal chamber,
or with the sorrowful Aphrodite lamenting the young
son of Cinyras you gaze at the sacred grove of the
blessed ones. All things, mistress, hail to all the gods;
we perform still your songs, of the immortals –
we who are their daughters.

Cinyras's son is Adonis, the most famous of the Aphrodisiac dying gods, and Hymenaios, according to Proclus, was a beautiful youth who vanished and was not seen again.[5]

As to the question, what Sappho's own religion was, we are relieved of the obligation to answer it by the great flexibility of Greek polytheism. The Greek priesthoods did not issue doctrines, but myths (that is to say, symbols and configurations of symbols) to guide the spiritual life of the devotees; Greek philosophers, in turn, (who were, almost to a man, religious devotees, i.e., guided by some or other of the priestly symbols) formulated high doctrines for those who might require them. It was not *belief* that was regulated, but certain ritual practices and symbolic currents. Sappho, like many another Greek, developed within the received symbolic frame (and most attracted to its centers of Aphrodisiac power – the cults of beauty, eroticism, youth, creativity, and death) a private religion thoroughly orthodox and yet peculiarly her own, about which enough has been said in the earlier parts of this book.

---

5 See *GMP* cxvii.

Nature, the Gods, and Romance

The question how *literally* Sappho believed in the whole pantheon of Greek mythology is an unsettled one, and it is connected with another question that has piqued scholars from time to time, viz., was Sappho a "Romantic"? Treu, for example, seems to feel that, for a Romantic, nature comes across as a vaguely sensed and vast wordless spirit – in some cases the comforter of the poet (as generally among German Romantics) and in others a symbol of a kind of universal and not altogether unpleasant Melancholy (as frequently among the English). Thus he holds Sappho to a literal level of polytheistic belief in order to rescue her from the purple shade of "Romanticism." "But that here we do not encounter a Romantic feeling for nature is easily understandable. Wherever the gods are present – and Sappho's life is grounded wholly in deep-rooted piety–, the role of comforter cannot fall to nature."[6] Further: "These lyrics, unlike their modern variety, cannot be lyrics of sentiment,"[7] and, "No Sapphic song ends in despair, none closes with a dissonance."[8]

It is true that we do not have in Sappho or, perhaps, in any Greek poet, the true note of Romantic despair, which did not become a standard lyric tone until modern times. There is nothing so glum in archaic art as Coleridge's "Dejection: An Ode." But perhaps no other Greek poet approaches so close to this note as Sappho does. The fact is that frr. 2, 94, and 96 are unquestionably "mood pieces" – whatever else they may be;

6 "Aber daß wir hier kein romantisches Naturgefühl antreffen, ist unschwer begreiflich. Wo immer die Götter gegenwärtig sind – und Sapphos Leben gründet sich ganz auf tiefe Frömmigkeit, – da kann nicht der Natur die Rolle der Trösterin zufallen." (Treu, *Sappho* [above, n.3], 139–40.)

7 "... diese Lyrik, anders als die moderne [kann] nicht Stimmungslyrik allein sein." (Ibid.)

8 "Kein sapphisches Lied endet in Verzweiflung, keines schließt mit einer Dissonanz." (Ibid.)

and that Ode 1, frr. 2, 16, 31, 94, and 96 – that is virtually all of the long normal pieces – end if not in despair then, at least, in expressions of unfulfilled desire; in all of these works the Romantic *Dissonanz* is, in fact, present, albeit uplifted and rendered simultaneously harmonious by a certain wholeness of feeling that is lacking among more modern Romantics. After all, no one is suggesting that Sappho was a nineteenth-century English or German Romantic, but that she was a Greek Romantic of the archaic period seems a safe enough assertion; along with the sense of *Dissonanz* – of being out of tune – we find also the balance, formal order, and restraint characteristic of the age. The *sweetness,* as Symonds says, is there – but it is not cloying like the sweetness of later ages.

Further, Treu's suggestion that there is a necessary antinomy between a classical polytheism and a Romantic sense of the self strikes me as unwarranted. We might compare the Romanticism of the later Yeats, which his adoption of the forms of thought of Irish polytheism had tempered into an austerity at once Romantic and classical – a Romantic feeling, as it were, held within a classical frame. Was Sappho's polytheism any more literal than that? Ode 1 does not seem so. And indeed in fr. 2 is it not the absence of the god, rather than her presence, which we are aware of? Are the gods really present in the lonely moonstruck universe of fr. 96? *Frömmigkeit* – "piety" – seems an unfortunate term to describe Sappho's religious feelings. I would guess (and all such statements are guesswork) that she was a true polytheist (more so than Yeats) and aware of the sense of a living universe, which is the great emotion of polytheism: at the same time that she took an elitist and nonliteral view of myths and personifications – and *also* that she felt that lonely and troubled sense of life – at times breaking into vague ecstasies – that is called Romantic. I would be perfectly happy to use another word, but how else really is one to name the combination of an overwhelming emphasis on the emotions with a religious feeling toward art and beauty?

Meters

In Sappho's day, a lyric poet was not a poet in our sense of the word, but a songwriter (as the tragedians of the next age might more accurately be called operatic composers than playwrights). Most (and perhaps all) of Sappho's songs were written for a solo singer accompanied (ordinarily self-accompanied) on the lyre. A later age thought highly of her as a musician and attributed to her the invention of the sensuous Mixolydian mode (or scale) and of the plectrum, or pick, to strike the lyre strings with,[9] but we can hardly judge, having lost the pitch indications of her melodies. How many, or varied, or interesting these pitch sequences were, we cannot say:[10] the rhythms, or time patterns, however, must have conformed to the meters of the poems (hence using only half and

9 For Sappho and the Mixolydian mode see pseudo-Plutarch, *De Musica 16,* where the information is cited from Aristoxenus; our mss. of the latter, however, attribute the mode to Terpander. For the plectrum see *Suda,* "Sappho," first notice; but the plectrum is known from Egyptian wall paintings of the New Kingdom, and according to Athenaeus it was the *pectis,* a type of lyre (probably Lydian) that Sappho was the first (probably among the Greeks) to use.

10 I cannot agree with M.L. West's statement, "It is a reasonable supposition that all songs in the same meter were sung to the same tune." ("Burning Sappho," *Maia* 19 [1970], 307.) Our ancient sources on music do not, as far as I know, support this. Further, the ancients attributed the introduction of a new mode and a new instrument to Sappho; her own works show a continual interest, almost a preoccupation, with music. Are we then to suppose that all the odes of Book 1 (possibly one third of her works) were sung to one tune, while the varied odes of Book 4 were graced with varied tunes? Had Sappho no sense of the appropriateness of music to words – the *ethos* of music? Would an interested, sensitive, and even innovative musician have sung odes 2 and 31 to the same melody? That melodies in one meter must be similar is obvious; that they were the same seems unlikely.

quarter notes), and these we will survey briefly in hopes that the reader (whether or not with knowledge of Greek) will read some of the poems aloud rhythmically and permit them to sing again their hushed, but still beautiful monotones.

The Æolic meters (as used by Sappho and Alcaeus) differ from other Greek meters in several ways: 1) They never admit resolution or substitution (the replacement of a long syllable by two shorts, or vice versa), and hence the number of syllables in lines of the same meter never varies; 2) they commonly employ at the beginnings of lines a "base" (the "Æolic base") of two ancipitia (syllables that can be either long or short); and 3) they tend to take stanzaic form (especially the Sapphic stanza and the Alcaic stanza), hence foreshadowing in smaller scale the stately grace of the later periodic structure.

The basic colon, or rhythmic length, is the glyconic:[11] x x – ⏑ ⏑ – ⏑ –, or: Æolic base, choriambic nucleus (– ⏑ ⏑ –) and extension (⏑ –) of choriambic nucleus. By catalexis (shortening of the ending) the glyconic becomes a pherecratean: x x – ⏑ ⏑ – –, and by hypermetrism (lengthening of the ending) a hipponactean: x x – ⏑ ⏑ – ⏑ – –, by acephaly (loss of the first syllable) a telesilleon: x – ⏑ ⏑ – ⏑ –; it is commonly expanded internally by the addition of one or more "dactyls,"

11 In what follows I have retained the traditional terms, glyconic, hipponactean, telesilleion, etc., despite some obvious disadvantages, such as the necessity occasionally of using the term bacchiac, which really should have no place in the prosody of Lesbian Æolic. The reader unfamiliar with the articles of A.M. Dale on "The Metrical units of Greek Lyric Verse" (*The Classical Quarterly* 44 [1950], 138–48; 45 [1951], 20-30 and 119-129) would do well to consult them, but her terminology, however revealing of underlying structure, is unwieldier than that of Hephaestion. I use the symbols x=anceps; – =long syllable; ⏑=short syllable; ∧=lack of an element, i.e, occurring before, it indicates acephaly; after, catalexis; ia=iamb; cr=cretic; ba=bacchiac; lec=lecythion; ith=ithyphallic; da=dactyl; ion=ionic; cho=choriamb; gl=glyconic; pher=pherecratean; hipp=hipponactean; tel=telesilleion; asc=asclepiadean.

xx–◡◡–◡◡–◡– (gl^{d}), xx–◡◡–◡◡–◡◡–◡– (gl^{2d}), etc., or by repetition of the choriamb, xx–◡◡––◡◡–◡– (gl^{1c}, "Lesser Asclepiadean"), xx–◡◡––◡◡––◡◡–◡– (gl^{2c}, "Greater Asclepiadean"). Further, the glyconic, hipponactean, pherecratean, and telesilleion, in *their* normal, catalectic, or hypermetric forms, may be compounded externally with various other cola, as, for example, in the Sapphic hendecasyllable, with the cretic: –◡–x–◡◡–◡–– (cr∧hipp).

We do not know what arrangement Sappho's poems were transmitted in prior to the Alexandrian Age. Certain facts can be recovered, however, about the Alexandrian edition, which consisted of eight books arranged by meters (and probably, within metrical groups, by subject matter), with a book of epithalamia at the end.

Book 1 contained the poems in the Sapphic stanza:

–◡–x–◡◡–◡––	cr∧hipp (Sapphic hendecasyllable)
–◡–x–◡◡–◡––	
–◡–x–◡◡–◡––	
–◡◡––	syncopated extended choriamb, –◡◡–(◡)–

Book 2 contained the poems in what has traditionally been called the Æolic dactylic pentameter, but might better be described as glyconic with two inserted dactyls, (or dactylic extensions of the choriamb) (gl^{2d}):

xx–◡◡–◡◡–◡◡–◡–

Book 3: the poems in what came to be called Greater Asclepiadeans (gl^{2c}):

xx–◡◡––◡◡––◡◡–◡–

Book 4: one of the ancipitia from the base of the Greater Asclepiad is moved to the end:

x–◡◡––◡◡––◡◡–◡–x

Book 5: various stanzas based on the glyconic.

(*a*)		(*b*)	
xx–⏑⏑–⏑–	(gl)	–⏑–xx–⏑⏑–⏑–	(cr gl)
xx–⏑⏑–⏑–	(gl)	xx–⏑⏑–⏑–	(gl)
xx–⏑⏑–⏑⏑–⏑–	(gl^d)	xx–⏑⏑–⏑–⏑–x	(gl ba)

(*c*)		(*d*)	
xx–⏑⏑–⏑–	(gl)	x–⏑⏑–⏑–	(tel)
xx–⏑⏑–⏑–	(gl)	x–⏑⏑–⏑–x–⏑–	(tel ia)
–⏑–xx–⏑⏑–⏑–	(cr gl)		

(*e*)

other stanzas not fully recoverable from papyri.

Book 6 is not identified by any of our ancient sources; it may have contained one or more of the meters at the end of this list.

Book 7:

⏑–⏑–⏑––/⏑⏑–⏑–⏑––

The line is difficult to analyse, as the positions of ancipitia (if any) are unknown. But the sound in general is that of an Ionic rhythm, jolly and life-affirming. The second half seems to be an anaclastic Ionic minore. Perhaps this book contained Sappho's poems in Ionic meters.

Book 8: various uncertainties shroud our evidence here.[12] The book probably contained a choriambic trimeter with a typical Æolic fillip at the end,

–⏑⏑––⏑⏑––⏑⏑–⏑–x

and at least one other meter that, at present, is unrecoverable.

Epithalamia: epithalamia not assigned to the ends of the other books exhibited a variety of meters including:

---

12 See the discussion of fr. 103 in chapt. 9 above, and *S&A* 118 n1.

(*a*)

heroic dactylic hexameters

–⏖–⏖–⏖–⏖–⏖–⏑

(*b*)

xx–⏑⏑–⏑⏑–– (pher[d])

(*c*)

xx–⏑⏑–⏑⏑–⏑⏑–– (pher[2d])

(*d*)

–⏑⏑–⏑–x–⏑⏑–⏑–x

(*e*)

–⏑–⏑–x–⏑⏑–⏑–x

(*f*)

the meter of fr. 111 is unclear; Lobel's emendations (based on Bergk), which present it as two short stanzas principally of "Æolic dactyls" (perhaps better: pherecratean, iambic refrain, acephalous pherecratean with inserted dactyl ... ?), are worth quoting:

ἴψοι δὴ τὸ μέλαθρον·
ὐμήναον·
ἀέρρετε τέκτονες ἄνδρες·

γάμβρος εἶσ' ἴσ' Ἄρευι
ὐμήναον.
ἄνδρος μεγάλω πόλυ μέσδων

(*g*)

fr. 141 is equally unclear. A.M. Dale regarded it as "incapable of metrical arrangement as it stands."[13] Again I simply give Lobel's version (of which he says "minime confido"):

13 "Metrical Units of Greek Lyric Verse III," *The Classical Quarterly*, n.s., 1.3/4 (1951), 124.

κῆ δ' ἀμβροσία μὲν ——⏑⏑——
κράτηρ ἐκέκρατ' ——⏑——
Ἔρμαις δ' ἔλων ὄλπιν θέοισ' ὠινοχόησε
——⏑——/———⏑⏑—⏑
κῆνοι δ' ἄρα πάντες ——⏑⏑——
καρχάσι' ἦχον ——⏑⏑——
κἄλειβον ἀράσαντο δὲ πάμπαν ἔσλα
——⏑———⏑⏑—⏑—⏑
γάμβρωι … ——

Miscellaneous meters attested in the fragments cannot be assigned definitely to one book or another.

(*a*)
The Alcaic stanza:
x—⏑—x—⏑⏑—⏑—
x—⏑—x—⏑⏑—⏑—
x—⏑—x—⏑—x
—⏑⏑—⏑⏑—⏑—x

(*b*)
xx—⏑⏑—⏑⏑—— (pher^{d})

(*c*)
xx—⏑⏑—⏑⏑—⏑⏑—— (pher^{2d})

(*d*)
xx—⏑⏑—⏑⏑—⏑— (gl^{d})

(*e*)
—⏑—⏑—⏑——⏑—⏑—⏑—x (lec lec x)
—⏑—⏑—⏑——⏑⏑—⏑—— (lec cho ba)

(*f*)
—⏑—⏑—⏑———⏑—⏑—— (2 ith)

(*g*)
x—⏑⏑——⏑⏑—⏑— (∧min. asc.)

(*h*)
x—⏑⏑—⏑—⏑—— (∧tel. ba)

(*i*)
x–⏑–⏑⏑–⏑–⏑–– (x gl ba)

(*j*)
xx–⏑⏑––⏑⏑––⏑⏑–– (maj. asc.∧)

(*k*)
⏑⏑––⏑⏑––⏑⏑–– (3 min. ion.)

(*l*)
–⏑⏑–––⏑⏑––
⏑⏑–––––⏑⏑–

(*m*)
x–⏑⏑–⏑––

(*n*)
x–⏑⏑––⏑⏑–⏑–⏑

A metrical index of the fragments discussed in this book follows:

Frr. 1–42	Book 1
Frr. 43–52	Book 2
Frr. 53–57	Book 3
Frr. 58–91	Book 4
Frr. 92–101	Book 5
Frr. 102	Book 7
Fr. 103	Book 8
Frr. 104–109	Epithalamia (*a*)
Fr. 110	Epithalamia (*b*)
Fr. 111	Epithalamia (*f*)
Fr. 112	Epithalamia (*d*)
Fr. 113	unknown
Fr. 114	Epithalamia, same as Book 8
Fr. 115	Epithalamia (*c*)
Fr. 116	Epithalamia
Fr. 117	unknown
Fr. 127	Miscellaneous (*f*)
Fr. 128	Book 8?

Frr. 130–31	Miscellaneous (*d*)
Fr. 132	Miscellaneous (*e*)
Fr. 133	Miscellaneous (*i*)
Fr. 135	Miscellaneous (*k*)
Fr. 136	Miscellaneous (*c*)
Fr. 137	Miscellaneous (*a*)
Fr. 140	Miscellaneous (*j*)
Fr. 141	Epithalamia (*g*)
Fr. 142	Epithalamia (*a*)
Fr. 146	Miscellaneous (*b*)
Fr. 147–48	unknown
Fr. 150.1	Miscellaneous (*g*)
Fr. 150.2	unknown
Fr. 154	Miscellaneous (*h*)
Fr. 158	Miscellaneous (*l*)
Fr. 160	unknown
Inc. Auct. 16	Miscellaneous (*n*)
Diehl 94	Miscellaneous (*m*)

Euphony

Sappho may have used a greater variety of meters than any other poet in any language - and most of them Æolic meters, which, as they fix both syllables and quantities rigidly, are unusually demanding.[14] Such a virtuoso display would be foolish for many poets - but this mysterious Lesbian poetess brought it off with no cracks appearing in her armor, shifting with apparent ease among the stateliness of the Sapphics of Ode 1, the lilting smoothness of the young girl's song of fr. 102, the plaintive and fretful experimental stanzas of Book 5, the hymeneal hexameters of fr. 105, crafted with such care, but so lightly, and many more. In our meager fragments we yet find much to praise and much that would reward careful analysis. As Demetrius said (*On Style* 166), "When Sappho

14 We cannot be certain how many meters Sappho used, as Draco of Stratonicea's book *On the Meters of Sappho* is lost.

sings of beauty, her words are full of beauty and sweetness." We will point out a few of the avenues into this melodious world for those who may wish to stroll on them at leisure by themselves.

Perhaps no Western poet has plaited vowel sounds with such consistent delicacy and grace. Ode 1, with its repeated chains of vowel transformations set off by frequent assonances and internal rhymes is a marvel of vocalic song. Line 14 is an example:

> *μειδιαίσαις ἀθανάτωι προσώπωι*
>
> smiling with her immortal countenance...

The vowel series

> *ei i ai ai a a a o o o o*

shifts its diphthongs around the central iota like the undulations of a falling leaf and glides smoothly from the high front to the low back vowels with a pattern of increasing repetitions that drives the series home: *ei,* once; *ai,* twice; *a,* three times; *o,* four – the immortal face has smiled with lovely laughter.

Other passages show less variety and gain from one strong note, such as the repeated alphas of fr. 34.1:

> *ἄστερες μὲν ἄμφι κάλαν σελάνναν*
>
> the stars around the fair moon...

Again, we find delicate frames and jewelwork patterns, as in lines 2 and 3 of the same fragment:

> *ἄψ ἀπυκρύπτοισι φάεννον εἶδος*
> *ὄπποτα πλήθοισα μάλιστα λάμπηι*
>
> ... quickly hide their shining light
> when at the full she shines...

The strong -*οις* sounds center each line like a pivot, framed in line 2 by repeated alphas and upsilons on one side, repeated epsilon sounds on the other, which emerge from the darker vowels like the hidden light of the stars; in line 3 the frame is omicrons on one side of the pivot and on the other, alphas leading into the (again luminous) -*η* of the rising moon. The vowel-rich Greek language lends itself to this type of song, and Sappho took full advantage of it.

Her alliterations are at times no less poignant in lending expressiveness to the verse. Do the pi's at the end of this line

> *ἠράμαν μὲν ἔγω σέθεν, Ἄτθι, πάλαι ποτά*
>
> I loved you once, Atthis, a long time ago...

not lend a pathetic, a mournful emphasis to the sense of time over and gone?

Perhaps no poet has used repetitions, asymmetrically placed within line or stanza, with such effectiveness. In fr. 105*a*, see how the height impossible to attain is neatly and clearly shown:

> *οἶον τὸ γλυκύμαλον ἐρεύθεται ἄκρωι ἐπ' ὔσδωι,*
> *ἄκρον ἐπ ἀκροτάτωι, λελάθοντο δὲ μαλοδρόπηες,*
> *οὐ μὰν ἐκλελάθοντ', ἀλλ' οὐκ ἐδύναντ' ἐπίκεσθαι*
>
> Like the sweet apple blushing on the tree top,
> high among the highest, and the pickers have forgotten it –
> no, they did not forget it, but were unable to reach it.

The second line of the Greek draws the reader to his tiptoes.

And: consider the intensifying effect of the repeated forms of *πόλυς* in frr. 94 and 96; in Ode 1, stanza four the plaited repetitions of *ὄττι* and *δηὖτε*, in stanza five the *τί* repeated in three different forms and line positions – all rhythmically strengthening their contexts *and* leading up to the relentless parallel repetitions of stanza six, when the imbalance of the repetition in the context of human weakness is replaced by the almost ominous perfection of the divine plan or edict.

Of course, Sappho is not so magnificent in metaphor as Pindar or Æschylus, nor so perfect in word order as Horace (indeed, the Greek language does not lend itself to Horatian effects as well as Latin does); but for supple grace in meters, for the sense of dancing and floating, she is perhaps the equal of any poet. Consider the Adonic line of the Sapphic stanza; in Horace's Sapphics, the Adonics are rather stiff and graceless, seldom enjambed or flowing nicely out of the hendecasyllable. In Sappho's verse, the Adonic flies out of the third hendecasyllable with incredible liveliness and concentrated impact, like the explosive end of a whiplash. For examples, turn to Ode 1, lines 19–20; fr. 16, lines 3–4; and fr. 31, lines 11–12.

The longer, glyconic-based, Æolic lines have a characteristic movement, which Sappho's poetry principally has given to them. They begin slowly, with, as it were, a hesitating or dragging step (the two ancipitia), stride quickly through the midline, and end (especially the catalectic, or pherecratean, forms) with the slow and grand pause of a completed pirouette. See, for example, how Sappho has brought out these qualities in fr. 115:

> *τίωι σ' ὦ φίλε γάμβρε, κάλως ἐικάσδω;*
> *ὄρπακι βραδίνωι σε μάλιστ' ἐικάσδω.*

> To what, O dear bridegroom, may I well compare thee?
> To a slender sapling I may best compare thee.

The ancipitia hold the question, in line 1, and, in line 2, the hesitating beginning of the answer; in the strenuous and quick-stepping midline we find the slender bridegroom himself, and in the grander end lines the solemn statements of (line 1) artistic purpose undertaken and (line 2) artistic purpose fulfilled. Lines more varied and subtle than such Æolic meters could hardly be found.

One general sign that distinguishes Æolic verse from other branches of Greek tradition is that it centers around the choriamb. There is a difference here that really goes beyond style and its effects. The iambic/trochaic distinction expands into dactylic/anapaestic, but in all four cases the force is plunging onward – it is committed to the idea of a future, whereas the choriamb, which constantly halts its onward flow and pauses, constantly returning to its beginning, points more to the present, or to a kind of eternal present.

The choriambic meters, with their sudden slowings, like pauses in a dance, after each measure, were at their best in Sappho's hands. In the invocation to the Graces and Muses (fr. 128),

> δεῦτε νῦν ἄβραι Χάριτες καλλίκομοί τε Μοῖσαι
>
> Come now delicate Graces and fair-haired Muses…

can those goddesses not be heard descending from heaven in airy and graceful steps? Similarly, in the asclepiads of frr. 53 and 54 we feel the approach of gods descending from heaven. But when preceded by the Æolic base, as in the asclepiad meters, the choriamb may take a sharper and more nervous tone, as of lamentation. Listen to the famous lines on Adonis (fr. 140):

> κατθνα<ί>σκει, Κυθέρη', ἄβρος Ἄδωνις· τί κε θεῖμεν';
> καττύπτεσθε, κόραι, καὶ κατερείκεσθε κίθωνας.
>
> He is dying, Cytherea, the delicate Adonis, what shall we do?
> Beat your breasts, O maidens, and rend your garments.

In the first syllable of each choriamb we hear a foot striking the ground in a weeping dance; in the last, a girl's head flung back, her long hair streaming. In the explosive kappa sounds (ten of them!) – listen: violent hands on young breasts, garments tearing…

Hardly less remarkable is the rhythm of the weaving hands in fr. 81*b*, or fr. 55, where again the choriambs reinforce a sense of descent (this time from earth to hell) and, combined with the Æolic base, convey in the fourth line with almost painful keenness the doom of endless wandering, flitting like a lonely cry, among the dead.

There would be little point in multiplying such examples further. The reader with an ear for poetry and the disposition to learn some Greek will decipher for himself or herself that "seal of absolute perfection and inimitable grace," which Symonds detects in "any two words of Sappho that survive in authentic juxtaposition... the ultimate and finished forms of passionate utterance, diamonds, topazes, and blazing rubies, in which the fire of the soul is crystallized forever..."[15]

Elegies

The Palatine manuscript of the *Greek Anthology* ascribes three funereal epigrams to Sappho. The ascriptions are doubtful, but there is nothing inherently unlikely in the thought that Sappho may have written some elegiacs. She was, as we have seen, interested in many meters and fond of trying her hand at them – including heroic hexameters. Further, it seems that she wrote poems commissioned for weddings (whether with or without pay is not the point), and she may on certain occasions have accepted funereal commissions also. The Oxyrhynchus biographer gives her a book of elegies, and the motto from the Athenian hydria indicates that some were ascribed to her in very early times, but the papyrus finds have not yet supported such ascription. Book 6 lies open to receive the elegies, if better evidence should ever connect them firmly to her name.

---

15 J. A. Symonds, *Studies of the Greek Poets*, 2 vols. (New York: Harper and Brothers, 1880), 1:291, 310.

Palatine Anthology 6.269 evidently adorned the base of a statue of a baby girl:

Παῖς ἔτ' ἄφωνος ἔοισα τόρ' ἐννέπω αἴ τις
ἔρηται
φώναν ἀκαμάταν κατθεμένα πρὸ πόδων·
Αἰθοπίᾳ με κόρᾳ Λάτως ονεθηκεν Ἀρίστω
Ἑρμοκλειταία τῶ Σαϋνϊάδα
σὰ πρόπολος, δέσποινα γυναίκων· ᾇ σὺ
χάρεισα
πρόφρων ἀμμετέραν εὐκλέϊσον γενίαν.

Although I am a child too young to speak, still, if anyone asks, I say with that untiring voice inscribed before my feet, "Aristo, the daughter of Hermokleitos (Saunaidas's son), dedicated me to the Æthiopian daughter of Leto. O mistress of women, she was your servant; do you favor her, and promote the good name of our family."

Palatine Anthology 7.505 demonstrates a more Leonidian awareness of the hard life of the common man and perhaps should be ascribed to a later age than Sappho's:

Τῷ γρίππει Πελάγωνι πάτηρ ἐπέθηκε Μένισκος
κύρτον καὶ κώπαν, μνᾶμα κακοζοΐας.

For the fisherman Pelagon his father Meniscus has set up his basket and his oar – a memorial of his hard life.

Finally, *Palatine Anthology* 7.489, which if it is not Sappho's is an imitation of her (the name Timas appears in the fragments), and is worthy of its ascription. I append the remarkable translation of E.A. Robinson:

Τίμαδος ἅδε κόνις, τὰω δὴ γάμοιο θάνοισαν
δέξατο Φερσεφόνας κυάνιος θάλαμος,
ἆς καὶ ἀπυφθιμένας παῖσαι νεόθαγι σιδάρῳ
ἄλικες ἰμμέρταν κρᾶτος ἔθεντο κόμαν.

This dust is Timas, who they say
Almost on her wedding day
Found her bridal hall to be
The dark house of Persephone
And many maidens knowing then
That she would not come back again
Let down their hair and all in tears
They cut it off with sharpened shears.[16]

Translations

No ancient lyric poems translate well into English (though Catullus's, lending themselves well to the modern idiom, come closest). English, for all its richness, has not the amplitude of Greek and cannot embrace the extremes to which the Greek poets went. Cowley's remark is justly famous, that to translate Pindar into English is to appear either a madman or a fool. Sappho, among the lyrists, stands at the opposite pole from Pindar; to translate her is to seem (which perhaps is worse) merely dull. That "peculiar and unmistakable perfume" Symonds smelled in every word of Sappho, detectable by every reader with some Greek and an ear for poetry, is not the stuff of which translations are made. Nevertheless, many have tried it, often led on, one would think, by no better reason than that the corpus is small and simple.

Ezra Pound decreed that the prose versions of Wharton[17] would not be surpassed, and the decree has not been broken at this writing. The reader with no Greek may profitably supplement Wharton with the various versions collected in *The Songs*

16 *The Poetry of E.A. Robinson*, ed. R. Mezey (New York: Modern Library, 1999), 50.

17 H.T. Wharton, *Sappho* (London: David Stott, 1887) and later editions; Wharton's versions are included in *The Songs of Sappho* (Mount Vernon, N.Y.: The Peter Pauper Press, 1942). Of course, Wharton and other nineteenth-century translators did not have access to the newly found fragments.

of Sappho by the Peter Pauper Press, and with Lattimore's metrical versions of Ode 1 and fr. 31 (unwarranted textual changes ruin his attempt at fr. 2).[18] But such readers must everywhere beware of translations based on the extensive *exempli gratia* restorations of J.M. Edmonds. Various more or less undistinguished recent versions have attempted to render the fragments in a modern free-verse idiom; they will at least do no, or little harm.[19] Something of the effect of the Sapphic stanza may be found in Swinburne's Sapphics ("All the night sleep, etc." is the best), which, to paraphrase Symonds again, are (metrically anyway) more Sapphic than Horace's.

Publication

Τάδε νῦν ἐταίραις ταὶς ἔμαις τέρπνα κάλως ἀείσω (For my companions fairly will I sing now these delights), Sappho wrote (fr. 160), and so the Athenian hydria portrays her singing to her friends, and so all modern authors have written: Sappho's poems were not written for publication, but for private recitation to the group of adolescent girls who are men-

18 R. Lattimore, *Greek Lyrics* (Univ. of Chicago Press, 1949), 38–39.

19 Paul Roche's version (*The Love Songs of Sappho* [New York-Toronto: Mentor/New American Library), 1966) is absurdly dependent on Edmonds's inflated text, but nonetheless has charming versions of the hymeneal fragments. Mary Barnard's *Sappho* (Univ. of California Press, 1958) also includes several long poems written primarily by Edmonds and must be criticized sharply for indicating nowhere in her text or notes the extent of his restoration, and I for one do not find her short lines a suitable vehicle for Sappho's characteristic long ones. Guy Davenport's *Sappho: Poems and Fragments* (Ann Arbor: Univ. of Michigan Press, 1965), while using the text of Lobel and Page, is in no way as successful as his Archilochus. *The Poems of Sappho* by Suzie Q. Groden (Indianapolis: Bobbs-Merrill Co., 1966) might as well at least be mentioned. And perhaps it is best openly to warn the reader against *Sappho: Lyrics in the Original Greek with Translations by Willis Barnstone* (New York Univ. Press, 1965), which includes a Greek text so miserably riddled with errors as to be virtually worthless; and, of course, the translation is based on it.

tioned in them. But the visual record is somewhat ambiguous on this point.

The oldest extant representation of Sappho is on a vase from the sixth century BCE.[20] It portrays Sappho apparently walking or dancing while holding in her left had a seven-stringed lyre and in her right a plectrum, which is attached to the lyre by a ribbon. Her lips are not parted to indicate singing. On the late-fifth-century hydria from Athens (National Museum 1260) she is portrayed seated with a female friend standing behind her and two others in front of her. Her head is bowed over a papyrus she holds in her lap in both hands. Her lips are not parted. She does not seem to be singing or reading aloud, but perhaps she is, as reading silently to oneself does not seem to have been practiced at that early a date. One of the girlfriends in front of her holds in her right hand a seven-stringed lyre, which she seems to extend toward Sappho as if handing it to her, though Sappho seems unaware of it, rapt in her reading (or possibly singing – though the angle of the head would suggest reading). In this picture, in other words, Sappho is not portrayed with her signature look of holding a lyre and also does not seem to be singing. She may be reading aloud to her friends. A third image is from a white-ground lekythos, probably from late-fifth-century Athens. This is the image that lies behind most modern ones such as Alma-Tadema's. Sappho holds and plays a seven-stringed lyre with her head slightly bowed down to it, though not as much as in the pose on the hydria. She is portrayed seated on Mt. Helicon, with a sparrow, the bird of Aphrodite, at her feet. Of these three early images, in other words, two show her with the lyre, and the third and most famous one shows her seemingly reading, without the lyre, though it is nearby.

---

20 Czartoryski collection 142333, in the National Museum, Warsaw. See M. Reynolds, *The Sappho Companion* (New York: Palgrave, 2002), 67.

In any case, the idea that Sappho did not write for publication, but for private recitation to schoolgirls has had an unfortunate effect on all Sapphic criticism: if Sappho's audience was made up of young unmarried girls leading sheltered lives, then her poems seem more likely to be simple, even primitive, works. Our alternative, namely that the mask that the poetess assumed was that of an older woman addressing young girls, is not mentioned. Yet Sappho knew well the example of Archilochus, who chose the mask of an older man speaking to a young boy, and indeed this mask was a standard one in the lyric age, and was adopted by Anacreon and Theognis also. No doubt most poets read to their friends at times, but we really should take the question more seriously than that.

The belief in an audience of young girls is not, I think, consonant with Sappho's expressed view of herself. The goals implied – to curry favor with adolescents in whom, after all, the poetess seems to have had an erotic interest, and to prepare them for adult life in Æolic society – are far too limited. Sappho never expresses a high estimate of herself as lover, friend, or teacher, but she was one of the first of ancient poets outspokenly to claim immortality on the merits of her poetry.

Πέρροχος, ὠς ὄτ' ἄοιδος ὀ Λέσβιος ἀλλοδάποισιν (Towering as the poet of Lesbos over those of other lands), she once wrote (fr. 106), probably comparing her predecessors Terpander and Arion to the native Dorian lyrists whose jobs they took, and we may assume that she exercised an international judgment in evaluating her own work also, and based her claim to immortality on professional criteria and an educated sense of proportions. Let us eschew this simple picture of a poetess writing for her friends alone, or relegate it to the sentimental grotesquerie of Alma Tadema's "Sappho."

It is apparent, since Sappho's poems survived into the Alexandrian age, that they were published in some broader way than closeted recitation. And it seems unlikely, in light of her open aspirations to immortality, that she left this to posthumous chance; probably she, like any poet desirous of such fame, published her poems herself and intended them primarily for an audience of her peers, contemporary and future, in her craft, and for those others who, while not practicing the craft, are its devotees – the "about two thousand souls" that Yeats says are the permanent audience of poetry. And how different is this from a captive audience of a handful of adolescent girls fidgeting in a boarding school classroom.

But in what would book publication consist in Greece in the early sixth century BCE? Writing was well-established, and papyrus had almost certainly been imported into Greece directly from Egypt since the establishment of the Greek trading quarters at Naukratis – say, after 625 BCE. It may well have been indirectly imported before that.[21] As Kenyon says, "Throughout the seventh and sixth centuries ... the poets were acquainted with one another's works, and enjoyed reputations among their contemporaries. Their poems must have been written down and must have been accessible to those who desired them ... It is evident that copies of the works of all these poets must have existed and circulated in sufficient numbers to insure their continued preservation."[22] Indeed, Polycrates and Peisistratus are said to have had large libraries.

Surely then there were book dealers who employed scribes to make copies of books that were selling well, keeping always one copy in stock to supply future orders; surely

---

21 See D. Page, "Archilochus and the Oral Tradition," and K.J. Dover, "The Poetry of Archilochus," in *Entretiens sur l'antiquité classique* 10: *Archiloque* (Geneva: Fondation Hardt, 1964).

22 F.G. Kenyon, *Books and Readers in Ancient Greece and Rome*, 2nd ed. (Oxford: At the Clarendon Press, 1951), 19–20.

also such dealers could obtain from abroad books they did not themselves have in stock. It is the number of such dealers that is uncertain. Would a native of Eresos on Lesbos, who wanted the poems of Semonides of Amorgos, be able to get them from a local dealer? Or would he have to order from Mytilene, or even from Miletus? We do not know, but really we do not need to know. Sappho lived in the age of writing and papyrus books, when the concept of publication was understood; she had read the poems of distant poets from such books and no doubt hoped that they would read hers and, ultimately, that "posterity," that is, we ourselves would read them too.

Then why are we today forced to deal with these tormented scraps, these "waifs and strays," when ancient scholars and publishers had placed all neatly in order for us? Of course, the handprint of Tyche lies heavy on all our inheritance from the past. But in this case it has been suggested that there is more to it. To the Christians, Symonds says, "to destroy an ode of Sappho was a good work,"[23] and perhaps he goes too far in implying that all "the Christians" were so educated in their zeal. But our evidence, though very slight, suggests that Christians both east and west conducted occasional burnings of pagan works, including Sappho's. The richest fires, most headily scented with the authentic Æolian and Ionian perfumes, have been attributed to Gregory Nazianzus in the fourth century, and to Pope Gregory VII in the eleventh century. Were the roses of Aphrodite, then, cut down by the masculine and celibate god of the Middle Ages? We will probably never be sure. We may only note that such gardening, if indeed it occured, was too little and too late. The seeds of Aphrodite's flowers had already been planted deep in the memory of all Western art.

23 Symonds, *Studies of the Greek Poets* (above, n.15), 275.

Posterity

Many have had the feeling that if we could only see the products of Greek literature between Homer and Æschylus (the "archaic age"), we would find that to be the richest and most important Greek period. But, of course, we cannot see; we have only the scraps of Heracleitus, Archilochus, and Sappho. Dimly, then, we see great moments in the growing mind of the West.

It is common, for example, to say that in that age the sense of individuality – the value of the peculiar and concrete personality rather than the archetypal – was born or invented. German scholars have attributed this new dimension in consciousness to the lyric poets, and especially to Sappho. Jaeger, for example, entitles one chapter of *Paideia*, "Ionian and Æolian Poetry: The Individual Shapes his own Personality"; he calls Æolian poetry, "the voice of pure emotion," and refers to "the marvellous process by which the inner soul of man shapes itself in Æolian lyric poetry..."[24] Snell, likewise, in *The Discovery of the Mind*, calls his chapter on the lyric, "The Rise of the Individual in the Early Greek Lyric," and discusses "personal poetry" as a particularly Æolic *genre*.[25] Treu extends this sense of individualism to include a heightened awareness of individual *objects*, a keener sense of vision, or of the poignancy of vision, as it were – an awareness of what has been called the *Thingness* of a thing...[26]

Truly, the lyrists do seem to exhibit these awarenesses, whereas Homer seems to have been more concerned with the

---

24 W. Jaeger, *Paideia: The Ideals of Greek Culture* [1939], vol. 1, trans. G. Highet (Oxford Univ. Press, 1965), 115, 130–31.

25 B. Snell, *The Discovery of the Mind in Greek Philosophy and Literature*, trans. T. G. Rosenmeyer (New York: Dover Publications, 1982), 43–70.

26 M. Treu, *Von Homer zur Lyrik: Wandlungen des griechischen Weltbildes im Spiegel der Sprache* (*Zetemata*, Heft 12) (Munich: C.H. Beck, 1968), 136–241.

great types of men, objects, and experiences. Neither Homer nor any contemporary or earlier Near Eastern literature contains an assertion of selfhood as confident as Alcman's little poem on the seasons:

Fr. 20 (P):

> *ὥρας δ' ἔσηκε τρεῖς, θέρος*
> *καὶ χεῖμα κὠπώραν τρίταν*
> *καὶ τέτρατον τὸ ϝῆρ, ὅκα*
> *σάλλει μέν, ἐσθίην δ' ἄδαν*
> *οὐκ ἔστι*
>
> Seasons he made three, summer,
> and winter, and autumn the third –
> and a fourth, spring, when
> everything blossoms, and I can't
> get enough to eat...

With playful perversity he asserts the traditional view of three seasons, then at once controverts it and appeals, as the authority for this innovation, not to Zeus who decreed three seasons, but to his own stomach, which tells him with as infallible a cosmic assurance as Zeus's that there is a fourth; really, the whole of individualism as a doctrine and a way of thinking and judging is here already, and before Sappho. G.M. Kirkwood suggests that Archilochus already displayed the qualities in question;[27] and indeed it does seem that if one individual embodies more than any other the great innovations of the age, it must be that wandering warrior of Paros.

Sappho, while adventuring in the new realm already explored by Archilochus and Alcman, rendered her reports in new psychological modalities that neither of her male predecessors had expressed and, above all, welded the new awareness to the practice of poetry with still greater strength of

---

27 *The American Journal of Philology* 79.1 (1958), 74-79 (in his review of M. Treu's *Von Homer zur Lyrik*).

vision. For Archilochus, the combination of the new sense of self and the old craft of verse led to the *genre* of satire – a great enough thing indeed. But when Sappho combined the new mind and the old craft, the effect, or rather effects for there were two, were still more profound.

Sappho's direct influence in antiquity was not the greatest.[28] There are echoes in Anacreon, Ibycus, Pindar, Euripides, Callimachus, Theocritus, Apollonius, Moschus, Bion, Catullus, Horace, Ovid, and hundreds of the pieces in the *Palatine Anthology*. But Sophocles and Æschylus contain none that can at present be identified, and it will be observed that such echoes are most common in the ages of the small poem, the archaic and the Hellenistic-Roman. It is her indirect influence that is massive, indeed, immeasurable, and here her name becomes connected with another poet's.

It was not, however, her contemporary and compatriate Alcaeus whom the ancients associated her with, but the singer of Teos, Anacreon. Socrates tells Phaedrus that he learned certain things from the beautiful Sappho or the wise Anacreon – and these things were involved with love (*Phaedrus* 235*c*). Pausanias, hitting the nail on the head, says, "Anacreon of Teos was the first poet after Sappho of Lesbos to make love the main subject of his poetry" (*Description of Greece* 1.25.1). The popularity of this new subject is well known. Plutarch says that the poems of Sappho and Anacreon were recited during dessert at banquets (*Symposiacs* 7.8.2), and Aulus Gellius describes how, while the wine was being poured, "young men and women were presented to us and sang in a pleasant way many songs by Anacreon and Sappho, and also some erotic elegies by recent composers" (*Attic Nights* 19.3). Athenaeus mentions

28 Two books investigate Sappho's influence on poets ancient and modern: D.M. Robinson, *Sappho and Her Influence* (Boston: Marshall Jones Company, 1924) and H. Rüdiger, *Sappho: Ihr Ruf und Ruhm bei der Nachwelt* (Leipzig: Diederichs, 1933).

their love songs together (*Scholars at Dinner* 13.605*e*), Gregorius Corinthius speaks of "erotic turns of phrase like those of Anacreon and Sappho" (*On Hermogenes* 7.1236), and Themistius magnanimously forgives "the unmeasured and excessive praises given by Sappho and Anacreon to their beloveds" (*Orations* 13.170*d*). Athenaeus, again, mentions that both sang of musical instruments (*Scholars at Dinner* 4.182*e*), and Pollux associated flowers and garlands with both (*Vocabulary* 6.107). That such new subjects (for they were, it seems, new) needed a style to suit them, and found one, was not lost on the ancients either. Dionysius of Halicarnassus cites Sappho and Anacreon among the lyrists as the representatives of the smooth style (*On the Admirable Style of Demosthenes* 40), and this is how he describes it: "...like the flowing of a swift stream...one continuous utterance...(like) finely woven fabrics, or pictures in which the lights melt subtly into the shadows. It requires that all its words shall be melodious, smooth, soft as a maiden's cheek..." (Ibid. 23.5.)

We even hear from Hermesianax (apud Athenaeus 598*b*), that although Alcaeus, too, loved Sappho, he was an annoyance to Anacreon – and it is easy to see why.

Anacreon, like Sappho, wrote of love and young favorites doomed to a world of ephemeral beauty – flowers, music, departures, gods of love; an implicit insistence on the higher importance of the small, but immediate event – an aching awareness of the poignancy of the concrete thing: when Cleuboulus cut his beautiful hair, all joy fell down to the dust with the abandoned locks.

In Sappho, and in her elegant creature Anacreon, we see a major shift in poetic sensibility that grew in importance until it put its stamp on all European literature. The subjects of earlier poets, and of later (for example, early Medieval) poets who had not yet felt her influence – heroism, morality, knowledge –, these had not been dreamed in the magic sleep of Aphrodite.

The Muses gave it to Sappho, before any other poet, to be concerned above all with beauty and with its effects on personality; and this concern subsequently became the mainstream preoccupation of all European lyric art. Further, it is principally Sappho's conception of what beauty is that has permeated all later literature. Her characteristic ways of describing the beautiful became its archetypal images, and have unleashed for thousands of years its central modes of feeling.

The exaltation of the small thing, the concentration on the paradox of immortal beauty lost in fleeting time, the preoccupation with personal feeling – with the joy and pain that follow awareness of this paradox – these are the attendants upon the Sapphic cult of beauty. The contrasting of imagination and reality, the emphasis on Romantic love as the only worthy subject of poetry, are its consequences.

Through Anacreon and the *Anacreontea,* through the *Anthology,* Catullus, and Horace, these mysteries were passed on through a barbaric age that had attempted to destroy them. But everywhere the roses of Aphrodite grew again, spawning their hypnotic blooms in the deep seedbeds of the mind.

When the anonymous Medieval lyrist sings,[29]

O, O, totus floreo
iam amore virginali
totus ardeo novus novus amor
est, quo pereo ...

Oh, oh, I am all aflower
now with a virginal love,
I am all afire, new,
new is the love
In which I perish ...

29 *Carmina Burana,* ed. A. Hilka and O. Schumann (Heidelberg: Carl Winter, 1930), 211.

he echoes, in the newness of his love, most ancient cries of a poetess whose name he may never have heard – or may associate only with devils. When Herrick's Julia walks in her silks, it is Anactoria's footstep that lurks behind the page. When Herbert, bidding adieu to life, says, "Farewell, dear flowers, sweetly our time ye spent," he uses a Sapphic image that has become all but universal. And there is hardly a poem in Heine or Yeats that does not dip into that storehouse of images that long controlled our conception of the beautiful and were stored up for the first time in the poems of Sappho.

> *Du bist wie eine Blume,*
> *So rein und hold und schön…* [30]
>
> Who dreamed that beauty passes like a dream?
> For these red lips with all their mournful pride,
> Mournful that no new wonder may betide,
> Troy passed away… [31]

Examples could be paraded here forever, but as we have promised two Sapphic innovations and have only told of one, let us proceed.

We have considered Sappho's influence on the subject matter of poetry (and, indeed, the subject matter of consciousness); on the basis of it alone she must rank high in any list of creative visionaries. But the matter does not stop there; her influence on the methods of poetry may be equally impressive.

Karl Shapiro once drew a distinction between what he called closed poems and open poems.[32] By the former term he meant those poems in which the wit of the structure and the wit of the relationships between the parts is of prime

---

30 "You are like a flower/So pure and sweet and fair" (H. Heine, *Book of Songs* 47).

31 W. B. Yeats, *The Rose* 20 ("The Rose of the World").

32 K. Shapiro, "A Malebolge of 1400 Books: Six Lectures," *The Carleton Miscellany* 5.3 (1964), 112–13.

importance; the forces that bring the poem to life are not necessarily inherent in its subject matter, but are a structural pattern created for it alone; through symbols, echoes, and allusions it works like a little closed universe or, as Shapiro said, a "gadget" – an ingenious machine in which everything is in better or worse working order depending on the quality of the poem. But the closed poem does not speak directly to the reader as does "open" poetry – gnomic poetry, say, or (Shapiro's example) the poetry of Walt Whitman; it speaks, as it were, with itself, and presents the reader with a functioning and supposedly beautiful miniature universe to behold and, perhaps, to attain some inner clarity from beholding (Yeats's poems were Shapiro's example of the "closed" kind). The terms "symbolist" and "metaphysical" might be appropriate, with in each case major reservations.

The large fragments of Sappho, with the exceptions of frr. 5 and 44, have seemed to us to be poems of this type. As far as we can tell, they are the first such poems ever written, or at least the first on a small scale (since it can be argued that the Homeric epics work this way). This type of poem, the brilliant self-enclosed intellectual *tour de force*, may seem to many to include the works of most of Europe's great modern lyrists – from Dante to Yeats –, and at our present state of knowledge we must say that it was invented by Sappho.

Glimpsed hazily (through the smoke of Medieval bonfires?), her poems seem to give us our first examples of the use of a contrived *persona* as the voice of song – the lyric "I" –, the emergence of beauty, and with it Romantic love, as the proper sphere of poetic interest, and the *structural* use of wit and imagination as the method through which this *persona* expresses this subject.

As we draw toward the close, some words of evaluation seem in order. Many have been spoken, from which we will select a few. "The voluptuousness of Æolian poetry," says

Symonds, "is not like that of Persian or Arabic art. It is Greek in its self-restraint, proportion, and tact. We find nothing burdensome in its sweetness."[33] And Mackail, describing, it would seem, the same quality: "Her fire is cool, like that of a gem." And: "Alcaeus among her contemporaries, Ibycus among her successors, perhaps reach the same level, but so far as can be judged from the fragments, *they do not apply their style to any material with the same unfaltering certainty.*"[34] The Poetess, the ancients called her, as Homer was the Poet, and various poets of the *Palatine Anthology* – including, perhaps, Plato – called her the Tenth Muse. Strabo, with his admirable matter-of-factness, said, "In all history you will find no woman who can challenge comparison with her even in the slightest degree"(*Geography,* 13.2.3). And perhaps it is so.

So, finally, what shall we say on closing? Only, we thank you, lady, whoever you are, whatever the true lineaments of your face behind the veil of time, sister and friend who first and more surely than any man guided us in the dream of female beauty – we thank you, and goodbye.

---

33 Op. cit. (above, n.14), 309.

34 J. W. Mackail, *Lectures on Greek Poetry* (London: Longmans, Green and Co., 1911), 101 (my italics).

PART TWO

The Garden of the Graces

The Survival of Bronze Age Religious Motifs into the Modern Lyric Poem

The love of the Æolian girl still breathes,
and her hot passions, entrusted to the lyre, still live.

– Horace, *Odes* 4.9

The Œuvre

The Sapphic corpus consists today of about fifty pages of fragments of lyric poems from the late seventh and early sixth centuries BCE. These are chance survivors of the winnowing of time, some gleaned from quotations in the works of other ancient authors, some recovered from torn and ravaged scraps of papyrus that the dry, hot Egyptian climate allowed to survive. This slender and partly incomprehensible body of text is of immeasurable importance in the story of our culture. Its significance goes beyond the question of the work's quality – though that has been much praised. Plato, for example, called Sappho the tenth Muse (*Palatine Anthology* 9.506), and Ezra Pound remarked that there was nothing better in literature than the one long passage (Ode 1) that was known when he wrote.[1] The scholar and translator Henry Wharton referred to Sappho in 1885 as "the Greek poetess whom more than eighty generations have been obliged to hold without a peer."[2] While judgments of quality are in general less stable nowadays than for a long time, this one seems to remain unvarying among those who bother to acquire the ability to read the relevant texts.

1 E. Pound, *ABC of Reading* (New Haven: Yale Univ. Press, 1934), 33–34.

2 H.T. Wharton, *Sappho: Memoir, Text, Selected Rendering and a Literal Translation* (London: David Stott, 1885), v.

Perhaps more important than the question of quality is the fact that Sappho's fragments constitute the central piece of evidence for an enormously important shift in human cultural and psychological history, one of a handful of specially formative moments in the Western tradition – what Bruno Snell, in *The Discovery of the Mind*, called "The Rise of the Individual in Early Greek Lyric."[3] Snell meant primarily the first expressions of subjectivity. The corpus of Bronze Age literature and of the literature directly derived from it, such as the Homeric epics, shows only communal modes of discourse. The poet speaks as a disembodied voice of tradition, or of the community, rather than as an individual center of subjectivity describing his or her experiences, feelings, and observations. The subjective voice does not clearly appear anywhere in the world until the Greek lyric age. There it is encountered in the seventh century BCE, in the milieu of the breakdown of feudal landholding aristocracies and the rise of a new competing elite based not on inherited land, but on wealth newly acquired through the opening of foreign markets to trade. In this situation, which was to recur in European history at a later age, the aristocratic tradition of wealth held by privilege was challenged by the emerging bourgeois tradition of wealth held by initiative; as a part of its ideology of personal initiative the new party began to make claims for the reality of the individual rather than the class. Not far behind was the age when artists would begin signing their works and poets expressing their private feelings. This is precisely the milieu in which Sappho lived; one of her brothers, Herodotus tells us, was an entrepreneur who marketed Greek wines in Egypt.

---

3 B. Snell, *The Discovery of the Mind in Greek Philosophy and Literature,* trans. T.G. Rosenmeyer (New York: Dover Publications, 1982), chap. 3.

The early phase of the monodic poem, insofar as it is visible from extant texts, extends from Archilochus in the seventh century to Sappho a generation or two later and from her, in another generation, to Anacreon. In this lineage it is really Sappho who predominates. The Archilochean remnants are very slight, though incredibly powerful in their freshness; the Anacreontic fragments, though more abundant, are already slightly overripe. It is the Sapphic fragments in which the voice of subjectivity speaks most extensively and plainly, and with more self-consciousness in its articulations, than any other voice from a comparably early culture.

Thirdly, the significance of this author in feminist history cannot be exaggerated. She is the *ur*-model of the female artist. Furthermore, she was, in terms of modern feminist trends, a radical. Her unabashed expression of a "lesbian" point of view (named indeed for the island of Lesbos, where she lived) and her direct and fundamental addresses to the question of gender attitudes - such as her reversal of male values in fr. 16 - laid the foundations on which the gender debate still stands.

Finally, Sappho's linguistic usage, along with her personally crafted body of poetic imagery, set the terms for much of the lyric tradition, not only for Catullus and Horace, but down to and including Hölderlin and Yeats. In the invention of the lyrical stance she forged fundamental innovations in the relations between signifiers and signifieds; the new linguistic methods she came up with made possible the hyperexpressive and intensified mood of the lyric, in which the individual voice seems to confront infinity, and have recurred, in a similarly fundamental role, in modern poetry. It would not take special pleading to argue that she was the most influential poet of the Western tradition.

The School?

Sappho is not as misty a figure as Homer – a name known to have referred to a medley of many voices contributing to a communal project over some eight centuries. The author of most if not all the fragments accepted into the Sapphic corpus by conservative editors such as Edgar Lobel and Denys Page[4] was clearly a single individual speaking in her own rather than a communal voice, resident in the city of Mytilene on the Ægean island of Lesbos around the year 600 BCE.

Her work, then, is far more subject than the Homeric corpus to a type of biographical reductionism that can trivialize it by preempting attention to other elements. In fact, a seemingly minor biographical question has exerted a questionable force on various issues surrounding this uniquely important corpus. This is the question whether or not Sappho ran a school somewhat along the lines of Plato's school two centuries or so later in Athens – an elite private institution to which young women of ruling class families from around the northeast Ægean world might have been sent for a finishing education in poetry, music, and cultic observance. Plato's school was dedicated as a sacred precinct to the Muses; Sappho's, if such there was, may have been devoted to the cultic service and poetic articulation of Aphrodite, or of Aphrodite and the Muses.

The evidence on the question is meager, amounting to about three words in ancient sources. The Medieval Byzantine encyclopedia called the *Suda* refers to the female associates whom Sappho mentions by name in the fragments as μαθήτριαι (students). Ovid uses the word *docuit* (taught)

4 *Poetarum Lesbiorum Fragmenta,* ed. E. Lobel and D. L. Page (Oxford: At the Clarendon Press, 1955) [=*LP*].

(*Tristia* 2.365) to describe Sappho's activity: "What did Sappho do," he asks, "but teach young women how to love," or, in a no doubt deliberate double entendre, "but teach how to love young women?"

Early in this century these hints fitted conveniently into a psychological need on the part of modern scholars to tame a certain aspect of Sappho's work. They were taken up by the influential German philologist Ulrich von Wilamowitz-Moellendorff, who, in his 1913 book *Sappho und Simonides,* constructed the theory of the *thiasos,* or private religious organization, which Sappho supposedly ran as a combination of a finishing school and a cultic group.[5] It is generally acknowledged that Wilamowitz-Moellendorff, who refused to acknowledge Sappho's homosexuality, hoped by this ploy to explain away the intimacies of Sappho's addresses to girls. On his view the girls for whom she expresses intensely loving feelings are her students, toward whom such feelings are seemly and quasi-parental.

Wilamowitz-Moellendorff's theory of the *thiasos* prevailed widely for half a century, establishing the direction for generations of essentially biographical interpretation. In this tradition, persons mentioned in the texts were interpreted as historical personages connected with Sappho's school; events glimpsed in her brief narratives were regarded as records of actual events, not as symbolic or allegorical or fantastic. The dominance of this approach weakened in the 1960s, when scholars began to confront more openly the sexual contents of ancient texts. At that time it began to be felt that the *thiasos* theory had been allowed to exercise an undue amount of influence. Not only was it widely perceived, with some sur-

5 U. von Wilamowitz-Moellendorff, *Sappho und Simonides: Untersuchungen über griechische Lyriker* (Berlin: Weidmannsche Buchhandlung, 1913) [=*SuS*].

prise, how weakly founded in the evidence the *thiasos* theory was, but there was also now a sense that it was wrongly motivated, having arisen from a phobia or psychological repression among moderns. Most important, the imagined milieu of the *thiasos* seemed to have precluded serious literary attention to Sappho's work; absorbed in reconstructing a picture of her social milieu, scholars had missed a staggering wealth of subtle esthetic and formal detail. In the 1960s and 1970s, a period when the *thiasos* theory was increasingly rejected, the New Criticism (which dawned late in classical philology) had a brief heyday in the Sapphic œuvre. Significant progress was made in deepening understanding of the fragments *as poetry*. But the biographical question did not go away; the redoubtable Wilamowitz-Moellendorff was not so easily to be dismissed. A later stage of the debate, inaugurated by new evidence, has seemed to revalidate his intuition, or genuinely to validate it for the first time.

The change in terms of the evidence has been primarily the publication in 1974 of a papyrus fragment – Pap. Colon. inv. 5860,[6] known in Sapphic studies as SLG s261*a*.[7] This lacunary text contains a reference to a commentary on Sappho by Kallias of Mytilene, a grammarian of the third century BCE, along with the words "She in peace and quiet educating (or teaching) young noble-women of both Lesbos and Ionia" (ἡ δ' ἐφ' ἡσυχία[ς παιδεύουσα τὰς ἀριστας οὐ μόνον τῶν ἐγχωρίων ἀλλά καὶ τῶν ἀπ' Ἰωνίας), which of course support the implications of the *Suda*'s μαθήτριαι and Ovid's *docuit*. Under the force of this tiny, but significant addition to the evidence, the recent reversal of approaches

6 M. Grönewald, "Fragmente aus einem Sapphokommentar: Pap. Colon. inv. 5860," *Zeitschrift für Papyrologie und Ephigraphik* 14 (1974), 114–18.

7 D. L. Page, *Supplementum Lyricis Graecis* (Oxford Univ. Press, 1974), fr. 261a.

to Sappho was re-reversed. Whereas for a decade or two the *thiasos* view had seemed old-fashioned, it has lately made a comeback. Recently various authors have shown a tendency, reminiscent of an era a half century earlier, to accept the *thiasos* without arguing the point.[8]

Any evidence on this question is welcome, but still it seems reaonable to point out that the new papyrus fragment is not all that could be desired. One problem that has been oddly ignored is that both the papyrus scrap and Kallias's book were written after the age of Attic comedy, which produced ten plays about Sappho's life, one or more of which may have wrongly forced her into the Athenian cult-school mold, as Aristophanes' *Clouds* did to Socrates; the whole *thiasos* theory could have arisen from such a comic *topos.*[9] If we did not have the biographical information on Socrates provided by

---

8 R. Merkelbach's "Sappho und ihr Kreis," (*Philologus* 101 [1957], 1–29) marked the end of the early period of this practice (Merkelbach called the *thiasos* a *Mädchenbund*). Examples of the revived practice can be seen in K. J. Dover, *Greek Homosexuality* (Cambridge: Harvard Univ. Press, 1978), 175 (Dover does not use the word *thiasos,* but "school"); E. Stehle, "Retreat from the Male: Catullus 62 and Sappho's Erotic Flowers," *Ramus* 6.2 (1977), 83–102 (e.g. 96); A. Burnett, "Memory and Desire, Sappho Fr. 94," *Classical Philology* 74 (1979), 26.

9 See W. K. Prentice, "Sappho," *Classical Philology* 13 (1918), 347–60. Let us suppose that no contemporary record of Socrates' life survived except fragments of Plato, which happened to include his declaration, in the *Apology,* that he was a servant of Apollo, and Aristophanes' *Clouds,* in which Socrates is made the headmaster of a school. Would we not all say that he was a schoolmaster in a *thiasos* dedicated to Apollo? We would all be wrong. We would have been misled by the comic tradition. Yet Sappho was misreported by the comic tradition far more than Socrates. Her school may have come from some such source as the *Clouds,* along with ambiguous fragments from here and there. Not a single author who has in the last few years accepted the revived *thiasos* theory makes mention of the problem of comic pollution. This is tantamount to accepting the Christian fathers as sources for Greek philosophy, or accepting Dictys and Dares (or even Benoît de Saint-Maure) as reliable paraphrases of Homer.

Plato and Xenophon, we would surely be dealing with the assumption that he ran a school, as Aristophanes shows him doing. Secondly, SLG s261*a* does not mention Sappho by name, and its authorship is unknown. A moment's reflection on the different value that we give to sources (say, Thucydides and Diodorus) casts a cloud of uncertainty over this evidence. Thirdly, even if, as far as it went, it were accepted, it would still leave unclear the relationship between the activity denoted by παιδεύουσα and the activity of a *thiasos*, that is to say, the shading of the emphasis in the distinction between "school" and "cult." It seems that either term as we know it is inadequate, and that the phenomenon in question may have been of a type that does not precisely occur in our culture.

It is here that Claude Calame's massive research into girl's choruses in ancient Greece, *Les chœurs de jeunes filles en Grèce archaïque*, published in 1977, enters the discussion.[10] Calame provided such a detailed and clearly defined description of the *thiasos* (troublingly vague since Wilamowitz-Moellendorff) as to make Wilamowitz-Moellendorff's theory seem new and positively compelling. He showed that cultic choral societies performed an educational function in both Sparta and Crete, and hence that there may be no problem to supposing a Lesbian parallel to the practice.

Several qualities in the relationships described in Sappho's poems seem to parallel the qualities of relationship between the chorus leader and chorus members in Sparta and Crete and, in short, in conjunction with SLG s261*a*, Calame's work has restored the *thiasos* to currency in Sapphic studies.

In this shift, however, two massive problems have remained unresolved. Choral societies, to begin with, can be ex-

10 C. Calame, *Choruses of Young Women in Ancient Greece: Their Morphology, Religious Role, and Social Functions* (Lanham, Md.: Rowman & Liddlefield, 2001).

pected to have pursued choral song, with its various rules of form and structure while individual lyrists observed the very different rules of monodic song. Sappho's poetry on the whole is of the monodic type and thus would seem to be outside the purview of a cultic choral society. The small number of her fragments that are in choral forms do not seem to most moderns to have been the center of her work – though the unexpurgated ancient edition might give a different impression. A composite picture might emerge of a choral society leader who wrote monodic poetry to express her private feelings about the choral society. Dover, for example, envisioned a school in which Sappho prepared girls to sing in the girls' choruses at festivals.[11] On this view, the comparative lack of choral poems in her extant œuvre might mean that her choruses sang traditional rather than new songs (though Alcman's did not), or that the vicissitudes of posterity have happened to edit out a greater proportion of her choral than her monodic work. But the fact that monodic or private reflections should be the main body of her œuvre rather renders the choral society idea irrelevant in any case.

In dealing with this problem Calame takes the daring path of denying the distinction between monodic and choral song[12] and further implying that Sappho's songs hitherto considered monodies may have been sung by a chorus of young girls expressing as a group the individual *persona* of the poet (as Alcman's choruses seem at times to have done). Whether the distinction between monody and choral song can be so lightly dismissed is highly questionable, and on this point, I think, the restoration of the *thiasos* must ultimately depend.

---

11 Dover, *Greek Homosexuality* (above, n. 8), 175.

12 Calame, *Les chœurs de jeunes filles en Grèce archaïque* (above, n. 10), 127 n171 and 369.

A second major problem with the recently revised *thiasos* model is a shocking discrepancy between the purpose of such an institution, as described by Calame, and its actual effects, as implied in the Sapphic corpus. Calame defines Sappho's function as *thiasos* leader as the preparation of girls for maturity and marriage.[13] The definition is sound in terms of anthropological evidence for girl's societies among modern traditional cultures that have been ethnographically described; Eliade, for example, says, "As for the women's societies, they are always concerned with the mystery of birth and fertility. The mystery of childbearing, that is, woman's discovery that she is *a creator on the plane of life,* constitutes a religious experience that cannot be translated into masculine terms."[14]

Yet something quite different from this seems to have taken place in Sappho's *thiasos* (assuming that there was one). Her poems emphasize homosexual relationships, whereas such groups as those described by Eliade feature mimetic preparation for sexual acts with men. Again, her poems seem to idealize the early adolescent phase (or anyway the premarital phase) of a girl's life – to invest it with a sense of eternality or perfection from which a heterosexual marriage must be viewed as a descent and even a betrayal. Finally, Sappho's poems seem to present no introduction to the reality of maleness at all: men are hardly ever mentioned in them, and almost never favorably. I do not think that a man who married a graduate of such a school would be very pleased with the "preparation for marriage" that it had dispensed. Indeed, as Stehle has pointed out,[15] Sappho's poems seem to inculcate a "retreat from the male" and a positive horror of maturation

---

13 Ibid., 448 n190, 440f., 444.

14 M. Eliade, *Myths, Rites and Symbols: A Mircea Eliade Reader,* 2 vols. (New York: Harper, 1975), 2:285.

15 Stehle, "Retreat from the Male: Catullus 62 and Sappho's Erotic Flowers" (above, n.8).

and parturition. Girls are, in effect, being subverted from the goals of maturity and marriage. The best place for a girl, Sappho declares again and again, is a virginal/homosexual milieu of dreamy symbols from which the real fertility message has been deleted in favor of an abstract poetic creativity. Only the dead male, Adonis, receives positive passion from these tight rosebuds.

This does not mean that Sappho could not have run such a school; it may instead mean either that the public goals of her school were quite different from the private goals that Sappho as teacher actually was motivated by, or that Calame has simply misidentified the goals of her school.[16] In the following it is not my intention to attempt to answer the question (which is still unanswerable) whether or not Sappho ran a school and/or *thiasos,* but to investigate its resonances and ambiguities and follow certain of its inner contradictions into new areas of thought about the Sapphic corpus and whose it was and what it means.

Bidirectionality

The surviving Sapphic fragments seem to express a multilayered religious sensibility. First of all, we see a convention-

16 If a school such as hers was in fact imagined to "prepare girls for marriage," then it may be that we are seeing into something of the inner tragedy of the relationship between the sexes in ancient Greece in the archaic and early classical periods. According to some interpreters of the Bronze Age mythological evidence, Sappho lived not too long after a period in which the male and female principles were in open conflict, both in the temple and in the bedroom. (See, e.g., E.A.S. Butterworth, *Some Traces of the Pre-Olympian World in Greek Literature and Myth* [Berlin: W. de Gruyter, 1966]). Sappho's *thiasos* (if such there was) may be a late cultic remnant of that conflict, and may suggest, in the company of other evidence, that this conflict was never properly resolved and that the tensions resulting from it contributed to the famous Greek preference for homosexuality.

al Greek cult, that of Aphrodite, with Anatolian overtones in the apparently special emphasis on Adonis and similar dying fertility gods. Secondly, by extending the word "religion" beyond the bounds of established cult to include the whole area of psychological experience where the sense of the sacred is encountered, we may say that Sappho seems to have created a kind of private religion somewhat along the lines of European Romanticism, emphasizing organic beauty, Romantic love, poetic creativity, and the sense of a coherent divine female presence (*das Ewig-Weibliche*) overseeing these areas and joining them into a single complex numinosum or a closely related group of numinosa, which reinforce and interpenetrate each other. This much I have said before.[17] Now, in addition to these two levels of religious meaning, I suggest that we can discern the dimly visible traces of a much earlier cult milieu. These traces lead us back to the Bronze Age of the ancient Near East, and may even preserve currents of thought and feeling that were religiously prominent in the Neolithic Age – and which would therefore have a special appropriateness to the female religion of a girls' *thiasos*.

Of the major Sapphic texts, fr. 2 has the most obviously cultic implications. It is an invocation to Aphrodite to appear before her female worshippers in a sacred grove that is described in some detail:

> Come, for my sake, from Crete to this holy temple,
> where is your lovely grove of apple trees,
> and altars are smoking with frankincense;
>
> therein cold water sings through the apple branches,
> and all the place is shadowed over with roses, and from
> quivering leaves a magic sleep flows down;

17 See above, Part One, chap. 2, 3, and 4.

therein a meadow with pasture for horses blooms with ...
flowers, and sweet breezes breathe ...

there, taking the garlands, Cypris,
pour into golden cups, luxuriously,
nectar mixed with good cheer

(for these my friends and yours.)

Elsewhere I have offered the view that the cultic overtones of this poem functioned as a symbolic analogue of the poetic process as Sappho experienced it.[18] In keeping with the pluralistic and malleable character of Greek polytheism, she combined elements of Aphrodisiac cult with worship of the Muses and Graces, the goddesses of poetry (and of adolescent girls). It was in this cultic displacement that the love poem in particular, and the lyric poem – the poem dedicated to the subjective experience of beauty – in general seem to have arisen. In Sappho's work, the primitive or archaic function of the poet as an "inspired oracle" whose "proper work as a poet [is] ... to reveal the god for whom he speaks"[19] has given way to an inspired introspection in which the poet's own creative imagination is the numinous force or transformative power that is worshipped as *mysterium*.

This point goes beyond the "rise of the individual in early Greek lyric," which Snell wrote about.[20] It amounts to a first appearance of the "literary sign" that, as Roland Barthes put it, "mingles in a single written substance both literature and the thinking about literature."[21] Modern critics have regarded this reflexive or self-referential mode of writing as peculiarly avant-garde. The Russian Formalist Victor Shklovsky identi-

---

18 See above, Part One, chap. 2, "The Song of the Sacred Grove."

19 N. Frye, *Anatomy of Criticism: Four Essays* (Princeton Univ. Press, 1973), 55.

20 Snell, *The Discovery of the Mind* (above, n. 3), chap. 3.

21 R. Barthes, *Essais critiques* (Paris: Seuil, 1964), 106–107.

fied *Tristam Shandy* as the first "novel about itself" and thus "a predecessor of modern avant-garde writing."[22] Barthes associated this reflexive "literary sign" with Mallarmé.[23]

It might seem strange to see such a Modernist concept applied to a poet of the sixth century BCE, but it is a critical commonplace that Greek literature underwent in a somewhat compressed sequence something like the developmental stages that European literatures have undergone since the Middle Ages.[24] In both cases the development in question was conditioned by the end of feudalism and the emergence of a bourgeois class with its ideology of the subject. There is, really, no need for special pleading in stating that Sappho, in the Greek tradition, exhibits the first emerging awareness of the mode of writing that would reappear with greater clarity with *symbolisme* in which, as Northrop Frye wrote, "poetic images do not state or point to anything, but, by pointing to each other, they suggest or evoke the mood which informs the poem."[25] Thus certain of Sappho's images[26] function as "objective correlatives" in T. S. Eliot's sense (which Frye explains as an "image that sets up an inward focus of emotion in poetry and at the same time substitutes itself for an idea"[27]). Enhanced through repetition and association, these images at times approach the *symboliste* "sense of a growing richness of meaning unlimited by denotation,"[28]

---

22 See *Russian Formalist Criticism: Four Essays,* ed. and trans. L. T. Lemon and M. J. Reis (Lincoln: Univ. of Nebraska Press, 1965), 25–57, and T. Hawkes, *Structuralism and Semiotics* (Berkeley and Los Angeles: Univ. of California Press, 1977), 66.

23 Barthes, *Essais critiques* (above n. 21).

24 For more on this, see T. McEvilley, "Development in the Lyrics of Aristophanes," *The American Journal of Philology,* 91/3 (1970), 257–76.

25 Frye, *Anatomy of Criticism* (above, n. 19), 81.

26 Primarily those emphasized above in Part One, chap. 4, "The Magic in Action."

27 Frye, *Anatomy of Criticism* (above, n. 19), 92.

28 Ibid., 81.

attaining the status of archetypal signifiers through an infinite regress, or circularity, of reflexivity: the poem expresses itself in symbols that refer back to the making and power of the poem.

Thus, on the one hand, the Sapphic poems show the first emergence of certain self-conscious structures that are basic to modern literature. On the other hand, they seem to reach back to an extremely archaic cultic milieu. It is precisely this bidirectionality that I wish to focus attention on. The Sapphic corpus seems to embody the "sudden replacement of an old problematics by a new one" which Bachelard and other French critics have called an "epistemological gap, or break, or discontinuity" (*une coupure épistémologique*).[29] On this view, she inherited the symbol-system expressing the "problematics" of an archaic cult, but, having herself emerged psychologically from the archaic attitudes, she experienced this system with a new problematics, that of a self-referential and self-validating poetic act. Thus her conflation of Aphrodite on the one hand and the Muses and Graces on the other acts as a bridge, so to speak, across the epistemological gap.

Cultic Background

In imagery such as that of fr. 2, it is of course possible, in the tradition of the biographical interpretation, that Sappho was simply describing what her *thiasos* (if such there was) actually did; on this view the rose bushes, apple trees, cold stream, and so on, are simply recorded from her experience. But here two problems arise: the cups of "nectar" cannot be literally called so, nor can the κῶμα, or "magical sleep," which some have felt suggests shamanic-style practices of incubation, with possible

29 See F. Jameson, *The Prison-House of Language: A Critical Account of Structuralism and Formalism* (Princeton Univ. Press, 1972), 135ff.

narcotic aids, which seem to belong to, or to survive from, a more primitive level of culture than Sappho's.

In fact, the flowering garden precinct with fruit trees, a stream, a bowl or pitcher of some sacred drink, a presiding goddess, a ritual of receiving the drink – both individually and as a meaningfully integrated group – these images had been elements of Near Eastern and Anatolian religious practice and myth for thousands of years before Sappho. And, while carrying with them a primordially ancient tone, they were still current, it seems, in her day in contexts not far from her own.

Turyn notices that a set of traditional Orphic paradisiacal images lies in the background of the goddess's garden in fr. 2.[30] This Orphic afterlife symbolism, in turn, has been traced by Zuntz to Sumerian and other Near Eastern prototypes.[31] It is possible, in following out this line of thought, to read the main images of fr. 2 as derived, at however great a distance and through whatever intermediaries, from the paradisiacal goddess symbolism of early-dynastic Sumer.

Sappho's grove of apple trees, with rose bushes twined among them and a cold stream rushing through, is obviously an image that could arise from everyday life and needs no traditional background; nevertheless, it has one, and the fact is probably significant. Widengren writes at length about the connection, in Sumerian symbolism, between the Tree or Plant of Life, the water of Life, and the Paradisiacal Garden.[32] The Tree of Life grows "near the streams of Life

30 A. Turyn, "The Sapphic Ostrakon," *Transactions of the American Philological Association* 73 (1942), 308–18.

31 G. Zuntz, *Persephone: Three Essays on Religion and Thought in Magna Graecia* (Oxford: At the Clarendon Press, 1971), 385–93.

32 G. Widengren, *The King and the Tree of Life in Ancient Near Eastern Religion,* Uppsala Universitets Årskrift 4 (Uppsala: Lundequistska Bokhandeln, 1951).

flowing in paradise."[33] The complex as a whole is associated with goddesses, especially aphrodisiac or fertility goddesses such as Ishtar and Nammu. A Sumerian text says,

> In Eridu there is a black kiskanu tree,
> growing in a pure place...
> In the foundation thereof is the place of the underworld,
> in the resting place is the chamber of Nammu.
> In its holy temple there is a grove, casting its shadow
> wherein no man goeth to enter.
> In the midst are the sun god and the sovereign of heaven,
> in between the river with the two mouths.[34]

The *kiskanu* tree happens to be a cedar, but the Tree of Life can take many other forms, too. In the *Epic of Gilgamesh,* for example, "vine grapes are hanging there, sweet to look at."[35] In an Akkadian text it is "the flower of the garden."[36] In Ugarit it becomes "an arbor of fruit clustering near a spring."[37] And in Egyptian versions the lotus blossom replaces the twig of the tree as a ritual object. The Tree or Plant of Life, in short, may be a cedar tree, a sycamore tree, a cypress tree, a date palm (or indeed any fruit tree), a water-growing plant, a land-growing plant, a flowering bush, or a sheaf of wheat.[38] There is, then, nothing to prevent Sappho's apple trees, rose bushes, and cold stream from participating in this ancient symbolism.

In Bronze Age contexts this symbolic garden is usually associated with one or another of the great goddesses. Sumerian texts connect it with Nammu and Ninsinna; an Akkadian

33 Ibid., 5.

34 Ibid., 5–6.

35 Ibid., 7.

36 Ibid., 11.

37 Ibid., 36.

38 See, in addition to Widengren, B. Goff, *The Symbols of Prehistoric Mesopotamia* (New Haven: Yale Univ. Press, 1963), figs. 251, 269, 376, 392, 705; A. Parrot, *Sumer: The Dawn of Art* (New York: Golden Press, 1961), fig. 190.

text places the Tree of Life "in pure Inanna's holy garden."[39] The Dilmun myth puts it in the garden of Ninhursag ("Lady Mountain").

Sappho's Aphrodite belongs typologically among these goddesses. As Kirk notes, "she is the Greek version of Sumerian Inanna ... and her famous cult at Paphos in Cyprus, where in Greek myth she was supposed to have been born, marks one stage in her passage from Asia to Greece."[40] The evidence is abundant to show that she did not come without portfolio, but brought elements of her cultic context with her. As Lanata says of fr. 2, "The mention of apples or roses always alludes to the presence or power of Aphrodite."[41]

This goddess's garden, with Tree and Water of Life, is associated also with the myth-rite complex of the Dying God, a subject that seems to have been especially important to Sappho, who wrote a lamentation for Adonis (fr. 140) and whose Phaon and Hymenaeus also shared in the Puer Æternus archetype. In the myth of Dilmun, the god Enki is brought back to life within the garden; in the Tammuz liturgies (ancestors of the lament for Adonis) that god is restored to life in the garden through a ritual of libation – which brings up a consideration of Aphrodite's pouring of nectar into golden cups.

Van Buren has analyzed the Sumerian icon of the Flowing Vase into three types, two of which involve divine figures, either gods or goddesses, holding a vessel that contains the

---

39 Widengren, *The King and the Tree of Life in Ancient Near Eastern Religion* (above, n.32), 9–10.

40 G.S. Kirk, *The Nature of Greek Myths* (New York: Penguin, 1974), 258.

41 G. Lanata, "Sappho's Amatory Language," in *Reading Sappho: Contemporary Approaches*, ed. E. Greene (Berkeley and Los Angeles: Univ. of California Press, 1996), 16.

"Water of Life."[42] In some cases the god or goddess holds a vase or goblet that he or she extends toward a group of worshippers.[43] The vessel itself is interpreted as a symbol of goddess-fecundity, so that the icon portrays the creative force as an anthropomorphic goddess offering herself as a vessel of liquid to the worshippers.[44] Clearly, a cult ritual is suggested by these icons as well as an archetypal symbolism. Many Sumerian cylinder seal impressions show worshippers drinking from a ritual vase,[45] and a few suggest the existence of an exclusively female cult involving a group (chorus?) of worshippers to whom the goddess appears in the sacred garden to hand out the fruit of the Tree of Life or distribute the Water of Life to drink.[46] The cup-holding figures from Tel Asmar are waiting for the god or goddess to pour out the Water of Life for them, as Sappho's poem implies one or more worshippers waiting for Aphrodite to pour out "nectar" for them.[47] The Water of Life, as the drink of the gods, which confers immortality, is directly equivalent to Greek nectar.

---

42 E.D. Van Buren, *The Flowing Vase and the God with Streams* (Berlin: Hans Schoetz & Co., 1933), 1.

43 See H. Prinz, *Altorientalische Symbolik,* Preisschrift der Königl. Preuss. Akademie der Wissenschaften (Berlin: Verlag von Karl Curtius, 1915), 137.

44 For goddesses holding the vase, see Van Buren, *The Flowing Vase* (above, n.42), figs. 32, 33, 45, 46, 55, and Parrot, *Sumer* (above, n.38), figs. 273, 300, 339. For interpretation of vessel-goddess symbolism, see E. Neumann, *The Great Mother: An Analysis of the Archetype,* trans. R. Manheim (Princeton Univ. Press, 1955), 39ff. and plates 27, 28, 31, 34, 40, 41, 55; and O. G.S Crawford, *The Eye Goddess* (London: Phoenix House, 1957).

45 See, e.g., H. Frankfort, *Cylinder Seals: A Documentary Essay on the Art and Religion of the Ancient Near East* (London: Macmillan and Co., 1939), plate 15, figs. a and f.

46 See especially ibid., plate 24, fig. d.

47 For the Tel Asmar figures, see Parrot, *Sumer* (above, n.38), figs. 129 and 135.

The correspondence I have sketched has several parts. Sappho's rose-covered apple trees correspond to the Tree of Life, her Aphrodite to Ishtar/Nammu/Ninhursag, Sappho's "cold water singing through the apple branches" corresponds to the river or rivers that traditionally flow through the Sumerian garden.[48] The vessel from which Aphrodite is about to pour nectar is the Sumerian Flowing Vase, which is associated both with the paradisiacal central garden and with the overflowing bounty of the sex-goddess Ishtar. The nectar itself is the mysterious Water of Life, which also is especially associated with Ishtar.[49] The *ὕδορ ψύχρον* of Sappho's grove brings with it Orphic afterlife associations,[50] and the whole motif of drinking life-water relates to the Orphic-Egyptian-Sumerian mythologem of the Thirst of the Dead, which is to be quenched in a garden compound by the Water of Life flowing from the base of a fruit-bearing tree.[51] (Sappho's connection with the "Leucadian Leap" also associates her with the Orphic-Pythagorean tradition.[52]) Finally, if one credits Butterworth's speculation that this Sumerian *cultus* involved recently domesticated shamanic practices, then Sappho's *κῶμα*, or visionary sleep, in which she will behold the goddess herself, may also correspond to the Sumerian prototype of the scene.[53]

---

48 See, e.g., *Ancient Near Eastern Texts Relating to the Old Testament*, ed. J. B. Pritchard (Princeton Univ. Press, 1955), 37–41.

49 Ibid., 52–57.

50 See W. K. C. Guthrie, *Orpheus and Greek Religion: A Study of the Orphic Movement* (New York: Norton, 1966), 177.

51 See Zuntz, *Persephone* (above, n.31), and any of the icons of the Egyptian goddess Nut, as goddess of the sycamore fig tree, pouring out the Water of Life in the afterlife (e.g. E.A. Wallis Budge, *The Gods of the Egyptians: Studies in Egyptian Mythology*, 2 vols. [New York: Dover, 1969], 2:107).

52 See J. Carcopino, *De pythagore aux apôtres* (Paris: Flammarion, 1956), 24–81.

53 E. A. S. Butterworth, *The Tree at the Navel of the World* (Berlin: W.

To posit Near Eastern influence on early Greek lyric poetry is not any stranger than to posit Near Eastern input into Homer, and the latter is abundantly documented and widely accepted. Elements of Demetrian myth and cult at Eleusis also "seem," as Kirk says, "to depend unmistakably on the Mesopotamian mythical background."[54] "The Greek flood myth," he goes on, "is unquestionably derived from the Mesopotamian exemplar by one means or another," and "it is an a priori probability that other important elements of myth came too."[55] Sappho's Mytilenaean milieu, only a few miles from Asia and with known contacts there, cannot have escaped such influences.

In fact, so many possible channels of diffusion are available in this case that the path can be reconstructed in a number of ways. Fr. 2 mentions Crete, a known stage in such diffusion events. The Cretan mountain goddess, worshipped in flowery fields and as a fruit tree, clearly relates to the Sumerian goddess of the garden, Ninhursag ("Lady Mountain"). Furthermore, Egyptian influence on Minoan Crete is well attested and through Crete, on Mycenae. The paradisiacal garden of the Egyptian coffin texts, the Field of Reeds (with sycamore fig, spring of life-water, and goddess pouring it from a vessel), seems to have diffused from Sumer into Egyptian afterlife myth, and from Egypt may have diffused into the Minoan/Mycenaean region, as the background of the Elysian Fields.[56] The golden scales found in the shaft graves at Mycenae, with butterflies inscribed on the weighing pans, indicate influence of the Egyptian idea of the Weighing of the Heart in the Court of Osiris, entering Greece by way of Crete, whence came the butterflies as symbols of the reawak-

---

de Gruyter, 1970), 138–61.

54 Kirk, *The Nature of Greek Myths* (above, n.40), 255.

55 Ibid., 263.

56 Ibid., 264–65.

ening in the afterlife. In addition both Minoan Crete and Mycenaean Greece had contact with Anatolian cultures that in turn purveyed Sumerian ritual forms in various provincial instantiations. The symbolic complex we are studying in fr. 2 could, then, have entered Greece in the Bronze Age by way of Anatolian, Cretan, Egyptian, Ugaritic and other Near Eastern influences.

Other channels exist during the Orientalizing period and in Sappho's own day. There was a Greek colony at Naukratis, in Egypt, by around 625 BCE (to which Sappho's brother traveled as a wine merchant). Furthermore, the Minoans had extensively explored the Levant, bringing back much cultural influence, and in the archaic age, Sappho's age, the main repository of Minoan culture was the west coast of Asia Minor, a thirty minute sail from her home in Mytilene.[57] The image-complex of the goddess's garden did not die out in the Bronze Age in the Near East, but was current in Assyria in the first millennium.[58] It occurs in the *Old Testament* in contexts approximately contemporary with Sappho.[59] It diffused from Bronze Age Syria into Asia Minor and Cyprus (along with the myth of the Cypriote birth of Aphrodite?).[60] Other parallels of this symbolism may be found in Greek literature, including, in the realm of archaic lyric, Ibycus's fr. 286P. In short, Sappho's world was surrounded by this symbol complex and, probably, permeated by it too. Finally, it should be noted that Gregory Nagy feels

57 See M. Cary and E. H. Warmington, *The Ancient Explorers* (Harmondsworth and Baltimore: Penguin, 1963), 25, 30, and 32.

58 Widengren, *The King and the Tree of Life in Ancient Near Eastern Religion* (above, n. 32), 32; Van Buren, *The Flowing Vase and the God with Streams* (above, n.41), 109.

59 Widengren, *The King and the Tree of Life in Ancient Near Eastern Religion*, 36–41, 53.

60 See Frankfort, *Cylinder Seals* (above, n.45), pl. 44, fig. m; Van Buren, *The Flowing Vase and the God with Streams* (above, n.42), 128f.

that Æolic lyric contains an inherited formulaic content even older that that of the epic, which is known to go back in parts to the fifteenth century BCE.[61] Of course, Sappho may have had in her backyard a setting like that of the poem. Nevertheless, the evidence, in my opinion, shows that this symbol complex was so widespread and fundamental that it was not possible for anyone of that world who was attracted toward cultic imagery to relate to those images without feeling resonances of their ancient origins. Even if Sappho had such a garden in her backyard, ancient religious associations would have clung round it very strongly in her hypersensitive, goddess-oriented receptive imagination.

A coupure épistémologique

The imagery of fr. 2, then, participates in the Sumerian symbol complex of central garden, goddess, Flowing Vase, Tree of Life, Water of Life, and the resuscitation of a seasonal Dying God. If Sappho was involved with a formal cultic association, its roots

61 G. Nagy, *Comparative Studies in Greek and Indic Meter* (Cambridge, Mass.: Harvard Univ. Press, 1974), 118–40. Nagy posits an extremely ancient background to the Æolic meters used by Sappho and Alcaeus – as ancient as the cultic background I am suggesting. He regards the Æolic dactyls, or expanded glyconics, of fr. 44, for example, as more ancient than the epic hexameters and as carrying with them a cargo of inherited formulaic content surviving from a hypothetical earlier age of lyric that had developed, along another line of descent, into the epic mode. He posits the actual persistence, into sixth-century Lesbos, of a pre-epic tradition going back at least to the Bronze Age and possibly to the proto-Indo-European period (148). We may see in fr. 44, then, an actual example, albeit very late, of the type of epyllion sung by Phemius and Demodocus or by their predecessors – a type of verse that may be as ancient in origin as the heroic lays of the Sumerians. (See S. N. Kramer, *The Sumerians* [Univ. of Chicago Press, 1963], 183ff.) On this view, the many apparent Homerisms in fr. 44 are not, in fact, borrowings from epic, but survivors of the literary tradition from which the epic sprang.

were very ancient; if she was not, she selected, from the common cultic environment of the Eastern Mediterranean in the Orientalizing period, images that hark back to ancient roots.

She did not, however, pass these symbols on as she had inherited them, but expanded them to contain a new level of meaning. Living as she did at a *coupure épistémologique,* or turning point in human awareness, she experienced them in two ways: on the one hand, as representing forces out there; on the other, as referring to her own mental processes in the poetic activity. Mental contents that had been projected outward in the Bronze Age, taking form as mythology, are now beginning to be gathered back into the mind, in subjectivist poetry. Sappho presents us with a *symboliste* meditation on the poetic process couched in terms of a Bronze Age fertility cult that she has redefined as a worship of cultural, not agricultural, fertility. The rose is a symbol of a poem, the goddess's epiphany is the power of the poet, nectar represents poetic inspiration, and so on.[62] A set of signifiers that had a longstanding association with a certain set of signifieds has suddenly acquired a new set of signifieds and backgrounded the old. The signifier's ability to function as a variable would seem to be a mechanism whereby culture adapts to alterations of consciousness. In Sappho's day, as Snell has shown, the age of cult art (the Bronze Age) was being replaced by the age of the individual artist pursuing his or her personal genius to its idiosyncratic ends. At this turning point the significations of the old cultic art were broken up; the signifiers were split off from the signifieds and became comparatively free variables available for the individual poet as he or she recast them in the shape of his or her personality.[63] From such

62 Much of this symbolism is worked out in detail above in Part One, chap. 4, "The Magic in Action."

63 Sappho's practice might be subsumed under one of several headings in Roland Barthes's *Elements of Semiology* (trans. A. Lavers and C.

subjective redefinitions the new age created for some of the old symbols relatively enduring new forms. The Water of Life, associated in the Bronze Age Near East with the quest for immortality, becomes – first for Sappho, then for the Greco-Roman period generally – a standard image for poetic inspiration and for the cultural type of immortality that, Sappho repeatedly states, literary posterity can confer.[64]

Sappho re-edited the Bronze Age symbolism in a characteristic way. In the first place, she more or less edited out the male figure that was featured so prominently in this *cultus* in the Bronze Age. According to Widengren, the central cultic function of the symbolic garden was as the site of the annual mating of the king with the high priestess of Ishtar, ritually renewing the annual lease on communal fertility. But in Sappho's setting, the marriage that takes place is not between male and female, but between female and female or, on another level, between mind and poetic archetype. Ishtar and Ninhursag, ancient proprietors of this garden, were god-

---

Smith [New York: Hill and Wang, 1973]). In what Barthes calls "staggered systems," the signifier-and-signified of the first level become a new signifier on the second level; Sappho's rose signification from the first level becomes globally connotative on the second level of the staggered system. In "transgression" the rose becomes metonymically part for whole of the goddess garden complex. In "neutralization" two signifieds refer to a single signifier, or vice versa; thus rose, bowl, spring, garland, girl, and so on, all have the same second-order signified, meaning that they have been "neutralized" or "emptied" somewhat as signifiers. At the edge between syntagma and system, Barthes says, "a great number of creative phenomena are situated, as if perhaps there were here a junction between the field of aesthetics and the defections from the semantic system." (86)

64 See N. B. Crowther, "Water and Wine as Symbols for Inspiration," *Mnemosyne* IV 32 (1979), 1–11. For related developments, see W. E. Forehand, "Symbolic Gardens in Longus' Daphnis and Chloe," *Eranos* 74 (1976), 103–12, and H. R. Fairclough, *Love of Nature Among the Greek and Romans* (New York: Longmans, Green and Co., 1930), 123–25 and 135–37.

desses of heterosexual union and procreation. But Sappho's Aphrodite presides primarily over sterile matings of girls. The bowl that had long represented the womb of the goddess in its connection with cosmic fertility has become symbol of homosexual desire and poetic sublimation.

In the myth of Dilmun, one of the Bronze Age texts that relate closely to this symbol cluster, the *mysterium* of the magic garden is the procreative sexuality of the god Enki and the goddess Ninhursag. When the two principles conflict, Ninhursag emerges triumphant yet still in conjunction with her male partner; it is never implied that her power could be effective without his complement. Sappho has retained the supremacy of the goddess, but has pushed it to an Amazonian extreme by the total exclusion of the god and the repression of the mystery of procreation. The cult of sexual fertility has become a "cult of virginity."[65] Various other symbols are redefined accordingly. In the myth of Dilmun, for example, it is food plants that are produced in the garden by the union of god and goddess. But for Sappho it is the precious nonfunctionality of the rose that represents the gift of the goddess: not physical fertility, but an abstract sense of ideal beauty is the numinosum worshipped in her goddess's garden.

Many Sumerian and Akkadian seal impressions show us the garden of the goddess, with the sacred tree, and female worshippers being "presented" to the goddess or "initiated into" her mystery. Sappho's *thiasos* (if such there was) may be seen as a late parallel (or perhaps even remnant) of these cults in outer form; but the inner meaning has been reversed: Sappho as cult leader seems to be working against the cause of life-renewing fertility. She supports instead a type of physically sterile relationship in which creative power has

---

65 See Stehle, "Retreat from the Male: Catullus 62 and Sappho's Erotic Flowers" (above, n. 8).

been sublimated into the emotional-aesthetic-spiritual realm. We may see in this a remnant of the cultic struggle of male and female principles in late Bronze Age Greece, but even more a manifestation of the growing tendency toward the abstract and sublime rather than the concrete and earthly in archaic Greek consciousness in general.

Dividing the Corpus

The fragments of the Sapphic corpus can be categorized according to the degree of redefinition that the Bronze Age cultic significations have received in them. At one pole are the poems that express without redefinition the Bronze Age values of vegetative fertility and heterosexual union; in these poems the values of the group, or of tradition, prevail. At the other pole are the poems in which Sappho's subjective or individual values of homosexual union and artistic sublimation have totally replaced the public communal values. Four groupings can convey the series of different balancings of the semiotic code.

Group 1 contains those poems written for performance at actual rituals of a public and traditional type. Here the Bronze Age values are largely maintained. The Dying God Adonis is lamented, with no hint of Amazonian "retreat from the male" – an apparently living memory of a Bronze Age cult that survives textually in the Babylonian *Laments for Tammuz*. Most of the Group 1 fragments are epithalamia, or wedding songs. In these Sappho takes a heterosexual point of view (speaking for society at large, not for herself in particular). Here the ancient vegetative signifiers (fruit tree, flowers) remain tied to the signifieds of fertility and sexual procreation. This group, which some of the ancients seem to have considered Sappho's most characteristic product, and which probably amounted to a large percentage of her work, tied her to the mainstream of social and cultural life and involved repression of her personal anti-procreative idealism.[66]

Group 2 contains the homosexual erotic poems, which employ the ancient symbols in redefined ways, sometimes reversing their values. The actual wedding poems, with their ancient fertility symbolism, seem to have formed a foundation stratum to Sappho's imagination, providing the set of signifiers to which in her homosexual poems she attaches new signifieds. In this group, the poetess imaginatively adapted the symbolism of the fertility and marriage rites to a homosexual viewpoint and lifestyle. Young girls are presented in pseudo-ritual attitudes that represent not their impulse toward marriage and procreation, but their inner dispositions; the emotional peak experiences of an aestheticized homoeroticism are sacralized as abstract aphrodisiac kratophanies. The power of poetry is employed in a Romantic-mystical way to heal the breaches between imagination and reality and to give to a private vision the ratification of cosmic authority. Typical is fr. 96, in which a girl is consoled at being parted from her

66 G. M. Kirkwood doubts that Sappho wrote many epithalamia (*Early Greek Monody: The History of a Poetic Type* [Ithaca: Cornell Univ. Press, 1974], 102 and 138–39.) But clearly she was most famous for this genre; "Hymen, God of Weddings, holding his bright torch, stands with you over bridal beds," wrote Dioscorides (*Palatine Anthology* 7.407). The textual evidence is inconclusive, but one reasonable interpretation of it indicates over eight hundred lines of epithalamia in book one alone. Himerius says that Sappho was foremost among poets of epithalamia (*Orations* 1.4), and Theocritus and Catullus both imitated her in this genre. Regardless of the quantity of the epithalamia, it seems certain that some of her examples were famous and popular standards in antiquity, known and imitated throughout the Greco-Roman world. Being mostly hymeneals, the choral songs do not seem to suggest a school setting; but Wilamowitz-Moellendorff speculated that Sappho would send her girls, upon graduation, into marriage, and sing them on their way.

female lover by a disguised wedding song that unites them symbolically in an inverted or lunar marriage.[67] This group includes Ode 1, the long frr. 2, 94, and 96, and several others whose imagery firmly connects them to one or more of these: frr. 22, 36, 38, 39, 46–49, 51, 53, 54, 57, 68*a* (?), 86, 92, 95, 120, 130, 134, 171, and 188. Sappho presents in these poems a world in which a value structure based on the admiration of beauty (of which the paradigm, for Sappho, is the young girl) has cosmic, rather than merely personal, validity. This ideal world is validated by conceiving its creation and celebration in poetry as a ritual offering to Aphrodite, of whom the poetess becomes the priestess and almost all-powerful agent, a stand-in not only for the Eros of Archilochus and Anacreon, but for the Orphic Eros-Phanes also, bringing a world into being out of herself. Aphrodite is redefined; no longer merely the goddess of sexual procreation, her realm is expanded to include beauty in general and the creation of it through poetry.[68] She is now the goddess of all beauty, imagination, and creativity; Sappho has gone halfway toward Plato's concept, at *Symposium* 180*d* ff., of a Celestial Aphrodite who presides over a realm of ideal beauty quite removed from such mundane matters as the mating of herds and the sprouting of crops.

The invocation of the goddess into the poem gave to Sappho's idealized poetic world a validation higher than that of the world of everyday experience; poetic invention emerges

---

67 See above, Part One, chap. 4, "The Magic in Action."

68 Sappho may first have conflated the worship of Aphrodite and the Muses, or there may have been earlier cultic associations. Eros is said to have had a festival in Thespiae that coincided with a festival of the Muses (see R. Flacelière, *Love in Ancient Greece,* trans. James Cleugh [New York: McFadden, 1964], 33). Euripides may be referring to Sappho or to an older tradition when he says "Eros makes poets even of yokels." (Ibid.) Anacreon says that while drinking one should "mingle the Muses and the splendid gifts of Aphrodite." (Fr. 116, Edmonds)

ontologically triumphant: the world as contemplated by poetic sensibility is declared more real than as perceived through the senses. Seen thus not as autobiography, but in a sense as escapes from autobiography, these poems contain not so much a plain record of facts as kernels of intense emotion, which have been isolated, idealized, intensified, and transformed through symbolic accoutrements to such an extent that the autobiographical aspect recedes into the background and is overshadowed by the selective and transformative power of daydream and ritual idealization.[69]

The Group 2 poems, which I have interpreted as an homage to the imagination, are those which Wilamowitz-Moellendorff, Bowra,[70] and others feel describe the secluded inner life of the *thiasos*. Group 3 contains the poems that I am willing, along with Wilamowitz-Moellendorff, Bowra, and others, to accept as plainly autobiographical. The distinction between the Group 2 and Group 3 fragments provides, I think for the first time, a somewhat objective way to decide what is autobiographical here and what is not. It was on the basis of very late ancient testimonia that Wilamowitz-Moellendorff constructed his appealing portrait of Sappho as an aristocratic poetess operating an elite girls' boarding school that was at the same time a *thiasos* or cult association devoted to the worship of Aphrodite. In doing so he chose to neglect the fact that all late sources on Sappho are polluted by the phantasies of authors of middle and new comedies.[71] Others followed more or less uncritically. An example is A. R. Burn, who, in *The Lyric Age of Greece*, presents a biographical sketch of Sappho that

69 For the element of daydream, see R. Bagg, "Love, Ceremony and Daydream in Sappho's Lyrics," *Arion* 3.4 (1964), 44–82.

70 C. M. Bowra, *Greek Lyric Poetry from Alcman to Stesichorus* (Oxford: At the Clarendon Press, 1936).

71 See Prentice, "Sappho" (above, n.9).

accepts late elements from Ovid, Athenaeus, Maximus of Tyre and the *Suda* without discussing the difficulties involved.[72]

In short, there has been no objective criterion for distinguishing fact from fiction in Sappho and scholars have chaotically followed the dictates of personal preference, selecting the "facts" they like and rejecting those they dislike.

The fragments contain many proper nouns, and commentators in general have regarded these as indications of autobiography. But, as I have indicated elsewhere, place names in Sappho are drawn from mythology and literature, not from autobiography, and the same must be said for many, if not most, of the personal names she mentions.[73]

The Group 2 poems express either an idealized world of poetic imagination or the sheltered and semi-sacred inner life of the *thiasos.* In either case they point to an idealized private realm dominated by the aura of symbolic meaning and cut off from, even opposed to, the external world of public life. There one can escape into a privileged arena in which all the practical concerns of the life of the ordinary citizen are bracketed. The Group 3 fragments may now be defined as those "normal" fragments, which run counter to the Group 2 fragments and represent the world from which the Group 2 fragments offer an escape. The distinction can be clarified through attention to Sappho's diction, which is a rather special case among ancient poets.

So extraordinarily limited and consistent is Sappho's diction that it led Lobel to postulate a Lesbian vernacular dialect with very inflexible rules that the poetess rather slavishly followed; the fragments that hold strictly to this dialect he

---

72 Burn even adds a few for which there is no ancient warrant whatever (that she "probably" married young and that her husband "probably" died early). (A. R. Burn, *The Lyric Age of Greece* [London: Edward Arnold, 1960], 227ff.)

73 Above, Part One, chap. 2, "The Song of the Sacred Grove."

called the "normal" fragments.[74] Others have argued, more plausibly as it seems to me, that the limitation of Sappho's diction is due not to dialectal restrictions, but to poetic choice.[75] This, in turn, is dictated by the special, quasi-ritualistic nature of Sappho's poetic vision – its connection with a sense of cultic intention.

The poetess presents us with a world of which only certain selected words can be used because in it only certain selected events can occur (or meanings be obtained). It is a dreamlike world (whether within Sappho's mind or within the garden of the *thiasos*) resulting from enormous censorship of the everyday world and correspondingly enormous censorship of language, from which "profane" everyday elements had to be eliminated to conform it to the ritual purity of the reality it posits. As external reality is purified, so is its linguistic sign system.

Within the world dominated by the symbols of the Bronze Age goddess, only meanings appropriate to those symbols may be acknowledged. This privileged world (whether *thiasos* or private imagining) is governed by rules like those of ancient religions, in which certain words will be efficacious, invoking the sanction of higher powers, and other will not. There is, as it were, a sacred diction and a profane one. The sacred diction describes the world of the benign Aphrodite (the Group 2 poems), the profane, the world of the "bitter" Aphrodite (Group 3), as Sappho calls her (fr. 15; cf. Plato's "terrestrial" and "celestial" Aphrodites),[76] who is not Sappho's Aphrodite, but that of

74 Σμ xxvff., and Αμ intro.

75 See esp. A. W. Gomme, "Interpretations of Some Poems by Alkaios and Sappho," *Journal of the Hellenic Society* 77 (1957), 255–66.

76 The double Aphrodite was not just a literary conceit, but had cultic echoes that are probably very ancient – perhaps Neolithic. Aphrodite was worshipped as ἐπιτύμβιος (goddess of the tomb) and as μελανίς (the dark one). Certain funereal services were performed in

the public world. Lobel's distinction into normal and abnormal fragments, then, is insufficient. We can discern a cleavage within the normal fragments, between those (Group 2) that employ the "sacred" diction of the bracketed world of ideal beauty, and those (Group 3) that employ the "profane" diction of the public world of sixth-century Mytilene.

Group 3 includes frr. 3, 5, 15, 20, 21, 58, 68*a* (?), 82, 121, 131, 133, 137, 144, 155, and 213. These poems, unlike those of Group 2, involve a profane diction and refer to scenes of conflict that are not resolved through poetic healing into a sense of transcendent harmony. They point to an area of experience that Sappho could not idealize, that remains strictly outside the brackets of the *thiasos* imagination, and that is treated with a diction that would not be possible in the poems of Group 2. Fr. 5 (the Charaxus episode) features terms of moral censure or approval ("sinned," line 5; "enemies," line 7; "evil," line 19), which have no place in the Group 2 poems where beauty, not morality, is the normative value. Conversely, the most typical features of the Group 2 poems – maidens, flowers, terms for beauty, musical imagery – are absent here. The viewpoint, in fact, is not private and "Sapphic" but public and Mytilenaean. Charaxus is exhorted not to love his sister, but to do honor to her, and the mention of πολίταν (citizen, line 14) at once removes us from the private realm and directs us to the world of public life. In this public world we find a negative image of the private world of Group 2. Here Aphrodite is not the benign goddess of the flowery grove, but a malevolent deity to be invoked in curses (as in fr. 15) – no longer the sweet, but the bitter Aphrodite.

---

her honor. She is ἀνδροφόνος (man-slayer.) Phaedrus's nurse in the *Hippolytus* of Euripides refers to the Aphrodite whom Sappho sent after Rhodopis when she says, "Kypris is irresistible when she attacks with violence. The foe who yields is gently treated, but woe to any whom she finds arrogant and haughty." (See Flacelière, *Love in Ancient Greece* [above, n.68], 31.)

Fr. 137 (the proposal by "Alcaeus" preserved by Aristotle) similarly speaks in the public language of Greek communal morality, not the private language of the poetic rite. "Shame" (line 2) and "right" or "justice" (line 6) occur nowhere else in the fragments that we have. The root κακ- (evil) occurs elsewhere only in fragment 5 (just considered) and fr. 3. The latter fragment also speaks of "reproach" (line 5), found nowhere else in the fragments; the conventional moral commonplace "fair and good" (line 3) recurs only in the reproach to Charaxus and the "reply to Alcaeus" (fragments 5 and 137). "Swollen" or "troublous" (line 6) expresses disgust, as does "to be glutted" or "to loathe" (line 7); "pain" (line 4) echoes "distressful pain" of fr. 5 line 10. This poem also seems to have been primarily concerned with moral judgments and to have lacked altogether the imagery of "gardens of the Nymphs, weddings, and love affairs," which, as Demetrius says (*On Style* 132), "are found in all the poems of Sappho." Fragment 20 describes a sea voyage and possibly a shipwreck. "Cargo" (line 13) reminds us of "citizens" in fr. 5.14, an image that directs our gaze to the world of goods, trade and citizens, which we would expect of Mytilene in the sixth century. Again the paradisiacal imagery of the erotic poems is absent.

Several fragments, which are customarily gathered together on the basis of a testimonium of Maximus of Tyre (*Orations* 18.9), seem to arise from a homosexual circle characterized by rivalry of certain dominant women for the affections of young girls. These fragments also contain the residue of nonliterary proper names mentioned above. Fr. 213 is a confused mixture of Sapphic lines and a grammarian's commentary. It seems to involve a pejorative or scurrilous description of one Pleistodika as the "husband" of one Gorgo. We see, again, Sappho in her sharp-tongued critical mood, outside the ecstatic reverie of the Group 2 poems. Fragment 68*a* seems sarcastically to apply the terms of a wedding song to Andromeda and another girl (possibly the *Suda*'s Megara [see line 12]); one of them is called a sinner (line 4), and the poem, like the preceding one, was probably a reproach arising from jealousy about a homosexual relationship. Frr. 82, 131, 133, 144, and 155 rise from the same milieu.[77] Surely, if any of the fragments are autobiographical, in the sense of relaying the plain facts of everyday life without poetic idealization, it is those discussed here as Group 3. These fragments show the poet in contact with a world outside her imagination and not subject to its manipulation, while the Group 2 poems show her in the sacred garden of Aphrodite to which the real and unblessed people and events of Mytilene did not penetrate. Sappho's normal fragments, in other words, show us two different realities: in the one, the imagery of the Bronze Age Garden of Youth; in the other, that of the profane marketplace; for the one, a diction of enraptured lyricism; for the other, an emotionally oppressed moralizing. That both groups are "normal" in dialect should not mislead us. They arise from separate chambers of the imagination; they relate to different orders of reality: Group 2 saturated by nourishing archetypal meaning; Group 3 offering only the desiccated husks of events cut off from sacred sources. The distinction transcends the question whether or not Sappho ran a school or *thiasos*. Group 2 portrays that aspect of Sappho's experience (whether imagined or lived in a *thiasos*) on which Aphrodite smiles; Group 3, that on which she frowns. For the first, the symbols of the ancient goddess cult are exclusively employed; from the other they are ruthlessly withheld.

---

77 It may be desirable to add to Group 3 several fragments featuring the imagery of old age (in sharp contrast to the emphasis on youth in the Group 2 poems): frr. 21, 58, and 121 (which, however, may be an exercise in a standard theme – the Rejected Suitor dialogue – as may fr. 137 and the New Sappho found in Cologne papyrus 21351 and 21376).

I have so far designated three realms within the Sapphic fragments. The relationship between them follows a clear progression. In the first realm, that of conventional ritual poems, the Bronze Age significations of the goddess-cult symbolism are maintained; the themes of earthly fertility and heterosexual procreation are treated in a traditional way. In the second, the Bronze Age goddess imagery is maintained, but its significations are broken apart; the signifiers are experienced as numinous variables that may be redefined according to the poet's personal vision, giving to the symbolic cosmos the shape of the poet's individual pathology, without regard for the conventions and attitudes of the social group at large. In the third realm, the ancient goddess imagery does not appear at all; it is deliberately withheld in order to convict that world of profaneness. This realm is not blessed by the goddess, who is invoked here not to unite lovers, but to sever them violently (as in fr. 5); here girls are not praised for their beauty, but scurrilously denounced for being "husbands" to each other. The three realms progress from religious ritual to poetic imitation of ritual to everyday life cut off from ritual sacralization. They compress three stages of human history in a single remarkable personality: the naive communal ritualism of the Bronze Age, the symbolic ritualism of the individual creator who no longer believes in the communal religion, but is still moved by its symbols and incorporates them into his or her private vision, and finally the age of complete secularism in which neither the traditional public religion nor any visionary remapping of its powers remains tenable. In this last realm (not unlike that of modern naturalistic novelists), separate egos not expanded by archetypal nourishment contend for sex, wealth, and power in ugly and egocentric chaos. Each of these sensibilities is a kind of grotesque parody of, or degeneration from, the one before.

At this point it may seem that, while my distinction between Groups 1 and 2 is clearly rooted in the internal and dialectal evidence, the distinction between Groups 2 and 3, being supported only by dictional and attitudinal evidence, is less strong. I have indeed withheld until now what I consider to be the strongest, indeed, the conclusive evidence for the separation and definitions of Groups 2 and 3. Several poems not yet considered show a clear awareness of the distinctions in question and confirm them rather conclusively. These fragments that comment on and clarify the relationship between the realms form a fourth group, the Linking Fragments.

Several of the most important Sapphic fragments deal with the discontinuities between the three realms of Sappho's work that I have so far described. The distinction between Groups 1 and 2 is that between the real weddings for which Sappho wrote the texts and the symbolic weddings or unions in her private religion of beauty where the partners are wedded, as are the first and second terms of a simile, by the magic of imagination. Foremost among the Linking Fragments is fr. 31, which I have dealt with elsewhere.[78] I have also analyzed fr. 96 elsewhere as a careful series of epithalamic allusions symbolically extending the sanction of marriage ritual to homosexual partners.[79]

By an implicit shifting and redefinition of signifiers, the Group 1 reality of outer events is annulled by the Group 2 reality of imagination; a healing has occurred. In fr. 96, for example, the departed girl has married a man in the real world; but for Sappho her truer state remains her state before the fall, as it were, her presence as maiden homosexual bride in the goddess's garden of night-blooming flowers. Fragments 31 and 96 both center on the distinction between Groups 1

---

78 See above, Part One, chap. 6, "The Face Behind the Mask."

79 See above, Part One, chap. 4, "The Magic in Action."

and 2 – between the real-world wedding and the imagined lunar union – but with reversed emphases: fr. 31 foregrounds the real wedding; fr. 96, the imaginary.

In fr. 16, Sappho systematically reverses the hierarchy of male or patriarchal values.[80] She adopts a standpoint that is above the different realms, analyzing and evaluating the relationships between them. Although monodic, the poem contains all the structural elements of the choral song (gnomic priamel, mythic exemplum, gnomic transition, personal exemplum, sphragis). In Sappho's intentionality, choral song expresses public, communal reality; monodic song, private, individual reality (Groups 1 and 2 respectively). In fr. 16, this contrast (in which formal elements implicitly carry contentual weight) is extended throughout the poem with a delicate irony. The hordes of cavalry, infantry, ships (choral, communal, public) pursue the fleeing Helen into the center of the poem (asserting implicitly that individual female beauty has greater power than communal male aggression). There follows the transition from mythic to personal exempla, from universal to particular (or from mythic universal to concrete universal), which takes us completely into the private reality, as the universal Helen is transformed into the particular Anactoria. At once the poem enters fully into the monodic mood and Sappho's most typical erotic subject appears – the sorrow of parting, separation, absence, and how this sorrow is healed by the inner sense of unity and well-being produced by the poetic "rite." Anactoria, representing the "sweet" Aphrodite of the private realm, strides through the poem with a power greater than that of outer history: the marching of troops (a Group 3 image) is subsumed by her delicate footstep (Group 2), the glitter of armor fading in the brightness of

80 See G. Wills, "The Sapphic 'Umwertung aller Werte,'" *The American Journal of Philology* 88/4 (1967), 434–42.

her smile. With her usual extraordinary subtlety, Sappho has transformed the traditional metaphor of woman preparing for a tryst seen as champion preparing for battle (e.g. *Iliad* 14) into a vehicle for her own opposition of private to public values. Finally, the poem is a complex ideological manifesto in which one set of values (female, homosexual, subjectivist, aesthetic, erotic) emerges victorious over another (male, heterosexual, dogmatic, conceptual, aggressive), the decision, characteristically, being handed down by means of a poetic trope. A value system emerges in which the small and still beauty of the *thiasos*/poetic rite overshadows, by its sublimity, the whole profane apparatus of worldly ambition.

Fr. 94 D involves a similar overview of the breach between the realities. The moon returns to the arms of her lover Endymion, the Pleiads sink into the sea to the bed of their husband Poseidon, all nature proceeds in the cosmic rhythm to its mating; only the homosexual poetess, wedded to the private cultivation of her inner vision, lies alone in a primal seizure of erotic loneliness.[81] Her supersession of the mythic leaves her alone in her particularity.

Others of the Linking Fragments leave aside the epithalamia proper and focus on the opposition between Groups 2 and 3, determinedly asserting the reality of the former to be the higher:

Fr. 55:

> When you die you will lie there
> and there will be no memory of you at all,
> for you do not share in the roses of Pieria,
> but unseen in the house of Hades, too,
> you will wander among the shadowy dead,
> having flown away (or, fluttering among them).

---

81 Cf. D. Clay, "Fragmentum Adespotum 976," *Transactions of the American Philological Association* 101 (1970), 119–29.

The flower, and especially the rose, is a central symbol – an objective correlative – in Sappho's poetry, as in much later poetry that (however indirectly) feels her influence. It has a double meaning in her work that results from her overlay of new signifieds on top of the inherited significations of these symbols. Both the gifts of the Muses (poems) and young girls she called roses; Aphrodite's garden (in fr. 2) is where such roses grow.[82] This double metaphor (or metaphor with two signifieds, or tenors) provides the formula that she made the basis of her life: the making of poems and the loving of girls are one and the same activity. Aphrodite, the goddess of female sexuality, becomes also the goddess of poetry; poetry, in short, emerges as a higher form of Eros.[83] The making of love poems is proclaimed as the essence of the Mysteries of Aphrodite, the sacrament of the religion of erotic love, pioneered by Archilochus and Alcman, of which Sappho was the primal High Priestess.

The Flower

The flower as a symbol of the goddess goes back to the same Bronze Age Near Eastern iconographic tradition that contains the Flowing Vase and the Tree of Life. In Sumer, Inanna-Ishtar (the prototype, according to Kirk, of Aphrodite) was worshipped (at Brak) in the form of an eight-petaled rosette. The rosette, says Frankfort, was "emblematic of the planet Venus, a manifestation of Inanna-Ishtar."[84]

---

82 See above, Part One, chap. 4, "The Magic in Action," for a fuller discussion of this symbolism in Sappho.

83 A sublimated or aim-inhibited form – but Sappho, like a mystic devotee, asserts, through her variable symbolism, the identity of the two.

84 H. Frankfort, *The Art and Architecture of the Ancient Orient* (Harmondsworth and Baltimore: Penguin, 1970), 40.

Although a flower, the rosette also appears as the fruit of the Tree of Life in the goddess's Garden (for example in the famous "Ram in the Thicket" offering stands from Ur, where the rams, representing the god of the herd, feed on the rosettes of the mother goddess). Also in "the temple of the Mother Goddess Ninhursag (Lady of the Mountain) ... [were a] large number of rosette flowers."[85] Dilmun and associated Sumerian goddess gardens being widely accepted as prototypes of the myth of Eden, we may say that the apple eaten by Adam and Eve was originally the rosette flower; Aphrodite's association with both roses and apples in Sappho's fr. 2 is not iconographically adventitious.

In related Bronze Age Egyptian contexts the flower represents the vagina of the goddess, "the great lotus flower, out of which rose the sun for the first time at the creation."[86] (Closely related is the Hindu goddess Padma, whose name literally means either "lotus" or "vagina.")

Both the Mesopotamian and the Egyptian traditions passed into Minoan Crete, where the association of the flower with female beauty, sexuality, and fertility is, of course, extremely widespread - seemingly foundational. The seals and rings that show the Minoan goddess seated among flowers and holding flowers while bare-breasted young women worship her are precise visual counterparts to some of the Sapphic fragments - including fr. 2. Eight-petaled Sumerian-style rosettes frame every panel of the Hagia Triada sarcophagus, which otherwise shows the influence of Egyptian afterlife ritual. As the rosette is associated in Sumer with the ram and the bull (both emblems of the Dying God), it appears in Crete also on the famous sacrificial bull rhyton.[87]

---

85 Ibid., 61.

86 Budge, *The Gods of the Egyptians* (above, n.51), 1:423

87 See F. Matz, *The Art of Crete and Early Greece* (New York: Crown, 1961), pl. 43.

The portrayals of ritual processions of women at both Tyrins and Thebes featured rosettes,[88] as well as a priestess carrying both flowers and a vase. The vase as symbol of goddess-womb has already been mentioned; in Sumerian iconography the two signifiers are conjoined in ritual vases adorned with rosettes.[89] Aphrodite's vessel of nectar shadowed over by roses participates in this tradition. The rosette remains prominent in Greek art through the Geometric and orientalizing periods (it is worth remembering that Sappho lived, a few miles from Asia, during the orientalizing period). In classical Greek architecture rosettes are prominent at sites with special goddess sanctity, such as Eleusis and the Athenian acropolis, or with other associations of rebirth, such as the temple of Asclepius at Epidaurus. Their special association with Aphrodite probably antedates Sappho, as roses are said to have grown from the blood of Aphrodite's Dying God consort, Adonis.[90] This tradition connects strongly to those Sumerian icons in which horned beasts, representative of the Dying God, await sacrifice, with the rosette mark upon them.[91]

The symbolism of the flower merges with that of the tree. In Sumer, the Tree of Life often has rosettes for fruit,[92]and the rosette may substitute for the ear of wheat, representing the Dying God in his vegetative form.[93] In fact, any of these images can stand for the deity itself. An Assyrian icon

---

88 See ibid., pl. 54; E. Vermeule, *Greece in the Bronze Age* (Univ. of Chicago Press, 1964), pl. 27.

89 See Goff, *The Symbols of Prehistoric Mesopotamia* (above, n.38), figs. 478–79.

90 M. Eliade, *Patterns in Comparative Religion* (Univ. of Nebraska Press, 1996), 302.

91 Goff, *The Symbols of Prehistoric Mesopotamia* (above, n.38), figs. 437, 454.

92 See ibid., figs. 251, 269, 376, and 272.

93 Ibid., compare figs. 254 and 256; 247 and 248.

shows a deity holding the Flowing Vase emerging from the Tree of Life, which has rosettes on the ends of its branches.[94] In closely related Egyptian icons, the goddess Hathor or Nut emerges from a sycamore-fig tree, which *is* her lower body, holding the Flowing Vase from which the "cold streams" flow whispering through the branches. The theophany in the tree, like the rest of this complex, entered Greece also, where Artemis and Helen are both worshipped in trees, and various Dying God types (Attis, Osiris, Dionysus) are sometimes worshipped as trees. Various Sumerian myths stand behind this tradition,[95] which diffused thence to the Indus valley and probably to Minoan Crete also, where many seal impressions associate the goddess so closely with the tree as to suggest that she was worshipped in the tree or as appearing from it.[96] Indeed, in Sappho's fr. 2, where Aphrodite has not yet appeared, but is expected momentarily, there is a strong sense that she is already present in the features of the site itself, echoing this ancient tradition of the goddess's theophany as tree, flower, and Flowing Vase.

In the tradition leading up to Sappho, then, the image of the flower is integral to the iconography of the mother goddess's sexuality and fertility. In later tradition, however, the flower/rose as signifier has a decreasingly sexual signified attached to it. In Christianity the rose is primarily a symbol of the virgin Mary[97] who inherited other Aphrodisiac motifs

---

94 Eliade, *Patterns in Comparative Religion* (above, n.90), 279.

95 Especially "Gilgamesh, Enkidu and the Nether World," in S. N. Kramer, *Sumerian Mythology: A Study of Spiritual and Literary Achievement in the Third Millennium B.C.* (Philadelphia: Univ. of Pennsylvania Press, 1998), 31ff., and the myth of Siduri, in Eliade, *Patterns in Comparative Religion* (above n.90), 284.

96 See, e.g., G. R. Levy, *The Gate of Horn: A Study of the Religious Conceptions of the Stone Age and their Influence upon European Thought* (London: Faber and Faber, 1963), figs. 94, 96, and 110.

97 See, e.g., G. Ferguson, *Signs and Symbols in Christian Art* (New

also, but without the ancient goddess's sexuality. Garlands of roses are said to signify the joy of the blessed in heaven, in a sublimation in which spiritual beauty and pleasure have replaced sexual beauty and pleasure. In the *Romance of the Rose,* the flower represents an eternally elusive and unidentified Beloved with whom the lover's passion is never consummated. In Dante, the rose becomes purely celestial and is located in the very empyrean of heaven; the ancient sexual symbolism has left only the chastest memory: "In form, then, of a white rose was shown to me the saintly host which Christ, with His own blood, made His bride."[98] By the time of Robert Fludd's *Utriusque Cosmi Historia,* in the seventeenth century, the rose represents the completely transcendent and nonmanifest *summum bonum.*

It is not going too far to say that Sappho was the hinge point in this shift from sexual, form-producing to spiritual, form-transcending signification. Standing, as it seems she did, at what has been called the "epistemological gap" between the concrete vision of the mythopoeic Bronze Age and the abstract vision of the philosophical Iron Age, she was the first (in the extant documentary record) to break the rose-as-signifier loose from the sexual signified and associate it with a sublimated creative force – that of poetry.

In this as in her other acts of sublimation, she was prompted in part by her homosexuality. The sexual root of the imagery is maintained by her association of girls with roses and other flowers; but it is not as procreators that Sappho loves girls, so the image must be at the same time de-sexualized. Since the writing of erotic poems seems to have been, for Sappho, a substitution for full sexual and procreative consummation,

---

York: Oxford Univ. Press, 1966), 37.

98 *The Divine Comedy of Dante Alighieri,* trans. J. D. Sinclair , 3 vols. (London: John Lane, 1948), 3:447 ("Paradiso," Canto 31.1–3).

the symbol of the flower becomes partly detached from girls and attached to poems. Roses, it turns out, are not only Aphrodite's flowers, but the flowers of the Pierian Muses, and they are also worn to please the Graces, who are equally goddesses of physical beauty and of song. In this connection roses symbolize poems.[99]

If we now turn our attention back to fr. 55, we will see this image at work in its Sapphically redefined form. The full weight of the redefined symbol is hurled against the "woman of no education" about whom Stobaeus tell us this poem was written. She has not worshipped in the magic rose garden of Aphrodite and the Pierian Muses. To worship there means to ennoble oneself by a love that, being nonprocreative, exists for its own sake only, or for the sake of the poems that, instead of children, this love produces as offspring.

Aphrodite and the Muses, as joint proprietors of the sacred rose garden, merge their attributes; sexual desire, prompted by Aphrodite, produces poems of love, under the guidance of the Muses. The woman of no education has not cultivated this garden where erotic poems bloom. Therefore, says Sappho, she will be forgotten, and for Sappho forgotten means unloved; she will be unseen, and for Sappho unseen also means unloved. The sublimated current of Aphrodisiac energy of which Sappho presents herself as high priestess passes by the unlettered woman who writes no poems. She is excluded from the garden of beauty of the Group 2 poems and exiled to the unblessed and unbeautiful secular world of Group 3, on which the Sapphic goddesses do not shed the radiance of their smiles.

Ælius Aristides was paraphrasing either this poem or a similar one when he wrote:

---

99 See above, Part One, chap. 4, "The Magic in Action," 85.

> I think you must have heard also how Sappho boasted to some women who were reputed happy, saying that the Muses had given her the real happiness, and made her enviable, and that when she died she would not be forgotten. (Fr. 193)

We can sense in such claims the vigilance with which Sappho had to defend her idiosyncratic personal values from the surrounding world that was evidently inimical to them. That those other women, although cut off from the Muses, *appeared* to be happy (as Ælius says, τῶν εὐδαιμόνων δοκουσῶν εἶναι γυναικῶν) can only mean that they were successful in the terms of the external world (the world of Group 3); but Sappho, whose values are inversions of those of the world at large, rejects conventional criteria of happiness; the *real* happiness, she insists, arises only when the internal world is blessed by the gifts of the Muses. Real happiness, in other words, is the happiness of the world described in the Group two poems, over which the roses of Aphrodite shed their magically altered consciousness (κῶμα).

In pre-Sapphic literature, the cults of Aphrodite and the Muses were not only separate, but even somewhat inharmonious. The Muses belonged to the Apollonian sensibility; Aphrodite, to the Dionysian. Sappho, who seems to have been both intensely sexual and intensely sublimated, fused these sensibilities into one – under the emblem of the rose. The resulting *numinosum*, both sexual and purified, earned her (or so she thought) an immortality that is somewhat beyond that claimed by ancient poets in general, and is the opposite of the oblivion awaiting the woman of no education.

In fr. 65, someone (perhaps Aphrodite herself) tells Sappho that she is dear to the queen of Cyprus and will have fame (perhaps it says: in every girl's heart) after she has gone to Acheron. The sense is somewhat conjectural, but it seems that here Sappho's claim to immortality is based on her service to Aphrodite, as in fr. 55 it depended on service to the Muses. Sappho clearly regarded herself as a servant of Aphrodite (cf. Socrates as the servant of Apollo in the *Apology*), and in fr. 150, addressed to her daughter (or so Maximus of Tyre says), she called herself servant to the Muses too:

Fr. 150:

> It is not right that the *threnos* should be sung in the house of those who serve the Muses; this would not be proper for us [or: for me].[100]

This passage indicates the extreme censorship that was a part of Sappho's activity as the guardian of the garden of the mysteries, who must keep thence what was impure or inappropriate.

The *threnos* is attested as early as the *Iliad* (e.g. 24.721) where it is sung round the biers of both Hector and Patroclus. Furthermore, the *threnos,* according to Horace (*Art of Poetry* 77), may have been the early form of elegiac verse – and it almost certainly was a respectable genre in Sappho's day. For virtually any other Greek poet, the Homeric sanction alone would be enough; but Sappho, who in fr. 16 in effect declares the Trojan war a profane topic in comparison with the charms of Anactoria, was a special case. She was performing a one-woman revolution in culture that was breathtaking in its extent. With the same rigorous censorship she denied the propriety of polemical, satirical, and obscene verses in frr. 137 and 158. Apparently the *threnos* is not proper to one who serves the Muses because such a one must serve Aphrodite as well and thus must sing of love, not of death. To sing the *threnos* within the goddess's magic grove would be a kind of

100 Sappho often used the first person plural; its use here is not necessarily a sign that there were other poets in the house. Cf. frr. 21.12, 24.3–4, 38, 147, and 121.1.

sacrilege. The musical imagery that is so common in Sappho occurs only in connection with girls, weddings, and praises of the beauty of girls. The service of song and the service of love, in her purified universe, are one and the same; they are two aspects of the new religion of erotic-poetic sensibility that lies at the heart of Sappho's poetry.

These fragments not only define Sappho's view of her own poetic activity, but clearly oppose it to other activities that people in general engage in – they clearly oppose the Group 2 sensibility to that of Group 3. They contain, in fact, a certain tone of alienation, the feeling of one who is convinced that her life is of a spiritually different, and higher, quality than those around her, and who resents the baseness of the outside world when it encroaches on her.

Other linking fragments convey the same lonely, but exalted message, not through comment on poetry, but through the plastic language of symbolic images.

Fr. 81*b*:

> Do you, O Dica, weave with your dainty hands
> garlands of anise sprays, and bind with them
> your lovely hair; for the blessed Graces
> love well-flowered things, and turn away
> from that which is not garlanded.

The diction of this fragment is solidly in Group 2, and the poem may be read as an invitation, or exhortation, for others to cultivate the spirituality of the rose garden too. Ἁπαλός (soft, tender, delicate, line 2) occurs only in the company of Sappho's most personal and highly charged images: a girl twines garlands around her "delicate neck" (fr. 94.16); maiden lovers lie on "soft and delicate beds" (fr. 94.22); flowers in the moonlight (perhaps the most central of all Group 2 images) are "tender" (fr. 96.13); a girl gathering flowers (again perhaps the most central of Group 2 images) is "tender" (fr.

122); a lover lies on the bosom of a "tender" companion (fr. 126); Gyrinno is "tender" (fr. 82a). Ἐρατόν (lovely, desire-arousing, line 1) in its only other Sapphic occurrence describes the footfall of Anactoria in fr. 16. Ὄρπαξ (spray, shoot, twig) describes the slender bridegroom of fragment 115.2. Flowers, of course, are the most characteristic of all Sapphic images. The Graces, for Sappho as later for Pindar, were goddesses of poetry as well as of beauty in general, and were to be invoked along with the Muses (fr. 128). Fragment 81*b*, then, in its diction, its imagery and its implied theology, clearly refers to that double service of homosexual love and monodic song that Sappho pays to Aphrodite and the Muses and Graces. It would be perverse to interpret these lines as the straightforward advice of a simple woman when, as we have seen, Sappho is far from being either straightforward or simple. Understood more deeply, this fragment is an invitation, couched in symbolic terms, to develop a new spirituality and participate in a new world, the world of art and imagination in which the servant of Aphrodite and the Muses spends her life. The unflowered things from which the Graces turn away include those unlettered women who have no share in the roses of Pieria. Dica is exhorted to turn away from the Group 3 life and enter that of Group 2; whether she is being invited to join a *thiasos* or simply to cultivate herself inwardly through love and poetry one cannot say – and in an important sense it does not matter. In terms of the structural dynamism of Sappho's poems the distinction hardly exists.

It remains, finally, to consider one of the most undervalued and misunderstood of the fragments, Sappho's so-called "Song to her Daughter."

Fr. 98:

(*a*)

For she who bore me used to say that in her youth
it was a great adornment for a girl to have her hair

bound with a purple ribbon. But it is better to have
hair more yellow than a torch, bound up with wreaths
of blossoming flowers [or: but it is better for a girl
who has hair more yellow than a torch to bind it
with wreaths of blossoming flowers.]
Just now ... a gay ribbon from Sardis ...

(*b*)

I do not know whence will come a gay ribbon for you, Cleis;
but for a Mytilenaean ... These relics of Kleanaktidas ...
the fugitive ... government ... [?] ... for these terribly
wasted away ...[101]

These lines are usually interpreted as belonging to a poem written in exile: Sappho and Cleis are in Sicily where the rich garments of Lydia are not available as they were in Mytilene, and the mother consoles her daughter, who wants a pretty headband, with the thought that flowers would be better anyway. But there is no good reason to believe in Sappho's exile, which has a poor footing in evidence, and the exile implied by the poem might as well (perhaps better) be that of of the embattled Mytilenaean politician Myrsilus, whom Sappho refers to by the patronymic Kleanaktidas.[102]

---

101 We cannot be sure that (*a*) and (*b*) belong to the same poem, nor whether *b*.1–3 come before or after *b*.4–9. I have followed Page's text (*S&A* 97).

102 Kirkwood, *Early Greek Monody* (above, n.66), rather credulously, accepts the exile, claiming that it represents a "respectable ancient tradition." But only the Parian Marble mentions it, and the Parian Marble falls after the comic pollution of the tradition about Sappho's life. Neither Athenaeus, the Oxyrhynchus biographer, nor the *Suda* mentions it, though they all garnered eagerly what information they could about Sappho's life; furthermore, since those authors evidently regarded the poems as autobiographical, their silence implies that the poems themselves did not mention it. It is not at all clear how "respectable" a tradition the Parian Marble represents; Polybius expressed contempt for that type of chronicle, which mixes legend and fact freely without seeming aware of the distinction. (For this quality of the Marble, see

It is equally plausible that for unknown reasons, possibly involving the political references in the last stanza (sumptuary laws passed by Pittacus?), Sappho is unable to get her customary luxuries in Mytilene and suggests an alternative to Cleis. The fragment is linked as strongly as possible to both worlds of Sappho's normal poems: the only unmistakable references to politics in the Sapphic corpus link it to the public world of Group 3, and Sappho's most basic and pervasive symbol – flowers for binding in a young girl's hair – place it in the private and symbolic world of Group 2.

The central action of the poem is the typically Sapphic presentation of conflicting realities – her familiar antinomy between the public and the private worlds. The imported Lydian ribbon, like the Lydian armaments of fr. 16, represents the public world of goods, citizens, and ships that the Group 3 fragments portrayed; over against it Sappho sets the central image of her religio-erotic poems, flowers for a girl's hair, expressing symbolically what the generalization *ὄττω τις ἔραται* ("whatsoever one loves") expressed in fr. 16. The exhortation that Dica received in fr. 81*b* – to enter the garden of the imagination where the Muses and Aphrodite tend the blossoms of songs and loves – is followed by an ugly picture of the alternative – the outside world of Mytilenean politics, exile, and Kleanax's son. The latter is the overbearing and sinister masculine world of the priamel of fr. 16 – identified here by the *only* nonmythological male name in the fragments; the former, the gentle and cloistered world of girls, like the garden of fr. 2. Desire for Lydian imports[103] embroils one in the problems of the outside world; devotion to the beauty of

---

J. Forsdyke, *Greece Before Homer: Ancient Chronology and Mythology* [New York: Norton, 1964], 50f.)

103 For Sappho, Lydia seems to represent hollow and pompous grandeur.

simple flowers leads to the inner peace or enchanted sleep (the κῶμα of fr. 2) of the garden of Aphrodite.

Fr. 81*b* explained its symbolism directly: to bind one's hair with flowers means to earn the favor of the goddesses of beauty and poetry, i.e., to serve them. Fr. 98, on the other hand, is a *tour de force* of immense subtlety. As in fr. 16, Sappho toys with the convention of the choral song to emphasize, in contrast to the sweep and size of choral technique, the stronger delicacy of her own preoccupation with Anactoria's footstep; as in fr. 31, she uses the conventions of public wedding song to set off the extreme privacy of her own emotions; and as in fr. 2, she disguises as a conventional invocation the symbolic picture of her inner rite. In this poem she has used the conventions of a mother's response to a request from her child to present a plea for the service of poetry. The smoothness with which the pieces of the disguise are put together is perhaps greater than for any other poem; everything follows reasonably from the possibly fictitious, but totally believable request of a young girl for a pretty ribbon: "My mother advised ribbons [i.e., the world of Group 3], but I chose to wear flowers in my hair [i.e., the world of Group 2] and I would wish the same for you; but you want a ribbon now, and I do not even know where I can get one, for the ugly business of politics blights our world."[104]

The lightness with which the picture is sketched, the gentleness of the exhortation, does not make it any less likely,

---

104 In paraphrasing thus I prefer to think that in line 6 Sappho gives her own view as distinct from her mother's; it might, however, be a continuation of her mother's advice. Fr. 71 seems to have been a poem of the same type, but there is hardly enough of it left to warrant detailed treatment. As in fr. 98, it seems, the world of politics is contrasted unfavorably with the world of "sweet song...gentle-voiced...clear-sounding" (lines 5–8), which a girl named Mika, ill-advisedly, had abandoned.

only more to be admired. The world of beauty, of the Muses, the Graces, and Aphrodite, is sketched in one sure and delicate stroke: it is the world where a girl wears flowers in hair more yellow than a torch; there is no care, no age, no death; a flower is a girl is a poem, and a poem is young forever. Outside the door of the house where the Muses' servant lives, ordinary men are singing the *threnos* as they waste away beneath the heel of Kleanax's son.[105]

The Flower and the Παρθένος

The flower is a key image not only in Sappho, but in Greek poetry in general (especially Pindar and the tragedians). It is in fact one of the most continuous and dominant symbolic images in human history. In extant remains of the past we can see a continuum of emphasis on the image of the flower in religious and poetic contexts from Minoan Crete through

---

105 It will have been noticed that in these lengthy remarks I have not tried to pass judgement on the revived *thiasos* theory. Not only is the question unanswerable, but for understanding the dynamic of Sappho's poems, as I have tried to show, it is not nearly as important as it has been deemed. Structurally, Sappho's corpus as it stands divides itself into an affirmation of certain private values and a condemnation of the opposed public values. The private values may be interpreted either as those of a *thiasos* or those of an individual imagination, without altering noticeably the meaning system that emerges from her work or the structural tensions that hold it together. In the past I have argued against the *thiasos* view because 1) it led to an anti-artistic interpretation of the poems, and 2) there was no good evidence for it. Objection 1 can be escaped by the realization that we can use both these models at once: if indeed Sappho conducted a *thiasos* in cultic activities, she seems nonetheless to have idealized it in a very personal way and to have added to the traditional resonances of the *thiasos* new dimensions of meaning. The publication of fragment SLG s261*a*, along with Calame's researches, has gone some distance toward eliminating objection 2 but certainly has not eliminated it altogether. We still lack external evidence from the pre-comic period.

Greece and Rome and into European lyric literatures. Farther back on the continuum, behind Minoan Crete, the image plunges back through the mythologies and iconographies of Egypt and Sumer, in both of which the flower was prominent. By dwelling on this continuum for a while, and looking for the cracks and gaps in it, or the changes in direction that the maintenance of similar imagery masks, we can approach answers to certain remaining questions about Sappho, her way of life, and its cultural meaning.

I have proposed that in Sappho's work the flower is a second order signifier with two signifieds.[106] Several signifieds of the first order coalesce as a signifier on the second, whose signified, in turn, is "general, global and diffuse; it is, if you like, a fragment of ideology."[107]The first signified is the one she inherited from the Bronze Age, which signified by the flower a whole complex of goddess traits including beauty, fecundity, beneficence, centrality, sexuality (the flower is the sex organ of the plant), and the year cycle of the Dying God or Goddess (when the plant flowers, it spills its seeds, and dies, to be reborn from its own seeds). In this signification Sappho uses the flower to refer to Aphrodite and to girls or young women through whom the luster of the goddess concept seemed to her to shine. The second signified is the one she added herself, as a response to the *coupure épistémologique* of archaic Greece (in which it may be said that Archilochus and Sappho did for poetry what Thales and Pythagoras did for philosophy). In this signification, the flower represents a poem, or the inspiration of poetry, or some related concept. It represents a mind-sprung thing.

The process of arriving at this double signification is simple and clear and rooted in the Sapphic texts. Sappho presented

---

106 See Barthes, *Elements of Semiology* (above, n.63), 89–92.
107 Ibid., 91.

herself as a servitor of both Aphrodite and the Muses. I take this to mean either that her *thiasos* (if she had one) participated in both these cults, or somehow fused them; or (if she had no *thiasos*) that her personal religion – her personal sense of the meaning of her life and of where the sacral centers of it were – bound her to those two archetypes. In the latter case, her declarations would be much like Socrates' assertion in the *Apology* that he was a servant of Apollo, despite the fact that he seems to have led no cult.

In addition to saying that she is the servant of Aphrodite and the Muses, Sappho associates the rose with both (fragments 2 and 55). The rose of Aphrodite is her vagina, along with all the intimations of pleasure and abundance that go with it. But the roses of the Muses must be poems, or songs, with all the associations of pleasure and creativity that they hold. Indeed, Sappho refers specifically to "the flower of song." Thus the rose in Sappho's work represents both girls and poems. She has expanded the ancient goddess symbol to a mentalist level complementary to its physical one; not only the births of crops, herds, and babies rise from Aphrodite, but also the births of poems and thoughts. Aphrodite and the Muses merge their two kinds of creativity in the symbol of the rose.[108]

No other author has proposed the second of my significations, and in fact some have proposed another signification altogether – one that I feel is in error. I propose to focus on one text of this type as a means to investigate certain previously hidden resonances or contents of Sappho's work – including an analysis of the changes in linguistic practice she

108 Pindar continues this signification when he speaks of tilling the garden of the Graces (*Olympian* 9.26–27 and *Pythian* 6.1–2). Meleager of Gadara, a late devotee of Sappho's poetic religion, called his anthology a "garland," meaning that the poems in it were flowers; Sappho's poems in particular he called "few, but roses."

wrought, and a sense of what she felt herself to be as a woman – as a person involved in gender politics.

In her 1977 article "Retreat from the Male: Catullus 62 and Sappho's Erotic Flowers," Eva Stehle[109] offers an interpretation of Catullus, Poem 62, which is based on the claim that while the flower signifies virginity, the fruit, in contrast, signifies mature sexuality. I will not discuss the interpretation of Catullus. The problem that I wish to focus on arises when Stehle seeks to confirm her interpretation of Catullus by finding the same symbolic system in Sappho, whom Catullus was following to some extent in his Poem 62. She focuses on Sappho's fr. 105*c*, which likens something, evidently a young girl, to a hyacinth crushed on a mountain path, and fr. 105*a*, which likens something, again evidently a young girl, to the last apple blooming high on a tree, too high for the pickers to reach it. Stehle's conclusion about these two Sapphic fragments involves the uncertain (and untestable) assumption that Greek men insisted on virgin brides.[110] The crushed hyacinth, on this view, is a girl who has advertised her beauty too openly and thus been raped or seduced; now, having lost her virginity,

---

109 Stehle, "Retreat from the Male: Catullus 62 and Sappho's Erotic Flowers" (above, n. 8).

110 Stehle asserts that when an unmarried girl had sexual contact with a man "it destroyed her in men's terms," thus rendering her unmarriageable.

As usual, there is insufficient evidence to be sure. Greece was made up of many cultures, in regard to matters like these. Lycurgus's reforms had sanctioned affairs by married women with their husbands' consent. In Athens, on the other hand, if a wife were adulterous, her husband was obliged by law to repudiate her or he would lose his civil rights.

This Spartan-Athenian contrast is seen again, for example, in the fact that King Ariston of Sparta married his friend's wife while Menander's *Arbitration* indicates rejection of a nonvirgin bride.

Flacelière, in *Love in Ancient Greece,* is of the opinion that "customs were undoubtedly very different [in Lesbos] from those at Athens" (above, n. 68), 65.

she is ruined permanently as no man will ever marry her. The apple, on the other hand, is a girl who "is ready for steady sexual intimacy and for becoming a mother...she denies men access, depending...on the promise of ripeness...to attract formal suitors."[111] The apple/girl, who wants to be fully integrated into the community as a mother, protects her virginity because she knows that without it she will be unable to marry and assume a respectable role in society.

In commenting on the images, Stehle constructs a dichotomy between "the sterile beauty of the flower,"[112] which represents either "virginity or at least sexual naivete,"[113] and the fruit (especially the apple), which is declared to be "an age-old symbol of sexual love and human fertility."[114] "A flower," Stehle feels, "unless it be the prelude to fruit, is beautiful, but alien to bread-eating men." "The apple is not irrelevant to the process of human nourishment and the cycle of fertility, as the hyacinth is."[115] Having established this construction on the basis of two short fragments, Stehle proceeds to apply it to the Sapphic fragments in general, meanwhile describing life in the *thiasos* in almost novelistic detail.

Her analysis concludes that both Greek men and Greek lesbian women were attracted only to virgins and were repelled from unmarried non-virgins; that all the girls whom Sappho associates with roses (and other flowers) are therefore virgins; that her *thiasos* was a "cult of virginity," in which girls "could enact passion" without endangering their marriage prospects because of "the physical inability to penetrate

---

111 Stehle, "Retreat from the Male: Catullus 62 and Sappho's Erotic Flowers" (above, n.8), 91.

112 Ibid., 91 n11.

113 Ibid., 91 n15.

114 Ibid., 91.

115 Ibid., 83 and 92.

one another."[116] This view does not seem inherently implausible. I will investigate first the flower-and-fruit linkage; second, the virgin bride; and last, the sex life in the "*thiasos*."

Sappho does seem to have favored physically sterile (but emotionally and artistically productive) relationships (a foreshadowing of the so-called "Platonic love"), and association with her may have discouraged girls from relationships with men; but a problem arises with the equations "flower = virginity" and "fruit = matronhood." In Bronze Age contexts, flower and fruit are both closely associated with goddesses and their sexuality; but they do not seem to represent different and contrasting stages of sexual development. Iconographically, they seem interchangeable. Each of them suggests the overall complex of positive goddess qualities – beauty, fecundity, beneficence, nourishment – just as certain other symbols may interchangeably signify the negative goddess qualities. There is no suggestion in the Bronze Age traditions that the flower equals virginity. The Egyptian lotus/vagina gives birth to the universe, as it does later in Hindu mythology and iconography. The Ishtar rosettes are associated with the vessel, symbol of the full and productive womb. Furthermore, the Ishtar rosettes are interchangeable with the ear of wheat in the iconic type called "Feeding the Temple Herd" and in others as well – hardly an image of sterility.

We are dealing here with signifiers that have the same signified, or to put it differently, with second-order or partially emptied signifiers, which were a basic mechanism of both Sumerian and Egyptian iconographies. In Sumer, for example, the basic message of religion seems formulable as "harmonious male-female interaction as the basis of the universe" combined with "Eros-Thanatos unity or interpenetration." In Lévi-Straussian bipolar terms, female-male and

116 Ibid., 92–93.

birth-death are two "structures" that are resolved by means of the emptying of the signifier or taking it beyond the level of denotation There were many signifiers in the very coherent visual language of Sumerian iconography that, in second-order significations, seem to have signified the whole ideological weight of the religion: tree, snake, mountain, flowing vase, flower, basket of fruit, horn, goat, stable, ziggurat, god-and-goddess, crescent moon, bull-and-lion. As first-order signifiers these terms have specific differences (their denotations), which prevent them from dissolving semantically into one another; but as second-order signifiers they have been emptied of specific differences and thus made interchangeable or, as Barthes says, general and diffuse." The flower is the goddess, and the fruit is the goddess, therefore the flower is the fruit. Egyptian mythology and iconography went even farther, especially in the revolutionary style of discourse developed in the Amon-Re cult, where, in effect, all signifiers are emptied of denotation and made to refer to an absolute called "Amon-Re."[117]

In Bronze Age religion, the empty signifier is a kind of theological device, either resolving opposites (as in Sumer) or unifying everything (as in Egypt) through mentally backgrounding the first order significations and foregrounding a second order signification in which assertions of unity abolish differences of denotation. As a religious process it seems to involve several mechanisms, including an assumption of language-reality isomorphism and the ability to shift the isomorphic modelling from one order of signifieds to another. Usually language-reality isomorphism involves the first order of signifieds; in the Bronze Age mythopoeic system, as in some other text groups such as religious allegory and par-

117 See, for example, "A Hymn to Amon-Re," in *Ancient Near Eastern Texts Relating to the Old Testament* (above, n.48), 365ff.

able, it is the second order of signifieds that is believed to isomorphically represent the world; since, in the second-order signification system, the differences of language are resolved into a single unspeakable word (such as the secret name of Amon Re), therefore reality, since it follows the structure of language, must also have a second-order that abolishes the first-order distinctions and either resolves opposition in the universe (Sumer) or unifies everything (Egypt).

The use of the empty signifier entered poetry later than religion. It may be possible to posit the practice for Homer, but only in limited and highly specified *topoi*, such as that which Turyn pointed out in connection with Sappho's fr. 96 of a lone person walking in sorrow by the waves at night. In such conventional images Homer encroaches on a vague or infinite second-order signified, but only momentarily and occasionally. Sappho, however, clearly displays the second order, and seems to foreground it in her most deeply felt poems – those of Group 2. By so doing she moved poetry into the mode that, for lack of a more focused critical term, could be called *symbolisme*. Ordinary language consists of a set of significations, that is, of attached pairs of signifier and signified. *Symbolisme* uses signifiers in such a way as either to abolish or at least to background the reader's awareness of denotation; that is, it uses signifiers without specific signifieds, and thus gives the impression of attaining meanings beyond language.

I have proposed that a number of Sappho's characteristic images have been opened up into broad second-order significations to such an extent that they become interchangeable – that is, they are partly emptied: viewed from the second order, they no longer refer to a specific concept, but to a whole cluster of related concepts. In this way each of Sappho's chief signifiers (of which the flower is one and the fruit another) signifies the whole central thematics of her poetry. Thus each of these images means something like

"Sappho's Aphrodite complex." The basic symbols of fr. 2 – apple, flower, meadow, tree, stream, goddess, sacramental drink, magic "sleep" – along with moonlight, the sound of music, the young girl, the feeling of longing, the fact of absence, and probably more – all of these mean more or less the same thing; that is, each of them means separately what all of them mean when together. Each of them is a partly emptied signifier that signifies something like "emotional exaltation achieved through the combination of eroticism with religious feeling and poetic creation."

There is another type of religious symbolism that seems closer to that suggested by Stehle. In this type, when signifiers are raised to the second-level signification, they are not emptied and made interchangeable, but each is assigned a specific new signified, quite as specific, in fact, as the signified that it has in the first order, its conventional denotation, although they will of course be different. An example is the orthodox signification system of Christian iconography. Different species of flowers and fruit, for example, in traditional Christian learned or priestly symbolism are quite different from one another. "The red carnation," one scholar says, "is a symbol of pure love." "The red, sweet fruit of the cherry symbolizes the sweetness of character which is derived from good works." "The clover... is a symbol of the trinity." The daisy is "a symbol of the innocence of the Christ child." "The hyacinth is... a symbol of Christian prudence." "The lily is a symbol of purity." "The laurel symbolizes triumph, eternity, and chastity." "The red rose is a symbol of martyrdom, while the white rose is a symbol of purity."[118] A body of symbolism with carefully worked out distinctions like these is usually a sign of a scholastic tradition. In the Bronze Age it seems that the cherry, for example, signified the goddess and her various

118 Ferguson, *Signs and Symbols in Christian Art* (above, n.97), 29–37.

attributes; the carnation, the same; the lily, the same; and so on. I have suggested that apple and flower, in Sappho, have more or less the same signified. Stehle, by assigning specific and very different signifieds to each seems to posit a scholastic type of closed symbol-system for archaic lyric and especially Sappho; I propose one more like both the Bronze Age iconographic and the *symboliste* – more intuitive and open than systematic and closed.

The many scenes of girls picking or wearing or plaiting flowers in Greek poetry suggest to Stehle virgins who are about to be raped; to me they suggest girls who are ready for sex – their flowers are open; they may indeed already have engaged in sex; that certainly would not disqualify them for the symbol of the opened blossom: virgins are buds not blossoms. Could one believe that Minoan religion, which constantly associates women and flowers, was a religion of virginity? Rather, the girl adorning herself in some way with flowers is advertising herself not as a virgin, but as a woman ready for sex.

Stehle assumes these equations not merely for Sappho, but for Greek poets in general, focusing especially on Ibycus's fr. 286, which describes a sacred garden precinct with flowers and fruit trees blooming. "The flowers," she writes, "... are not so much significant in themselves as reminders of the fruit to follow."[119] But the passage in question mentions the ripening fruit first, and then the flowers, the opposite of the sequence in which the flowers would presage the fruit. Probably they are meant to be visualized simultaneously as partly emptied signifiers that reinforce one another by making the same statement twice. Edmonds translates the phrase in question (Κυδώνιαι μηλίδες ἀρδόμεναι) as "the quince

119 Stehle, "Retreat from the Male: Catullus 62 and Sappho's Erotic Flowers" (above, n. 8), n. 35.

trees...grow green," which could support Stehle's view. Lattimore goes to the other extreme; neglecting the hinted flowers altogether he translates, "the Kydonian quinces...and grapes...ripen,"[120] eliminating Stehle's dichotomy. The grammar most obviously suggests something in-between the two. "The quinces...and vine-blossoms...ripen," thereby reversing the order, which Stehle needs for her interpretation. This passage is not a strong support for the flower-fruit opposition (of which she says, "The contrast of flower and fruit is not a commonplace in Greek thought; I think it is an undercurrent."[121]) (But *anything* can be suggested as an "undercurrent.")

A basic problem with the equation flower = virginity is that, as Stehle herself notes, the flower basically represents "the female genitals."[122] Against those who, following that signification, call the site of Ibycus's poem a "garden of love" she notes that Ibycus specifically calls it Πάρθενων κῆπος ἀκήρατος, which she translates "a garden of virgins,"[123] relating Ibycus's vision to a cult like Sappho's supposed "cult of virginity."

Both the *thiasos* and the attitude toward virginity are as much topics in the history of religion as in Sapphic literary criticism. And once more it is necessary to look behind Sappho, at the influences she inherited, to understand her. One cannot interpret Sappho by Catullus, though one can, to some extent, interpret Catullus by Sappho. Sappho was (whether institutionally or personally) a scion of the ancient goddess religion. Cultic associations of girls and women devoted to a goddess extend back through the Bronze Age and

---

120 *Greek Lyrics*, ed. and trans. R. Lattimore (Univ. of Chicago Press, 1960), 37.

121 Stehle, "Retreat from the Male: Catullus 62 and Sappho's Erotic Flowers" (above, n. 8), n. 16.

122 Ibid., n. 15. Why was so important a fact relegated to the middle of a long footnote?

123 Ibid., n. 35.

probably into the Neolithic. Whatever we feel about the alleged gynaicocracy or matriarchy of the Neolithic Age, we cannot deny at least that the female principle was more independent then than in the so-called patriarchal ages. Studies of sexual and marriage practices among modern Neolithic primitives illustrate this, though it is already apparent from an analysis of ancient texts and iconography.[124]

What is found among such societies is a female social role that the resolutely patrilineal cultures – such as the Judeo-Christian and Islamic – do not exhibit. Among modern Neolithic primitives, as one scholar notes, young girls "are guarded ... against violence and especially from 'incest' with their 'clan brothers' but with men of a clan into which they may marry they can follow their own wishes ... A girl belongs to *herself* while she is ... unwed, and may not be compelled either to maintain chastity or to yield to an unwanted embrace."[125] In the Neolithic societies of the ancient Near East and Eastern Mediterranean, unmarried women seem to have enjoyed the same independence. During the Bronze Age, while male dominance slowly and steadily asserted itself, this custom was prohibited in some, but by no means all areas. The concept at least still survived into Sappho's day and was denoted by the word *παρθένος*, which almost everyone translates "virgin." This translation, however, may apply only to certain uses and certain times.

"The word *parthenos*," Frazer wrote, "applied to Artemis, which we commonly translate virgin, means no more than an unmarried woman, and in early days the two things were by

124 I mean the type of analysis that was begun by J. J. Bachofen, in *Myth, Religion, and Mother Right* (*Mutterrecht und Urreligion* [1861], trans. R. Manheim [Princeton Univ. Press, 1973]), and extended by many scholars down to, say, James Mellaart and Marija Gimbutas.

125 M. Esther Harding, *Women's Mysteries: Ancient and Modern* (New York: Pantheon, 1955), 103.

no means the same ... there was no public worship of Artemis the Chaste; so far as her sacred titles bear on the relation of the sexes, they show that, on the contrary, she was, like Diana in Italy, especially connected with the loss of virginity and with child-bearing ... Nothing, however, sets the true character of Artemis as a goddess of fecundity though not of wedlock in a clearer light than her constant identification with the unmarried, but not chaste Asiatic goddesses of love and fertility, who were worshipped with rites of notorious profligacy at their popular sanctuaries."[126]

Robert Briffault concurs: "The word virgin is, of course, used in those titles in its primitive sense as denoting 'unwed,' and connoting the very reverse of what the term has come to imply. The virgin Ishtar is also frequently addressed as 'The Prostitute'; and she herself says, 'a prostitute compassionate am I.' She wears the 'posin' or veil, which, as among the Jews, was the mark of both 'virgins' and prostitutes. The hierodules, or sacred prostitutes of her temples, were also called 'the holy virgins' ... children born out of wedlock were called *parthenioi*, 'virgin-born.' The word 'virgin' itself has not, strictly speaking, the meaning which we attach to it; the correct Latin expression for the untouched virgin is not 'virgo,' but 'virgo intacta'. Aphrodite herself was a virgin."[127] Another scholar notes, "The Great Mother is always represented as *virgin*. In spite of the fact that she has many lovers and is the mother of many sons."[128] The word *παρθένος*, on this view, means "unwed and independent or self-governing." "It may be used of a woman who has had much sexual experience; it may even be applied to

126 J. G. Frazer, *The Golden Bough: A Study in Magic and Religion* (Oxford Univ. Press, 1998), 18.

127 R. Briffault, *The Mothers: A Study of the Origins of Sentiments and Institutions*, 3 vols. (London: Allen & Unwin, 1927), 3:169–70.

128 Harding, *Women's Mysteries* (above, n. 125), 101.

a prostitute. Its real significance is to be found in its use as contrasted to 'married.'"[129]

And yet it seems impossible that the Artemis of the *Hippolytus* is merely recommending that Hippolytus remain unmarried; she seems to require chastity. Similarly, in the Homeric *Hymn to Aphrodite*, Athena, Artemis, and Hestia are declared to avoid not just marriage, but sex also. The discrepancy arises from the fact that in the age of these texts the term is changing denotation, as the history of culture and religion, to which it belongs, undergoes changes. Theoretically these "unwed" or "independent, self-sufficient" goddesses represent a type going back to the Neolithic and Bronze Ages – a goddess of sexuality who remained unbound to any single man. It refers to a period when goddesses were sexual adventurers as the Greek gods Zeus and Apollo were later to be (a period of which there are explicit memories in, for example, the *Epic of Gilgamesh*). During the course of Greek culture the denotation was drastically altered. To a Mycenaean Greek it presumably had its earlier meaning; to Euripides in the *Hippolytus* it means "chaste." Where does Sappho stand in regard to this term?

In connection with the Ishtar type of independent unwed goddess, who takes different lovers at will, the goddess-garden archetype is a "garden of love," and in connection with the later, patriarchally revised sense of the word the παρθένων κῆπας is a "garden of virgins." There are signs of the earlier

129 Ibid., 103. Cf. K. Kerényi, *Athene: Virgin and Mother in Greek Religion*, trans. M. Stein (Putnam, Conn.: Spring Publications, 2008): "In Greece the relation to sex is not exhausted by the alternatives of chastity and unchastity. There are many combinations and mixtures; 'chaste' is not always identical with 'virginal' nor even with 'temperate.'" (20) And: "'Parthenos' and 'Kore' also do not particularly stress this, but they certainly do refer to the girlishness of the goddess concerned." (35)

meaning surviving well into the Greek period alongside the emerging new meaning. In the *Hippolytus,* for example, there is a reference to the Garden of the Hesperides, "the apple-bearing Hesperian coast... where ambrosial fountains flow by Zeus's bed in his chambers, where life-giving earth increases happiness for the gods" (742ff.). Here is the garden of fr. 2 again, with apples, springs, ambrosia-or-nectar, goddesses – and sexuality. Earlier in the *Hippolytus,* Euripides describes a "garden of virginity"; Hippolytus, offering flowers to Artemis, says,

> This woven garland I have made from a pure meadow,
> O queen, where no shepherd dares feed his flock,
> no steel of sickle comes; only the bee roveth the
> undesecrated springtime meadow... They who have
> self-control in all things, purity inborn, may gather
> flowers there, but none impure. (72ff.)

Yet Euripides does not believe in this garden, which he regards as a pathological ideal. Later in the same play he reveals the hidden presence of sex in Artemis's garden:

> The terrible goddess [Aphrodite] breathes on all things,
> flying about like a bee. (563–64)

Euripides, in other words, seems to be aware of both kinds of gardens, and to regard the Aphrodisiac garden as the more fundamental type. Pindar, in *Olympian* 2.71ff., also describes this garden, which he calls Elysium, shadowed by red roses and incense trees, with golden fruit hanging about. Here again are Sappho's roses, trees, and apples. Pindar does not specify whether the garden is devoted to sexuality or to chastity. Sappho's "roses of Pieria" come from just such a garden as the first Homeric *Hymn to Hermes* reveals, speaking of Pieria as "a place of untouched and lovely meadows" (72). The Homeric *Hymn to Pan* takes us to this garden again: a mountain meadow where nymphs sing and dance, clear springs flow, crocuses and hyacinths blossom (375ff.). Euripides, in *Iphigenia at Aulis,* gives us yet another example: "to dwell by the silvery waters, by the nymphs and their fountains, by that meadow green and abundant, with roses and hyacinths gathered for goddesses" (129ff.). The first Homeric *Hymn to Aphrodite* presents the ancient garden again:

> As for the child, as soon as he sees the light of the sun, the deep-breasted mountain Nymphs who inhabit this great and holy mountain shall bring him up. They rank neither with mortals nor with immortals, long indeed do they live, eating heavenly food and treading the lovely dance among the immortals, and with them the sileni and the sharp-eyed Slayer of Argus mate in the depths of pleasant caves; but at their birth pines or high topped oaks spring up with them upon the fruitful earth, beautiful flourishing trees, towering high upon the lofty mountains (and men call them holy places of the immortals, and never mortal lops them with the axe.) (256ff.)

This again is clearly a garden of sexuality; yet it is specifically off-limits to human beings – not unlike the situation in the book of Genesis, where Adam and Eve are forbidden access to the garden.

The ambiguity of this evidence – the fact that this archetypal garden is seen in directly opposite ways – as a precinct of sexual intercourse or as a precinct of chastity – can be explained in terms of the history of religion. The goddess-worshipping cultures of the third millennium BCE, in Sumer especially, seem to have had garden cults in which initiations involving ritual performances of sexual acts were conducted. This may be seen as a remnant of the Neolithic Age, in which sexuality was a powerful *numinosum* and female sexuality was perhaps even more prominent than male. With the appearance, sometime before 2000 BCE, of Semitic and Indo-European cultures with male dominated structures, sexual morality changed – and so did attitudes toward the garden, and the unwed and sexually independent woman. The earlier customs probably were generated in matrilineal societies, where the paternity of a child is irrelevant for purposes of inheritance; but in the patrilineal Indo-European and Semitic cultures much energy was expended in guaranteeing accurate knowledge of paternity. In Israel, Yahweh closed off the garden and female sexuality was radically repressed. The sexually independent woman was rejected violently, in an attempt to establish clear patrilineal dynasties. In Greece the garden was shut off, but less violently and unambiguously. The garden of the Hesperides remains sexual, but is relegated to the edge of the universe where only the hero Heracles can find it. The garden in the Homeric *Hymn to Aphrodite* is still sexual – but is inhabited only by demigods, sileni, and the phallic Hermes. In the *Hippolytus,* Euripides actually shows awareness of this process, when he first posits Artemis's garden of chastity, then reveals that Aphrodite herself is hidden in it as the bee mating with flowers.

We are, then, dealing with two psycho-sexual structures – the garden of sex and the garden of chastity – of which the second is later than the first and represents a deliberate censorship and distortion of it (as does the story of the Fall in Genesis). One cannot simply assert that one level or the other is *the* (one and only) Greek archetype. Rather, we find some gardens of the first type, some of the second, and some that cannot be identified. Both Sappho's and Ibycus's gardens are of the unidentifiable type.

The same ambiguity exists in uses of the word παρθένος and in assignations of flower and fruit imagery. We have seen that there are two meanings of the word παρθένος, "unwed and independent" with no implications of either chastity or unchastity, and "virgin." The two meanings seem to correspond to the customs of Bronze and Iron Age Greece, respectively. As Flacelière says, "In classical Greece neither unmarried nor married women were regarded as legally entitled to act independently ... Their position contrasted strikingly with that of women under the Minoan and Achaean civilizations."[130] What I am suggesting is that Sappho's sense of herself in her society partook to a degree of the earlier role of the independent woman; that this was a part of the cultic context that her garden of Aphrodite brought with it.

There are many references to this female social role in Greek literature, though many if not all of them may have been remembered from an earlier age rather than observed. One example of the Bronze Age type of independent unwed παρθένος is Atalanta, whose son is named Parthenopaeus, "born of a παρθένος" or unwed mother; Euripides refers to "his archer mother the κόρη of Maenalus" (*Phoenician Women* 1062), where κόρη, like παρθένος in her son's name, cannot have the meaning "virgin." Κόρη also has the meaning of "young wife" in *Iliad* 6.247, and in Euripides' *Orestes* 1438. It refers to a concubine, Briseis, in *Iliad* 1.98, 1.337, and 3.689. In Pindar's Eulogy of Xenophon of Corinth, it refers to prostitutes, as it does at *Palatine Anthology* 5.4. Obviously κόρη does not carry the primary meaning of "virgin" but simply "girl," whether chaste or not, or married or not.

Παρθένος was a more limited term, signifying either a virgin or an unmarried woman who may even be a mother. The word means "unwed non-virgin" in *Iliad* 2.514, referring to Astyoche, who bore sons to Ares, and who is perhaps a survival of a Bronze Age παρθένος or self-governing goddess. In the archaic period one can still see this role passing away or being redefined. In Pindar's third *Pythian Ode*, Coronis is in the position of a self-governing παρθένος from the "matriarchal" age, who is punished violently by the patriarchal Apollo

130 Flacelière, *Love in Ancient Greece* (above, n. 68), 75.

for precisely her insistence on her own sexual freedom. Artemis, whose cult was once itself extremely licentious, has by this time been converted to true anti-sexual virginity from the self-governing sexual freedom of her earlier period, and goes as the agent of Apollo to destroy this girl who still maintains the old way (*Pythian* 3.30ff.). As part of the classical redefinition of the role, *πάρθενος* came to have disreputable moral associations. Sophocles, in *The Women of Trachis* (1219), refers to Heracles' mistress Iole as *παρθένος*. Aristophanes, in the *Clouds* (530), seems to use the word in the same way. A concubine may be called *παρθένος*, and perhaps a courtesan.

One can see in the changing meanings of this word the remains of a social order being given the last nudge into invisibility. Granted that the concept of the matriarchy *per se* – a state in which both inheritance and political office are exclusively in the hands of women – is widely regarded nowadays as mythical, in the sense that there is no strong evidence for ascribing such social systems to the ancient Neolithic stratum of the Mediterranean and Near East. Burials at Çatalhöyük, the leading candidate for a couple of decades now, show women's remains buried with cosmetics and kitchen utensils, men with weapons and tools.[131] Something not unlike patriarchal social roles is suggested. Still, such societies have been observed on a small scale among modern Neolithic cultures in Oceania, so they are not completely mythical. And there is something, indeed, behind the type of mythic evidence that Bachofen proposed the matriarchy as a solution to – and that something may have involved the effects of matrilineality. One anthropologist offers the estimate that fifteen percent of the world's

131 J. Mellaart, *Çatal Hüyük: A Neolithic Town in Anatolia* (London: Thames & Hudson, 1967).

cultures are matrilineal, eighty-five percent patrilineal.[132] In a matrilineal society, the identity of the father doesn't matter in terms of inheriting office, goods, or social position. The child is raised in the mother's clan, and the men of her family, not the biological father, sponsor the child in the world. There is room then for a social gender role that becomes untenable under patrilineal systems – that of an unmarried woman who makes her own decisions about sexuality and childbearing, and is not accountable to any authority in these decisions. This is a type of female social role that has been coming back in the last generation or two in the West, after long disappearance. We do not know what the social situation in seventh and sixth century Lesbos was, but clearly the sexes lived separately to a large extent. At Alcaeus's drinking parties there are only men; in Sappho's social world men are totally absent except at wedding ceremonies. In Sappho's seemingly sheltered life – without judging how much of it is fantasy (hers and modern scholars') and how much fact – she maintained the stature of the mature and self-determining female, which is built into the aphrodisiac cultic milieu of her verses.

It would seem then that to call Aphrodite's garden in Sappho's fr. 2 a "garden of virgins" may be to import a puritanical patriarchal tone that she managed to keep more or less attenuated in her milieu (localizing it in Group 3). Ibycus's "Garden of the Parthenoi," similarly, is not necessarily a "garden of virgins," as Stehle calls it, but may just as well mean a garden of sexually independent Bronze Age-type females.[133]

132 See M. Harris, *Cows, Pigs, Wars, and Witches: The Riddles of Culture* (New York: Random House, 1974).

133 The same is true of Sappho's use of the word; even as homosexuals these girls were not necessarily *virgines intactae:* Sappho's fr. 99 seems to mention a dildo. It is true, as Campbell notes, that "the lines may be by Alcaeus." (D. A. Campbell, *Greek Lyric with an English Translation*

Sappho's poetic cult, whatever its status as private, public, or something else, seems to preserve many Bronze Age elements. These may be expected to go beyond matters of culture – say, a poetic meter or a myth – and to preserve suggestions of social forms from earlier ages. There are still other survivals of this character type, which can be glimpsed through certain kinship terms. Both Aristotle (*Politics* 1306*b*29) and Strabo (*Geography* 6.3.2) use the masculine noun παρθένιας, to refer to the son of a concubine, and both Homer (*Iliad* 16.180) and Pindar (*Olympian* 6.31) use ὁ παρθένιος to mean the son of an unmarried woman. Euripides, in the *Ion* (1472), employs the term νόθον παρθενεύματος to mean "child of an unmarried woman." These examples extend the usage throughout Greek literary history – from Homer to Strabo – and make assertions about "virginity" without the full and unambiguous term problematical. There are uses of the word παρθένος, which, context establishes, do clearly imply "virgin," but it seems that the unambiguous phrase for that meaning was παρθένος ἀδμής, "an unmarried woman who has not yet been overcome by love, or by a lover." (See, e.g., Homeric *Hymn to Aphrodite I* 82, 133; Æschylus, *The Suppliants* 149; Homeric *Hymn to Demeter* 145; Sophocles, *Electra* 1239; Hesiod, *Catalogue of Women* 88, where the term is used of Coronis.)

For example, in Sappho's epithalamic fragments 107, 112, and 114, there can be no certainty about which usage is intended. In fr. 114, for example, the bride may not be saying "virginity, virginity, leaving me where do you go?" but "independence, independence, leaving me where do you go?" Many

---

[Cambridge, Mass.: Harvard Univ. Press, 1987], 125.) West notes that ὄλισβος can also mean *plectrum,* and either translation makes sense of the passage. (M. L. West, *Iambi et Elegi Graeci ante Alexandrum cantati* (Oxford: At the Clarendon Press, 1971–72.) The fragment belongs in Group 3 (compare it to fr. 155 with its testimonium by Maximus of Tyre).

uses of the word are simply unclear as to meaning. Hesiod, for example, says, "marry a παρθενικὴν so you can teach her careful ways" (*Works and Days* 699), and it is not certain that he means a "virgin" rather than "a woman who has not been married before" (lest her former husband have taught her uncareful ways). In 519ff. he specifies a παρθενικὴν "who knows not the deeps of Aphrodite," hence a virgin; but why did he have to specify what kind of παρθένος he meant, unless he was aware of the two uses of the word? Sophocles, in *The Women of Trachis* 144ff., has Deianeira say, "Like us, the tender young thing is reared and nurtured in some closed garden; neither heat nor rain nor any breath of air disturbs it, but it leads a life effortless with pleasures (ἡδονάι) until, wife instead of παρθένος, she receives her share of worries in the secret night, fearing for her husband or children." "Παρθένος" here may or may not mean "virgin," but in any case this passage seems much more likely to be the source of Catullus's garden-enclosed flower than do the fragments of Sappho, which Stehle attempts to derive it from (frr. 105 *a* and *c*). Later in the same play (536), we read, "not a κόρη, but married," suggesting again the sense of "unwed" for κόρη.

Flower and Fruit

The use of the imagery of flower and fruit, which Stehle interprets as virginity and sexuality respectively, is just as ambiguous as that of the words for "virgin." The pattern that she discerns may indeed be there as "an undercurrent" (as she says); but it is clearly not a widespread or dominant practice. Some examples will illustrate the range of uses involved in these two images in early Greek poetry. While there are examples that could involve virginity, other usages indicate that the flower means maturity or ripeness.

1) Homeric *Hymn to Hermes I* 375: The infant Hermes, competing with Apollo, complains that the older god "has the rich flower of glorious youth (Hebe), but I was just born yesterday"; he associates flowers, then, not with early childhood, but with adolescence or young adulthood; they cannot then have the simple denotation of virginity, since the very young, of course, possess that quality; it is the ripeness of full-blown beauty that the very young lack and the flower here intends.

2) Homeric *Hymn to Aphrodite I* 284: "Offspring of a flower-like nymph" indicates that the identification with a flower (here *καλυκώπιδος*, not *ἄνθος*, is used) does not mean virginity; this flower has already given birth.

3) Both Homeric *Hymns to Aphrodite* associate the goddess, no virgin, with flowers: she wears flower-shaped earrings and necklaces, as in *Hymn to Aphrodite II* 10.

4) Homeric *Hymn to Aphrodite III* 3: "The erotic flower (*ἱμερτὸν ἄνθος*) of her face" describes again the goddess not of virginity, but of sexuality.

5) Hesiod, in *Catalogue of Women* 18, says, "Because of their wantonness they have lost their tender flower (*τέρεν ἄνθος*), for he gave them leprosy." Here the flower is associated not with virginity, but with surface beauty.

6) Mimnermus (fr. 1.1–3) says that love, gifts and the bed are the "flowers of youth" – clearly not virginal flowers.

7) In Sophocles' *The Women of Trachis* (547ff.), Deianeira complains about a younger rival, noting that "the eye loves to pluck the flower of those who are still gaining [beauty], but from those who are decreasing [in beauty] the foot turns away." That is, Deianeira herself, though no virgin, still has the flower – only her flower is withering; her younger rival's flower is still opening. The flower then represents not virginity, but beauty and desireability. (This passage may be related somehow to Sappho's fr. 105*a*.) Deianeira does not say, "once they have plucked the flower they turn away" but

"when the flower is old, they turn away." The suggestion is that this flower may be plucked again and again; it is not the hymeneal membrane, but the whole beauty-and-sexuality of women.

8) In Euripides' *The Phoenician Women* 88, Antigone is called the "flower of her father's house" (θάλος, not ἄνθος). Is this more likely to mean "its virgin" or "its ornament, its delight"?

9) In Euripides' *Iphigenia at Aulis* 1224–25, Agamemnon, speaking to Iphigenia (in Iphigenia's flashback), says: "O child, surely one day I shall see you happy in your husband's home and like a flower blooming for me and in my honor." That is, even after her marriage, Antigone will have her "flower"; it does not vanish with her virginity.

10) There are still other examples where the intention is more vague and generalized than this distinction would suggest. In the Homeric *Hymn to Gaia,* we read that in communities blessed by Mother Earth, "the daughters in flower-laden bands play and skip merrily over the soft flowers of the field." This image by itself could comport with the equation flower = virginity, but it is unclear either way, and if we review usage in the Homeric hymns overall, the equation becomes so muddied as to be almost meaningless.

11) Stehle seems to feel that her strongest example is in the Cologne Epode of Archilochus (SLG 478.27), where the suitor "has spurned Neoboule on the grounds that she has 'lost her virgin flower.'"[134] But literally the text says, her "flower has flowed away," and the "flowing" suggests the passage of time, that is, Neobuole is now too old, like Deianeira in *The Women of Trachis*. Her flower is withering, while her sister's is still opening.

---

134 Stehle, "Retreat from the Male: Catullus 62 and Sappho's Erotic Flowers" (above, n.8), 95.

Liddel-Scott-Jones's Greek-English lexicon defines ἄνθος (flower) as "generally *anything thrown upon the surface*." In terms of girls, it means their surface beauty. Many other usages of the word rob it of the specificity of "virginity." Æschylus, for example, speaks of "culling the flowers of grief" (*The Suppliants* 73), grief having come to the surface of consciousness. Sophocles similarly speaks of the "flowering of madness" (*The Women of Trachis* 999). Pindar prays that "wealth may flower" (*Pythian* 10.18). The "flower of wine" is the froth that rises to the surface. In Pindar, "prosperity flowers" (*Isthmian* 5.13) and "happiness blooms" (*Pythian* 7.21). Ares "flowers" among the spears (*Olympian* 13. 23).

12) Many examples connect the images of flower and fruit with the general sense of well-being or ripe maturity of life. Winners at the games are wreathed with flowers to associate them with the whole complex of well-being that goes back to the Mother Goddess and the Dying God; they are assimilated to the dying flower god.

The dead receive flowers to return them into the care of the ancient goddess; here the flower may have its root meaning of vagina. In Sophocles' *Electra,* flowers *and milk* are left on Agamemnon's grave (893ff.), strongly suggesting the ancient afterlife hope of returning to the mother's care (or into the pre-Oedipal state).

The land flowers around Dionysus (and runs with milk!) in the *Bacchae* (105). In the *Homeric Hymn to Dionysus,* the ship's mast blossoms with flowers, vines, and grapes. In the Homeric *Hymn to Delian Apollo* (135ff.), Delos blossoms when the god first walks there.

Finally there is the common phrase "flower of youth" (ἥβης ἄνθος). The age designated as ἥβη is said to be around 16 to 18 years old. But clearly the phrase is used more widely than that and simply means something like "life viewed as a positive value." Athenian battle inscriptions down to the end of the fifth century declare that the dead have "lost the flower of their youth," though most of the soldiers involved must have been older than 16 or 18. In Æschylus's *The Persians* (58) it is related that "the flower of the Persian nation" fell, meaning no more than men in the fullness of maturity. In *Iliad* 13.484 Diomede declares that he fears Æneus because the latter has "the flower of youth," meaning simply that he is "in his prime." In Æschylus's *The Suppliants* (663) it is prayed, "may the flower of this land's youth be unculled" in war, again suggesting not virginity, but mature strength, not budding strength, but full-flowering strength. The same passage expresses the hope that "Ares may not shear off the bloom of the nation's men," and here we can see the mutability of this image: Ares himself "flowers" in battle and also "cuts off the flowers" in battle. I suggest that Archilochus's *ἄνθος παρθένιον* relates to the common image of the "flower of youth" and simply means "the flower of girlhood." The same usage occurs in the Homeric *Hymn to Demeter*, where we find Persephone described as "maiden… sweet flower" (*κουρὴν… γλυκερὸν θάλος*, 66), the daughters of Celeus described as "like goddesses with the flower of girlhood" (*κουρήϊον ἄνθος*, 108), the goddess's newborn son described as her "new flower" (*νέον θάλος*, 187), and (as if to confute and confound the flower/virginity linkage) Aphrodite called "garland-loving." Indeed, Aphrodite is constantly associated with flowers while Artemis, Athena and the Eumenides never are. The implication is clear, that the flower does not denote virginity at all, but beauty and desirability, which Aphrodite has and those other goddesses lack. Surely this is the meaning that Sappho, the servant of Aphrodite, intended in her obsessive repetitions of this image.[135]

135 In reconstructing Sappho's "personal religion" of Aphrodite, the Muses and Graces, we will find confirmation in Pindar, the most

In light of these and other examples, it would seem ill-advised

---

Sapphic of all Greek poets (more than half of whose extant work is in Æolic meters). Several key points may be made briefly:

1) *Olympian* 9.48: ἄνθεα δ' ὕμνων νεωτέρων (the flowers of new songs); Pindar continues Sappho's implied practice of regarding poems as flowers.

2) *Nemean* 5.54–55: "Bring the grassy garlands of flowers and the yellow-haired Graces."

3) *Olympian* 1.30: "Charis (Grace) creates all sweet delights for people."

4) *Olympian* 3.6ff.: "Garlands bound in the hair exact from me this god-commanded duty...to mingle the harp's note and the flute's cry and the patterns of words." As in Sappho, flowers bound in hair and songs go together as by a religious law. This is Sappho's religion, adopted by Pindar. No other poet contains statements so close to her use of her central symbols.

5) *Olympian* 2.49ff.: "The Graces made him share the flowers with his brother."

6) *Isthmian* 8.9: "So let us not give in and go without garlands." To go without garlands would, as Sappho noted, offend the Graces. To go without garlands means to cease to be glad to be alive, to cease to find life beautiful. The flower of youth is not something (like virginity) for another person to take; it is the delight in life that the possessor himself or herself enjoys.

7) *Isthmian* 3.8: "We must exalt [the victor] with the gentle Graces."

8) *Isthmian* 8.66*a*: "Weave a delicate [ἁβρόν] wreath of myrtle for Kleandros."

9) *Isthmian* 4.35ff.: Describing the change in a family's fortunes: "Now after the winter's dark, the ornamented earth has blossomed with purple roses."

10) *Paeans* 3 (Sandys): "Hail, holy Graces, companions of the Muses, enthroned in splendor."

11) *Pythian* 6.1–5: "Is it Aphrodite of the sudden glances or is it the Graces whose field we are ploughing now?" As in Sappho, the ancient fertility goddess and her garden are converted to the creation of poem-flowers rather than plant flowers.

12) *Pythian* 6.48: "Not violently plucking [the flower of] youth, but plucking the flower of wisdom in the secret places of the Pierian [Muses]." As in Sappho, flowers of song grow in the Pierian garden.

13) *Pythian* 12. 26–27: "The song...blown through the reeds that grow near the fair-spaced city of the Graces, the garden of the Nymph of Kephisos."

to accept the simple equation flower = virginity. It may occasionally work like that, but if the usage is not regular, how are we to be sure it is there at all? The situation with imagery of fruit is just as bad. Stehle rightly observes that "the apple is an age-old symbol of sexual love and human fertility,"[136] but her scholastic distinction between fruit and flower does not seem sustained in the literary tradition.

13) In Æschylus's *The Suppliants* 998ff., Danaus, addressing the suppliant maidens, who are of course virgins, calls them not flowers, but fruit: "The tender fruit of summer is hard to protect... The Cyprian spreads the news of fruit bursting with ripeness." Clearly the equation fruit = matron does not hold. It seems that flower and fruit are interchangeable images for the beauty and sexuality of young adulthood.

14) Not once in the *Suppliants*, a play that features virginity above all others, is the image of the flower used to describe the virgin girls. The image of fruit, or summer, however, is used three times.

15) Often the flower and fruit images are combined in such a way as to indicate that they merely reinforce one another – there is no rigid distinction between them. In *Pythian* 9.110, when a girl is offered in marriage, Pindar says that her suitors "wished to pluck the flowering fruit of the gold wreath of Hebe."

---

14) *Olympian* 14.1ff.: "The waters of Kephisos belong to the place of fine horses where you dwell, Queens of Song, in sparkling Orchomenos, Graces... By your help all sweet and delightful things belong to men."

136 Stehle, "Retreat from the Male: Catullus 62 and Sappho's Erotic Flowers" (above, n. 8), 91. On this subject see further B. O. Foster, "Notes on the Symbolism of the Apple in Classical Antiquity," *Harvard Studies in Classical Philology* 10 (1899), 39–55; E. S. McCartney, "How the Apple Became the Token of Love," *Transactions of the American Philological Association* 56 (1925), 70–81; J. Trumpf, "Kydonische Äpfel," *Hermes* 88 (1960), 14–22.

16) Pindar, *Isthmian* 8.45*a*: "The fruit of her words did not wither."

Finally, it seems clear that the images of fruit and flower, which abound in Sappho's work, were not scholastically opposed as, say, the lily and the rose are opposed in the iconography of the Virgin Mary. This is not the way her imagery worked – as an arbitrary set of second-order significations that is in a one to one correspondence to the first-order significations, so that in each set one has a signifier, a first-order signified, and a second-order signified, each set different in all three elements from each of the others. Rather, in Sappho's method, the set of second-order significations is much fewer in number than that of the first-order signifieds because the point is not simply to redescribe the world in every detail, but to partly melt it down into an assertion of an underlying unity. Her imagery then was not separate units, but a cumulative process in which mutually reinforcing signifiers repeatedly and from many directions affirm the self-sustaining viability of the female in particular and of the richness of life in general. Whether homosexual or heterosexual, this is the common ground.

"Symbolisme"?

In past articles I have analyzed some of Sappho's work primarily from the standpoint of the so-called "New criticism." That type of analysis was sufficient to show how the poems "work" as "gadget-poems" (Karl Shapiro's term) or self-referential aesthetic systems. At the moment I am less concerned with how individual poems work than with their relationship to the overall tradition of Western literature. It is possible to discern cracks or gaps in Sappho's poetic mask that reveal discontinuities in the history of sensibility, and seem to place her at the forefront of a crisis in consciousness that she resolved by retaining the signifiers of the older age while assigning them a new order of signifieds, a mentalist and *symboliste* order that would not, it seems, have been possible to an earlier poet.

The use of the word "*symboliste*" is not meant polemically, nor is it intended as a general comparison. The point is that in the history of European (as opposed to Greco-Roman) literature, a similar *coupure épistémologique* occurred in the *symboliste* movement and was worked out there by means not totally different from Sappho's. She, of course, was much closer to the body of archaic tradition than was, say, Mallarmé, and for a variety of reasons – some cultural, some dealing with the stage of language awareness at her time – she could not break away from the old ways as freely or radically as he did. The positive point I wish to make is that Sappho's imagery has several aspects at once, some attempting to maintain an impression of continuity with tradition, others more revolutionary. The Group 1 poems are primarily those that maintain continuity with the ancient tradition. In the Group 2 and 4 poems we find the more radical aspect of Sappho's imagery, and my point is simply that in its most radical aspect Sappho's imagery begins the process that was begun again (and carried much farther) by Mallarmé for the modern age. The French poet used language as a group of more or less free variables – some having no value at all assigned to them, others with rather loose and vague values far less explicit than the denotations. Words then became pure signifiers with no signifieds attached to them – signifiers not yet involved in any act of signification. Used thus, words become "empty"; a certain infinity opens up in them. They exist as pure potentiality without any limiting actual meaning; language itself becomes like the blank page that Mallarmé says is the ultimate poem, since containing nothing it suggests everything. Similarly his image-words, since they assert nothing, imply everything (or anything). Used in this way, words become, as Mallarmé intended, icons of the absolute, of a meaning beyond any conceivable form. All words then become interchangeable since all open into the same infinite (or indeterminate) signified. The page filled with words is then, in a mysterious way, both the same as the blank page and again obviously different from it.

Sappho's poetry of Groups 2 and 4 is *symboliste* in its constant "centripetality," in its concern for "isolating the hypothetical germ of literature" and its "tendency to equate this isolation with the entire creative process."[137] Her poems, like those of the *symbolistes,* are based less on assertive meaning than on "a unity of mood," "the state of mind directed toward the ... contemplating of beauty."[138] Sappho's flowers, girls, enchanted groves, moonlit seas, are signifiers that have been partly pried loose from their signifieds. They are relatively free or empty compared with the range of ordinary linguistic denotation. They palpitate with implications of translinguistic meaning; they become mysteries, *numinosa.* Those signifiers that Sappho has emptied become more or less interchangeable; the rose or other flower, the goddess, the pretty girl, the garland, the sound of music, even a smile or a footfall – all these images (and others) may be used more or less interchangeably since all refer to the same expanded or emptied signified, an ideal realm in which perishable beauty is transmuted through art into archetypal eternality.

In Sappho's poetic language those holes into infinity have just begun to open up here and there. In certain of Mallarmé's poems the whole language was emptied out. Sappho's main second-order signifiers are in contrast only partially empty; their denotation remains effective at the more or

137 Frye, *Anatomy of Criticism* (above, n. 19), 80.
138 Ibid.

less inconsequential level of the primary signification; but as second-order signifiers they point to very broad areas of emotion and sensibility through "a growing richness of meaning unlimited by denotation." Sappho retains coherence at the level of first-order signification, or lexical denotation, because she is still bound by the "plausibility-principle," "the necessity of shaping [the poem] into a form acceptable to the poet's and his reader's waking consciousness, and of adapting [it] to the sign-meanings of assertive language well enough to be communicable to that consciousness."[139] Clearly the innermost meaning of her poems reaches beyond the daylight world of the plausibility principle into dreamy lunar realms where the processes of waking life are inverted: vegetation is nourished not by the sun, but by the moon, and has no practical purpose; the products of the earth are not eaten (in fact, no one eats in this phantomlike world "on the other side of the mirror") but used for adornment; unions are severed by presence (fr. 94) and united by absence (fr. 96); the tumults of empires are silenced by the footfall of a girl (fr. 16). This is a nighttime world where a dreamlike trance (*κῶμα*, fr. 2) presides and annuls the reality of the day (not unlike the world evoked in *symboliste* poems). It bespeaks a deep discontent with ordinary reality and a longing to escape it through those expanded symbols that open into infinity, which we dimly sense behind their residual opacity, or the inertia of their denotations. The poetic image becomes a kind of membrane through which we can feel the rippling of transcendent winds. The various images become like the panes of many-colored glass that, in Shelley's line, "stain the white radiance of eternity." The inertia of their denotations produces the opacity or "stain," yet behind them all the same numinosum can be sensed. This use of the lyric genre became

139 Ibid., 272.

common in the Romantic and Symboliste movements and was the basis of the abstract or nonrepresentational modern verse in which denotation (like representation in painting) becomes irrelevant or at least problematic.

Judging from the present state of the evidence, it seems that Sappho was the first to open poetry to a sense of a signification beyond language itself, by beginning the process of freeing the signifier from the signified.[140] Being the first to move in that direction, she could not possibly have gone all the way without losing the audience still conditioned to Homer's discursive parataxis. Pindar, following her lead, was able to take the process, at times, altogether beyond the arena of denotative coherence, into a realm closer to that of Mallarmé.

In fact, Sappho's innovations were made in response to the *coupure épistémologique* that only she and a handful of other Greek poets of that age seem to have been sensitive to. She discovered for poets what mythographers had discovered in the Bronze Age, that signifiers can be broken loose from their signifieds and thereby, paradoxically, attain greater meaning. She first composed the type of closed, self-referential poem, which Karl Shapiro called the "gadget-poem," and of which Yeats's works are the most famous examples in our time. She was the first lunar poet (which is in a sense the same as saying that she was the first truly lyric poet), who understood that events in a lyric poem are closer

140 David Shapiro and I have repeatedly discussed whether the Egyptian texts "translated" by Ezra Pound as "Egyptian Love Poems" were, in fact, such pure expressions of subjectivity as they seem. Still, if one were to look for expressions of lyrical subjectivity before Archilochus and Sappho, or of contemplative subjectivism before Protagoras and Gorgias, where would one look except to late New Kingdom Egypt, the culture that produced the paradox-intoxicated "Hundred Stanza Hymn to Amon-Re"?

to those of dream than those of waking and that, being simply parts of consciousness, they need no external warrant. She first produced poems based on what Frye calls "centripetality," the awareness that her "intention can only be expressed by some kind of tautology."[141] She first featured her own subjectivity as the subject of poetry and she first associated the poetic urge with the quest for love and beauty exclusively. Finally, she first wrote the reflexive "avant-garde" literature that has as one of its chief subjects its own composition and power.

These qualities, which I am attributing to Sappho's work are, of course, the qualities that have come to characterize the "modern" lyric poem. It does, in fact, seem the case that the lyric poem as so defined first fully appears in her work. Her influence then, by way primarily of Theocritus, Catullus, Horace and the *Palatine Anthology*, passed the genre on to the European tradition. Her conception of beauty, and of poetry as veneration of beauty, have permeated all later literature. When Pindar, describing his poetic ability, says, "with blessed hand I garden the secret precinct of the Graces" (*Olympian* 9.26–27), it is Sappho's rite in Aphrodite's grove, her redefinition of the Bronze Age symbolism, that lies at the root of his tradition. When an anonymous Medieval poet writes,

O, O, totus floreo
iam amore virginale
totus ardeo,
novus, novus amor
est, quo pereo ...[142]

Oh, oh, I flower entirely
now with a virginal love,

141 Frye, *Anatomy of Criticism* (above, n. 19), 86.

142 *Carmina Burana*, ed. A. Hilka and O. Schumann (Heidelberg: Carl Winter, 1930), 211.

> I burn utterly,
> new, new is the love
> in which I perish...

he is echoing a poetess whose name he may never have heard. When Herrick's Julia walks in her silks, it is Anactoria's footstep that lurks behind the page. When Herbert, bidding farewell to life, says "Farewell, dear flowers, sweetly our time ye spent ..." he uses a Sapphic image that has become all but universal. When Mallarmé's faun ("crowning myself with roses") says, "I would perpetuate these nymphs," he echoes Sappho's "eternalization" of her girls. Rilke's "solitude... which falls like rain in that gray doubtful hour when all the streets are turning toward the dawn" replays the loneliness of the poetess in fr. 94 D. The list could be extended indefinitely. Sappho's free signifiers sprung loose from the Bronze Age cults of which they were remnants, have permeated all later literature, as have her subtle structural wit and her deliberately ambiguous concentration on the antinomy of dream and reality. History assigned to her the task of bringing literature across the epistemological gap between the communal myths of the Bronze Age and the personally created mythologies or hierophanies of the "modern" age. "Is there any comparable achievement in European art before Goethe?" asks Jaeger.[143]

143 W. Jaeger, *Paideia: The Ideals of Greek Culture,* 3 vols. trans. G. Highet (New York: Oxford Univ. Press, 1965), 3:135.

PART THREE

The Clear-Voiced Song-Loving Lyre

Recent Explorations in Sapphic Studies

Sexual Politics

The main change in Sapphic studies in the last generation is that philology, which still exercised an hypnotic power during the years when Part One of this book came into being, has since been put somewhat in the background, as if it were a thing of the past, in favor of a more journalistic approach centered in gender studies. There is a hint in the air that philology came to occupy a patriarchal position, that its analytic approach was more or less androcentric and thus inherently opposed to Sappho. As Sapphic scholar Ellen Greene has observed, in a book in whose editorial foreword Sappho is referred to as "proto-queer": "In the past thirty years...with the feminist wave of the 1960s and 1970s, Sappho's poetry has begun to be reevaluated."[1] One of the books Greene discusses in this respect is Page DuBois's 1995 book *Sappho Is Burning*.[2] That book features an element that would not have been encountered in previous generations of Sapphic scholarship, namely the statement that "both the classicists and the gay and lesbian theorists and historians have much to contribute to our readings of Sappho."[3] It is notable that until rather recently the great Sapphic scholars have almost all been men – Wilamowitz-Moellendorff, Snell, Schadewaldt, Treu, Bowra, Turyn, Kirkwood, Lobel, Page – it

1 "Introduction," in *Reading Sappho: Contemporary Approaches*, ed. E. Greene (Berkeley and Los Angeles: Univ. of California Press, 1996), 1.

2 P. duBois, *Sappho Is Burning* (Univ. of Chicago Press, 1995).

3 Ibid., 18.

is a daunting patriarchal lineage, Germanic in its roots, that inherited the words of this ancient woman and worked its way on them. The tables seem to have turned, after centuries, to something perhaps more like Sappho's day; there is a primal urge "to discover," as one Sapphic scholar has put it, "the originary voice of female poetic consciousness."[4] A group of primarily female scholars has come of age and claimed a special right to the field. They comprise what might be called a contemporary academic *thiasos* of Sapphic studies. There can be no doubt that, as Greene says, "the last several decades of Sappho studies have been enormously productive."[5] Indeed, the field has almost become what it studies, a new "female initiatory discourse ... conducted in the sheltered atmosphere of the *thiasos*"[6] – the *thiasos* in this case being the sheltered and cultic atmosphere of classical studies in academia.

No Men Allowed

Several years ago I went to Lesbos to spend a few days on the island where Sappho seems to have lived most of her life. I had been there three or four times before, beginning in 1969.

After a day or two in the port city of Mytilene (where one can see the shore of Turkey across the water) I went to the other side of the island to the beach town of Eressos, which the first account of Sappho's life in the *Suda* says was her home. Perhaps that was her family's country home where she presumably grew up before moving to Mytilene as a young adult and conducted at least some of her activity as a poet.

---

4 M. Williamson, "Sappho and the Other Woman," in *Reading Sappho* (above, n.1), 245.

5 Greene, "Introduction," in *Reading Sappho* (above, n.1), 8.

6 M.B. Skinner, "Woman and Language in Archaic Greece, or, Why Is Sappho a Woman?" in *Reading Sappho* (above, n.1), 190.

I had not been to Eressos for twenty years and it had changed. From being a sleepy little town with an empty sun-bleached plaza it had become a specialized holiday resort – a resort for lesbians, primarily German, but not exclusively. Women crowded the tables at the little sea-front restaurants and lay everywhere about the beach. I went into a hotel, approached a woman standing behind the desk, and began to say, "I would like a room please," but before that brief sentence could be uttered she cut me off, saying simply, "No men allowed." She didn't look at me or say another word. In a little while I did find a room, but a point had been made.

The Group 2 Poems

An important contribution to the resources of Sapphic studies has been made by two collections of essays edited by Ellen Greene: *Reading Sappho* [7] and *Re-Reading Sappho,* [8] both published in 1996. The first essay in *Reading Sappho* is Giuliana Lanata's "Sappho's Amatory Language." [9] Indeed, Greene, in her introduction, uses this essay to mark a turning point in Sapphic studies. "With Giuliana Lanata's article, 'Sappho's Amatory Language,' originally published in 1966...," she observes, "Sappho scholarship turns decidedly away from the obsession to reconstruct Sappho's biography and to rationalize away the homoerotic aspects of her poetry." [10]

The year of Lanata's article, 1966, was also about the time when I began writing about Sappho. Actually Lanata's text and mine seem to have a similar content, perhaps born of

7 Above, n.1.

8 *Re-Reading Sappho: Reception and Transmission,* ed. E. Greene (Berkeley and Los Angeles: Univ. of California Press, 1996).

9 In *Reading Sappho* (above, n.1), 11–25. First published as "Sul linguaggio amoroso di Saffo," *Quaderni urbinati di cultura classica* 2 (1966), 63–79.

10 "Introduction," in *Reading Sappho* (above, n.1), 1f.

that transformative period – the late 1960s. The distinctions I made among four groups of fragments arranged by their content or by the poet's attitude toward their content features the Group 2 fragments – the ones in which the imagery that led into the *thiasos* theory was overwhelmingly dominant. These are among the poems that the ancient critic Demetrius meant when he uttered a really defining statement, saying, "Virtually the whole of Sappho's poetry deals with nymphs' gardens, wedding songs, and eroticism" (*On Style* 132). The diction, imagery and mood of the Group 2 fragments constitute what Lanata calls "Sappho's amatory language." In my formulation the mood of the Group 2 fragments was contrasted with that of the Group 3 fragments that seem to portray Mytilenean *haute-bourgeois* society thriving in the Age of the Tyrants rather than the sheltered vision of the *thiasos*. Lanata's formulation did not involve my Groups 1, 3, and 4, but focused deeply and intently on the Group 2 world, which does seem to be the poetic center of the *œuvre* insofar as we can see it. The structure of thought underlying Lanata's approach, however, has much in common with my position of forty years ago and, in fact, this approach seems to have become rather dominant recently.

The distinction between Groups 2 and 3 has come up repeatedly in recent criticism. It is found, for example, in John Winkler's essay, titled after the description of Demetrius, "Gardens of Nymphs: Public and Private in Sappho's Lyrics,"[11] where what he calls the private and public worlds generally correspond to Groups 2 and 3. Winkler observes that "Sappho's consciousness ... is necessarily a double consciousness, her participation in the public literary tradition

---

11 In *Reading Sappho* (above, n.1), 89–109; first published in *Reflections of Women in Antiquity*, ed. H.P. Foley (Philadelphia: Gordon and Breach, 1981).

always contains an inevitable alienation."[12] "There are two sides to double consciousness," he goes on. "Sappho both re-enacts scenes from public culture infused with her private perspective as the enclosed woman and she speaks publicly of the most private, woman-centered experiences from which men are strictly excluded."[13]

Centering the argument on fr. 2 (as I had done, following Turyn), Winkler writes, "Virtually every word suggests a sensuous ecstasy in the service of Cyprian Aphrodite (apples, roses, quivering followed by repose, meadow for grazing, spring flowers, honey, nectar flowing)."[14] He remarks on the distinction between Homeric and lyric verse, "I have tried to sketch two areas of Sappho's consciousness as she had registered it in her poetry: her reaction to Homer, emblematic of the male-centered world of Greek public culture, and her complex sexual relations with women in a world apart from men."[15] He opposes Groups 1 and 3 (both public in different ways – the Homeric and the seventh-century Mytilenian) to Group 2 (the *thiasos*).

Another scholar who has focused on the distinction between Groups 2 and 3 is Charles Segal who speaks of "an interplay between one level of style that is close to the ritual and public discourse and another that is freer and more private."[16] He describes the situation: "The new expressiveness of personal emotion interacts with the older public forms and finds its realization both through and against the conventions."[17] (The conception that Sappho worked "both

12 Ibid., 95.

13 Ibid., 101.

14 Ibid., 108.

15 Ibid.

16 C. Segal, "Eros and Incantation: Sappho and Oral Poetry," in *Reading Sappho* (above, n.1), 74.

17 Ibid., 75.

through and against the conventions" was another major point in my 1967 formulation that seems to have come to the forefront of scholarly discourse more recently.)

Another scholar who has focused recently on this dualism in Sappho's expressiveness is Jane McIntosh Snyder in "Public Occasion and Private Passion in the Lyrics of Sappho of Lesbos."[18] Snyder distinguishes between the public songs, mostly wedding songs (Group 1), private songs like frr. 94 and 96 (my Group 2) and a third group, equivalent to my Group 4, the linking fragments, which use conventions of public song, but often for parodic purposes (as in frr. 1, 2, 16, and others) ("both through and against the conventions"). Snyder calls her own approach to Sapphic studies "a woman-centered perspective"[19] (Winkler had referred to the "man-centered world" of Homer).

This widespread shift of emphasis suggests that the preoccupation with biography, so important to Wilamowitz-Moellendorff, Bowra, and others of earlier generations, has given way, at last, to an emphasis on the poetic imagination. This contrast can also be seen in the essays of both Gregory Nagy and Claude Calame in the same collection.[20] Something like it seems to underlie Eva Stehle's work too.The realization is summed up by Greene when she attributes to Sappho "an ability to speak bilingually, that is, in the languages of both the male public arena and the excluded female minority."[21]

---

18 In *Women's History and Ancient History*, ed. S.B. Pomeroy (Chapel Hill: Univ. of North Carolina Press, 1991), 1–19.

19 J. McIntosh Snyder, *Lesbian Desire in the Lyrics of Sappho* (New York: Columbia Univ. Press, 1997), 1.

20 G. Nagy, "Phaethon, Phaon, and the White Rock of Leukas: 'Reading the Symbols of Greek Lyric'"; Claude Calame, "Sappho's Group: An Initiation into Womanhood," both in *Reading Sappho* (above, n.1).

21 E. Greene, "Apostrophe and Women's Erotics in the Poetry of Sappho," in *Reading Sappho* (above, n.1), 234.

Ironically, for a long time it was only male scholars who presumed to speak about what Winkler describes as "the most private, woman-centered experiences from which men are strictly excluded." Beginning with Lanata's essay, this has not remained the case.

Adonis

"The Garden of the Graces," Part Two of this book, traces the diction and imagery of the Group 2 fragments (whether they are regarded as documents of an historical *thiasos* or as a poetic reverie on a group of religious symbols) back to the iconography of ancient Near Eastern Bronze Age fertility religions. Sappho lived within the geographical purview of the Near East and seems to have been fairly saturated with remnants of religious motifs and themes inherited from the Bronze Age. In addition it seems that she was personally drawn to that milieu. We actually encounter the name Adonis in a cultic setting in her fragmentary remains.

Fr. 140:

> He is dying, Cytherea, the delicate Adonis, what shall we do?
> Beat your breasts, O maidens, and rend your garments.

This would seem to be the first reference to the annual Adonia festival in Greek literature. Adonis is a representative of the mythic type that C. G. Jung and Erich Neumann, and others in that tradition, have called the Dying God – a male fertility deity whose early death fuels the agricultural cycle.[22] In addition, Dioscorides refers to Sappho as a fellow

22 For comments on "the flowerlike youthful god" and "the divine boy," see C.G. Jung, *Symbols of Transformation,* Collected Works, trans. R.F.C. Hull, vol. 5 (Princeton Univ. Press, 1956), and *Archetypes of the Collective Unconscious,* Collected Works, trans. R.F.C. Hull, vol. 9.1 (Princ-

mourner with Aphrodite (*Palatine Anthology* 7.407) as the latter mourns the death of her beautiful young lover, and Pausanias also mentions that Sappho sang of him (*Description of Greece* 9.29.8). A haunting Sapphic fragment contains only the words, "Oh, for Adonis!" (fr. 168).[23] The name occurs four times in the extant fragments, more than any other male name except Eros. This would seem to underline and highlight a Neolithic/Early Bronze Age level of cultural rootedness in the fragments.

Sappho was involved with the Dying God (or, in its male instances, the Puer Æternus) motif because of her cultic identification with Aphrodite, but in addition it seems she was drawn to this archetype in general. "Sappho apparently sang of Linus (fr. 140*b*)," one scholar notes, "who also died young and who is mourned in the dirge described on Achilles' shield in the *Iliad*."[24]

---

eton Univ. Press, 1959); E. Neumann, *The Great Mother* (Princeton Univ. Press, 1991), and *The Origin and History of Consciousness* (Princeton Univ. Press, 1954). Marie-Louise von Franz (*The Problem of the Puer Æternus* [Toronto: Inner City Books, 2000]) uses the term as a description of a modern psychological type, like the popular idea of the "Peter Pan complex"; every child has to deal with the memory of childhood as a paradise he or she has lost. In Franz's terminology, the Puer Æternus fails to resolve this problem and embodies it in various ways. But in terms of the history of religion in antiquity, it points to a more important archetype, which is more or less parodied in a degraded form in the Peter Pan idea. The phrase Puer Æternus may have been originated – at least it is preserved – by Ovid who in the *Metamorphoses* applies it to the god Iacchos in the Eleusinian Mysteries, a Dying God of a Neolithic type who is sometimes a counterpart to Dionysus. In Sappho's day and in her eastern Ægean orientation it signifies an earlier archetype that includes Dumuzi, Tammuz, Adonis, and other fertility gods who die young, a lineage in which Dionysus and Iacchos appear.

23 Also, M.L. West ("Burning Sappho," *Maia* 22 [1970], 328) suggests a restoration for Sappho, fr. 96.23 that mentions Adonis.

24 M. Williamson, *Sappho's Immortal Daughters* (Cambridge, Mass.: Harvard Univ. Press, 1995), 67, 128.

Of course, Sappho is most closely associated with Phaon, another beautiful young man loved by Aphrodite who was often identified with Adonis – "The flowerlike youthful god," as Jung calls him, "like Tammuz, Attis, Adonis."[25] Greek mythology encompasses many cases of a mortal who is sexually engaged with an immortal. As Stehle points out in "Sappho's Gaze: Fantasies of a Goddess and Young Man,"[26] the myths of Aphrodite and Adonis and of Aphrodite and Phaon are myths of the same type or structure. Stehle describes it in a neutral and general way as a myth of an older goddess with a younger mortal man, but in terms more laden with cultural history it is what Jungian commentators on mythology have called myths of the Double Goddess and the Dying God. This is perhaps the most characteristic mythic structure of the Neolithic and Early Bronze Ages, which is the root level from which both the imagery and the themes of Sappho's poems of Group 2 seem ultimately to emerge. Stehle also notes some other myths of this type that Sappho mentions: Selene and Endymion, Eos and Tithonos. These mentions all belong to the "amatory language" of the Group 2 fragments and are not out of the ordinary for Sapphic discourse. In keeping with a family background that may have been somewhat aristocratic, Sappho appears to have been old-fashioned in her religious associations and to have continued to believe and, to some extent, to exercise the religious commitments that lingered as cultural shadows of an earlier age. As one scholar says, "ancient ways seem to have lingered in one culture especially, the Æolian culture of Lesbos."[27]

---

25 Jung, *Symbols of Transformation* (above, n.22), 258.

26 E. Stehle, "Sappho's Gaze: Fantasies of a Goddess and a Young Man," in *Reading Sappho*" (above, n.1), 193ff.

27 L. Crompton, *Homosexuality and Civilization* (Cambridge, Mass.: The Belknap Press, 2003), 18.

Sappho's apparent expression of archaic gender roles must have been subversive in terms of the patriarchal ideology of her day; as Stehle puts it, "Adonis is the Greek conception of the effeminate ineffectual Near Eastern man, marked by all that the Greek man considers to be antithetical to himself. Adonis is a failed hero."[28] He belongs to "the category of youths who fail to make the transition to adulthood."[29] Sappho's spirituality, in other words, veered over toward the sacrificial theme of the Puer Æternus (who never grows up because he always dies young).

The Ancient Near East

Sappho supposedly was born in Eressus, but she spent her adult years in Mytilene. Eressus is on the west side of Lesbos, looking over the Ægean toward mainland Greece in the far distance. Mytilene, however, is on the east side of the island, facing nearby Asia, specifically the kingdom of Lydia in northwest Anatolia. In fact, on the Lydian coast across from Mytilene there were several small Greek settlements in contact with Lesbos and dependent on it economically and in other ways. These settlements may figure in Sappho's relations with Lydia – especially in fr. 96, where she and Atthis lament the departure of an unnamed girl who evidently has gone to Sardis to marry a Lydian man.

Lydia is mentioned in the Sapphic fragments as a source of fine clothing and as a symbol of something like imperial splendor. Twice Sappho uses Lydia as a symbol of great wealth; in fr. 132: "I have a beautiful child like golden flowers, my darling Cleis, for whom I would not take all Lydia…"; and in fr. 16, where Sappho similarly declares that

28 Stehle, "Sappho's Gaze" (above, n.26), 200.
29 Ibid., 206.

Anaktoria's beauty and charm are such that they would outweigh "the Lydians' chariots and armed infantry." One of the functions of Sappho's circle seems to have involved "forging international links between noble families."[30]

In Sappho's day Mytilene was a center of trade; Greek and Lydian goods passed constantly back and forth through its excellent port. The prosperity of seventh-century Lesbos was dependent in part on this trade, but with this prosperity came danger. In the sixth century the Lydian king Gyges attacked several eastern Greek cities, including Miletus and Smyrna, and conquered one, Colophon. Xenophanes remarked that his Colophonian compatriots were somewhat corrupted by Lydian luxuriousness (*DK* 21*b*3). Sappho's style of writing has been categorized as "Asian" in terms of the ancient dispute between Attic (plain, masculine) and Asian (flowery, feminine) literary styles.[31] One scholar calls Sappho "Asianizing and effeminate herself,"[32] and notes that Sappho's own family may have had roots in Asia Minor, as her father (Skamandronymos) seems named after the Trojan river Skamander, and Zuntz has argued that Sappho's own name may also have been Asian.[33] Sappho's aesthetic is characterized by an emphasis on the quality of ἁβροσύνη (Æolic, ἀβροσύνη), tenderness/delicacy, and this is the very quality Xenophanes says the Colophonians learned from the Lydians: in other words, Sappho's ἁβροσύνη would seem to be a Lydian trait, acquired by her, as by the Colophonians, through Lydian influence.

As one scholar says, "The precious objects of Sappho's world come from the East."[34] An example of the somewhat

30 Williamson, *Sappho's Immortal Daughters* (above, n.24), 87.

31 See DuBois, *Sappho Is Burning* (above, n.2), 168ff.

32 Ibid., 173.

33 G. Zuntz, "On the Etymology of the Name Sappho," *Museum Helveticum* 8 (1951), 15–25.

34 DuBois, *Sappho Is Burning,* (above, n.2), 182.

Asianized milieu Sappho lived in is the mention in fr. 2 of frankincense smoking on the altar in Aphrodite's sacred grove. As Page observes, "this is the earliest extant mention in Greek of *frankincense*... There is no mention [of it] in Homer... [though] in Egypt it was a common practice long before the Mycenaean era. Frankincense was presumably an article of the Phoenician trade."[35]

Another cultural article that seems to have passed from Asia into Greece via the Lydia-Lesbos connection in the archaic period was the Adonia festival, which can perhaps be traced back to the annual laments of Ishtar and her priestesses for Dumuzi's death that very likely passed over into Lesbos in some Lydian version. Dumuzi was a forerunner of Adonis incorporating the same Neolithic Near Eastern archetype of the Dying God. As Burkert writes, "What can be identified [in the Adonia festival] is the spread of the Mesopotamian Dumuzi-Tammuz cult. Old Testament prophets speak of it as an abomination: women sit by the gate weeping for Tammuz, or they offer incense to Baal on roof-tops and plant pleasant gardens. These are the very features of the Adonis cult."[36] Indeed, as Jones and Pennick say of this era in *A History of Pagan Europe*, "The culture of the eastern Mediterranean was one large interrelated continuum. Its deities interacted, many of its religious practices remained constant..."[37]

The Adonia was celebrated in parts of June and July – in the Babylonian calendar the month of Tammuz. It was not, however, a part of the state calendar of rituals and, in comparison with the Thesmophoria, a festival to Demeter, was relatively raw and more upfront about sexuality. The women

---

35 *S&A* 36.

36 W. Burkert, *Greek Religion: Archaic and Classical*, trans. J. Raffan (Cambridge, Mass.: Harvard Univ. Press, 1985), 177.

37 P. Jones and N. Pennick, *A History of Pagan Europe* (London and New York: Routledge, 1995), 11.

who practiced the Thesmophoria were enjoined to remain chaste through its three days, but the Adonia seems to have been closer to the Neolithic roots of festivals of this type. Little Adonis gardens were planted in the terracotta roof tiles of houses, watered for a while, then sprouted and allowed to wither and die, whereupon they were thrown into some natural body of water along with an image of Adonis. This, the climactic, night was characterized by women wailing lamentations from the rooftops that had borne his gardens. Indeed, some of the private cultic celebrations mentioned in Sappho's poems may have derived from women's rites that had endured in a continuous though winding trail from the Neolithic Near East to Sappho's Lesbos. A number of Greek goddesses – Artemis, Hera, Athena, Demeter, Persephone, Aphrodite – share cultic traits that probably go back quite far in that lineage. As Williamson says of these goddesses, "they can all ... be honored by groups of young girls who are dedicated to them for a fixed period, and they all delight in singing and dancing and in female beauty and charm ..."[38] Another sign that parts of Sappho's cultural attitude may go back to pre-Greek, Near Eastern roots is her uniformly positive feeling toward Aphrodite, who is often portrayed (as in Euripides' *Ion* and *Hippolytus*) with ambivalence and distrust; for Euripides she is beautiful, but represents the sinister and dangerous aspect of beauty.

The "first creative act," says Jung, "... is matricide."[39] This act is committed by "the divine boy, the Puer Æternus."[40]

---

38 Williamson, *Sappho's Immortal Daughters* (above, n.24), 114.

39 Jung, *The Archetypes of the Collective Unconscious* (above, n.22), 187.

40 Ibid., 96.

Sappho's Circle

One of the conspicuous features of the world portrayed by Sappho's fragments is that she speaks of, and at times addresses herself to, what seems to have been a social circle, or actually two of them. The essential one seems composed of young women or girls who participated in the *thiasos* (as Wilamowitz-Moellendorff called it) or, in terms advocated by Calame, in the choral society devoted to Aphrodite; this is the social circle associated with the Group 2 fragments. The other social circle is very different; it belongs to Group 3, the world of Mytilenians, mostly women, who were, it seems, somehow at odds with Sappho. It has long been a central problem of Sapphic studies how her social circle of close, but seemingly younger friends like Atthis and Anactoria was composed – how they happened to come together.

The basic requirement for the structure of Sappho's circle has been described thus: "Sappho used the special condition of lesbian love to create an alternative world in which male values, those same values that denied Greek women an outlet for erotic fantasy, are not dominant ..."[41] Three visions of this circle have been proposed: that it was a kind of school in which Sappho was the schoolmistress to young girls of aristocratic families from several cities in the northeast Ægean; that it was a kind of choral society in which Sappho was the poet or songwriter and the choral director (*χορηγός*), somewhat on the model of what seems to have been Alcman's situation in Sparta about a generation earlier; that it was a *ἑταιρεία*, or association of friends who met privately for events more or less like what we today might call cocktail parties cum poetry readings.

41 E. Stehle, "Romantic Sensuality, Poetic Sense," in *Reading Sappho*" (above, n.1), 149.

In all three versions, Sappho's circle fulfills the basic function of providing a mechanism for female bonding. According to a somewhat influential anthropological work of 1970, *Men in Groups* by Lionel Tiger, a basic distinction between male and female groups is that male groups supposedly will bond among themselves, with or without the presence of women and children, whereas women, in his view, bond only with family, under the domination of a male, and do not bond among and by themselves. The position seems obviously, as Carolyn Heilbrun called it, an "ardent masculinist point of view."[42] Nevertheless, it may apply in general to patriarchal societies, including archaic Greece. Sappho seems to have put together a female group that was more or less sheltered from social pressures and male domination and provided a matrix for female bonding outside of male proclivities. This matrix may have survived from earlier eras in which female independence seems to have been more widely accepted.

The School

The school idea goes back to three ancient sources. Above all is a fragment of a work by an Æolic grammarian, probably Kallias of Mytilene, who seems to have lived in the third century BCE: "She lived a tranquil life, teaching young women of good families from both Mytilene and Ionia..." Neither Kallias nor Sappho is named in the fragment. Still, there is no other candidate for the identity of the person being described, and the fact that the prose fragment is Æolic in dialect reduces the chance of an error about the authorship greatly. It's only a phantom of a fact, but there it is: this ancient fragment says that Sappho was a teacher.

---

42 C.G. Heilbrun, *Reinventing Womanhood* (New York: Norton, 1979), 214 n1.

The principal alternative is to dismiss the fragment on the basis of comic pollution. It is well known that Aristophanes, in *The Clouds,* portrays Socrates as director of a school; the school has a building, in which Socrates teaches comically silly things to his students. *The Clouds* expresses an anti-intellectual strain in Aristophanes that was shared by other comic playwrights. At least ten ancient comic plays were written about Sappho, and it is quite possible that one or more of them may have used this comic topos.[43] It was in the comic plays that the tradition about Sappho and Phaon rose to prominence and almost took over the view of Sappho for thousands of years, though there is no reason whatever to regard it as historical. Sappho's school could have come from the same place Socrates' school came from, or the affair with Phaon.

On the other hand, the fact that the prose in the fragment attributed to Kallias is Æolic makes it unlikely to have come from an Attic play. Even though there is only one evidential word (*παιδεύουσα,* a feminine participle meaning "teaching"), and its authorship is uncertain, still, in the absence of other evidence, it is powerful. Without some actual Æolic source, how could an Æolic verb form have intruded there?

Two other details support the word *παιδεύουσα*. The *Suda,* the Byzantine encyclopedia of the tenth century, says in an article on Sappho, "her friends were..." and then mentions three names from the fragments, then says, "her students were [using the unambiguous word *μαθήτριαι*]..." and names three others from the fragments – these all apparently girls who had come from Ionia. On the one hand, the *Suda* is

43 The comedies about Sappho that are known to have existed include plays entitled *Sappho* by Ameipsias, Amphis, Antiphanes, Diphilus, Ephippus, and Timocles; *Phaon* by Plato Comicus and Antiphanes (if not identical with his *Sappho*); *Leucadia* by Menander and Diphilus; and *Antilais* by Epikrates.

absurdly later than Sappho (maybe fifteen centuries); on the other, Byzantium is close to Mytilene, and there is reason to think that many of Sappho's poems survived in Byzantium until the ninth century or so, and along with them, no doubt, some tradition about her.

The third piece of ancient texual evidence on the school theory is the famous double entendre by Ovid: "Sappho quid docuit nisi amare puellas?" (*Sorrows* 2.365). Either "What did Sappho teach except to love girls?" or "What did Sappho teach girls except to love?" In either case Sappho is teaching.

Since about 1960 the school theory has seemed to many to arise from sexual shame or moral disapproval of Sappho's homosexuality. The idea was that a schoolmistress could dote on and adore her charges just to promote the educational process, without gay overtones. As Holt Parker says, "In its form Sappho Schoolmistress is the well-known creation of Wilamowitz-Moellendorff, who was concerned with defending Sappho from charges of homosexuality, in particular Pierre Louys's recently published *Chanson de Bilitis* (1895)."[44] In the 1960s this motivation itself came to seem the shameful element in the situation, and a huge wave broke for banishing the school theory and in its place accepting Sappho's homosexuality. But of course you could have both. Indeed, there may be more in favor of the school theory than defending Sappho from charges of homosexuality. Recently the school theory has been making a comeback.

Feelings have become somewhat twisted about this issue, and often nowadays scholars seem to support the school theory without explicitly saying so. Even Denys Page, the most outspoken and influential critic of the idea, seems to assume that it is true to some unspecified degree. On the one hand, he repeatedly denies it in his discussions of fragments. "In none

44 H.N. Parker, "Sappho Schoolmistress," in *Re-Reading Sappho* (above, n. 8), 150.

of these places," he says, "is there anything to indicate that Sappho was a priestess or pedagogue ..." Again: "... no suggestion of cult or academy ..." "In none of these places is there any indication that Sappho was a priestess ... nor is there the slightest suggestion that she was a *teacher* or that her companions were her *pupils*."[45] Indeed, in the whole corpus of fragments there is "nothing that suggests, let alone enforces, the recognition of a priestess or the principal of an academy." Yet a few pages later he says, "Pre-eminent among her rivals is Andromeda, who was evidently another Sappho, the leader of a company of young women," and again: "There was another leader of a rival society, Gorgo."[46]

Another example is Claude Calame who does not overtly advocate the school, yet he says, "The education of her group prepared young girls to be adult, married women by teaching feminine charm and beauty."[47] Also: "The instruction leading to marriage given by Sappho has as its corollary homoerotic relations between mistress and pupils."[48] Getting more explicit, but still using the term circle instead of school, Calame says: "... the education in Sappho's circle consisted of preparation for marriage through a series of rites, dances, and songs, mainly dedicated to Aphrodite."[49] The "circle" then was in one sense a school and in another a cult association, and in either case probably was a choral society. Calame refers to "the educational and social role of Sappho's homophilia"[50] and calls her verse "a ritual and collective poetry with an educational purpose."[51] Calame deeply

45 *S&A* 128.

46 Ibid., 111, 133f.

47 C. Calame, "Sappho's Group: An Initiation into Womanhood," in *Reading Sappho* (above, n. 1), 119.

48 Ibid., 121.

49 Ibid., 123.

50 Ibid.

51 Ibid., 124.

connects the school hypothesis with the tradition of the chorus. "... especially among the Dorians," he says, "school was often called *choros* (χορός) and the school master was called *choregos*." Lesbos of course was not Doric, but still he applies this tradition to Sappho, saying, "In Sappho's group, there is no doubt about the didactic relationship between the poet and her companions," and, "Sappho's circle offered a form of instruction and education by frequenting the Muses."[52]

Judith Hallett, too, seems to imply the school theory, saying, "Sappho's sensually expressive verses may be viewed as an institutional force in and a reflection of her social setting – a social vehicle for imparting sensual awareness, and sexual self-esteem, to women on the threshold of marriage and maturity."[53] But here is the real point: that "Greek lyric poetry for and by women ... appears to have functioned as a type of institution."[54] "Throughout ancient Greece festivals glorified the beauty of boys simply as a religious and aesthetic ideal. It only stands to reason, therefore, that Greek society would have similarly institutionalized the sensual education and affirmation of upper-class young women."[55] "One of Hera's holy festivals, held on Sappho's native Lesbos, was devoted to a female beauty contest."[56] Stehle also implies a school when she says that in Sappho's circle: "... separation, if only by virtue of the inevitability of marriage, was inevitable."[57]

---

52 C. Calame, *Choruses of Young Women in Ancient Greece: Their Morphology, Religious Role, and Social Functions* (Lanham, Md.: Rowman & Liddlefield, 2001), 222 and 225.

53 J.P. Hallett, "Sappho and Her Social Context: Sense and Sensuality," in *Reading Sappho* (above, n.1), 134f.

54 Ibid., 138.

55 Ibid., 136.

56 Ibid., 137.

57 Stehle, "Sappho's Gaze" (above, n.26), 145.

The view of Sappho as a choral leader for adolescents depends to a large extent on the case of Alcman as analyzed by Calame. "Alcman's maiden songs may have influenced Sappho's 'personal' poems," says Hallett, who goes so far as to refer to Sappho as "a member, and perhaps a follower, of Alcman's literary tradition."[58]

The idea of choruses of girls singing hymns to Aphrodite seems to hark back to earlier ages than Sappho's. In terms of broad spiritual ages it seems most natural and at home in the Neolithic and Early Bronze Ages of Old Europe and the ancient Near East. Mytilene is of course virtually a part of that area of the world, and it is not unreasonable that in Sappho's time there may have been residual cultic survivals of that ancient tradition of goddess worship. And it is also not unreasonable to suppose that Sappho may have found that her own sensibility and her own poetic goals could be sheltered and supported in such a setting. In contemplating the cultic meeting around the altar in fr. 2, one should remember that "many sanctuaries in ... Greek culture centred on a sacred tree, and the Cretan icons reveal a similar practice. The single tree, fenced or walled off with or without an altar beside it, is a universal feature of European sacred culture ... Sometimes a goddess appears hovering in the air above ... perhaps seen by [the worshippers] in a visionary state brought on by their activity."[59] It may be accurate, as Skinner puts it, that "on archaic Lesbos a socially segregated group of girls and women devised its own symbolic system."[60] But it also seems to have been true that, as argued in "The Garden of the Graces," a good deal of their symbolic system was derived from more ancient cultic symbolism

58 Hallett, "Sappho and Her Social Context" (above, n. 53), 140 and 142.

59 Jones and Pennick, *A History of Pagan Europe* (above, n. 37), 6.

60 Skinner, "Woman and Language" (above, n. 6), 183.

going back, through whatever lengthy shifts, to the heritage of the Bronze and Neolithic ages. "Thus Sappho would have inherited both her social role and her craft from a long line of female predecessors," says Marilyn Skinner.[61] Finally, it would not be unreasonable to say that Sappho was in part a Near Eastern poet as well as a Greek one.[62]

The Θίασος

In addition to the school model of Sappho's biography, Wilamowitz-Moellendorff added the term *thiasos* to the discussion – meaning a loosely conjoined cult organization involving singing and dancing, in this case for adolescent girls. Θίασος was a common term, more or less equal to guild, in Hellenistic inscriptions. At Pergamon in the Hellenistic period, the followers of Dionysus formed a *θίασος*, led by two *ὑμνοδιδάσκαλοι*, or song-masters, and a *χορηγός*, or choral director. This celebration was in honor of "the divine boy, the Puer Æternus."[63] In that period, *θίασοι* for women "only had a cult function and were essentially colleges of

61 Ibid.

62 Sappho's position living on the edge of the Lydian world and participating in its musical and mythological traditions is still more or less the situation of Lesbian musicians today who are her artistic descendants. Nikos Dionysopolous says, "Lesbos or Mytilene was for centuries along with most of the other Eastern Ægean islands, a distinct geopolitical, historical and cultural area indissolubly linked to the nearby coast of Asia Minor. It lies geographically between Asia Minor and the Ægean and symbolically between East and West." (*Lesbos and its Music: Songs and Dances of Lesbos*, Greek Traditional Music Series 5 [Iraklion: Crete Univ. Press, 1997], 19). On p. 16 he notes: "Lesbos is, even today, an enclave of unknown, rich and vigorous music, full of direct references to the recent past of musical life in Asia Minor and in Smyrna in particular…"

63 Jung, *Symbols of Transformation* (above, n.22), 127.

priestesses."[64] In the classical period, *θίασος* "refers to a troupe or gathering of people dancing and singing, generally in a cult context."[65] In Euripides, "the words *χορός* and *θίασος* were practically synonymous."[66]

Granted the variation in such usages from one local community to another – probably depending in part on the personality of the presiding teacher or *χορηγός* – there is no problem fitting what we know about Sappho into such a tradition. The problem is simply that no ancient text, including her own, uses that term *thiasos* to describe her operation (though that is the term Alman used for his). It was used by nineteenth-century scholars such as Paul Foucart in 1873 and Erich Ziebarth in 1892,[67] though they did not apply it to Sappho's circle. So in 1913, a generation or so after Foucart and Ziebarth, Wilamowitz-Moellendorff reached back for the term and gave it new life, for better or worse, by applying it to Sappho.

Without necessarily using the word *θίασος* at all, it is difficult to avoid something like the idea. Lanata, for example, says, "The *μοισοπόλος* Sappho addresses herself above all to the *ἔταιραι* united to her... by the ties of the cult of Aphrodite" – tacitly accepting the *thiasos* theory.[68] And Calame writes, "The life of Sappho's companions unfolded almost completely under the sign of Aphrodite, in an atmosphere and in a setting represented on the mythical level by the famous gardens of the goddess."[69] He, too, seems to assume

64 Calame, *Choruses of Young Women* (above, n. 52), 209.

65 Ibid.

66 Ibid., 210.

67 P. F. Foucart, *Les Associations religieuses chez les grecs. Thiases, Eranes, Orgéons avec le texte des inscriptions relatives à ces associations* (Paris: Klincksieck, 1873); E. Ziebarth, *Das griechische Vereinswesen* (Stuttgart: S. Hirzel, 1896).

68 Lanata, "Sappho's Amatory Language" (above, n. 9), 17.

69 Calame, "Sappho's Group" (above, n. 47), 118.

some type of *thiasos*. André Lardinois says "the whole poem [fr. 94] ... is, I would suggest, concerned with choral performances."[70] And in Sappho's case choral performances might constitute what Skinner calls "a female initiatory discourse," conducted "in the sheltered atmosphere of the *thiasos*."[71]

The Ἑταιρία

A third reconstruction of Sappho's circle is Merkelbach's *hetairia*, or group of friends. On this view, Sappho's circle wouldn't have been much different from that which Alcaeus gathered around himself for symposiac purposes, but presumably with more attention to cultic atmosphere.[72] This view appeals to scholars, such as Stehle and Parker, who would rather imagine Sappho spending her time with other mature women than with immature girls. Unfortunately this view belongs to the world of the Group 3 fragments, where female social leaders like Gorgo and Andromeda are found, and does not seem to meet the needs of the Group 2 poems, which demand something like the *thiasos*.

---

70 A. Lardinois, "Who Sang Sappho's Songs?" in *Reading Sappho* (above, n.1), 163.

71 Skinner, "Woman and Language in Archaic Greece" (above, n.6), 190.

72 Different positions have been expressed on the *thiasos/hetairia* issue. Parker, who seems to find it exciting to rehearse the positions of Denys Page forty years later as if they were brand new, says about the *thiasos*: "I am officially announcing its death. It should never be used again in connection with Sappho" ("Sappho Schoolmistress" [above, n.44], 176). Well, perhaps it should never be used again by *him*. On the other side, Lardinois, seemingly missing the school or the *thiasos*, expressed some skepticism about the *hetairia* idea, saying, "Parallels have been drawn between Sappho's circle and the *hetaireia* of the Lesbian poet Alcaeus, but there is quite a difference between a gathering of politically active, adult men and a group of young girls" (Lardinois, "Who Sang Sappho's Songs?" [above, n.70], 156).

Χορός *or Monody?*

In nineteenth- and early twentieth-century scholarship, the distinction between monody and choral song was taken for granted. Pindar was considered a pure choral poet, and Sappho a pure monodist. This categorization associated Sappho with the modernist tradition of the individual subjectivist lyric poet expressing predominantly his or her feelings or emotions. This is one of the modernist shibboleths about ancient Greek song that sprang in part from Bruno Snell's famous essay "The Rise of the Individual in the Early Greek Lyric"[73] and has relaxed its grip somewhat in the last generation or so. Not only is Sappho regarded nowadays as having written both choral and monodic song, but one also encounters the opinion that the same poem would sometimes be sung monodically and sometimes chorally,[74] as seems to have been the case with Alcman.

In general the milieu suggested by the extant fragments of Sappho's poems is compatible with the idea that she was a chorus leader – specifically the leader of a chorus of παρθένοι or maidens as Alcman had been in Sparta a generation or so before her. Indeed, it seems that choruses of young girls were a common enough feature of archaic Greek culture. Calame, in his influential book *Les Chœurs des jeunes filles en Grèce archaïque* (1977; it appeared in English translation in 2001[75]), understandably uses Alcman's παρθένεια, or maiden-songs, as the principal example from which most of his argumentation is spun.

---

73 In B. Snell, *The Discovery of the Mind in Greek Philosophy and Literature,* trans. T.G. Rosenmeyer (New York: Dover Publications, 1983), 43–70.

74 Lardinois, "Who Sang Sappho's Songs?" [above, n.70], 150–72.

75 *Choruses of Young Women in Ancient Greek* (above, n.52).

There were other cases, though less richly documented. Homer, for example, mentions a chorus of girls singing and dancing in honor of Artemis. The *Hymn to Delian Apollo* mentions a chorus of maidens who sing hymns to various gods including Apollo, and at Delphi, too, there was a girls' chorus to sing hymns to him. Pindar (*Pythian* 3.78) indicates that at Thebes there was a chorus of girls who sang at nocturnal festivals to the Mother of the Gods, and the Hyperboreans, too, he says, had girls' choruses. Great choral poets including Pindar, Bacchylides, and Simonides composed *παρθένεια*, or songs to be sung by choruses of maidens. That such illustrious poets should write songs for children shows, as West put it, "the importance attached to attaining the highest artistic quality in these girls' choral performances."[76] There is no difficulty in presuming that Sappho was another such poet, entering the field after Alcman, but before Simonides, Bacchylides, and Pindar.

Indeed, Lardinois has suggested that all Sappho's poems were chorally performed. But the image of Sappho holding a harp and singing solo in front of a small audience of adolescent girls will not go away. From Greek vase paintings to Alma Tadema, the tradition shows Sappho holding the type of harp called a *πηκτίς* (Æolic, *πακτίς*). The *πακτίς*, says M.L. West, was "characterized by the playing of octave concords, or echoing of the melody at octave intervals, and strongly associated with the Lydians."[77] Remember that from the port of Mytilene you can *see* the Lydian shore, and some of Sappho's students or choristers either came from Lydia and returned there or married and moved there. Her use of the *πακτίς*, like her invention of the Mixo-Lydian mode, is another factor placing her in the Lydian tradition. The *πακτίς* is the type

76 M.L. West, *Ancient Greek Music* (Oxford Univ. Press, 1992), 18.
77 Ibid., 71.

of stringed instrument that West calls a harp, an instrument with strings of different lengths, as opposed to the lyre or the lute, both of which have strings of equal length that are pressed against a board to change the pitch of the note, like a guitar or a zither.

Anacreon calls his instrument a *πηκτίς* and mentions twenty strings, which implies an instrument capable of three octaves, for the sake of the doubling or octave consonance mentioned above. The harp was associated with "sensual, erotic, and adulterous songs, and ... appears in contexts of love and pleasure, from Sappho's time on ... its players in the classical period are nearly always women."[78]

Æolic Meter

Æolic culture was somewhat peripheral in both archaic and classical Greece, yet a bright and brilliant area of periphery it was. Poetry and music and dance were regular parts of life, it seems, and Lesbian practitioners were sometimes recognized as pre-eminent or at least prominent in these activities. In addition to Zeus and Hera, Dionysus and Aphrodite were worshipped on the island. A satisfying synthesis of older and newer levels of developing Greek culture arose there in the seventh and sixth centuries. A part of this was the system of Æolic meters, which embodied the somewhat eccentric brilliance of archaic Lesbian culture in general.

Sappho and Alcaeus composed primarily in four-line stanzas, which was not a common practice in other parts of the Greek tradition. They were born when Homer was still dominant, and stichic construction (meaning lines all the same metrical type) in dactylic hexameters seemed a cultural universal. At the same time, two other prosodic modes were

78 Ibid., 75.

growing and spreading: iambic trimeter, which was a stichic form associated with satire and Archilochus; and elegiac couplets, associated with Theognis, Mimnermus and others, in which the first line is dactylic hexameter and the second concluding line of each couplet a slightly abbreviated form of this.

The construction of one-line metrical units and two-line metrical units was expanded by the Lesbian poets into their customary four-line stanzas. It is notable in terms of the whole long tradition of poetry that the four-line stanza became the basic form of the lyric poem through the great height of modernism in the nineteenth and twentieth centuries.

Aside from the stanzaic form, the Æolic meters are unusual in the types of internal units they use, which feature the choriamb (–⏑⏑–), a kind of synthesis including both the iambic and trochaic units, and the Æolic glyconic (–⏑⏑–⏑–). The typical Sapphic line, which was the form of the first three lines of the Sapphic stanza, preceded the glyconic with two ancipites or "doubtful" syllables (which could be either long or short). The anceps is not found in other types of Greek meters and may be a survival of a very ancient stage of the Indo-European tradition that has not survived elsewhere.[79] Overall, the effect of the Sapphic line was kind of like syncopation in modern musical meters. The glyconic seems to skip, inserting an extra short length with which the line takes off and rushes to its end. These special meters may have an almost religious or sacral identity. They seem dance-like. A succession of choriambs gives an impression like a falling leaf or a repeated balletic sequence. These meters may have been specially associated with cultic songs to the Muses and Graces,

---

79 A. Meillet, *Les Origines indo-européennes des metres grecs* (Paris: Les Presses universitaires de France, 1923); M.L. West, "Indo-European Metre," *Glotta* 51 (1973), 161–87, and *Greek Metre* (Oxford: Clarendon Press, 1982).

as in fr. 97, which Hephaestion in his *Handbook of Meters* identifies as choriambic tetrameter (–∪–––∪∪––∪∪–∪––): "Hither now tender Graces and fair-haired Muses ..."[80]

Through incorporation in the glyconic the choriamb expanded itself into a five stress line, which, like the four-line stanza, was enshrined in Western verse since the Renaissance. Modern English verse (and to an extent prose too) is so caught up in the iambic flow that it has come to seem natural and inevitable. Meters like the choriambic or the glyconic do not occur naturally in English, though Swinburne and others have demonstrated that the Sapphic line can in fact be achieved in English.

Sappho was, it seems, a considerable metrist. It has been said that she used a greater variety of meters than any other poet. She wrote some Homeric hexameters, and with Alcaeus (and with prior input by Terpander and other Æolic singers) formed the unusual Æolic stanzas. They are extremely rare in that they do not accept the Homeric bards' rule of substitution that, with the positioning of the caesura, creates the stately, rolling and powerful surge of the Homeric line.

The Sapphic line is –∪–x–∪∪–∪––. It is composed of a cretic (–∪–), an anceps, and an Æolic glyconic (–∪∪–∪–) with a one-syllable extension. This is the meter of the first three lines of the Sapphic stanza, no substitutions being allowed. There is a mysterious focus on the anceps functioning like a hinge in the middle of the line. Then the fourth line is just basically the choriambic part of the glyconic: –∪∪––, also called the Adonic (or Adonius). Evidently, all the poems of the first book of the Alexandrian edition of Sappho's poems were in this line and stanza. It seems a noble and somewhat severe line – severe in its rejection of substitution. It is

80 *Hephaestionis Enchiridion* IX.2, ed. M. Consbruch (Leipzig: B. G. Teubner, 1906), 30.

fit for Sappho's great classic statements like frr. 1, 16, and 31. According to modern reconstructions of the Alexandrian edition of Sappho,[81] it seems that all the poems in the "Sapphic stanza" were grouped in Book 1. Thus that book contained Ode 1 and frr. 2, 16, and 31 - four of the eight main fragments. In fact, one might say that these are the most "official" poems of the major fragments; they practically advertise the *thiasos*.

The other book about which we now know rather a lot is Book 5, since the publication of the Berlin Parchment (P. Berol. 9722) in 1907,[82] containing frr. 92–96. This book seems perhaps to have been less "official" and more personal than Book 1. There is almost a split here in Sappho's poetic sensibility - like the distinction between Groups 2 and 3. This time it is not just two different Sapphic moods, but two different metrical Sapphos. The text of what might be called the "Old Sappho" primarily consisted of lines from Book 1, which dealt only in the Sapphic stanza. The "New Sappho," unearthed in the twentieth century, now provides special insight into Book 5. All three of the great poems of the Berlin Parchment (frr. 94, 95, and 96) were from Book 5, and fr. 98 was metrically related. This is a powerful new Sappho, and fr. 96 may be the greatest poem or near-poem we have from her hand. It's understandable that Ezra Pound was so sold on fr. 1; for one, the Berlin Parchment was not known yet, and for another, he was favoring the strict clean beauty of lines and images in Book 1. Book 5 is different - drenched in moonlight and swooning in a dreamy meltdown.

81 E.g. *S&A* 318–23.

82 *Berliner Klassikertexte* 2 (1907), 12.

The Χορός

It seems that the Bronze Age was primarily choral, and the early Iron Age brought the possibilities of monody into focus (in the train of early capitalism and individualism). In the dim vision we have of Sappho's *œuvre*, it may be that Book 5 was more purely monodic than some others; at least, some of the Book 1 poems seem more clearly choral (maybe frr. 1, 2, 16). Greek tragedies and comedies, both probably with roots in the Bronze Age, had choruses, Greek comedies had choruses, and lyric poems seem first to have been performed primarily by choruses, then to have increasingly become monodic. The *Suda* says tragic choruses had fifteen members, comic twenty four. The lyric choruses of the archaic period seem commonly to have had ten or eleven members – both numbers from Alcman, fr. 1.98–99. Various representations of female choruses in the visual arts generally have ten.[83]

What evidence we have suggests that "female choruses, particularly those made up of girls, are more frequent on the whole than male choruses."[84] In addition there seem to have been mixed choruses of adolescents, perhaps rarely. Female choruses are either of "maidens" (*παρθένοι*) or of married adult women (*γυναῖκες*). Calame cautions that "the term *παρθένος* [usually translated virgin or maiden] by no means denotes a physical state of virginity, but simply the status of a young woman who is not yet married."[85] The two statuses, *παρθένοι* and *γυναῖκες*, as another scholar says, "were kept apart," [86] and "the surviving poetry is largely for performance by *παρθένοι*." This is clearly the type of chorus for

83 Calame, *Choruses of Young Women in Ancient Greek* (above, n.52), 22.

84 Ibid., 25.

85 Ibid., 27.

86 E. Stehle, *Performance and Gender in Ancient Greece* (Princeton Univ. Press, 1997), 73.

which Alcman functioned as *choregos,* and probably Sappho too. The members of a chorus were ordinarily of about the same age, sometimes almost exactly. In fact, "a new Papyrus fragment of Alcman… describes the *choregoi* as being of the same age as the girls in the choruses they lead"[87]– a quality that after a while anyway did not apply to Sappho, who in fr. 58 as augmented by the new Cologne papyrus says she is a good deal older than her chorus members.

Though maidens' choruses were similarly constituted, still a variety of cults was involved. Sappho's chorus (assuming there was one) was primarily dedicated to cultic songs addressed to Aphrodite; Alcman, working in more conservative Sparta, addressed primarily the cults of Hera and Artemis, and refers to himself as "servant of Artemis," as Sappho called her home "the house where the Muses' servants live" (fr. 150). All these cults, and others, maintained "this relationship between female adolescence and chorus participation…" Euripides, for example, "associates dancing in a chorus (*χορεῖαι*) with the activities proper to adolescent girls (*παρθενεύματα*)."[88] In addition to the bonding suggested by their shared age and choral activity, there was usually an element of "family association" based on mythical motifs like Homer's referring to the chorus of Nymphs around Artemis as "daughters of Zeus" (*Odyssey* 6.105). Calame stresses also that there was a geographical association because in any specific chorus the girls probably all came from the same town or neighborhood.

In addition there seems to have been a bond of friendship involved. In Pindar's third *Pythian,* for example, each of the choristers seems to have been a friend of the bride for whose nup-

---

87 Calame, *Choruses of Young Women in Ancient Greek* (above, n.52), 28.

88 Ibid., 30.

tials they performed. Other authors, from Euripides to Vergil, echo this view, and seem to support Merkelbach's description of the Sapphic "circle" as a *ἑταιρεία* or group of companions.

Lyric choruses are generally represented as standing, or dancing, in a circle around a center occupied either by a cult object such as a statue or by a person. This person was usually the *χορηγός*, sometimes, as in Sappho's case, playing the lyre, sometimes the aulos. This configuration is commonly referred to in myth. In Callimachus's *Hymn to Artemis*, for example, the Nymphs "make a circle of their chorus round Artemis."[89] The virgins of Delos "dance in a circle when they sing the paean in honor of Apollo." "In one of the *Orphic Hymns*, the Fates and Graces together form a circular chorus."[90] Calame notes "a link between 'circularity' and 'lyric chorus'... and more specifically between the semantic features 'lyric chorus' + 'female' + 'adolescent.'"[91]

Initiation

Merkelbach, writing in the 1950s, felt that Sappho's *Kreis* or circle was an initiation society.[92] Sappho, he thought, was an initiation leader for young girls of her community and roundabout. Something similar comes up in "The Garden of the Graces" (Part Two of this book) where I compare the training of young girls in Sappho's circle with tribal initation rites in which adolescents boys and girls, in separate ritual societies, are prepared for and escorted into adulthood. A similar view has been expounded at greater length by Calame in *Choruses of Young Women in Ancient Greece*.

89 Ibid., 35.

90 Ibid.

91 Ibid.

92 R. Merkelbach, "Sappho und ihr Kreis," *Philologus* 101 (1957), 1–29.

Calame points out that "in almost all societies that have no education system like that in the West, such an institution appears to be a system aimed at integrating adolescents into the community of adults."[93] "Hellenic chorality... offered characteristic features of tribal initiation:"[94] the smallness of the lyric chorus ("fewer than twenty chorus-members"), the fact that they are all "young women... bound together by age similarity, by ties of companionship" and bearing "a collective appellation. These features are also present among adolescents undergoing initiation..."[95]

It seems unclear how traditionally-based Calame feels Sappho's circle to have been. At one point he notes that in many tribal societies the initiation of young girls is accompanied by excision or circumcision, and he connects initiation to "acts of violence... committed on adolescent girls."[96] But in the Greek case there seem to have been no such acts of violence, and Calame explains that he is referring to myths associated with the choruses of young girls.

More pertinently, he writes that "one of the most significant features in Greece of the passage from childhood to adulthood is homoeroticism."[97] He notes that "homoerotic practices seem to have been used to imitate adult heterosexual relations within a group composed only of women." Furthermore, as in tribal societies, the neo-initiates are presented to their community in the practice of song, dance, and music. He even remarks that "it is possible that the term χορός originally meant the 'group of initiates.'"[98] Theologi-

93 Calame, *Choruses of Young Women in Ancient Greek* (above, n.52), 258.

94 Ibid.

95 Ibid.

96 Ibid., 260.

97 Ibid.

98 Ibid., 261.

cally the essence of initiation was to prepare the girls "to abandon Artemis and Apollo, the gods of adolescence, and enter the domain of Dionysus, Aphrodite, and Hera," the so-called Lesbian trinity.

He concludes: "The ritual activity of the lyric chorus of adolescent girls ... is comparable to the institution of tribal initiation." This system is "dependent on a certain type of society in which the specialization of labor and the differentiation of social roles are reduced; its members live in a system of relationships all the more coherent because less numerous."[99] The main pivot of the evidence is not Sappho, but Alcman, from whom the argument is extended to Sappho by analogy.

The initiation theory is attractive on several counts, not least because it provides an explanatory principle for the whole phenomenon of the lyric chorus of young girls. Yet it has not gone unquestioned.

In her 1997 book *Performance and Gender in Ancient Greece*, Eva Stehle demonstrates a certain flimsiness to the evidence on which Calame has based such an important conclusion. She notes that in only one fragment does Sappho specify who her audience were:

> Now for my companions [feminine gender] I will sing delightful things beautifully. (Fr. 160)

In other words, Sappho here says her listeners are her female "companions" (*ἑταίραι*) and does not specify their age or class or profession or anything else at all but her common theme of companionship among women.

Stehle argues against the idea that Sappho's circle of companions involved mostly young women who were past puberty, but not yet married – *παρθένοι*, usually translated virgin, but perhaps meaning only unmarried. In the personal fragments

99 Ibid., 262f.

of Sappho – mainly the Group 2 fragments – Sappho never uses the word, which she does use sometimes in epithalamia and poems with a mythic subject, such as fr. 44. The connection of Sappho's Group 2 poems with an audience of *παρθένοι* comes from later authors such as Himerius (who says it twice), and the two Philostratuses. Clearly, then, it is possible to reject the idea as unsupported by direct evidence. And the rejection of the idea that Sappho's Group 2 poems (at least) were addressed to a number of *παρθένοι* would be a devastating setback to Sapphic criticism of thousands of years.

Stehle also argues against the view that Sappho conducted an educational process to prepare girls for marriage. In regard to the three poems 16, 94, and 96, in each of which a girl seems to be absent, she says: "They may have left because they were getting married ... but nothing in the poems indicates as much."[100]

Stehle points out that for both Merkelbach and Calame the lynch pin of the argument is the comparison with Sparta, which also she rejects. "The analogy between Sparta and Lesbos must be demonstrated independently of Sappho's poetry before it is used to interpret her poety."[101] She points out that for both Merkelbach and Calame "choral performance was ... an institution unto itself" and a certain ideology came with it. Another part of the institution was its initiatory function. She denies that choral performance was an institution, regarding it instead as a medium in which different credos could be expressed. In fact, she seems to deny that Sappho's poetry performed any function for the larger community, as initiation does: "Sappho's love poetry

100 Stehle, *Performance and Gender in Ancient Greece* (above, n.86), 269.

101 Ibid., 271f.

does not speak to or for a community; it confines its subject to the emotions of the speaker."[102]

Stehle has shown that the initiation is no more proven than the *thiasos*. She prefers to "posit a circle of adult friends for whom Sappho performed and who performed in turn."[103] "Sappho ... addressed her personal poetry to her peers, not to a group of παρθένοι."[104] At one point she professes to be "enamored of the idea" "that women were traveling to study professional work at the end of the seventh century."[105]

But despite such anti-Wilamowitz-Moellendorff argumentation, "there is," as another scholar remarks, "quite a bit of evidence to support the idea of a link between Sappho's poetry and *parthenoi*."[106] To begin with, several poems specify the status of παρθένος (27.10, 44.25, 56.2, 112.2, and 153), and other features imply "a focus on this stage of life,"[107] such as the frequent invocations of the Graces and Muses, the goddesses specially concerned with παρθένοι. Hera and Aphrodite both have to do with the transition from παρθενία to marriage. Philostratus (*Imagines* 2.1) and Himerius (*Orations* 9) both describe Sappho as surrounded by young women.

In addition, other modern authors have bought into the theory that Sappho's cult process culminated by initiating young girls into womanhood. Williamson says, "... for both young women and young men alike, the approach to adulthood was negotiated through a period of quasi-initiation." This process "involved for both boys and girls a period of

---

102 Ibid., 275.
103 Ibid., 276.
104 Ibid., 277.
105 Ibid., 278.
106 Williamson, *Sappho's Immortal Daughters* (above, n.24), 80.
107 Ibid., 81.

segregation from the rest of society in single-sex groups."[108] As to how Sappho's "circle" was composed, "religious ritual and the initiation of maidens both figured prominently among the occasions that brought them together."[109]

Virginity

Calame says that παρθένος simply means unmarried; it does not mean never having experienced intercourse.[110] This is a view common in anthropological literature, but for a long time not predominant in Sapphic studies. Yet, recently, it has come to the forefront there too. Guilia Sissa approaches the issue from Greek medical texts. She encountered what she calls "the problem of the hymen."[111] This problem about conceptualizing the female body existed in ancient Greek culture, but was not confronted until the second century of the Roman Empire, possibly under Christian auspices. In the Greek tradition, Hymen was a male deity of the Dying God type at least as early as the archaic period. A wedding or fertility god, he was invoked in a Pherecratean refrain in wedding hymns: "Hymen O Hymenaeus," as in Sappho, fr. 111, where the refrain appears more briefly as ὑμήναον.[112] But it seems that later in Greek culture the word became a medical term meaning a thin membrane. This was in place in Aristotle's time, but not with the connection to virginity. Sissa finds the earliest mention of the idea of the virginal

108 Ibid., 77.

109 Ibid., 84.

110 Calame, *Choruses of Young Women in Ancient Greek* (above, n.52), 27.

111 G. Sissa, *Greek Virginity*, trans. A. Goldhammer (Cambridge, Mass.: Harvard Univ. Press, 1990), 2.

112 See R. Muth, "'Hymenaeus' and 'Epithalamium,'" *Wiener Studien* 67 (195), 5–45.

hymen – a membrane obstructing entry to the vagina, which bleeds when first punctured – in the *Gynaekia* of Soranus, a medical author of the second century CE. At this point in the argument, she is faced with two options: either the earlier mentions have not happened to survive, or earlier Greek culture did not have at all the idea of a virginal hymen. She seems to lean toward the latter conclusion, in which case the issue of virginity in Sappho's Greece did not involve the situation of the groom's family checking the potential bride's hymen to confirm her eligibility for marriage that became featured in the Christian era.

This line of argumentation then flows together with the anthropological argument about the status of the independent woman – neither wife, nor virgin, nor courtesan – who might bear and raise children herself – a role that has been coming back gradually as the influence of Christianity wanes. So finally one must recognize two different meanings of the words παρθενία and παρθένος, obtaining in different times and places. In the one case, virgin means simply unmarried; in the other, unmarried and also untouched – *virgo intacta*. There are indeed cases (some of them are reviewed in Part Two of this book) in which, as Sissa says, "a girl could lose her *parthenia* and continue to be called *parthenos*."[113] She could be maiden without maidenhead. *Parthenos,* she says "was the term assigned to all young women between childhood and marriage." The text implies that this eligibility was founded on a *virgo intacta* requirement. (This embroiled issue is another aspect of the hymen.)

This situation creates a lot of ambiguity, for the two denotations have not been clearly distinguished in linguistic

113 G. Sissa, "Maidenhood without Maidenhead: The Female Body in Ancient Greece," in *Before Sexuality: The Construction of Erotic Experience in the Ancient Greek World,* ed. D.M. Halperin, J.J. Winkler, and F.I. Zeitlin (Princeton Univ. Press, 1990), 348.

usage. Anne Burnett says that virginity was "of supreme importance" in Sappho's "circle."[114] Does she mean that the state of being unmarried, and hence autonomous, was of supreme importance or the state of having an unbroken hymen? It seems that this question cannot be answered with certainty from ancient documentary evidence. Lyn Hatherly Wilson suggests that "segregation from the larger community, and the danger of seduction ... could provide viable reasons for the presence of these women in Sappho's establishment. Within the seclusion of this community, a woman's virginal status remains intact in both a physical and a social sense."[115] The two times when Sappho uses the word *παρθενία* (virginity), she is referring to its loss. Fragment 107: "Do I still long for virginity?" Fr. 114: "'Virginity, virginity, deserting me, where have you gone?' 'Never again shall I come to you, never again.'" Is Sappho referring to autonomy lost through marriage or to a lost maidenhead?

The theme of virginity and its loss in a ritual setting implies a rite of passage/initiation. Williamson goes so far as to observe "There is even the possibility, suggested by parallels with the initiation of boys elsewhere, that lovemaking itself was part of a socializing process for girls at this transitional phase of life."[116] In fact, the custom can be found both in girls' and boys' initiation groups, but generally in what have been called primitive societies - primarily to set them apart from Greek and Greek-influenced cultures. This may be yet another example of how Sappho's circle, and indeed seventh century Lesbos in general, was more archaic, closer

114 A.P. Burnett, *Three Archaic Poets: Archilochus, Alcaeus, Sappho* (Cambridge: Harvard Univ. Press, 1983), 218.

115 L. Hatherly Wilson, *Sappho's Sweetbitter Songs: Configurations of Female and Male in Ancient Greek Lyric* (Milton Park: Routledge, 1996), 91f.

116 Williamson, *Sappho's Immortal Daughters* (above, n.24), 125.

to the Bronze Age than much of Greece. Choruses of girls in the Bronze Age may have been "maiden without maidenhead" – in other words, bachelor women – but after the seventh century, or the sixth, in which the Greek patriarchy solidified, it seems unlikely that this continued to occur. At that point the distinction became inconvenient: both meanings of *παρθένος* were conjoined or indissolubly linked as if conjoined. That was the phallogocentric patriarchy fully in place, even to its neuroses.

Sappho, living in the somewhat slow Æolic swath of Greek culture and in closest possible proximity to the Lydian empire, seems to have stood at one of the points in history where a change of cultural episteme was occurring – a epistemelogical break (*coupure épistémologique*). Her milieu seems on the one hand to have felt strong links to the ancient Near Eastern tradition about gender relationships in which the female seems to have been more independent than she was to be as the other side of the *coupure* came into place. It is plausible to suppose that Sappho represented a more ancient goddess-oriented culture with roots in the Early Bronze Age and the Neolithic, where virginity meant unmarried autonomy, and at the same time to have lived at the moment when the male dominated Greek culture led into Christianity and its obsession with virginity not as autonomy, but as physical intactness. She herself, probably aware of both currents of feeling, may have occupied somewhat different attitudes at different times.

The Lesbian-Æolic Tradition

Æolic was the least extensive of the major dialects of ancient Greek – having fewer native speakers than the Ionic, Doric, or Attic. It was tucked away on rather distant islands such as Lesbos and Chios or found in comparatively backward areas of the mainland, such as Thessaly and Boeotia. It may represent an archaic form of Greek culture that did not progress after the Dark Age as much as some other parts of Greece did. It may have clearer links with earlier eras, back to the Mycenaean age, than the other cultural strains of the Greek Ægean. Certain characteristics of the meters of Æolic poetry compare to metrical features of the *Rig Veda* and other early Indo-European lineages. The first two syllables of the Æolic line in the works of Alcaeus and Sappho can be either short or long, without recognition of the quantitative principle whereby two shorts can be substituted for one long. This trait, it seems, is "a relic from a very ancient type of song..."[117] and is part of "the archaic-looking tradition represented by Sappho and Alcaeus."[118] It seems that features of Sappho's work and her social role may go back to earlier models rather than pointing progressively ahead toward modern models influenced by feminism, industrial capitalism, and other things. That Aphrodite's cult should be practiced almost as a Bronze Age ritual society does not seem inappropriate.

Lesbian culture is regarded as peaking in a period of great accomplishment in the seventh and sixth centuries BCE – especially in music. In that period, Lydia expanded its domain to the Ægean coast opposite Lesbos and seems to have influenced it. Sappho's songs, for example, are said to have used a Lydian mode, the Mixolydian. "Lesbos and Sparta," says West, "stand out as the great centres of musical excellence in the seventh century."[119] Two important seventh-century *citharodes* – poet-musicians who sang while accompanying themselves on the lyre – were Terpander and Arion. Terpander is credited with significant innovations,

117 West, *Ancient Greek Music* (above, n.76), 147.
118 Ibid., 335.
119 Ibid., 334.

especially increasing the number of the lyre's or cithara's strings from four to seven. Probably Alcaeus and Sappho played seven-string lyres, which were not only common by their time, but had been invented either in their homeland or at least by a compatriot. Other famous citharodes are known by name only and are referred to as children of Terpander. Terpander went to Sparta as, more or less, municipal music director, where he founded the Karneia, games that featured musical competitions. Lesbian citharodes were especially prominent in these competitions, and Sappho has the line "Outstanding like the poet of Lesbos over those of other lands" (fr. 106).

The Rise of the Individual

In "The Rise of the Individual in the Early Greek Lyric,"[120] Snell argues powerfully that the poems of Archilochus, Sappho, Anacreon, and others are the first known expressions of individualism and subjectivism anywhere in the world – that, in effect, they represent a new age in the development of the human personality. The Greek mind or personality emerges as the first modern mind or personality; it stands midway between the apparently communal expressiveness of the Stone Age and the subjectivism of, say, eighteenth- to twentieth-century Europe. In this sense, the mental stance expressed in the early Greek lyric is the primal stereotype of the modern personality, indeed of modern civilization.

There are dissenters, however. Ann Burnett, for example, begins with the observation, based on Snell, "Archilochus has been saluted as the first 'individual' of Greek

---

120 Above, n.73.

antiquity"[121] – also, "a rebel against worn-out values, a debunker of artistocratic ideals, a brawling upstart with a vein of music in him." She proceeds to argue that the existence of steles that indicate there was actually a cult of Archilochus in the third century BCE shows that he was not regarded as a disreputable character in antiquity, as he has been in modern times at least since Snell's essay. "Antiquity did not regard Archilochus as a rebel or an iconoclast. The elder traditions do not put him in any way at odds with society."[122] Similarly, she says, the archaic lyric poets in general "refuse to be as spontaneously passionate as they are asked to be." "The idea of a sudden outburst of ego does not find much support in the surviving work of the archaic lyricists, for this work is more artful and less passionate, more conventional and less individual than the advocates of this notion might have wished."[123] Consequently, "they are forced to ask themselves why this important psychic phenomenon should have appeared just when it did…"[124]

The question is certainly worth asking, and the history of the moment – the seventh to sixth centuries BCE – suggests that it would be reasonable to attribute this event to the development of free-market capitalism and overseas trade. In the so-called Dark Age that was ending, wealth was only land; passed by inheritance from father to eldest son, it didn't usually abandon a family line. The only way to get wealth was to inherit it or to get it from someone who had inherited it. Meanwhile, many Greek cities and areas were experiencing population pressure leading to colonization. Also in the seventh century, sons of aristocratic families (like Sappho's brother Charaxus) began to take goods abroad for trade and

121 Burnett, *Three Archaic Poets* (above, n 114), 15.
122 Ibid., 17.
123 Ibid., 2.
124 Ibid.

return with new mercantile wealth that was not bound to the land as the feudal wealth of the "Dark Age" had been. This development of early capitalism coincided with the period of colonization. Greek colonists already in place offered sheltered ports and markets, as at Naucratis in Egypt, where Charaxus traded. The avenue of self-aggrandizement through travel and competition for markets (whatever kind) quickly caught on and spread through society. The Olympic and other games were established with competitions including music. Entrepreneurship spread. Soon artists were signing their works (for the first time, it seems, in history) and poets were writing with an emphasis on the subjective utterance. Individualism and subjectivism characterized much of Greek culture from that point on.

Generation Gap

There is a kind of generation gap among scholars of Sapphic studies in the last few decades. The dividing line is primarily the *thiasos* theory and Wilamowitz-Moellendorff, and with them goes the milieu of παρθένοι and the educational role of the poet.

Burnett's writing, with its echoes of Wilamowitz-Moellendorff, illustrates how coherently a scholarly position extends its embrace. "Sappho's audience," she writes, "was not yet mature. Some indeed were hardly more than children."[125] Furthermore, "the group met in daily intimacy ... and ... most of Sappho's songs were first performed before this assembly."[126] This assembly was, at least in part, a finishing school for girls: "Evidently one learned, chez Sappho, not only how to walk with elegance ..., but also how to

125 Ibid., 209.
126 Ibid., 209 n2.

dress according to the latest mode."[127] "Cult, deportment and dress were all apparently matters for study among Sappho's girls, but music was at the core of their curriculum."[128] Having said "curriculum," she proceeds to use the dread word "school": "Nothing survives to suggest that the music of any other school gained a reputation..."[129] Then the word school seems to become interchangeable with *thiasos*: "...within the *thiasos*, music seems to have been the natural mode of expression." Furthermore: "Soon the girls of these youthful groups would marry, and it was to this end that their elegant accomplishments were acquired."[130] And in explanation of the poems of separation, especially frr. 94 and 96: "The need to marry well was evidently what brought the members of the Sapphic group together, but the marriages they made moved them apart again."[131] This sounds like a school, and is a view of Sappho's "circle" that Wilamowitz would have been happy with; in fact, it is based on his *Sappho und Simonides*.[132]

Fragment 31

The drama that seems to have taken place repeatedly in Sappho's circle was in three acts: the formation of homoerotic attachments during school years (Group 2); after a few years the abandonment of these attachments in a heterosexual marriage (Groups 1 and 3); and loneliness and longing in the absence of the beloved (Group 2 again). This is seen most

127 Ibid., 213.
128 Ibid., 215.
129 Ibid.
130 Ibid., 216.
131 Ibid., 223.
132 For other views of Wilamowitz-Moellendorff's interpretation of fr. 31, see M. R. Lefkowitz, "Critical Stereotypes and the Poetry of Sappho," and J. P. Hallett, "Sappho and Her Social Context: Sense and Sensuality," both in *Reading Sappho* (above, n. 1), 29f. and 129 n17.

clearly in the three poems or long frr. 16, 94, and 96. Fragment 31 occupies a special position in all this.

Like the view that Sappho may in some sense have led a school, the view that fr. 31 was in some way a wedding song or epithalamion was held by prominent earlier scholars, including Wilamowitz, Snell, Schadewaldt, Merkelbach, Fränkel, Bowra, and others and then fell out of favor[133] in the 1960s along with the school. In 1967 I, too, came out somewhat on the Germanic side of the issue in writing the chapter on that fragment in my thesis (later published as "Sappho, Fragment Thirty One: The Face Behind the Mask";[134] see Part One, chap. 6, above).

The evidence for the wedding-song view is powerful. First, men and women of seventh-sixth century Lesbos seem never to have mixed together socially except at weddings. It may be objected that we don't have enough information about archaic Lesbian society to be sure. Still the evidence, such as it is (some of it from Sappho and Alcaeus), counts. Second, the first line of the poem looks clearly like the *μακαρισμός*, or blessing of the groom that would occur in this position in an epithalamium. The *μακαρισμός* typically consists of the assertion that the groom seems like a god or the bride and groom together seem like gods. This is not a comparison that is usually made in poetry about the everyday world, but it is characteristic of the hymeneal fragments. The wedding rite,

---

133 *SuS* 58; B. Snell, "Sappho's Gedicht *phainetai moi kenos,*" *Hermes* 66 (1931), 82; W. Schadewalt, *Sappho: Welt und Dichtung* (Potsdam: Eduard Stichnote, 1950), 98; R. Merkelbach, "Sappho und ihr Kreis" (above, n. 92), 6; H. Fränkel, *Early Greek Poetry and Philosophy,* trans. M. Hadas and J. Willis (New York: Harcourt Brace Jovanovitch, 1973), 176; F. Lasserre, "Ornements érotiques dans la poésie lyrique archaïque," in *Serta Turyniana: Studies in Greek Literature and Palaeography in honor of Alexander Turyn* (Urbana: Univ. of Illinois Press, 1974), 22; et al. – again a strong Germanic patriarchal lineage.

134 *Phoenix* 32 (1978), 1–18.

in other words, was privileged as a transformative and transcendentalizing experience. In the moment of marrying, the bride and groom seem like gods.

Fragment 31 has appeared in another context among the sexual issues that surround Sappho's fragments. Jane Snyder refers to the view that the poem was in some way either an epithalamium or based on ironic references to the epithalamium as an "androcentric interpretation [that] got its start in 1913" with the publication of Wilamowitz-Moellendorff's *Sappho und Simonides* in which, noticing the traditional *μακαρισμός*, he referred to the man mentioned in the first line as a groom. Snyder's own approach eliminates the groom, the wedding, and the epithalamic references, and sees the poem as a celebration of lesbian values, which she calls "gynocentric."[135] But these categories don't seem to fit together to make a whole. Snyder seems to say that heterosexuality is androcentric, while lesbian homosexuality is gynocentric. Then there is no place in this dichotomy for male homosexuality, which, judging from the use of gynocentric, would seem to be androcentric – in which case heterosexuality is in the middle, neither androcentric nor gynocentric. But Snyder seems to feel that, since heterosexuality is mandated by the patriarchy, it can be called androcentric.

Along with the *thiasos,* Wilamowitz-Moellendorff's view of fr. 31 became the most passionately rejected part of Sapphic theory by those who saw themselves as twentieth-century rationalists opposing nineteenth-century idealists. The leading voice of this group was Page, who in his comments on fr. 31 asks: "With what pleasure will they listen, 'father and wedding guests,' to this revelation of uncontrollable ecstasy ... ? There was never such a wedding song in the history of society; and there should never have been such a

135 Snyder, *Lesbian Desire in the Lyrics of Sappho* (above, n.19), 29.

theory in the history of scholarship.'"[136] One scholar dismissively calls Wilamowitz-Moellendorff's wedding theory of fr. 31 "absurd"[137] – despite the impressive list of scholars who have signed on to it.

But Page's vehement rejection of the wedding-song theory does not allow for the possibility of irony. It is based on Wilamowitz-Moellendorff's literalistic form of that theory – and really that is not the point. Sappho was neither a straightforward monodist nor a straightforward choralist. In my view of fr. 31, as presented in an earlier chapter of this book,[138] the fragment's connection with the genre of the epithalamion is mediated by a deep irony in the practice of which Sappho's meaning may be very different from a simple literalistic one. It seems that Sappho was not using epithalamic echoes in a straightforward way here. In recent years, Sappho-as-ironist is becoming a dominant theme in Sapphic criticism. Increasingly, scholars are noticing how cunningly Sappho plays the conventions of genre expectations against one another. Her monodist often hid behind choral conventions, and vice versa. This cunning interplay of genres informs my discussions of the major frr. 16, 31, 96, and several others.

So cunning is Sappho in fact that the decision can't seem black and white one way or the other. Probably many nowadays would agree with Larindois when he says, "I would not want to exclude the possibility that it was sung at a wedding, as Wilamowitz-Moellendorff declared."[139]

136 *S&A* 33.

137 Parker, "Sappho Schoolmistress" (above, n.44), 174.

138 Part One, chap. 6: "The Face Behind the Mask."

139 Lardinois, "Who Sang Sappho's Songs" [above, n.70], 167–68.

Subversion

It might be worth looking at Sappho's seizure in fr. 31 in terms of Julia Kristeva's psychology of speech.[140] Her categories of semiotic and symbolic are connected with female and male speech practices, in a sense with mother and father, and also with Groups 2 and 3. The essence of the distinction is the dichotomy between pre-Oedipal and post-Oedipal uses of speech. The semiotic represents the use of speech in the child's life before the onset of the Oedipus Complex; the symbolic, on the other hand, occurs after the resolution of the complex. Sappho's γλῶσσα ἔαγε – the moment in fr. 31 when her "tongue breaks' – seems meaningfully related to the process one scholar describes like this: "Subversion of the rational symbolic process occurs ... through irruption of a repressed linguistic core, the 'semiotic' – affiliated, though not explicitly identified, with the cultural category of the feminine."[141] This irruption is in a sense an infantile regression, as the "repressed linguistic core" that "erupts" is the habit of pre-Oedipal speech, the baby talk of the infant. The infantile nature of this reversion is hinted also in Sappho by its physicality and immediacy: as Yopie Prins points out, "γλῶσσα displaces φωνή, the word that usually designates voice in the Sapphic fragments."[142] Jesper Svenbro proposes that the poem expresses Sappho as "a subject displaced by writing,"[143] that is, as a preliterate subject who is, even as

140 See J. Kristeva, *Desire in Language: A Semiotic Approach to Literature and Art,* trans. T. Gora, A. Jardine, and L.S. Roudiez (New York: Columbia Univ. Press, 1980).

141 Skinner, "Women and Language in Archaic Greece" (above, n.6), 176.

142 Y. Prins, "Sappho's Afterlife in Translation," in *Re-Reading Sappho* (above, n.8), 43.

143 J. Svenbro, "Death by Writing," in *Phrasikleia: An Anthology of Reading in Ancient Greece,* trans. J. Lloyd (Ithaca: Cornell Univ. Press,

she composes this poem, heralding the demise of the oral mode. Sappho "emerges as female lyric subject at the precise moment when the tongue breaks."[144] The lyric subject speaks semiotic, not symbolic; the semiotic is both the pre-Oedipal and the feminine mode, associated with the mother as the symbolic order is connected with the father. Poetry, like baby talk, is integrally connected to the semiotic modality, while prose is more useful for expression of the symbolic modality.

There are also some meaningful points of connection with Giulia Sissa's discussion of the role of the vatic priestess, especially the Pythia. To begin with, she points to Plato's declaration, in the *Phaedrus,* of the superiority of "the prophecy of inspiration over that of omen reading."[145] She notes that the prophecy of inpiration, in which the god speaks through the body of a possessed prophet, is performed primarily by women and the prophecy of omens, which is a more scholarly approach, by men. Here is another way of defining a mode of speech conceived as female and another conceived as male. There is a noticeable parallelism with Kristeva's semiotic/symbolic distinction. In the speech of inspiration, "no artifice or code intervenes." The woman's body, meaning especially the Pythia, "becomes ... a wall of glass, a blank page, speech does not find a symbolic order." The Pythia, she concludes, was the inception of a form of language that was at once divine and feminine."[146]

Aspects of this description parallel Sappho's predicament in fr. 31. "If," Sissa says, " the equilibrium between god and priestess was transformed into tension, the integrity of the

---

1992), 152.

144 Prins, "Sappho's Afterlife in Translation" (above, n.142), 54.

145 Sissa, *Greek Virginity* (above, n.113), 10.

146 Ibid., 14.

Pythia's utterance was destroyed and her voice was stifled by congestion in her throat."[147]

Pseudo-Longinus, in whose text *On the Sublime* fr. 31 is preserved, presents the poem as a Sapphic sublime, and several modern scholars have attempted to unravel the idea. Prins, in commenting on fr. 31, sees the disarticulation and scattering of the body or the decentering of the self (the symbolic self is centered), as an experience of the sublime. Fragment 130, in which Eros, "loosener of the limbs," stirs or shakes the poet, seems to involve the same idea of sublime disarticulation or tearing apart.[148] Gregory Nagy further regards the "intolerable" hiatus in line 9 ("tongue is broken," γλῶσσα ἔαγε) as mimetic or performative, embodying the theme of disarticulation.[149] In a similar vein Paul Fry says, "the 'broken tongue' of Sappho could be an emblem of the Longinian sublime," embodying the disarticulation of syntax under the impact of the sublime; "the moment of dismemberment ... will be represented in language that risks inarticulateness."[150] The idea of the sublime as disarticulation and scattering also encompasses the Homeric example "Longinus" gives, and shows the link between the two exempla.

Again it is worth attending to Kristeva's theory of early linguistic development. Her distinction between the semiotic and symbolic uses of language is based to an extent on Jacques Lacan's theory of language's role in developmental psychology, which in turn developed from Freud's Oedipus Complex. Freud's idea (in all its simplicity) was that the child

---

147 Ibid., 30.

148 Y. Prins, *Victorian Sappho* (Princeton Univ. Press, 1999), 17.

149 G. Nagy, *Comparative Studies in Greek and Indic Meter* (Cambridge, Mass.: Harvard Univ. Press, 1974), 45.

150 P.H. Fry, "Longinus at Colonus: The Grounding of Sublimity," in *The Reach of Criticism: Method and Perception in Literary Theory* (New Haven: Yale Univ. Press, 1983), 47–86, esp. 56f.

stays mostly at home with its mother till it is about three or four; then the father begins to displace the mother and occupy center stage in the child's view of the world. The process should be over by about age seven. The father strides into the infant's consciousness wielding his phallus as a rod of authority, and in Lacan's view the phallus is symbolic language. The significance of the Oedipal moment is that the child is introduced to a new use of language. In the early years with the mother, language did not have to be based on logic. It was enough that it was based on feeling. It could be baby talk/nonsense, but it was a means of intimate communication that did not involve the outside world. The father, however, represents the outside world or society and introduces a new use of language that is based on logic and a concept of truth rather than feeling and imagination. In a terminology based partly on Lacan, Kristeva calls the early (pre-Oedipal) linguistic phase the semiotic and the later (post-Oedipal) use of language the symbolic. The symbolic is regarded as the narrower of these domains, based on logic and often dealing in binary oppositions such as "man/woman, mind/body, reason/emotion, symbolic/reality."[151] As Hélène Cixous and Catherine Clément remark, "Is the fact that Logocentrism subjects thought – all concepts, codes and values – to a binary system, related to 'the' couple, man/woman?"[152] Logocentrism denotes the symbolic order of language, the male-centered order, which is inseparable from society; it represents society. The semiotic is more private, it is the language mode of intimacy (*jouissance*) between mother and infant, and it is also the mode of poetic speech, surrealism, and the chaos of the Menippean Satire, in which category Kristeva includes

151 Wilson, *Sappho's Sweetbitter Songs* (above, n.115), 10-11.

152 H. Cixous and C. Clément, *The Newly Born Woman*, trans. B. Wing (London: I.B.Tauris, 1996), 64.

great modernist works like James Joyce's *Ulysses*. Kristeva expressed the view that the semiotic use of language implies the pre-Oedipal stage of dual unity, as Géza Róheim called it; the symbolic use of language on the other hand represents a kind of alienation: "Language as symbolic function constitutes itself at the cost of repressing insti nctual drive and continuous relation to the mother."[153] Jungian scholars have not been taken seriously on the whole. Yet early Jungians like Neumann have made valuable contributions to the discourse.

There seems to be a meaningful parallelism between these pairs of concepts – on the one hand, Sappho's private world and the public world roundabout; on the other the semiotic and the symbolic. Even after the conversion to the cause of the Father, one can revert to the stage of the semiotic, a gesture that characterizes many works of late modern and postmodern literature, basically everything that can be called a Menippean Satire, from Joyce's *Ulysses* and Ezra Pound's *Cantos* on down. It is not just a structural style that is involved in such works, but a mode of subjectivity. Sappho's "modes of subjectivity," says Skinner, "differentiate her to an extraordinary degree from her male counterparts."[154] That is because Sappho's "mode of subjectivity" is in some determined way pre-Oedipal. In keeping with the mother-child analogy, "Her model of homoerotic relations is bilateral and egalitarian in marked contrast to the rigid patterns of pursuit and physical mastery inscribed into the role of the adult male *ἐραστής* ..."[155] "... the subject position extracted from Sappho's monodies and choral compositions does not replicate patriarchal modes of awareness, but rather affords

153 Kristeva, *Desire in Language* (above, n.140), 136.

154 Skinner, "Woman and Language in Archaic Greece" (above, n.6), 186.

155 Ibid.

a substitute basis for organizing female experience."[156] "The ultimate purpose of Sapphic song, we may conclude, was to encode strategies for perpetuating women's culture."[157] "Compositions of Sappho and other women poets ... formed part of a widespread female oral tradition handed down from mother to daughter, and [...] those compositions served, in effect, as a mechanism for opposing patriarchy."[158] This goes along with the Kristevan interpretation: Sappho's circle, and indeed the whole tradition of women's poetry for women, involves the era before the father intrudes on the dual unity that speaks only to itself. This is one notion from which the idea of "mechanism for opposing patriarchy" can be approached. "Alcman in his maiden songs is most likely appropriating a Spartan female initiatory discourse akin to the one Sappho herself inherited and making it conform to a masculine symbolic order."[159] His case then is not so different from those of male authors of Menippean satires as recognized by Kristeva, for example Joyce and Pound. The fact that Kristeva recognizes them as authentic authors of Menippean satires implies that they, and other male authors, were able to regress deliberately into something structurally like a pre-Oedipal mode of subjectivity, "to enter imaginatively into states of awareness foreign to them."[160] Kristeva and others in the discourse have recognized surrealist poetry in general as a semiotic or pre-Oedipal use of language (it lacks the demand for responsibility that comes with the symbolic use of language). In terms of their mode of subjectivity, it seems, artists of this ilk have taken the mother's side rather than the father's.

156 Ibid., 188.
157 Ibid.
158 Ibid., 189.
159 Ibid.
160 Ibid., 192.

Girl Talk

Eva Stehle has remarked that Sappho created "an alternative world in which male values, those values which denied Greek women an outlet for erotic fantasy, are not dominant."[161] In a nearby passage she seems to explain what she means: "Sappho does not picture love relations as domination by one partner over the other." Ellen Greene notes that Jessica Benjamin, in *The Bonds of Love,* speaks of the fact that in a love relationship "one is always up and the other down." This "pattern of erotic domination" is "a specifically masculine mode of thought and practice that permeates all social organization."[162] Observations to similar effect have been common in the last generation of Sapphic studies. Margaret Williamson, for example, speaks of "an erotic reciprocity which evades the structures of phallic domination..."[163] Most authors who have made this point have been women, but not all. John Winkler speaks of Sappho's "private woman-centered" world, which he contrasts with male public culture.[164] Williamson also remarks that Sappho represents "the originary voice of female poetic consciousness."[165] Marilyn Skinner calls Sappho's poetry a "woman-specific discourse... an elaborate complex of coding strategies differing perceptibly from those of the dominant symbolic order." These strategies are "open, fluid, and

161 Stehle, "Romantic Sensuality, Poetic Sense" (above, n. 41), 149.

162 Greene, "Apostrophe and Women's Erotics in the Poetry of Sappho," in *Reading Sappho* (above, n. 1), 235.

163 M. Williamson, "Sappho and the Other Women," in *Reading Sappho* (above, n. 1), 250.

164 J. J. Winkler, "Double Consciousness in Sappho's Lyrics," in *The Constraints of Desire: The Anthropology of Sex and Gender in Ancient Greece* (London: Routledge, 1990), 165.

165 Williamson, "Sappho and the Other Woman" (above, n. 163), 249.

polysemous – and hence conspicuously nonphallic"[166] (and hence also conspicuously pre-Oedipal). "A pattern of mutuality emerges in Sappho's poetry in sharp contrast to a hierarchical mode of eroticism that is prevalent in male patterns of erotic discourse." Stehle: "Sappho can represent an alternative for women to the cultural norm."[167] Her poetry "dramatizes an experience of desire as mutual recognition,"[168] says Greene. It would be easy to multiply such citations.

It might be useful, again, to compare this distinction between female and male modes of communication, or pre- and post-Oedipal uses of language, with a third context where a roughly parallel distinction is made. Alongside the distinction between androcentric and gynocentric on the one hand and symbolic and semiotic on the other is a distinction made in feminist discussions of aesthetic theory. Heidi Göttner-Abendroth has written an influential essay called "Nine Principles of a Matriarchal Aesthetic."[169] One principle is that "matriarchal art is not 'text'... [but] a process which gives a pre-existing inner structure, found in the ritual of dance, external expression... a process in which all participate collectively..."[170] Another is that the participants "operate simultaneously on the levels of emotional identification, theoretical reflection and symbolic action."[171] Another is that genres are not sharply differentiated, but overlap, as poetry, dance, and song seem to have done in Sappho's world. Another is that

166 Skinner, "Woman and Language in Archaic Greece" (above, n.6), 234.

167 E. Stehle, "Sappho's Private World," in *Reflections of Women in Antiquity* (above, n.11), 108.

168 Greene, "Apostrophe and Women's Erotics in the Poetry of Sappho" (above, n.162), 234.

169 In *Feminist Aesthetics*, ed. G. Ecker, trans. H. Anderson (Boston: Beacon Press, 1986), 81–94.

170 Ibid., 82.

171 Ibid.

"the erotic is the dominant force and not work, discipline, renunciation."[172] Matriarchal art is "the ability to shape life and so change it; it is itself energy, life, a drive towards the aestheticisation of society."[173] It seems that these principles, and perhaps some of the others, apply to the private world evoked in Sappho's poems - the Group 2 fragments.

In an essay entitled "Toward a Feminist Aesthetic," Julia Stanley and Susan Wolfe describe women's literary style as a "discursive and conjunctive style rather than the complex and subordinating linear style of classification and distinction"[174] (a dichotomy paralleling that between the semiotic and the symbolic). Josephine Donovan writes of a "nondominative aesthetic" based on "women's domestic aesthetic praxis ... Such art remains embedded in the everyday. It is not extracted and commodified as a 'masterpiece.'"[175] Later she remarks, in a way that seems relevant to Sappho, that "art does not simply reflect everyday reality ... rather, it expresses the ontic illuminations that inhere in everyday life."

Marilyn French remarks that "the feminist perspective is partly a reversal of patriarchal views." A remark that seems to apply to Sappho's work: "To endorse women's experience, feminist art must present it honestly, wholly."[176] Also: "Women seem to feel legitimated not by power and authority, as men do, but by experience itself. And experience is made up of feeling."[177]

---

172 Ibid., 83.

173 Ibid., 84.

174 J.P. Stanley and S.J. Wolfe (Robbins), "Toward a Feminist Aesthetic," *Chrysalis* 6 (1978), 57–71.

175 J. Donovan, "Everyday Use and Moments of Being: Toward a Nondominative Aesthetic," in *Aesthetics in Feminist Perspective*, ed. H. Hein and C. Korsmeyer (Bloomington: Indiana Univ. Press, 1993), 53.

176 M. French, "Is There a Feminist Aesthetic?" in ibid., 70.

177 Ibid., 74.

It seems, finally, justified to attribute to Sappho the "originary impulse of women's poetry." She seems first to have defined and acted out principles that underlie modern feminism in both psychology and aesthetics.

Some Distinctions in Feminist Theory

The idea of different language modes that correspond roughly to masculine and feminine has been prominent in recent feminist theory. It seems to arise from a synthesis of Freudian theory and developmental psychology, with considerable influence by first Lacan and then Kristeva. Lacan stressed the difference between pre-Oedipal and post-Oedipal speech. Pre-Oedipal speech, in the developmental phase in which the infant relates more to its mother than its father, he characterizes as "the imaginary." It is an area of loose connectivity and free flow of signifiers expressing the emotions of the moment. The Imaginary is where Baby Talk comes from (also Surrealist poetry and Menippean satire). It's not so concerned with information as with feeling. Post-Oedipal speech arises after the intervention of the father, who insists that the developing child must begin to take responsibility for the truth value of his or her utterances. Language is now called the symbolic – meaning that it actually relates to something – and the process of maturing consists precisely of entering the realm of the symbolic and establishing oneself in a subject position there. The subject is one who exercises the power of the symbolic and navigates the world through use of this power. Again there is a parallel with the different approaches to language in Groups 2 and 3: Group 2 resonates to the vibrations of the imaginary while Group 3 is focused on the symbolic.

Kristeva redesignated the imaginary as the semiotic, which is defined as specifically pre-Oedipal and, at the same time, specifically feminine. The semiotic is linked to pre-Oedipal primary processes, predominantly oral and anal.[178] The semiotic is a special almost pre-birth realm designated by the Greek word *χώρα*, space or womb. It is whole or unbroken in the sense that birth or actualization has not happened to it yet. It has not undergone differentiation. The wholeness of this semiotic continuum must be split in order to produce signification and move along its stages into the symbolic reality. The threat of castration in the Oedipal phase propels the achievement of this splitting.

The *χώρα*, the unbroken place of primal motherly speech, equates perceptibly with Sappho's *thiasos* as the "house of the Muses' servants." Music is specifically based on the *χώρα*, and lyric poetry, a type of song, is similarly based – but perhaps toward the edge of the whole space, where its Wholeness begins to break up in the differentiations of language. Julia Kristeva, in *Revolution in Poetic Language*, asserts these two "modalities" of language, the semiotic and the symbolic, equating them roughly with feminine and masculine, or the age of the mother and the age of the father.[179] Again, these two modalities relate to the distinction between Group 2 and Group 3 fragments, what John Winkler calls Sappho's "double consciousness"[180] or private and public uses of speech, and again what Charles Segal calls "an interplay between one level of style that is close to the ritual and public discourse and another that is freer and more private,"[181] and what Jane Snyder calls "public occasion and private passion."[182]

---

178 The probable word ὄλισβος (dildo) in fr. 99 seems an exception in Sappho's diction.

179 See J. Kristeva, *Revolution in Poetic Language*, trans. M. Waller (New York: Columbia Univ. Press, 1984), chap. 1.

180 Above, n.172.

181 Above, n.20.

182 Above, n.22.

What Kristeva calls the semiotic modality is what Giuliana Lanata refers to as "Sappho's amatory language."[183] Kristeva says that "pre-Oedipal semiotic functions... connect and orient the body to the mother... The oral and anal drives... are oriented and structured around the mother's body."[184]

Kristeva also connects the concept of the imaginary/semiotic with Mallarmé's idea of the mystery in language: "Enigmatic and feminine," this mystery is a space (*χώρα*) "underlying language... rhythmic, unfettered, irreducible to its intelligible verbal translation; it is musical, anterior to judgment"[185] – and specifically allied to the feminine.

A similar argument is found in Luce Irigaray's *This Sex Which Is Not One,* where she speaks of female language patterns as having an auto-erotic quality that is supposedly lacking in male speech. "One must listen to her differently in order to hear an 'other meaning' which is constantly in the process of weaving itself, at the same time ceaselessly embracing words and yet casting them off to avoid becoming fixed, immobilized."[186] It is masculine language of the symbolic order that desires to become fixed and immobilized in service of a belief in an objective unchanging reality that, in turn, upholds the patriarchy.

It is this latter – fixed and immobile – aspect of the symbolic use of language that Hélène Cixous focuses on. The phallogocentric symbolic order attempts to separate the child from its mother's body; the mother's body is the real, and without separating from the real the child cannot enter the symbolic. The symbolic order is only phallic and thus cannot represent the mother's body or the female body in general.

183 Above, n.13.

184 Kristeva, *Revolution in Poetic Language* (above, n.179), 27.

185 Ibid., 29.

186 L. Irigaray, *This Sex Which Is Not One,* trans. C. Porter with C. Burke (Ithaca: Cornell Univ. Press, 1985), 103.

Is it possible for a woman to write at all, Cixous asks? Since the symbolic order is exclusively phallogocentric, it not only cannot express the female body, but it may even be lifeless in female hands. When one writes or speaks, Cixous says, one does so always "as a man." Women are close to the margins of the symbolic order and thus not as fixed or anchored in stable meaning as men in a patriarchy are. So it seems hopeless that women should be written by men. Rather, Cixous says, "Woman must write herself." "Woman must write woman." That sounds like a clear and concise description of how Sappho spent her life. From "The Laughter of the Medusa":

> Woman must write herself : must write about women and bring women to writing, from which they have been driven away as violently as from their bodies – for the same reasons, by the same law, with the same fatal goal. Woman must put herself into the text – and into the world and into history – by her own movement.[187]

When woman writes herself, the result is *"l'écriture feminine,"* a writing that is possible only in poetry and not in realist prose or other genres that posit a stable language with one to one fixed relations of signifiers and signifieds. Poetry is closer to the unconscious and thus closer to the repressed. When woman writes her own body the structure of language itself will change: *l'écriture feminine* will become an inherently deconstructive language that deconstructs the linear rationality of the symbolic order. *L'écriture feminine* is too fluid to be anchored or limited within a stable system. It cannot be theorized, coded, or understood. What makes that impossible is that there is a basic difference in focus. As one feminist scholar says, "A lesbian feminist perspective situates

---

187 H. Cixous, "The Laugh of the Medusa," trans. K. and P. Cohen, *Signs* 1 (1976), 875–93.

centrally what is marginal to or absent from the heterosexual version of reality."[188] What Annette Kolodny suggests for feminism seems to have been true of Sappho's circle:

> A communal frame of mind which encourages debate and dialogue among individuals ... who are, first and foremost, committed to the validity of the shared effort.[189]

Jane Gallop redraws the distinction between feminine and masculine approaches to language in terms of genre: "Women write letters – personal, intimate, in relation; men write books – universal, public, in general circulation."[190] (And many of Sappho's poems, especially those in the Berlin Parchment seem to be letters.)

Challenges to Homer

Much writing on Sappho in the last generation has focused on the idea that she created a discourse that escaped male domination – a discourse that has been described by the terms "woman-centered" and "woman-specific" and by other similar terms. Perhaps this is most clearly and bluntly stated in what Garry Wills called "The Sapphic 'Umwertung aller Werte'";[191] this is specifically a revaluation of masculine values (of which Homer was the model) by feminine ones (of which Sappho became the model). It is said that in antiquity

188 E. Messer-Davidow, "The Philosophical Bases of Feminist Literary Criticisms," in *Gender and Theory: Dialogues on Feminist Criticism*, ed. L. Kauffman (Oxford: Basil Blackwell, 1989) 93.

189 A. Kolodny, "Some Notes on Defining a 'Feminist Literary Criticism,'" *Critical Inquiry* 2 (1975), 91.

190 J. Gallop, "Annie Leclerc Writing a Letter, With Vermeer," in *The Poetics of Gender*, ed. N.K. Miller (New York: Columbia Univ. Press, 1986), 139.

191 *The American Journal of Philology* 88 (1967), 434–42.

if one heard the phrases "the poet" or "the poetess," one knew immediately that Homer or Sappho was referred to.

Jane Snyder suggests that Sappho was not simply using Homeric meter and dialect forms as part of the common poetic inheritance, but that she specifically used these allusions to challenge the epic tradition. "May Sappho perhaps," she asks, "be presenting herself as a 'consciously anti-heroic persona'?"[192] It does seem to be the case. "Sappho is producing her own new version of Homer - minus the warriors carrying on warfare - rather than merely reproducing epic themes in a lyric mode."[193] Fragment 16 is the standard exemplum. Wills calls it Sappho's "revaluation of all values," meaning, it seems, her challenge to Homer. The rise and fall of Anaktoria's footstep replaces the rise and fall of empires. "The military focus of the opening and closing of the fragment, so obviously male-centered in terms of the Homeric background, may then be seen as contrasted with the female singer's point of view"[194] Fragment 44, though the most Homeric of the fragments in terms of its dialect, rigorously excludes images of war in favor of Sappho's most common public event, a wedding reception with the emphasis, as usual, on rich garments, the sounds of flute and lyre, the chorus of maidens singing a holy song. The bride and groom are described as godlike, as in the *μακαρισμοί* at frr. 31.1 and 96.4. Though these are the great examples, the "challenge" to Homer appears in many small utterances too, like the phrase "be my ally" at the end of Ode 1 or "the rosy-fingered moon" at fr. 96.8. Whereas men rise at dawn to go to war, the women's time, Sappho seems to mean, is when the moon rises and the only ally is Aphrodite.

---

192 Snyder, *Lesbian Desire in the Lyrics of Sappho* (above, n.19), 63.
193 Ibid., 64.
194 Ibid., 65.

Sappho's Aesthetics

Snyder has addressed the question how to describe the Sapphic aesthetics.[195] To leap to the conclusion of her interesting and thoughtful presentation: "*Charis* and the *Charites, habrosune*, and *poikilia*: these are the distinctive qualities that stand out as hallmarks of Sappho's worldview."[196] Χάρις, usually translated as "grace," is a basic concept of Sappho – more so than any other poet. Commenting on a use of the word by Homer (*Iliad* 14.183), Snyder sees it as "a quality that radiates visibly from... enticingly beautiful" objects. This enticing beauty is not described in more detail except that "it is not a question of symmetry and proportion."[197] The χάριτες are the "three Graces," maiden goddesses whom Sappho often mentions along with the Muses, as in fr. 103.5: "Hither divine Graces and Pierian Muses," and in fr. 128: "Come hither now, tender Graces and beautiful haired Muses." Ἀβροσύνη seems to mean something like delicate or tender or both at the same time.[198] Ἀβρός, the adjectival form, is one of Sappho's most common words, occurring seven times, and is used, for example, to describe the Graces. "The positive light in which Sappho views the *Charites* and the special prominence she grants to the quality of *charis*... throughout her poetry give the Sapphic corpus its unique stamp."[199] Ποικιλία (variegation or variety) could apply either to poetic style or to things being described inside the world of the poem. Sappho often says that beautiful things are multicolored or dappled or variegated (like Aphrodite's throne), applying it to the world portrayed in the poem rather than to the poem itself. Like

195 Ibid., chap. 5: "The Aesthetics of Sapphic *Eros*."
196 Ibid., 95.
197 Ibid., 80.
198 Snyder says "lushness" (ibid.).
199 Ibid.

ἀβρός, the adjective form πόικιλος occurs seven times (the same as the word παρθένος). Indeed, it is the very first word in Sappho's book.

This analysis strikes me as a valuable contribution to the discussion of Sappho's aesthetics – though in a sense these are not really aesthetic qualities in the way that, say, "symmetry and proportion" are (but perhaps those are qualities of the symbolic realm). Πόικιλος, especially, seems not to describe the verses, but the fictional world viewed in the imagination. It does not occur in the Group 3 fragments. Sappho's devotion to the Three Graces is indeed distinctive, as much as her devotion to Aphrodite, and seems virtually cultic. In her little backyard shrine Sappho put a religion together. Hesiod's description of the Graces (*Theogony* 910–11) shows that in the eighth and probably the seventh centuries BCE they were not bland charming presences, as in the Renaissance, but full-blooded spirits of life:

> *Eros,* limb-loosening, drips from their eyes as they
> glance about;
> Beautifully do they glance from beneath their brows.[200]

Ancient authors show two conflicting approaches to the problem of characterizing Sappho's aesthetics. Dionysius of Halicarnassus (*On Literary Composition*) uses Sappho as the leading example of the style he calls γλαφυρός, usually translated "smooth." For Homer, the word seems to have meant hollow and later polished, finished, subtle. One might think it referred to the way Sappho's verse usually sounds smooth and natural rather than stilted and poetic – something like what Yeats meant when he said that one might work all day on a single line only to make it seem as if it were effortlessly tossed off. But Dionysius himself gives a more

200 Translation by Snyder. (Ibid., 81.)

physical definition: "There are very few clashings of semi-vowels with semi-vowels or mutes, and of mutes and vowels with one another, such as cause the sound to oscillate...As a natural consequence the language has a certain easy flow and softness; the arrangement of the words in no way ruffles the smooth waves of sound."[201]

Pseudo-Longinus, in his text of about 200 CE, *On the Sublime*, uses Sappho's fr. 31 as one of two examples of the sublime. First, there is the Homeric sublime, involving the anger and supernatural conflicts of gods, in which the world "might be turned upside down and torn apart." Then there is the sublime of the seizure that comes over Sappho in the experience described in fr. 31. How exactly are these two examples sublime? Well, in terms of later European views of the sublime, which were supposedly derived, at however great a distance, from Pseudo-Longinus, the Homeric example is an instance of the "terror sublime" expounded by Edmund Burke in *Philosophical Enquiry into the Origin of Our Ideas of the Sublime and the Beautiful* (1757). The Sappho example, however, bears more affinity to Immanuel Kant's analytic of the sublime in the *Critique of Judgment* (1790), which is based simply on otherness - of any kind. The condition Sappho experiences in fr. 31 is so different from the normal condition of one's body and senses as to be both sublime and dreadful.

Writing about the same time, Demetrius (*On Style*) applied several critical terms to Sappho's verse. He especially praises her figures of speech (the epiphoneme, or ornamental simile), hyperbole ("more golden than gold"), reduplications, or rhythmical repetitions ("Parthenia, parthenia..."), and so on (106). Still, he maintains that grace "may reside in the subject

---

201 Dionysius of Halicarnassus, *On Literary Composition*, ed. and trans. W. Rhys Roberts (London: Macmillan, 1910), 237–41.

matters... gardens of nymphs" and such (132). Again the dual approach – to Sappho's style and to the properties of her inner world.

Back to the Stone Age

It has become usual to think of the culture of the Paleolithic age as preceding much social definition of gender differences. The Neolithic age, in this way of thinking, tilted toward the female principle presumably in connection with agriculture – both its symbolic association with the fertility of the female body and its acknowledgment of woman's role in both the discovery and the practice of agriculture. It is possible that in the Neolithic Age there was a woman-centered discourse in a fairly prominent place in society. In the Bronze Age change happened only slowly. The early Bronze Age seems to have been psychologically largely a continuation of the late Neolithic (or Chalcolithic) with, however, an increasing tilt from the female to the male side, which became increasingly prominent as the Bronze Age continued.

Sappho, though born into the early Iron Age, seems to have lived in a place and milieu that bore within it a strong memory of the more female-dominated discourse or ideology of earlier periods. It is possible to see seventh-century culture of the northeast Ægean as still closely bound to the old way of thinking and feeling while, at the same time, colonialism and primitive democracy brought the logocentric spirit to the center of the stage. So Sappho's position in cultural history is multifaceted. While she occupies a *coupure épistémologique* as described by Bruno Snell in his essay on "The Rise of the Individual in the Early Greek Lyric," she seems to occupy another *coupure* in which a shift in gender roles and attitudes is occurring. The male principle begins to assert itself through ideas of its own purity that developed into the Platonic soul and the Christian emphasis on female chastity.

Many of the scholars who have focused on Sappho's "woman-centered" discourse are professed feminists who are celebrating her achievement. But usually they fail to mention that Sappho's discourse, in all its woman-centeredness, does not seem to be eerily forecasting modern feminism, but rather preserving a discourse from an older, pre-patriarchal (pre-Oedipal) age. Most of these authors are rightfully impressed – and shocked – by the truth that Luce Irigaray stated in her famous caption: "Any theory of the 'subject' has always been appropriated by the 'masculine.'"[202]

This pungent observation seems to possess a striking and relentless truth, but it may need some qualification. The word "always," for example, is a problem. After the establishment of the unbounded power and authority of the "phallogocentric" patriarchy, it is probably true that this appropriation has always happened. But in earlier more woman-centered eras like the Early Bronze Age or the Neolithic Age, woman-centered discourses presumably existed unthreatened by masculine appropriation.[203] Sappho seems to be standing on the edge. For her and the little community that gathered somehow around her it was possible to maintain a woman-centered attitude because the male and female groups seem to have been pretty much segregated in archaic Greece. In the οἶκος, or home, the private woman-dominated realm, women's discourse seems not to have been intruded upon much until the fifth century. Clearly, Sappho lived in a world where the patriarchal

202 L. Irigaray, *Speculum of the Other Woman*, trans. G.C. Gill (Ithaca, New York: Cornell Univ. Press, 1985), 133.

203 A reading of the Sumerian texts should establish the point. See, e.g., *Inanna, Queen of Heaven and Earth: Her Stories and Hymns from Sumer*, trans. D. Wolkstein and S.N. Kramer (New York: Harper & Row, 1983).

attitude was in place, but not in the οἶκος; it was in place in the πόλις (the public sphere), not the οἶκος (the private). Behind closed doors a much more ancient approach could still survive – for a while.

But not, it seems, for a very long while. With the rise of the New Comedy in the fourth century the male world intruded as directly as possible into Sappho's discourse and found ways to make her its own. Menander's apparent first mention of Sappho's suicide from love of the young man Phaon began the appropriation, which Ovid, in *Heroides* 15, elevated to a stature from which it deeply influenced attitudes toward her for thousands of years. As Marylin Skinner remarks, "Ovid's radical reinscription of Sappho bears the marks of sexual mastery or theft."[204] The Roman and later Christian preference for seeing her as corrupt or sinful was the second step of this appropriation by the masculine. Sappho's incorporation into philology in the nineteenth and twentieth centuries was the third level of this appropriation. Wilamowitz-Moellendorff stepped into the shoes once occupied by Ovid and Menander and was followed by the dreary modern lineage of patriarchal discomfort with Sappho. These recent scholars with their interest in the woman-centered attitude are taking her back, in a sense freeing Sappho from that wholesale male incorporation.

Different Sapphos

So little is factually known about Sappho that commentators inevitably project into the emptiness; they may not project a specific position on evidence (like that she was or wasn't a schoolmistress), but at least they project their own sense of

204 Skinner, "Women and Language in Archaic Greece" (above, n.6), 176.

reality, choosing to emphasize the mystic grove or Kleanax's son or Cleis's multicolored headband or some other element recovered from the meager heap of fragments via the critic's excited imagination. So there arises a flickering cinematic quality as of film superimposed and edited polyphonically – a *Rashomon* or *Citizen Kane* quality of different visions afforded by different points of view and pointing to an enigma.

The New Sappho is the phrase that has come to be used of a poem reconstructed by combining fr. 58 with two recent fragments called the Cologne Papyrus (P. Köln Inv. 21351 and 21376), published by Michael Grönewald and Robert Daniel of the University of Cologne in *Zeitschrift für Papyrologie und Epigraphik* 147 and 149 in 2004. The Cologne Papyrus contains some 33 lines that seem to include parts of three poems. Approximately the middle 12 of the 33 fit together with Sappho fr. 58, which had earlier been recovered from an Oxyrhynchus Papyrus. This reconstructed twelve-line poem is considered to be more or less complete. There's no absolute guarantee that it is by Sappho, but no other explanation of its existence has surfaced. It has not yet been included in the corpus and given a fragment number. It is simply called "the New Sappho."

It is new in the sense that it is *a* new Sappho, – a new specimen of Sappho's work. Yet in other senses, too, it might be called the New Sappho. For one, the Sappho presented here is not one among her girls, but a white-haired and slow-moving elderly woman living among young girls. It is a poem about old age, whereas we have usually encountered a Sappho who sounds young. We had previously had two fragments – 21 and 58 – that clearly deal with old age, but are only partially intelligible. Now that fr. 58 has been completed by the Cologne Papyrus, we have a more or less complete poem about old age in Sappho's voice. And it is clearly her own old age she is talking about. Here is the Greek text, followed by my translation:

> Ὕμμες πεδὰ Μοίσαν ἰ]ο̣κ[ό]λ̣πων κάλα δῶρα, παῖδες,
> σπουδάσδετε καὶ τὰ]ν̣ φιλάοιδον λιγύραν χελύνναν·
> ἔμοι δ᾽ἄπαλον πρίν] π̣οτ̣᾽ [ἔ]ο̣ντα χρόα γῆρας ἤδη
> ἐπέλλαβε, λεῦκαι δ᾽ ἐγ]ένοντο τρίχες ἐκ μελαίναν·
> βάρυς δέ μ᾽ ὀ [θ]ῦμο̣ς̣ πεπόηται, γόνα δ᾽ [ο]ὐ φέροισι,
> τὰ δή ποτα λαίψηρ᾽ ἔον ὄρχησθ᾽ ἴσα νεβρίοισι.
> τὰ <μὲν> στεναχίσδω θαμέως· ἀλλὰ τί κεν ποείην;
> ἀγήραον ἄνθρωπον ἔοντ᾽ οὐ δύνατον γένεσθαι
> καὶ γάρ π̣[ο]τ̣α̣ Τίθωνον ἔφαντο βροδόπαχυν Αὔων
> ἔρωι φ . . α̣θε̣ισαν βάμεν᾽ εἰς ἔσχατα γᾶς φέροισα[ν,
> ἔοντα̣ [κ]ά̣λ̣ο̣ν καὶ νέον, ἀλλ᾽ αὖτον ὔμως ἔμαρψε
> χρόνωι π̣ό̣λ̣ι̣ο̣ν̣ γῆρας, ἔχ[ο]ν̣τ̣᾽ ἀθανάταν ἄκοιτιν.

> Girls, seek eagerly the lovely gifts of the violet-bosomed
> Muses and the clear-voiced song-loving tortoise-shell lyre.
> But as for me, old age now seizes once tender flesh
> and my hair that once was black is white.
> My spirit is heavy, my knees,
> which once were fleet in the dance like fawns,
> hardly hold me up.
> Often I complain about these things, but what's to be done?
> For a mortal it is not possible to be unaging.
> Even Tithon once, they say, rosy-armed Dawn,
> smitten by love, carried off to the ends of the earth
> When he was handsome and young, but in time grey age
> caught up with him, while he lay with his immortally
> youthful bride in his arms.

It does indeed sound like a schoolmistress or music teacher exhorting her students to work hard at poetry and music, and then there is a sort of soft farewell. Though Sappho does not mention her death, it is lurking behind the description of bodily decrepitude. In terms of the mythic parallel, Sappho takes the role of the male hero Tithon rather than the female goddess Eos; Sappho's girls – students or whatever – in their youth and beauty represent Eos. As Tithon lay in bed impotent with old age, yet with his eternally youthful bride in his arms, so Sappho no longer relates sensually to her girls, who, because they leave and are replaced by others, are always young like Eos. Do we think that Sappho wrote more poems in her youth than in her old age? At least, our surviving corpus seems to contain only these two fragments about old age alongside dozens that express joy in youth, both her girls' and, by implication, her own. So is this the new Sappho: this elderly white-haired Sappho?

There are other senses also in which one might see the meaning of the phrase "The New Sappho." Many of the most important Sapphic fragments were recovered from papyrus and parchment finds in the twentieth century. Thus the Sappho known to the Middle Ages, the Renaissance, and the Enlightenment was a very different Sappho from the one we know today. Today our Sappho has been enriched and filled out by the discovery of the Berlin Parchment, containing frr. 94–96, the poem on the ostracon (fr. 2), and numerous Oxyrhynchus papyri. This is arguably the most important part of the Sappho corpus, perhaps even beyond the great long fragments from ancient sources, Pseudo-Longinus's fr. 31 and Dionysius's Ode 1. So, in a sense, the Sappho of Longinus and Dionysius is the Old Sappho and the Sappho of the Berlin parchment and the Oxyrhynchus finds the New Sappho – and they are two very different expressions from a multi-voiced poet.

Yet another sense in which the phrase "different Sapphos" is involved in this book is the way the book itself came into being. The enigma Sappho is experienced through one sensibility at different ages of its life in shattered fragments. Putting her together is like a philological project undertaken by the reader. First the Sappho of New Criticism, then the Sappho of *Kulturwissenschaft*, and finally this late journalistic ribbon with which I tie them up. But they are not really tied up; the place where we imagine Sappho (or project our pictures of her) is still somewhat empty – to be filled by other Sapphos yet to come.

THE END.

INDEX